EDENS ZERO

16

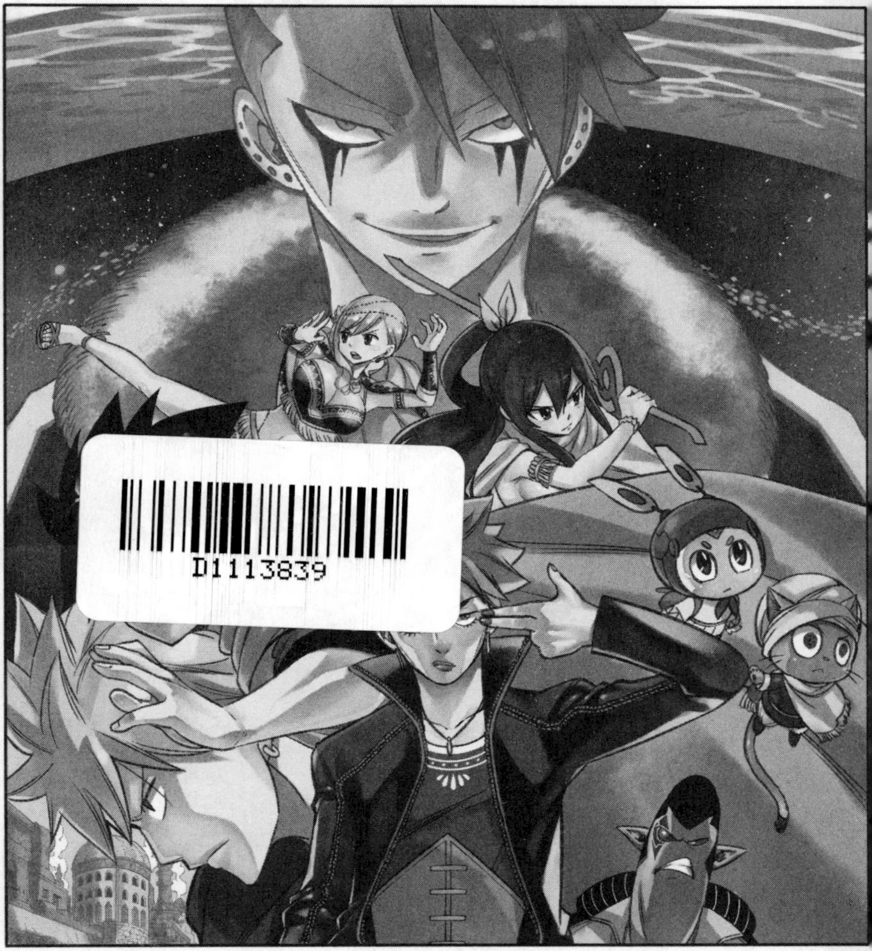

HIRO MASHIMA

EDENS ZERO 16 contents

EDENS ZERO

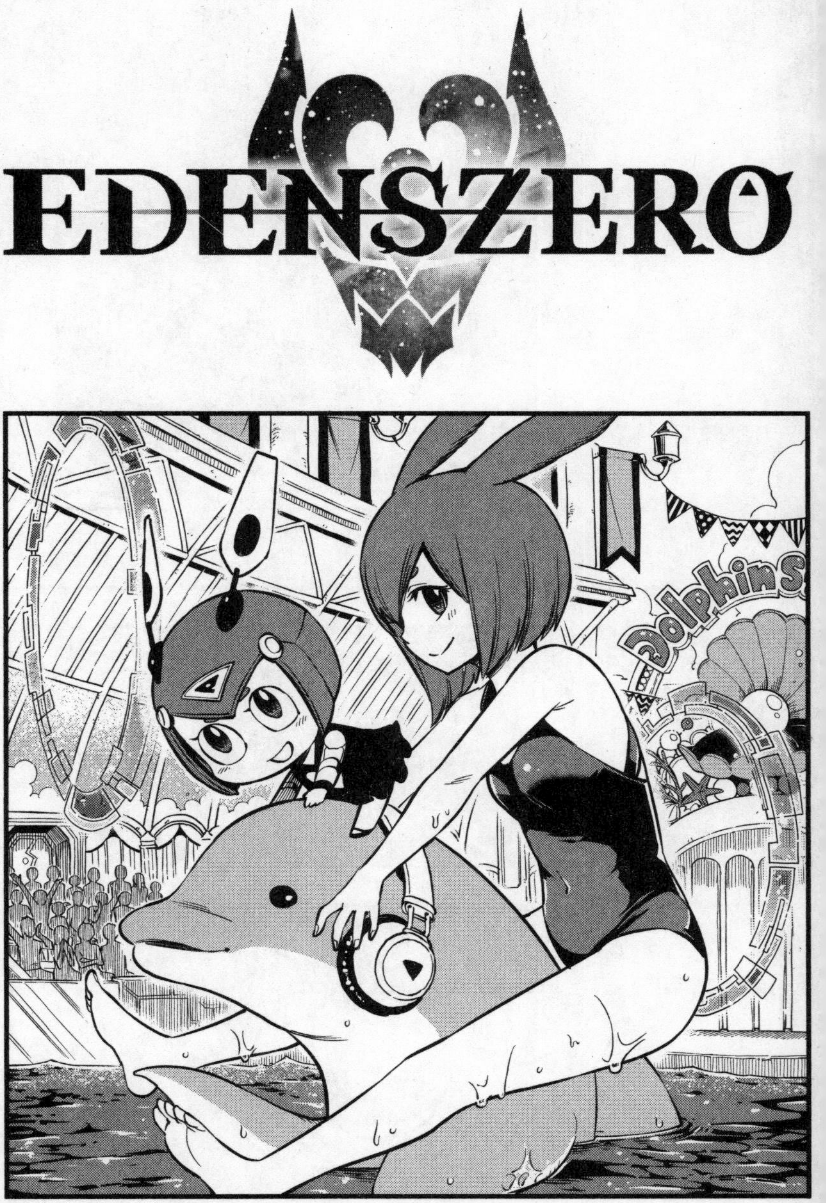
Dolphins

CHAPTER 132: CHRONO WITCH

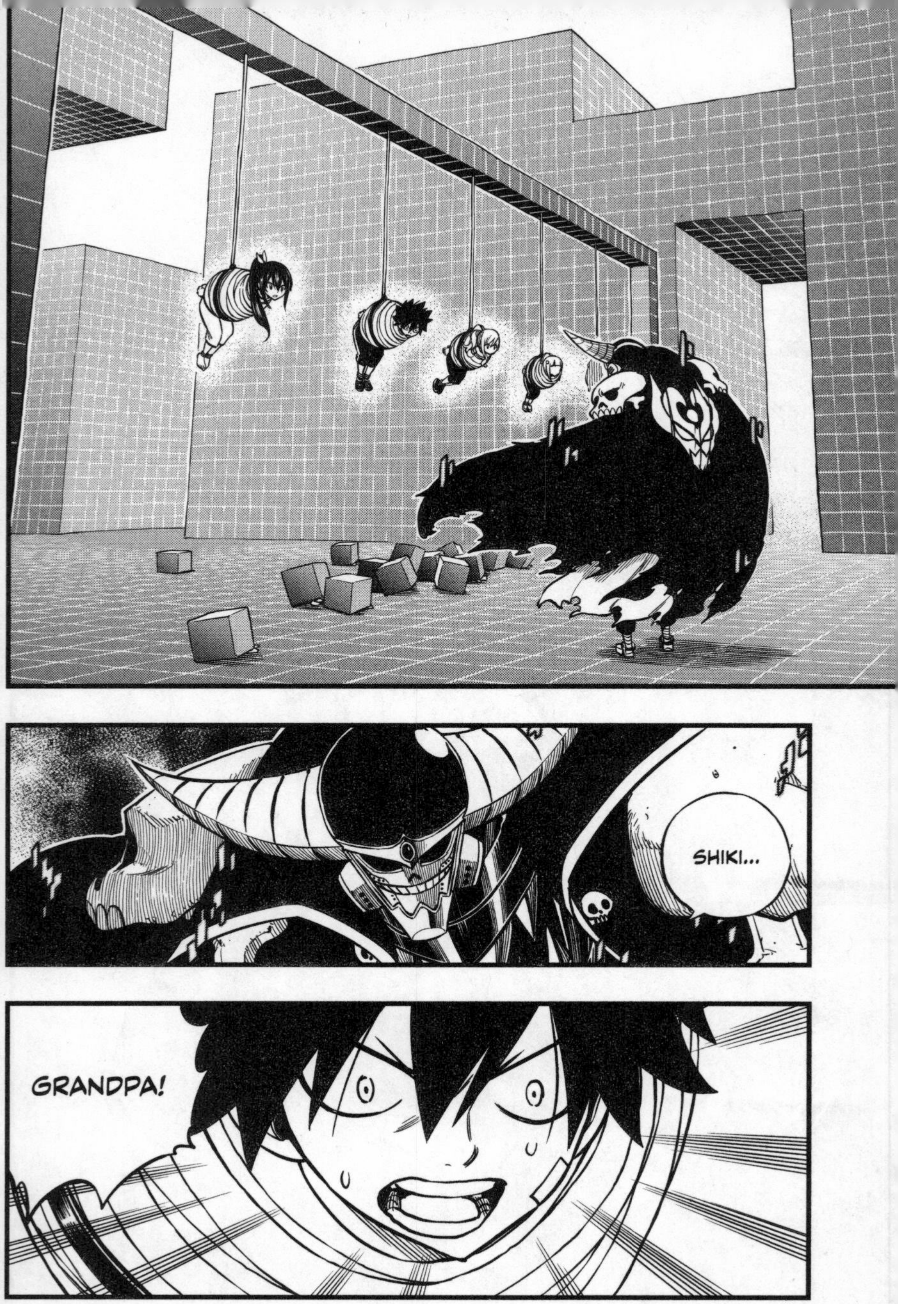
SHIKI...
GRANDPA!

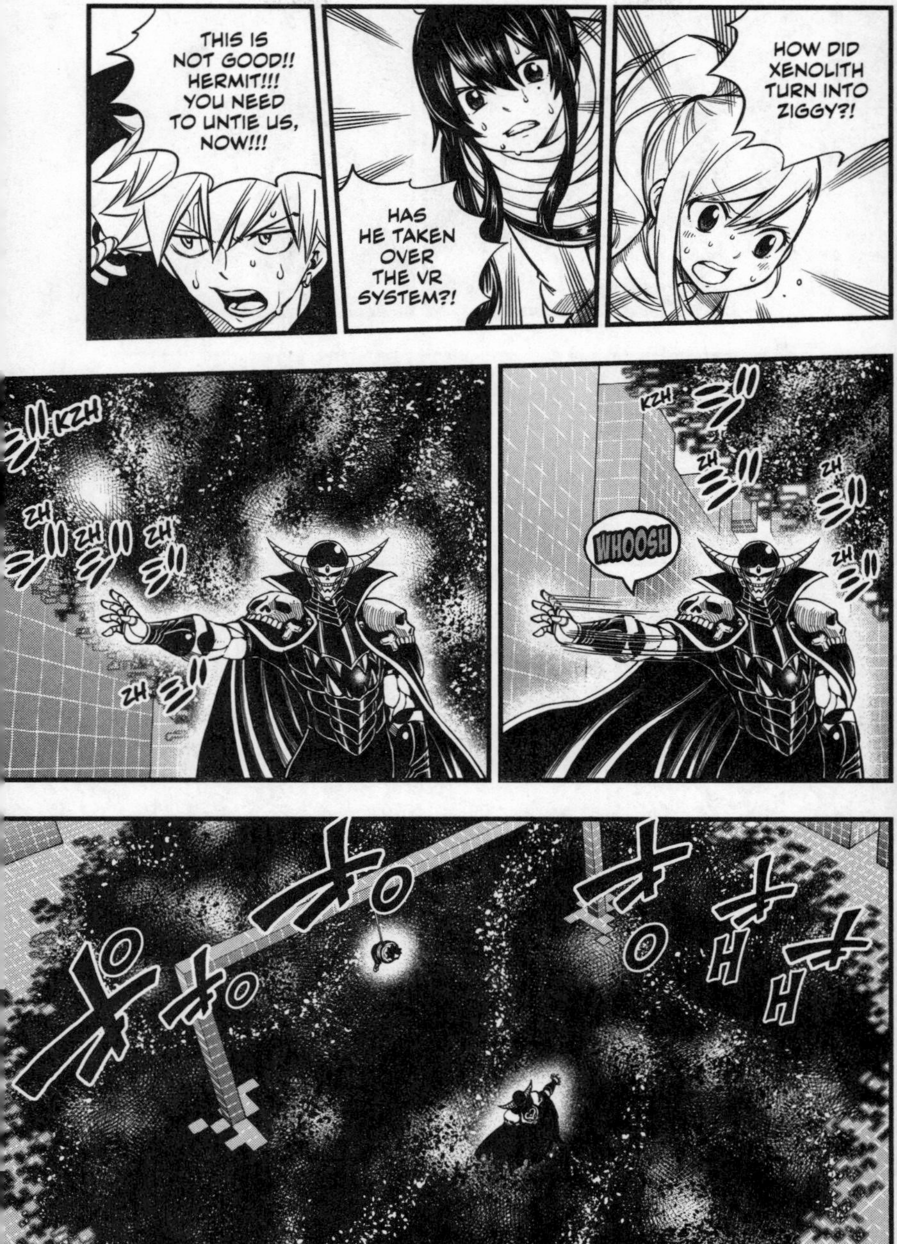
HOW DID XENOLITH TURN INTO ZIGGY?!
HAS HE TAKEN OVER THE VR SYSTEM?!
THIS IS NOT GOOD!! HERMIT!!! YOU NEED TO UNTIE US, NOW!!!
KZH
ZH
ZH
ZH
WHOOSH
KZH
ZH
ZH
ZH
ZH

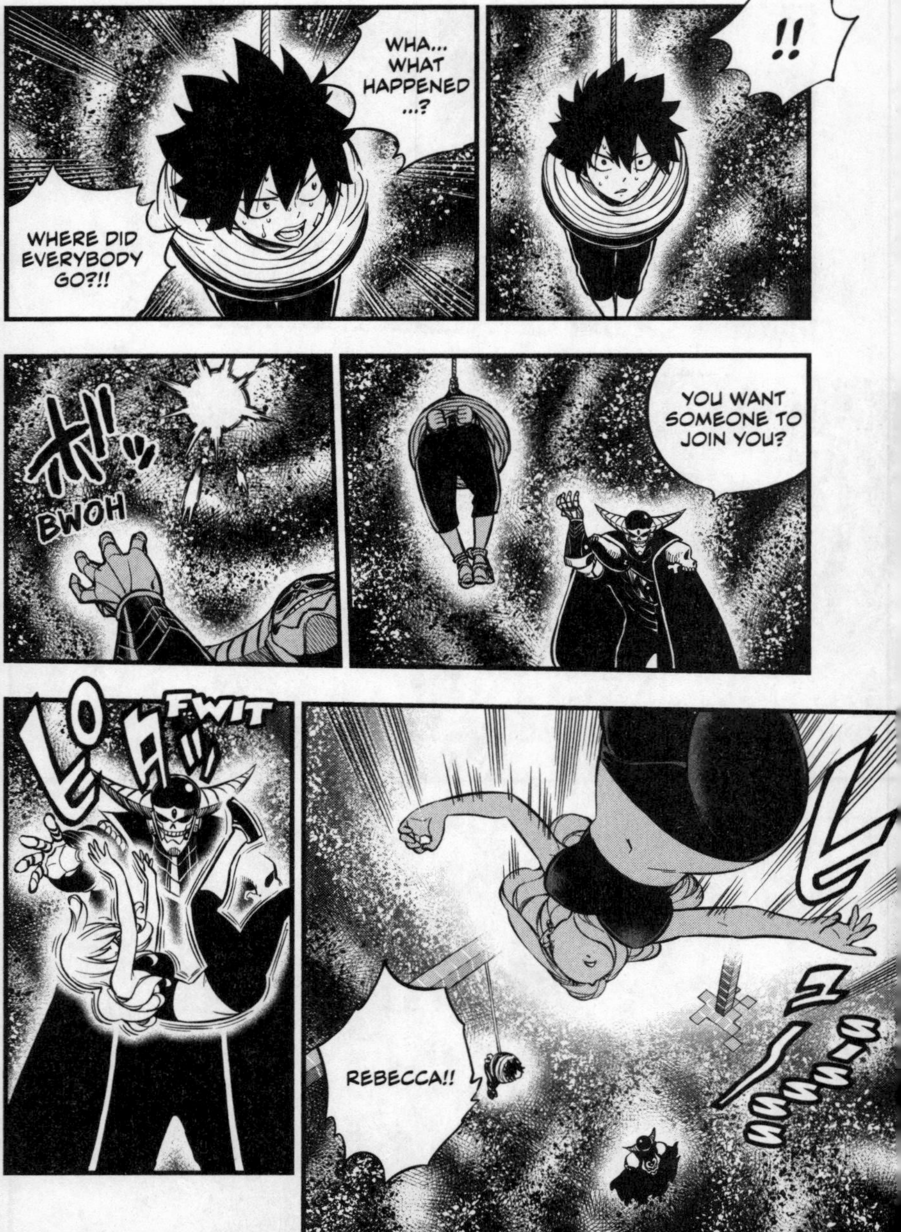
!!
WHA... WHAT HAPPENED ...?
WHERE DID EVERYBODY GO?!!
YOU WANT SOMEONE TO JOIN YOU?
BWOH
REBECCA!!
FWIT

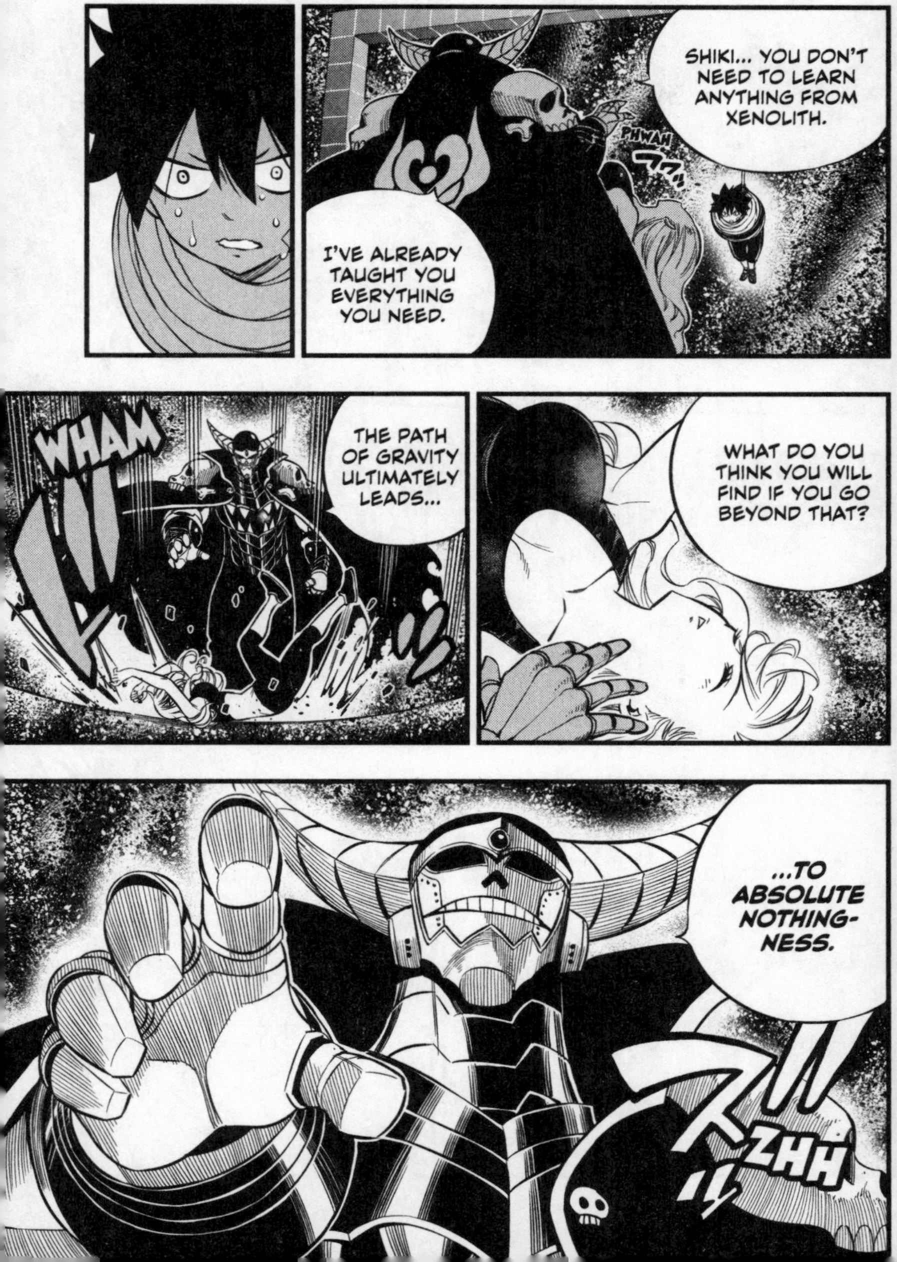
SHIKI... YOU DON'T NEED TO LEARN ANYTHING FROM XENOLITH.
PHWAH
I'VE ALREADY TAUGHT YOU EVERYTHING YOU NEED.
WHAT DO YOU THINK YOU WILL FIND IF YOU GO BEYOND THAT?
WHAM
THE PATH OF GRAVITY ULTIMATELY LEADS...
...TO ABSOLUTE NOTHING-NESS.
ZHH

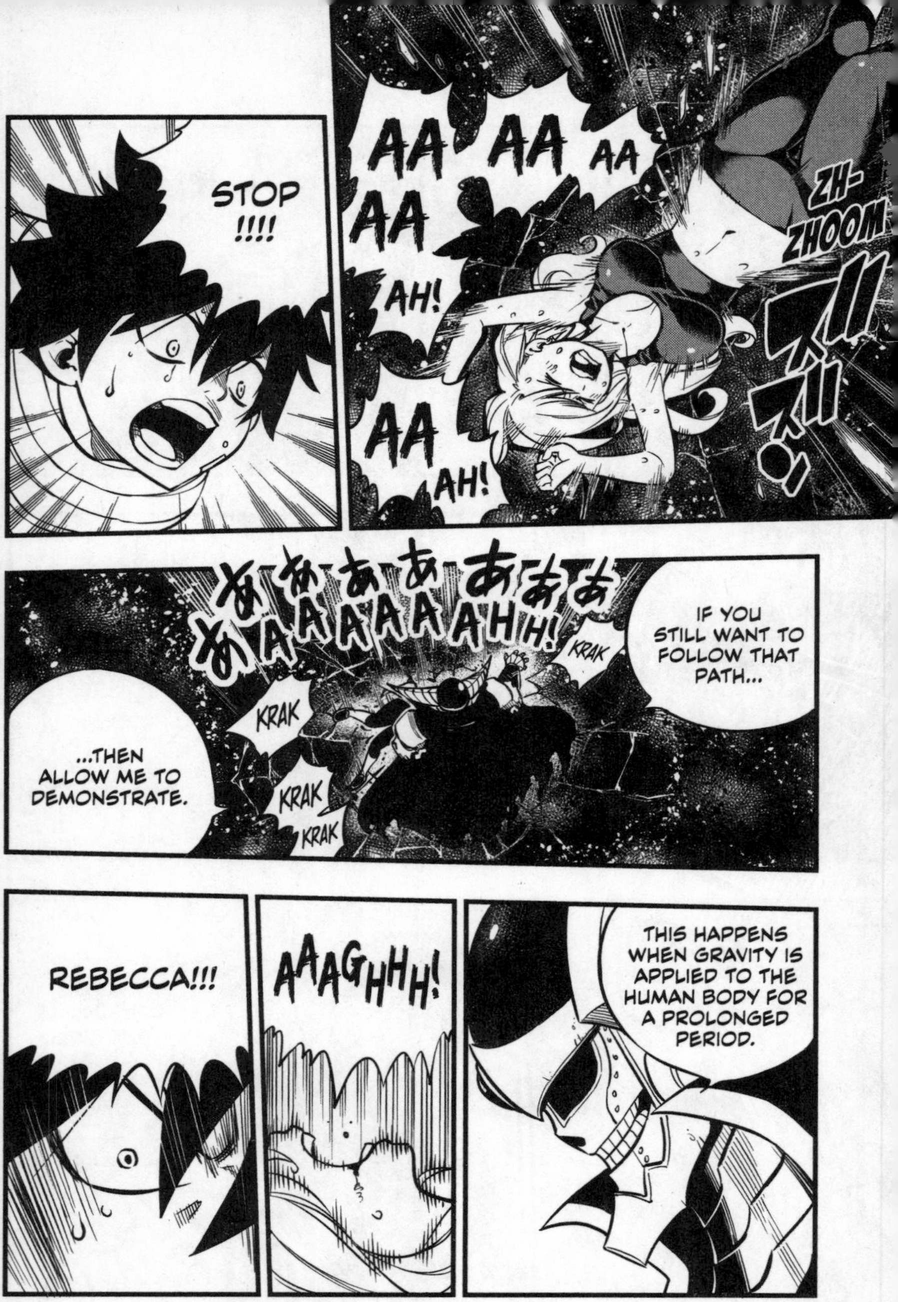
AA AA AA
AA
AH!
AA
AH!
ZH-ZHOOM
STOP
!!!!
AAAAAAAHH!
IF YOU STILL WANT TO FOLLOW THAT PATH...
KRAK
KRAK
...THEN ALLOW ME TO DEMONSTRATE.
KRAK
KRAK
THIS HAPPENS WHEN GRAVITY IS APPLIED TO THE HUMAN BODY FOR A PROLONGED PERIOD.
AAAGHHH!
REBECCA!!!

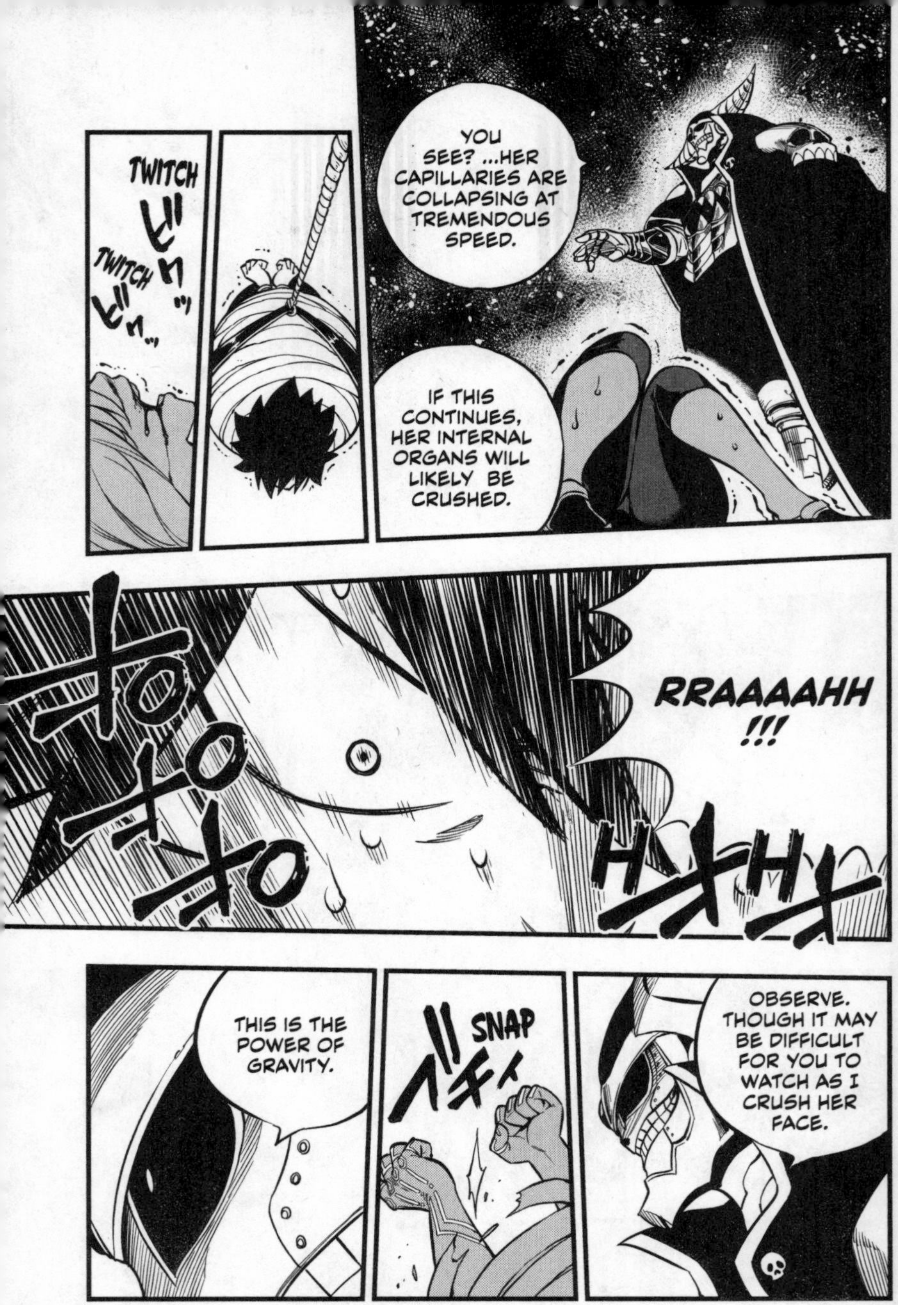

YOU SEE? ...HER CAPILLARIES ARE COLLAPSING AT TREMENDOUS SPEED.
IF THIS CONTINUES, HER INTERNAL ORGANS WILL LIKELY BE CRUSHED.
TWITCH
TWITCH
RRAAAAHH !!!
OBSERVE. THOUGH IT MAY BE DIFFICULT FOR YOU TO WATCH AS I CRUSH HER FACE.
SNAP
THIS IS THE POWER OF GRAVITY.

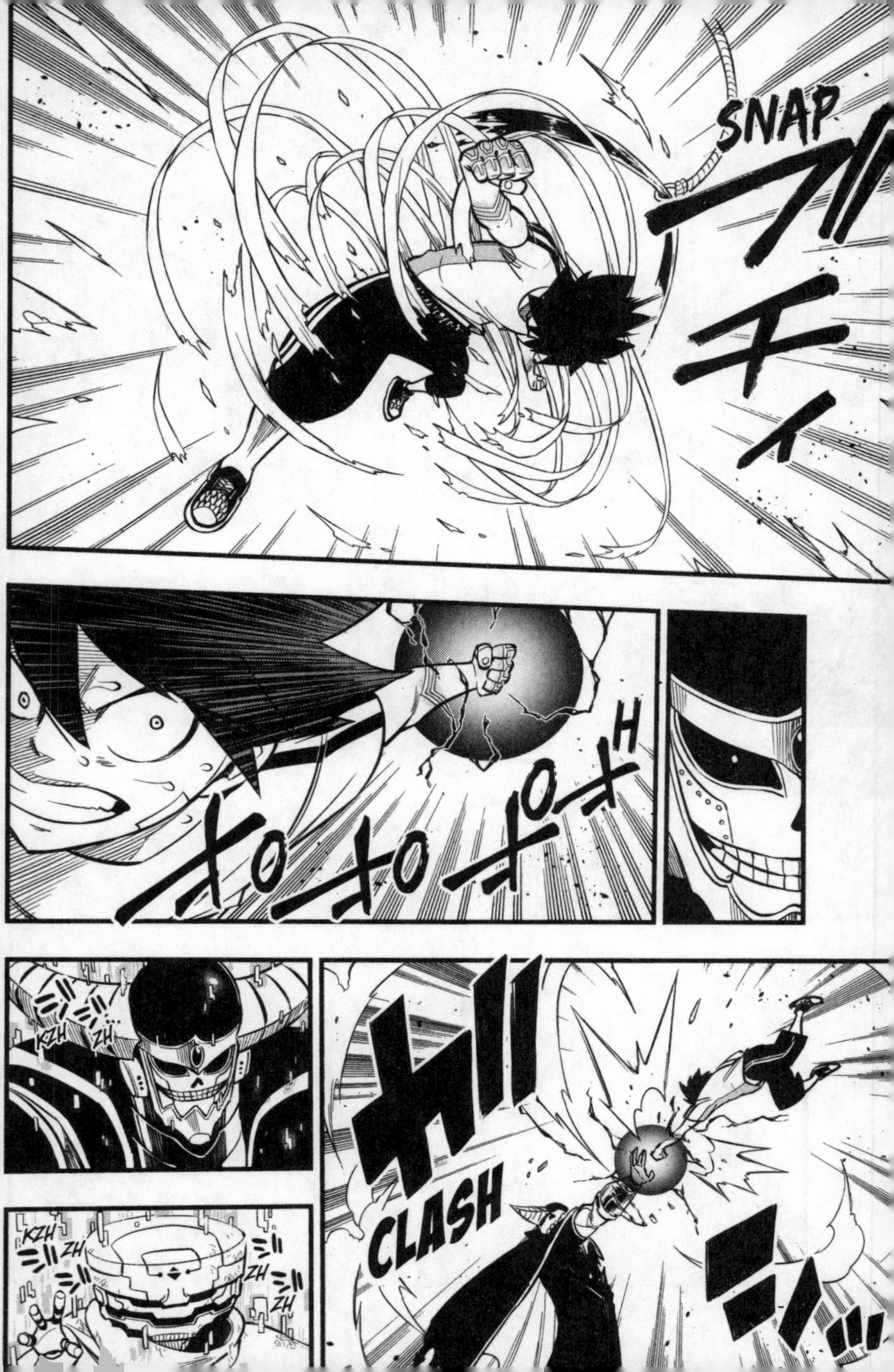
SNAP
H
CLASH
KZH
ZH
KZH
ZH
ZH
ZH

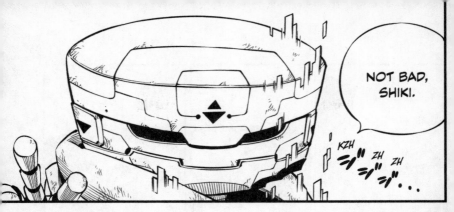

NOT BAD, SHIKI.
KZH ZH ZH...
HUH?!
YOU ACTIVATED YOUR ETHER GEAR DESPITE YOUR RESTRAINTS AND MANAGED TO ESCAPE.
WOW!! HOW DID YOU DO THAT?!
I...I AM TRULY IMPRESSED.
...
S-SO NOW JUST TIE ME UP THE NORMAL WAY, OKAY?! RIGHT?!!
THE WAY YOU'RE TIED UP. IT'S CREEPY.
STAY AWAY FROM KLEENE, YOU PERVERT!!

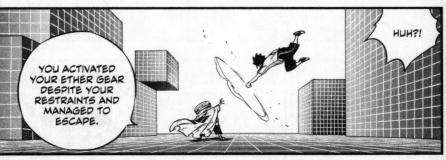

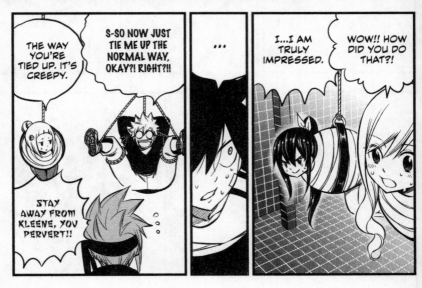

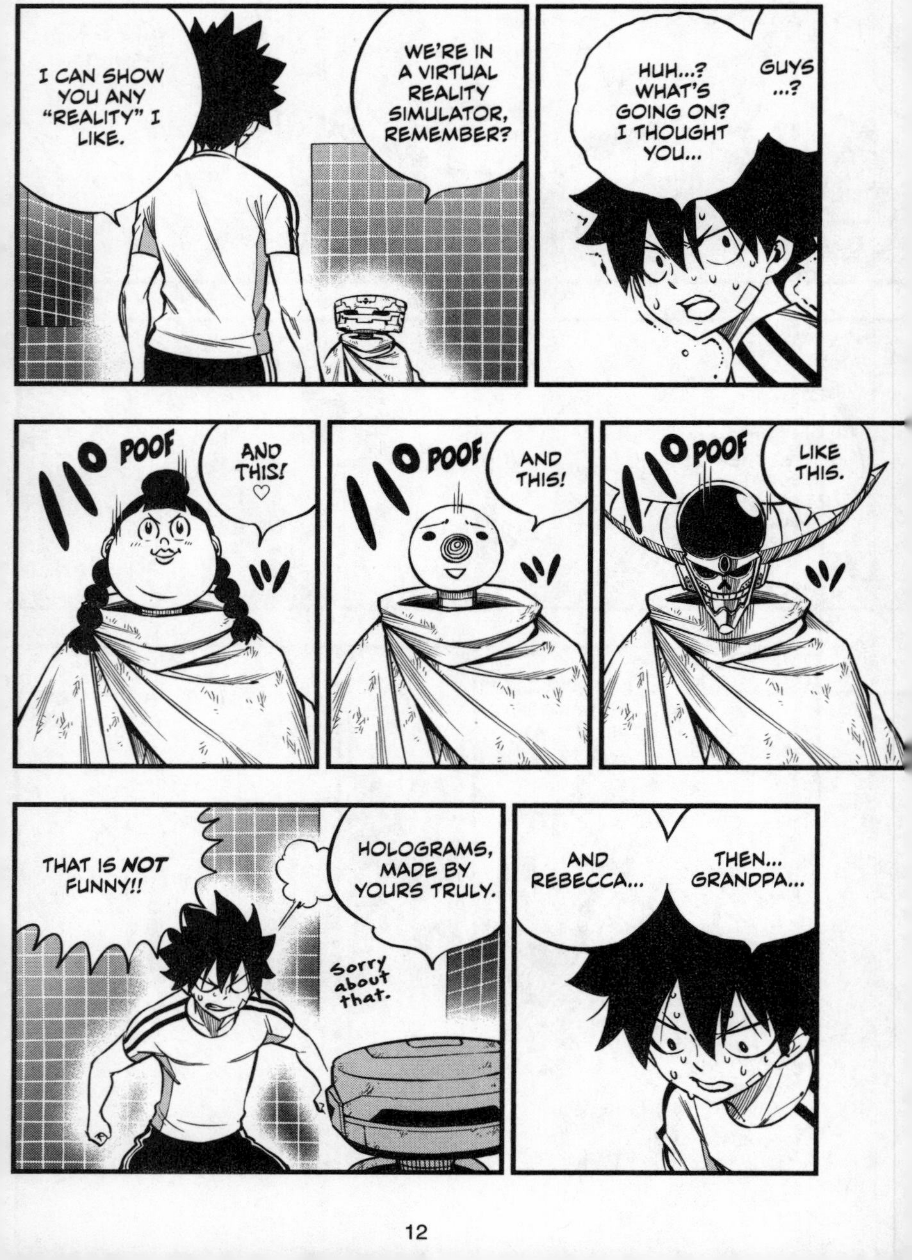
GUYS ...?
HUH...? WHAT'S GOING ON? I THOUGHT YOU...
WE'RE IN A VIRTUAL REALITY SIMULATOR, REMEMBER?
I CAN SHOW YOU ANY "REALITY" I LIKE.
POOF
LIKE THIS.
POOF
AND THIS!
POOF
AND THIS! ♡
THEN... GRANDPA...
AND REBECCA...
HOLOGRAMS, MADE BY YOURS TRULY.
Sorry about that.
THAT IS NOT FUNNY!!

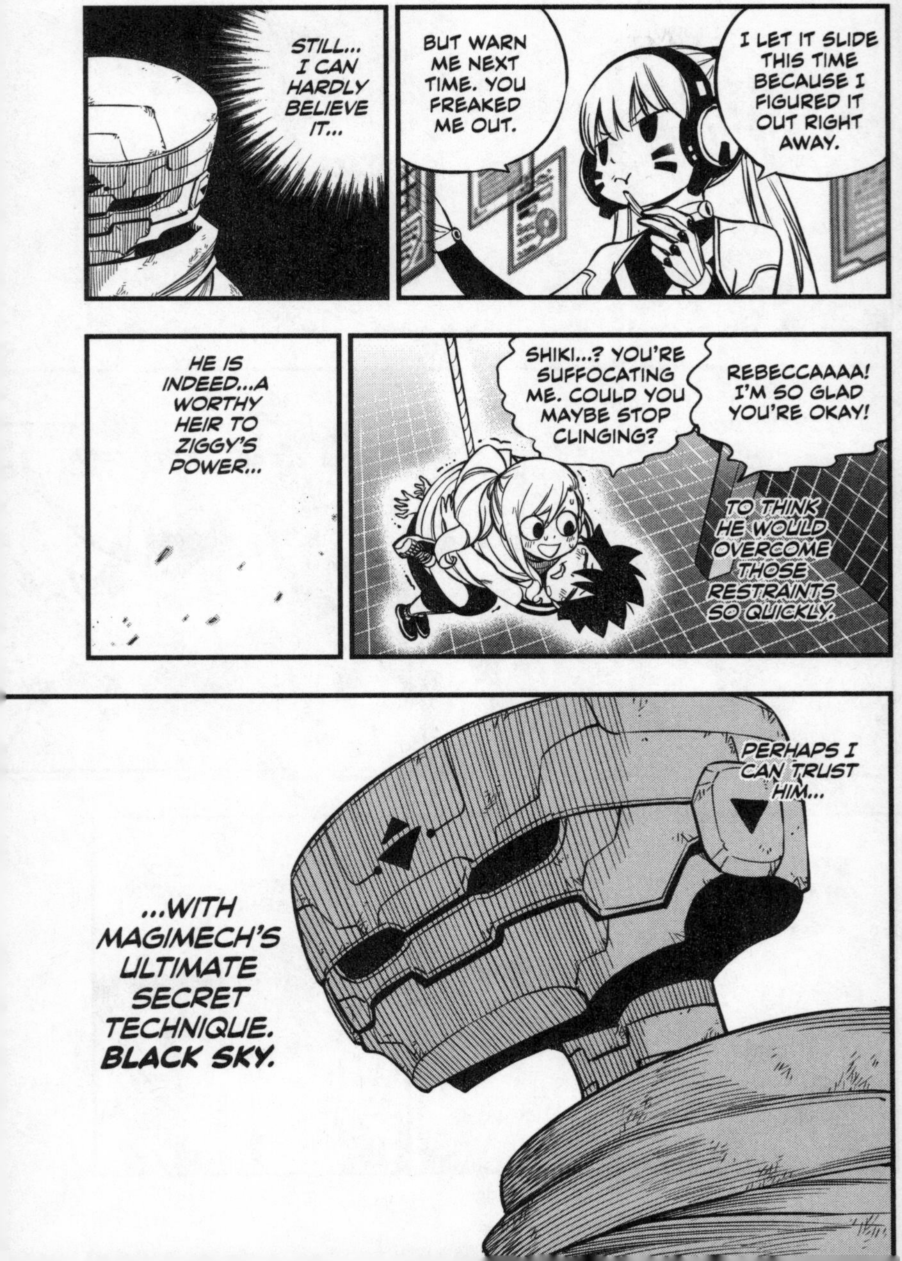
I LET IT SLIDE THIS TIME BECAUSE I FIGURED IT OUT RIGHT AWAY.
BUT WARN ME NEXT TIME. YOU FREAKED ME OUT.
STILL... I CAN HARDLY BELIEVE IT...
REBECCAAAA! I'M SO GLAD YOU'RE OKAY!
SHIKI...? YOU'RE SUFFOCATING ME. COULD YOU MAYBE STOP CLINGING?
TO THINK HE WOULD OVERCOME THOSE RESTRAINTS SO QUICKLY.
HE IS INDEED...A WORTHY HEIR TO ZIGGY'S POWER...
PERHAPS I CAN TRUST HIM...
...WITH MAGIMECH'S ULTIMATE SECRET TECHNIQUE. BLACK SKY.

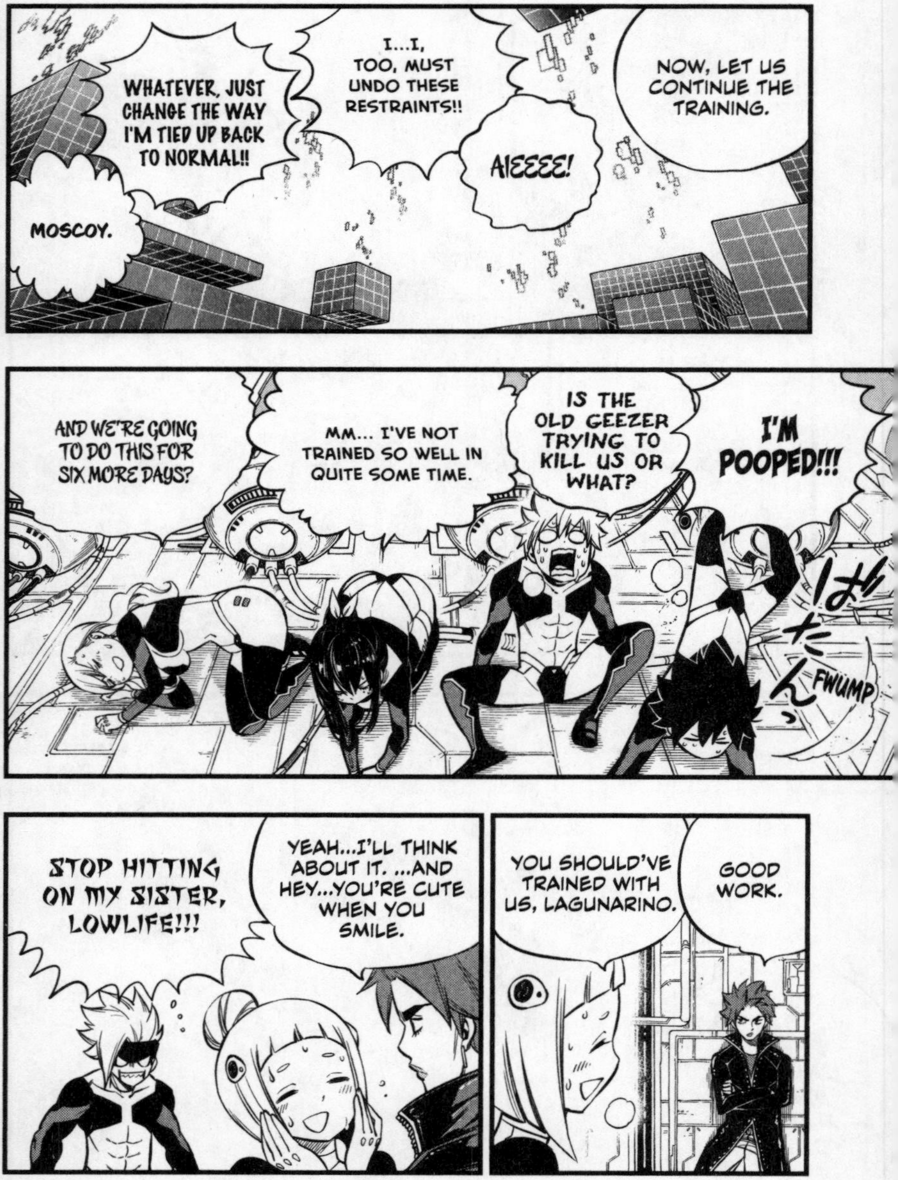
NOW, LET US CONTINUE THE TRAINING.
AIEEEE!
I...I, TOO, MUST UNDO THESE RESTRAINTS!!
WHATEVER, JUST CHANGE THE WAY I'M TIED UP BACK TO NORMAL!!
MOSCOY.
I'M POOPED!!!
FWUMP
IS THE OLD GEEZER TRYING TO KILL US OR WHAT?
MM... I'VE NOT TRAINED SO WELL IN QUITE SOME TIME.
AND WE'RE GOING TO DO THIS FOR SIX MORE DAYS?
GOOD WORK.
YOU SHOULD'VE TRAINED WITH US, LAGUNARINO.
YEAH...I'LL THINK ABOUT IT. ...AND HEY...YOU'RE CUTE WHEN YOU SMILE.
STOP HITTING ON MY SISTER, LOWLIFE!!!

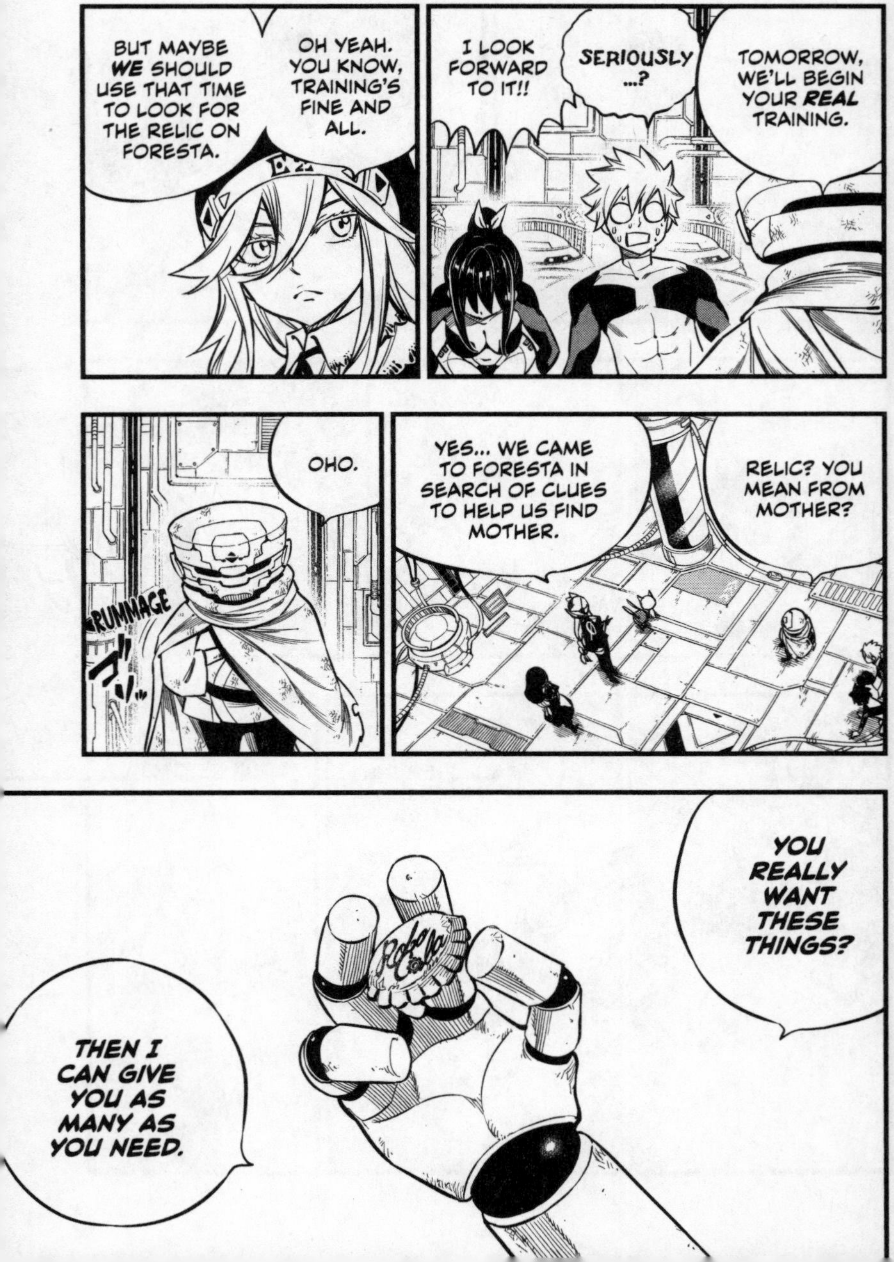
TOMORROW, WE'LL BEGIN YOUR *REAL* TRAINING.
SERIOUSLY ...?
I LOOK FORWARD TO IT!!
OH YEAH. YOU KNOW, TRAINING'S FINE AND ALL.
BUT MAYBE *WE* SHOULD USE THAT TIME TO LOOK FOR THE RELIC ON FORESTA.
RELIC? YOU MEAN FROM MOTHER?
YES... WE CAME TO FORESTA IN SEARCH OF CLUES TO HELP US FIND MOTHER.
OHO.
RUMMAGE
YOU REALLY WANT THESE THINGS?
THEN I CAN GIVE YOU AS MANY AS YOU NEED.

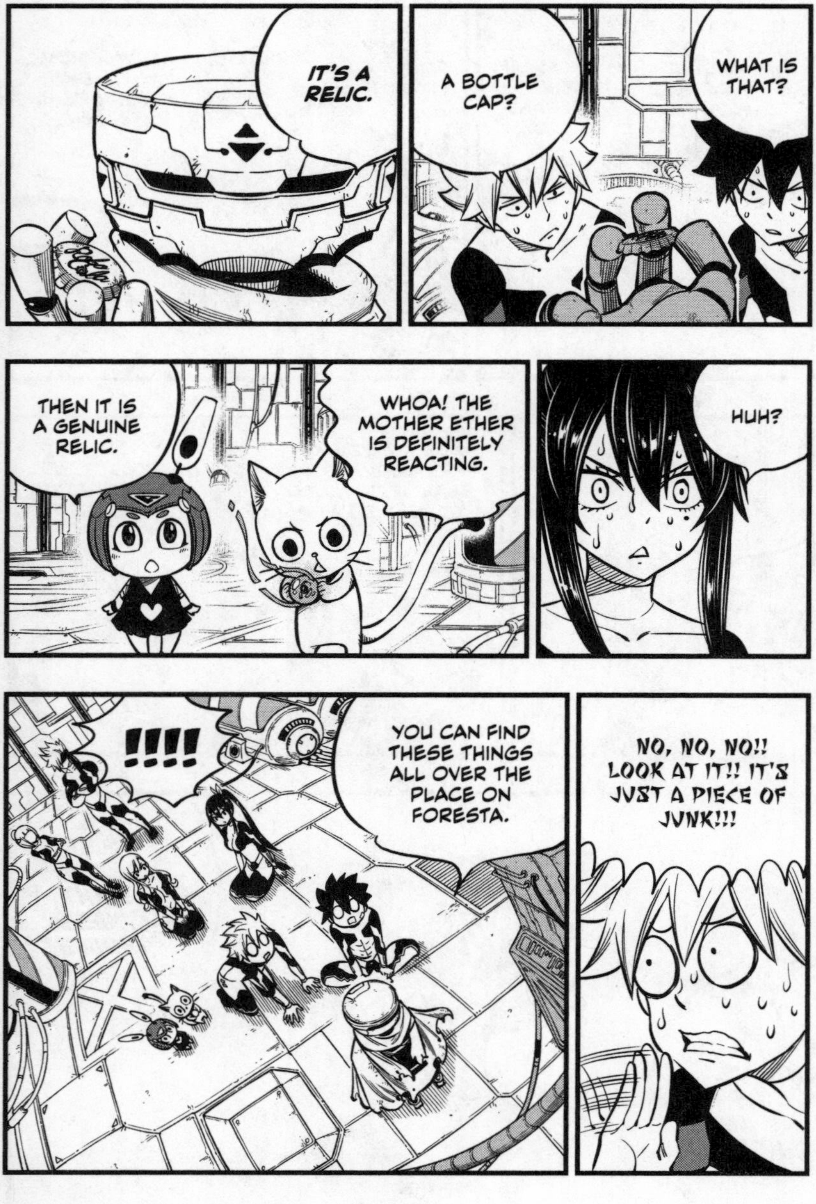
WHAT IS THAT?
A BOTTLE CAP?
IT'S A RELIC.
HUH?
WHOA! THE MOTHER ETHER IS DEFINITELY REACTING.
THEN IT IS A GENUINE RELIC.
NO, NO, NO!! LOOK AT IT!! IT'S JUST A PIECE OF JUNK!!!
YOU CAN FIND THESE THINGS ALL OVER THE PLACE ON FORESTA.
!!!!

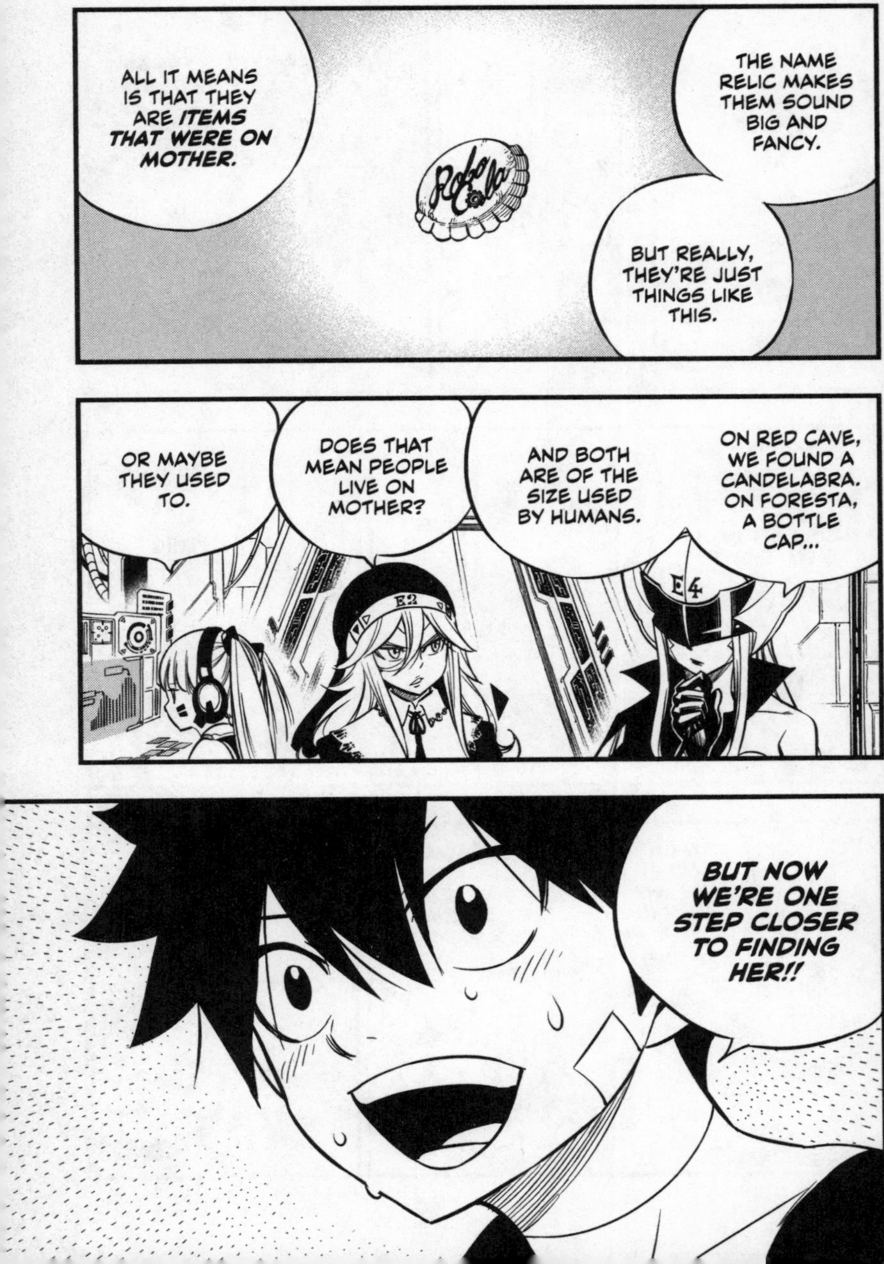
THE NAME RELIC MAKES THEM SOUND BIG AND FANCY.
BUT REALLY, THEY'RE JUST THINGS LIKE THIS.
ALL IT MEANS IS THAT THEY ARE *ITEMS THAT WERE ON MOTHER.*
ON RED CAVE, WE FOUND A CANDELABRA. ON FORESTA, A BOTTLE CAP...
AND BOTH ARE OF THE SIZE USED BY HUMANS.
DOES THAT MEAN PEOPLE LIVE ON MOTHER?
OR MAYBE THEY USED TO.
BUT NOW WE'RE ONE STEP CLOSER TO FINDING HER!!

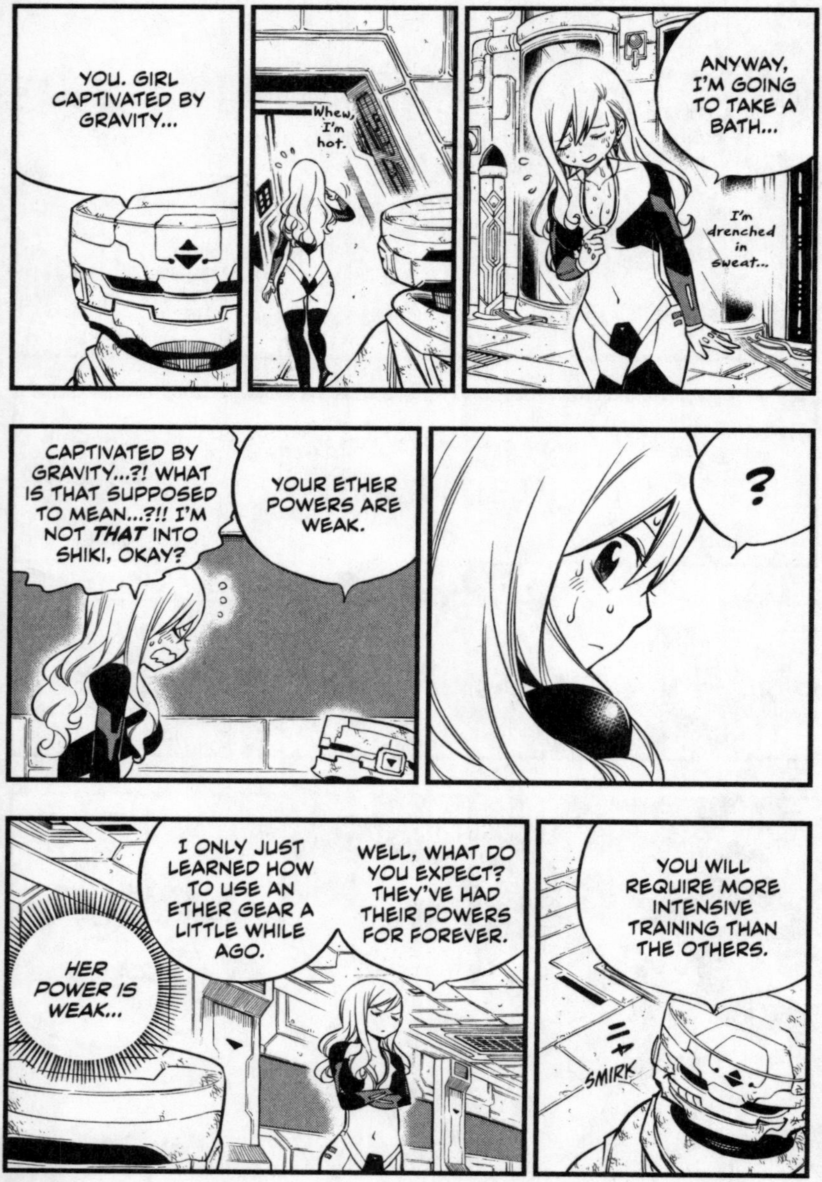
ANYWAY, I'M GOING TO TAKE A BATH...
I'm drenched in sweat...
Whew, I'm hot.
YOU. GIRL CAPTIVATED BY GRAVITY...
?
YOUR ETHER POWERS ARE WEAK.
CAPTIVATED BY GRAVITY...?! WHAT IS THAT SUPPOSED TO MEAN...?!! I'M NOT *THAT* INTO SHIKI, OKAY?
YOU WILL REQUIRE MORE INTENSIVE TRAINING THAN THE OTHERS.
SMIRK
WELL, WHAT DO YOU EXPECT? THEY'VE HAD THEIR POWERS FOR FOREVER.
I ONLY JUST LEARNED HOW TO USE AN ETHER GEAR A LITTLE WHILE AGO.
HER POWER IS WEAK...

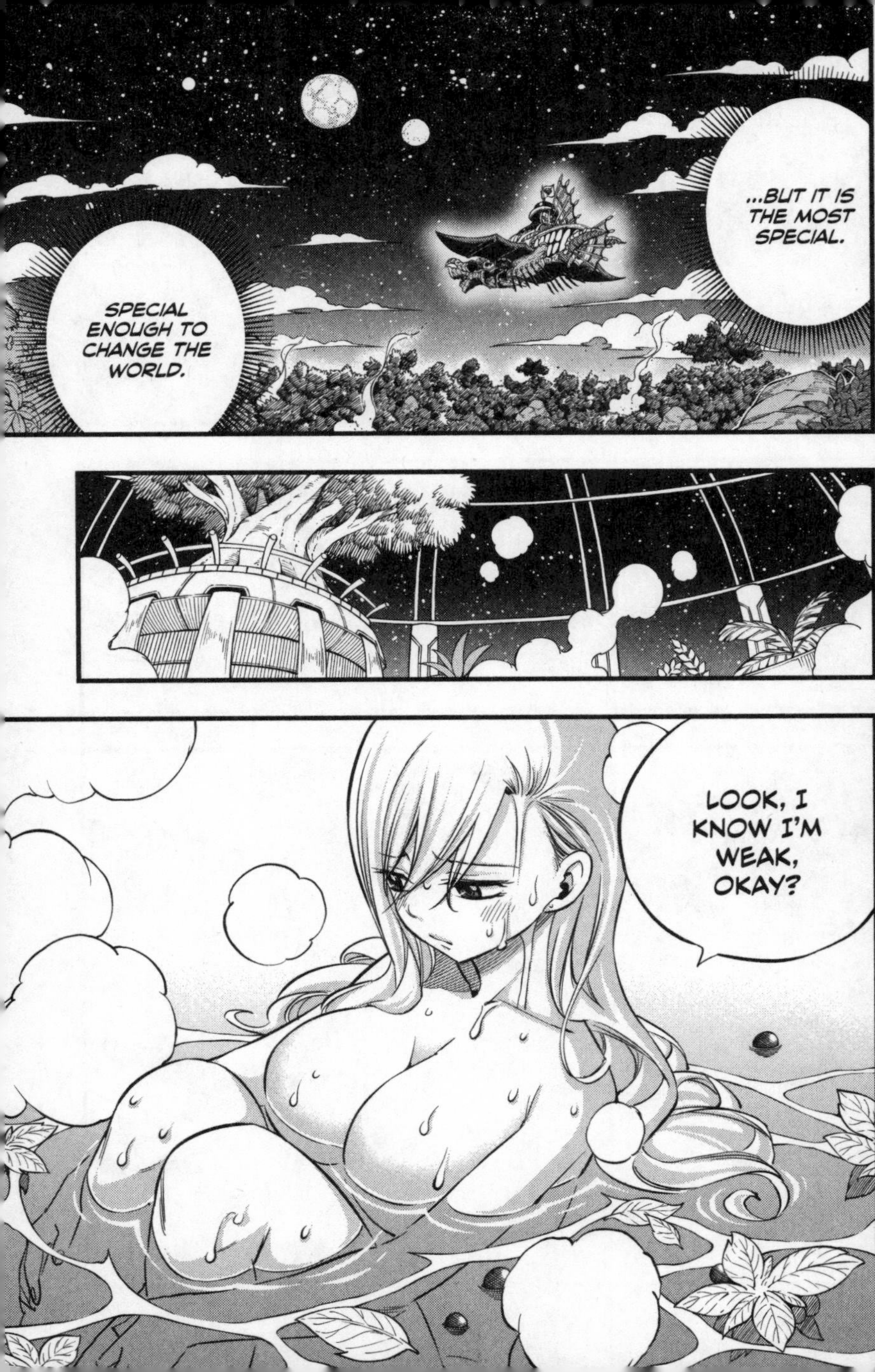
...BUT IT IS THE MOST SPECIAL.
SPECIAL ENOUGH TO CHANGE THE WORLD.
LOOK, I KNOW I'M WEAK, OKAY?

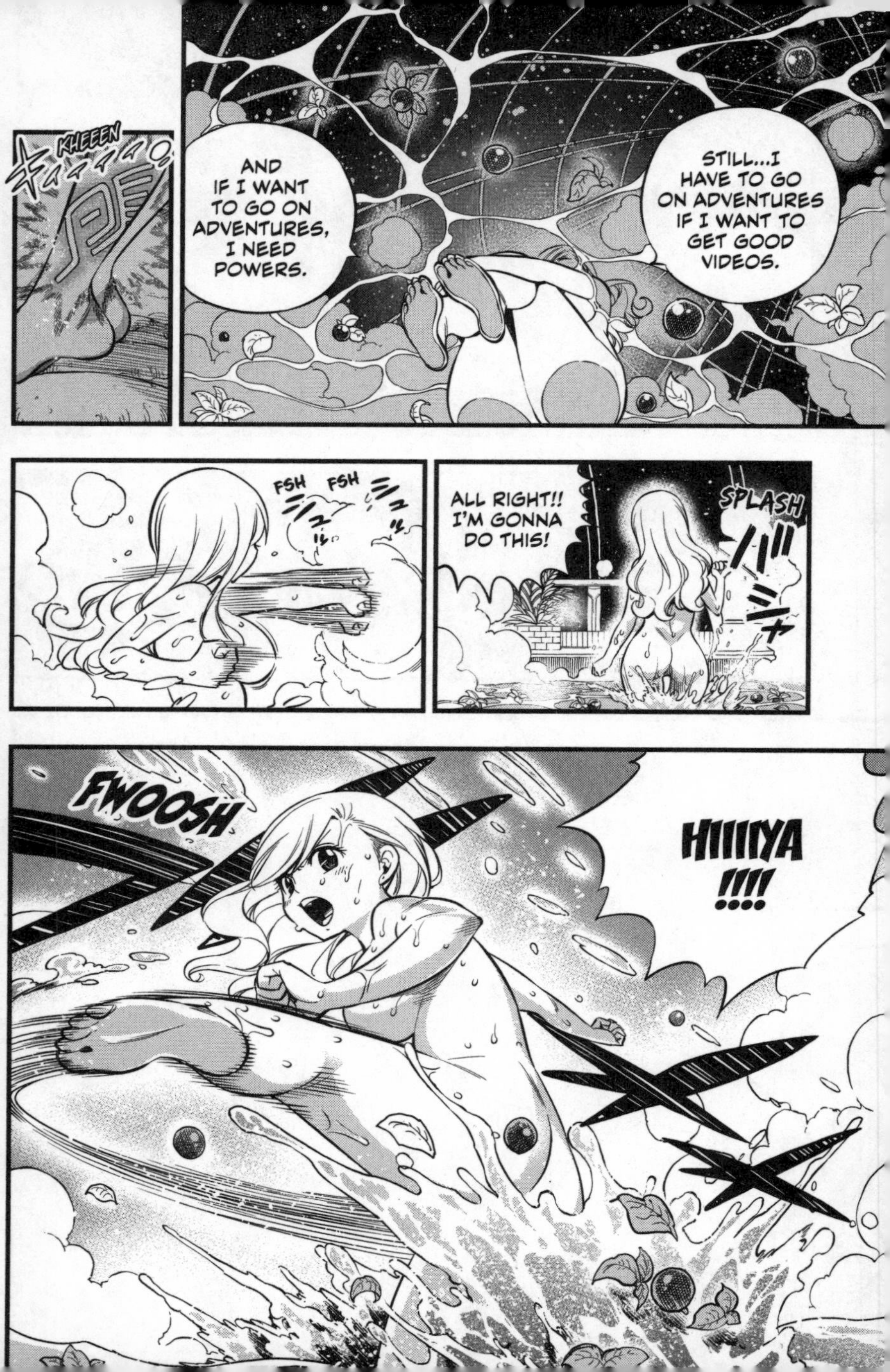
STILL...I HAVE TO GO ON ADVENTURES IF I WANT TO GET GOOD VIDEOS.
AND IF I WANT TO GO ON ADVENTURES, I NEED POWERS.
KHEEEN
SPLASH
ALL RIGHT!! I'M GONNA DO THIS!
FSH FSH
HIIIIYA !!!!
FWOOSH

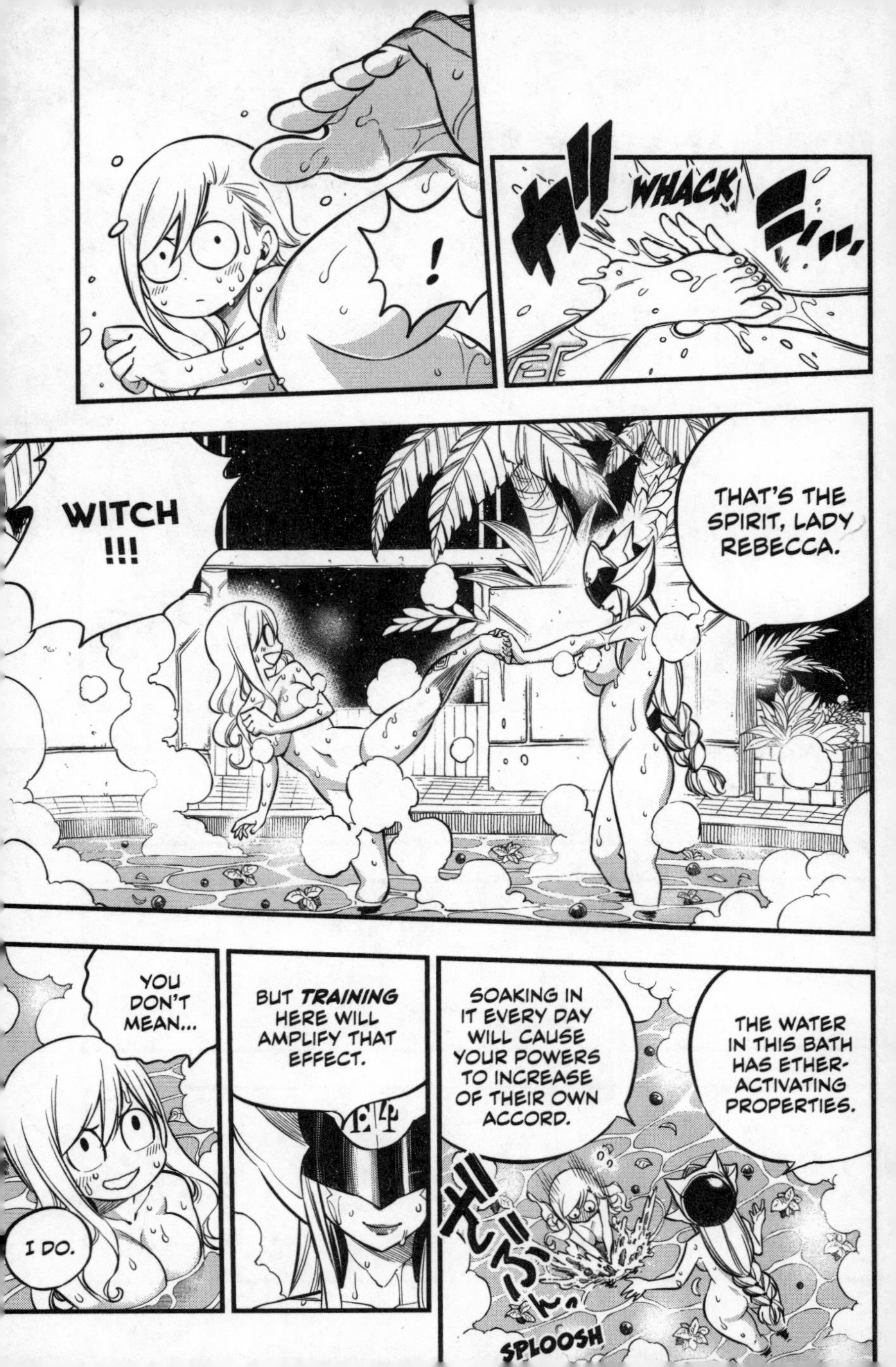

WHACK
!
THAT'S THE SPIRIT, LADY REBECCA.
WITCH!!!
THE WATER IN THIS BATH HAS ETHER-ACTIVATING PROPERTIES.
SOAKING IN IT EVERY DAY WILL CAUSE YOUR POWERS TO INCREASE OF THEIR OWN ACCORD.
SPLOOSH
BUT *TRAINING* HERE WILL AMPLIFY THAT EFFECT.
YOU DON'T MEAN...
I DO.

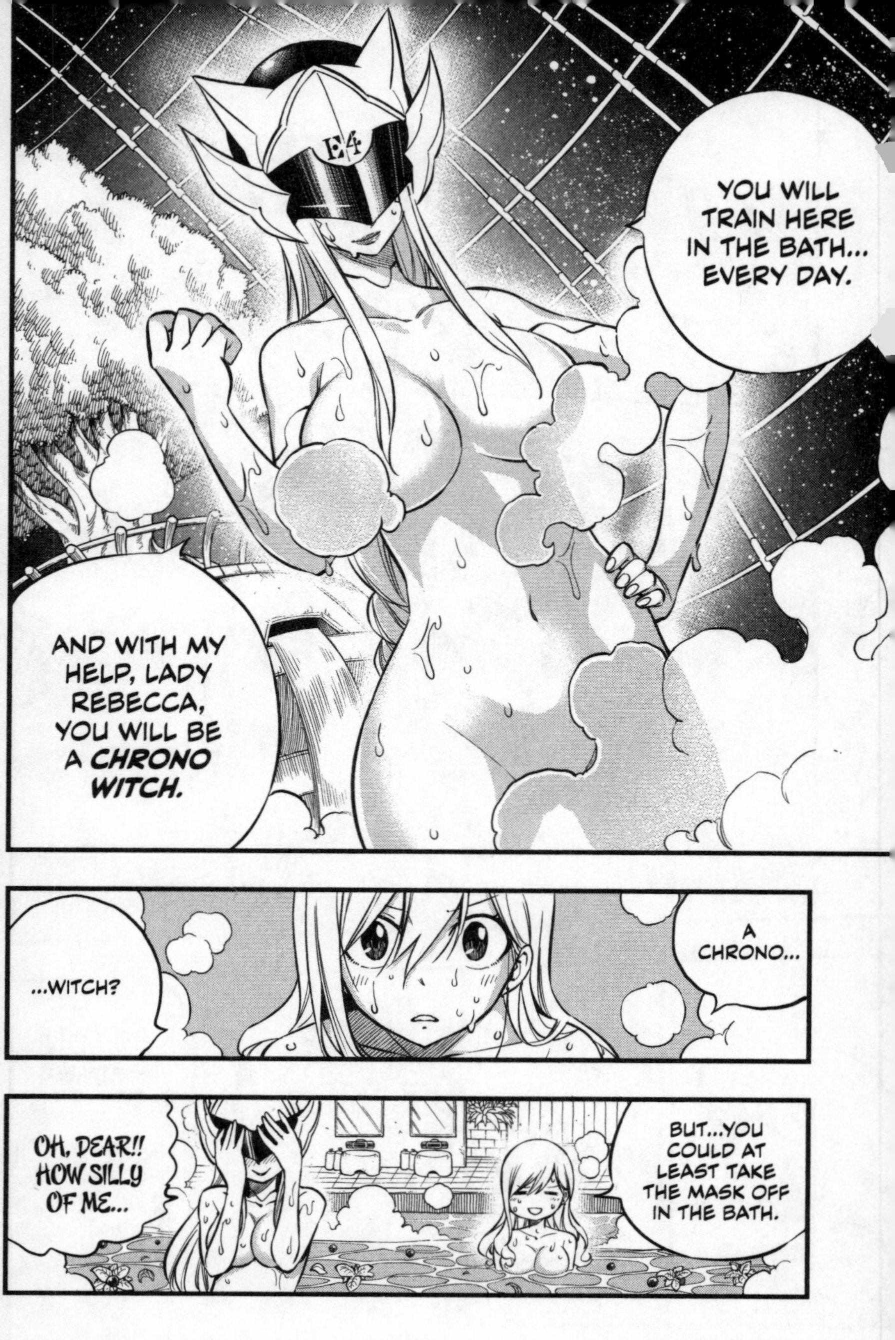
YOU WILL TRAIN HERE IN THE BATH... EVERY DAY.
AND WITH MY HELP, LADY REBECCA, YOU WILL BE A *CHRONO WITCH.*
A CHRONO...
...WITCH?
BUT...YOU COULD AT LEAST TAKE THE MASK OFF IN THE BATH.
OH, DEAR!! HOW SILLY OF ME...

EDENS ZERO

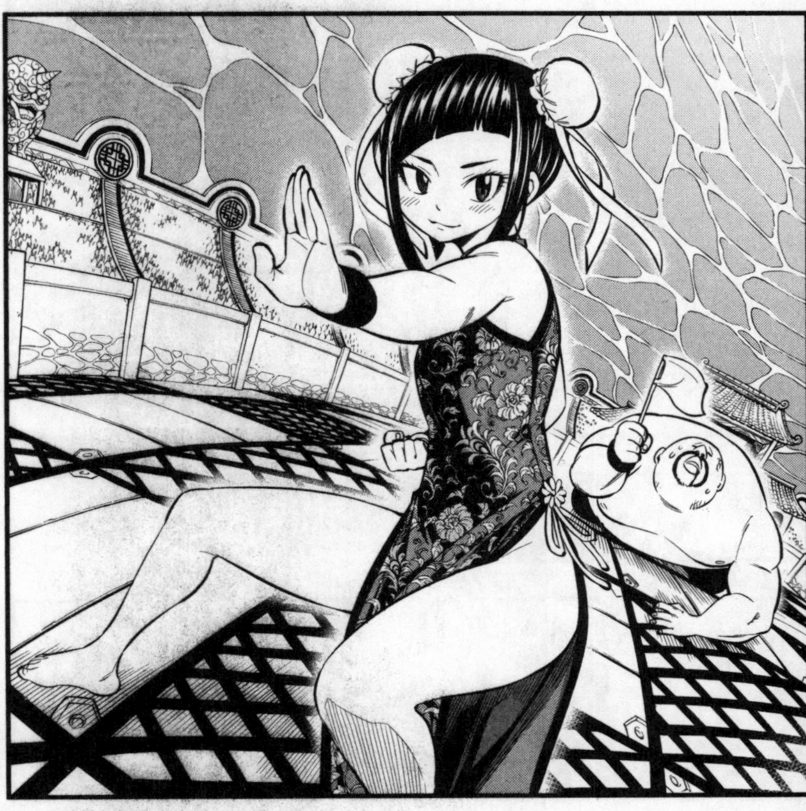

CHAPTER 133: FOLLOWING ZIGGY'S PATH

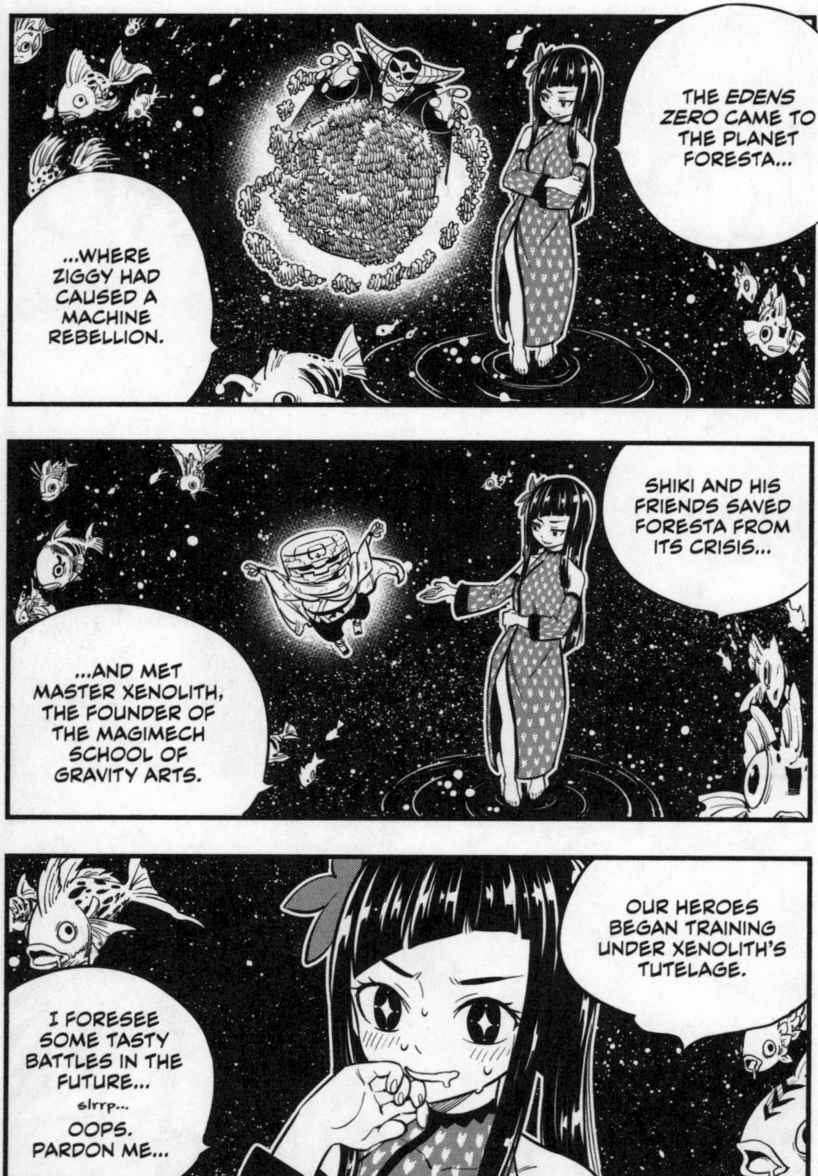
THE EDENS ZERO CAME TO THE PLANET FORESTA...
...WHERE ZIGGY HAD CAUSED A MACHINE REBELLION.
SHIKI AND HIS FRIENDS SAVED FORESTA FROM ITS CRISIS...
...AND MET MASTER XENOLITH, THE FOUNDER OF THE MAGIMECH SCHOOL OF GRAVITY ARTS.
OUR HEROES BEGAN TRAINING UNDER XENOLITH'S TUTELAGE.
I FORESEE SOME TASTY BATTLES IN THE FUTURE...
slrrp...
OOPS. PARDON ME...

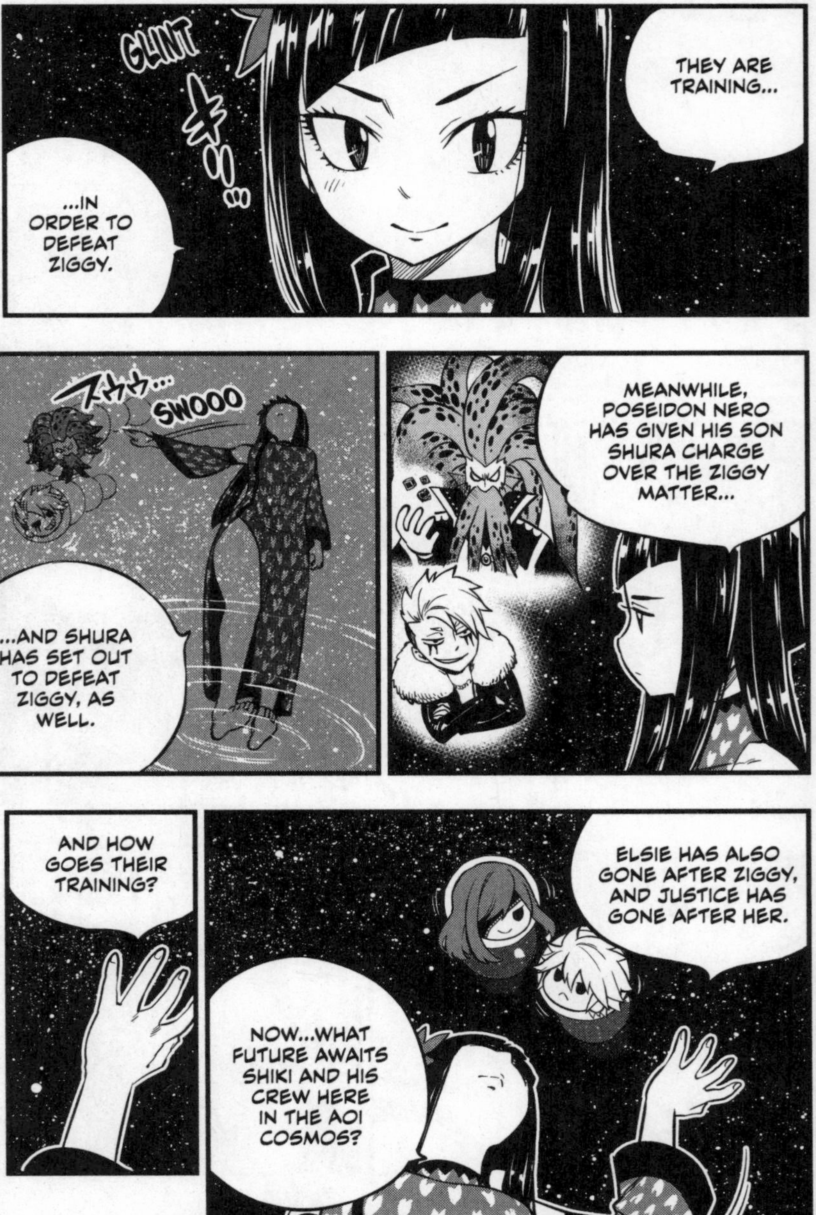
THEY ARE TRAINING...
GLINT
...IN ORDER TO DEFEAT ZIGGY.
MEANWHILE, POSEIDON NERO HAS GIVEN HIS SON SHURA CHARGE OVER THE ZIGGY MATTER...
SWOOO
...AND SHURA HAS SET OUT TO DEFEAT ZIGGY, AS WELL.
ELSIE HAS ALSO GONE AFTER ZIGGY, AND JUSTICE HAS GONE AFTER HER.
NOW...WHAT FUTURE AWAITS SHIKI AND HIS CREW HERE IN THE AOI COSMOS?
AND HOW GOES THEIR TRAINING?

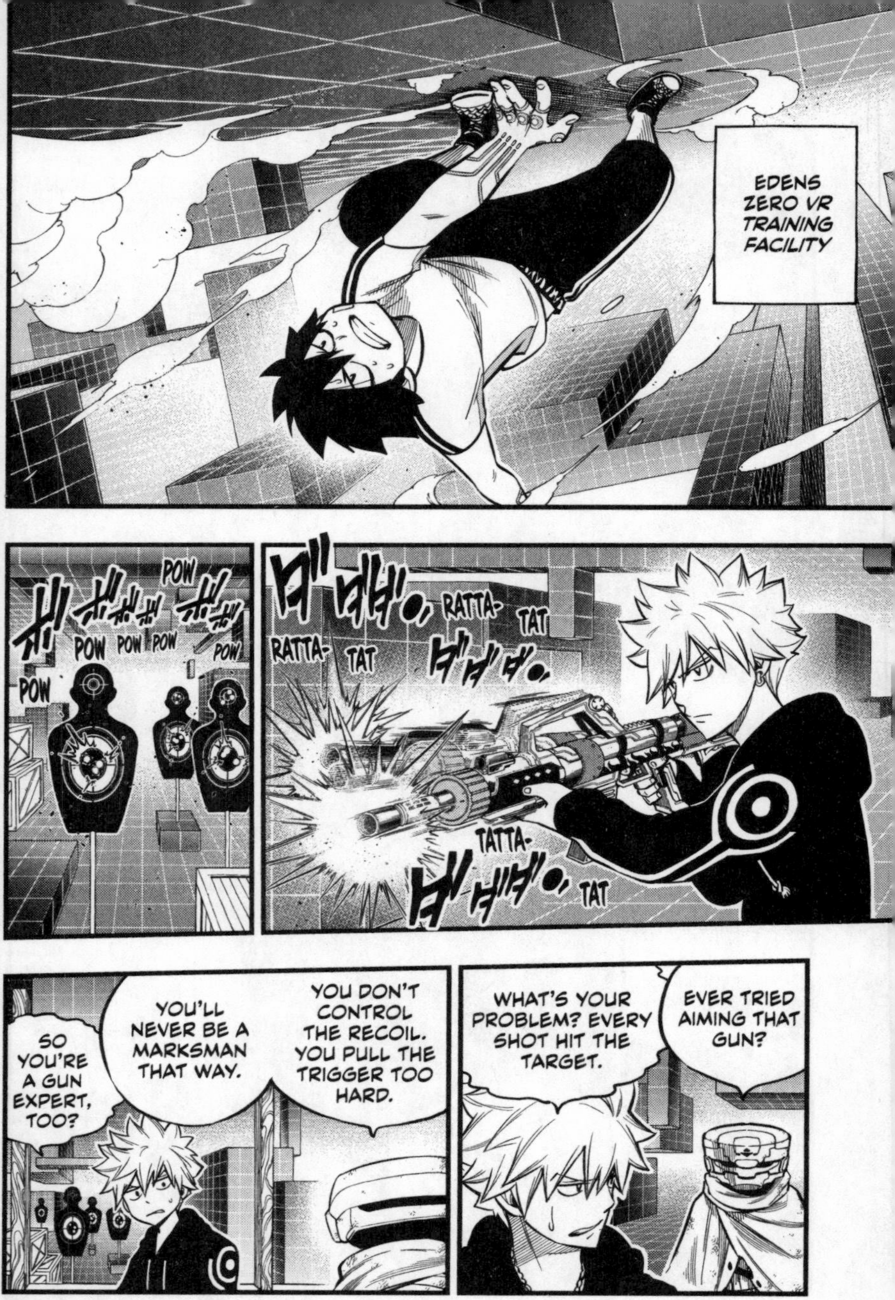
EDENS ZERO VR TRAINING FACILITY
RATTA-TAT
RATTA-TAT
TATTA-TAT
POW
POW
POW
POW
POW
POW
EVER TRIED AIMING THAT GUN?
WHAT'S YOUR PROBLEM? EVERY SHOT HIT THE TARGET.
YOU DON'T CONTROL THE RECOIL. YOU PULL THE TRIGGER TOO HARD.
YOU'LL NEVER BE A MARKSMAN THAT WAY.
SO YOU'RE A GUN EXPERT, TOO?

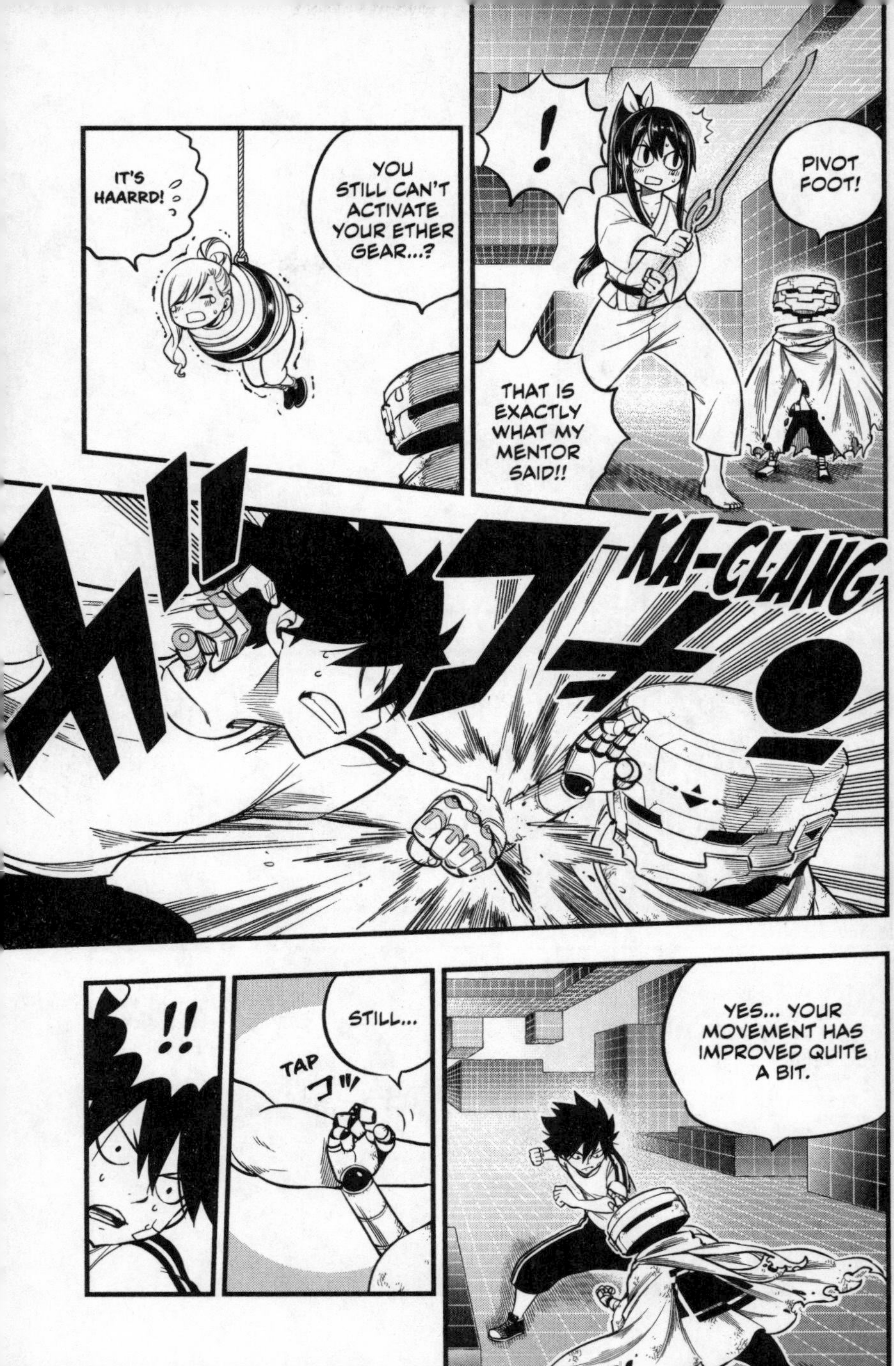
PIVOT FOOT!
!
THAT IS EXACTLY WHAT MY MENTOR SAID!!
YOU STILL CAN'T ACTIVATE YOUR ETHER GEAR...?
IT'S HAARRD!
KA-CLANG
YES... YOUR MOVEMENT HAS IMPROVED QUITE A BIT.
STILL...
TAP
!!

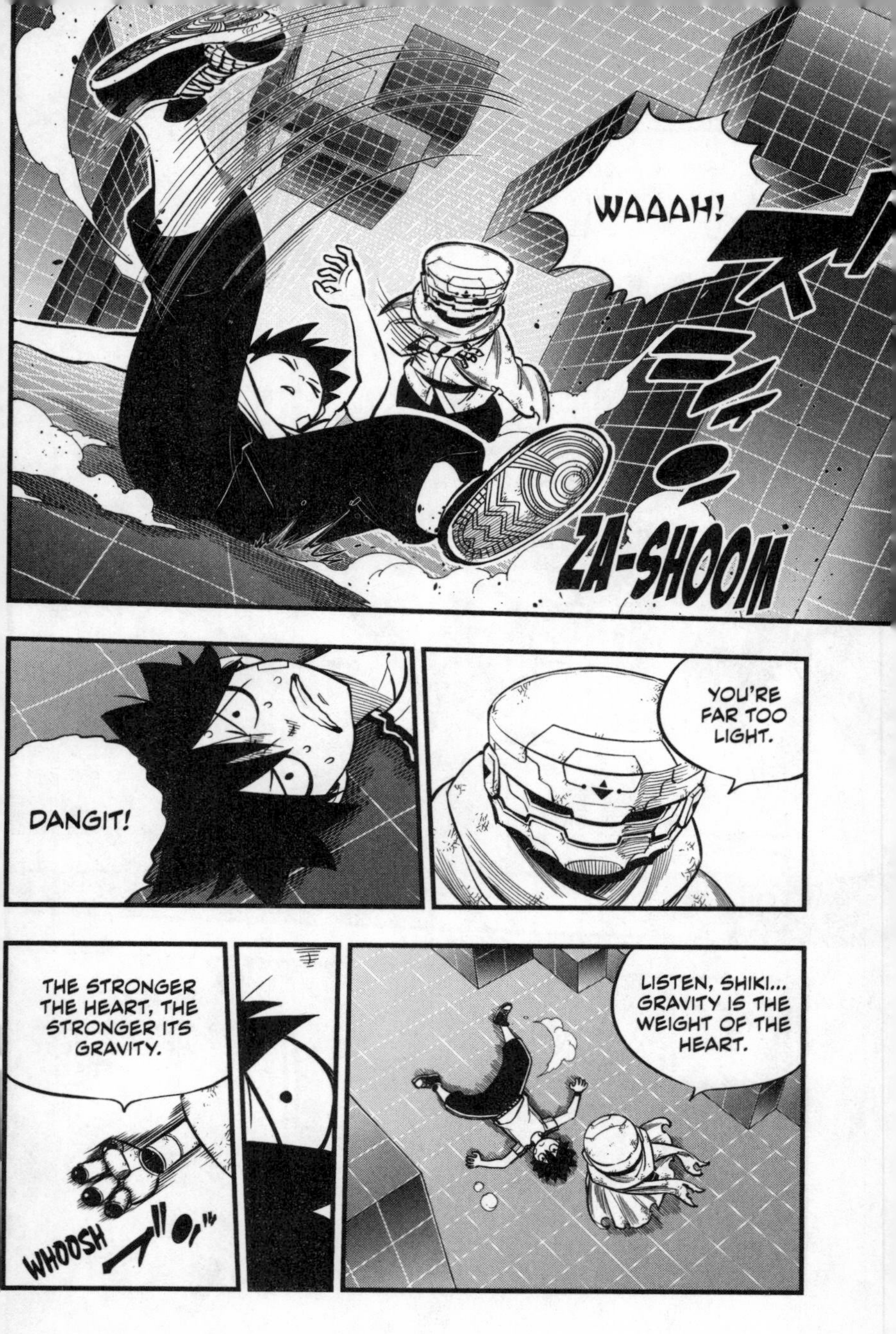
WAAAH!
ZA-SHOOM
YOU'RE FAR TOO LIGHT.
DANGIT!
LISTEN, SHIKI... GRAVITY IS THE WEIGHT OF THE HEART.
THE STRONGER THE HEART, THE STRONGER ITS GRAVITY.
WHOOSH

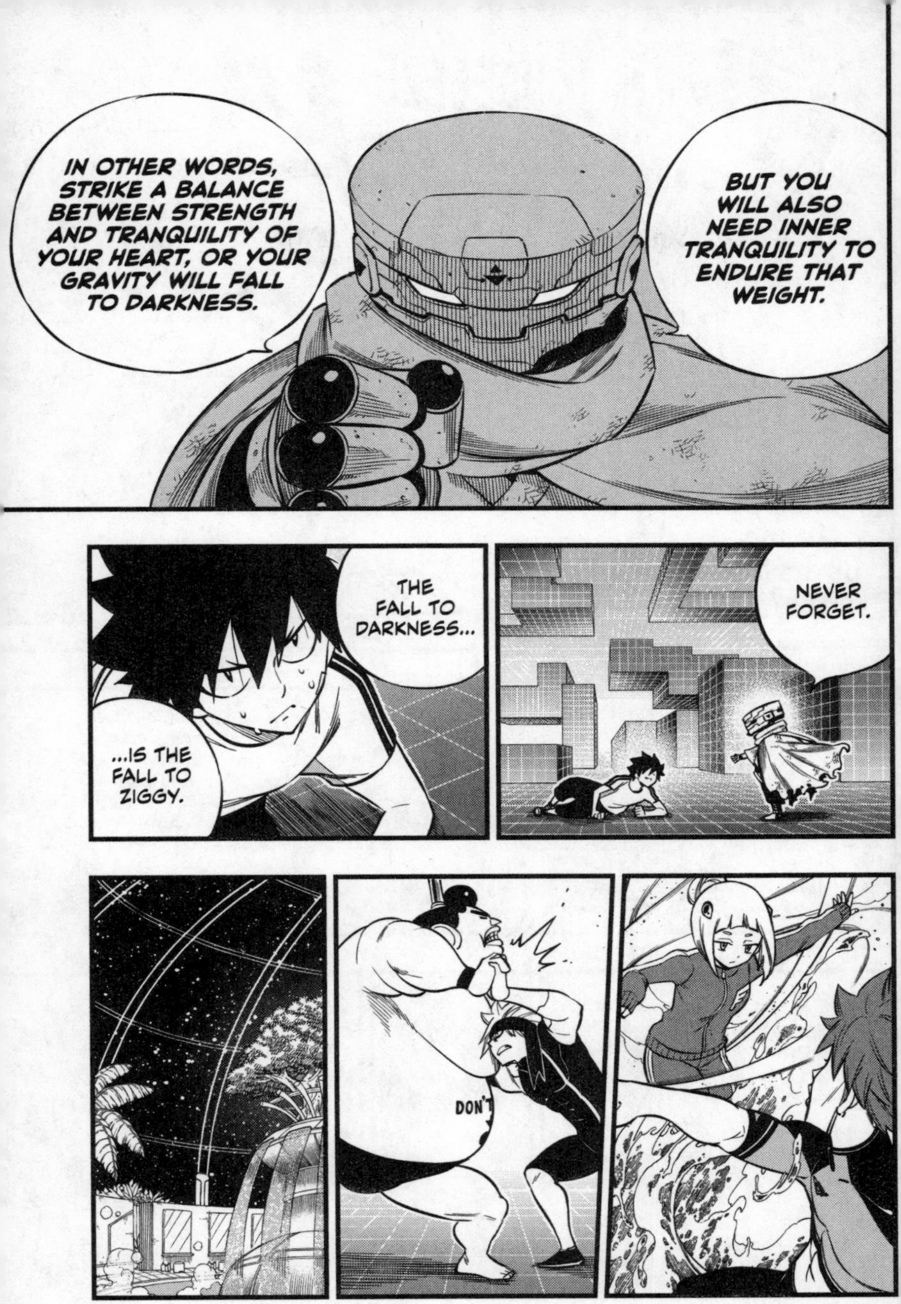
BUT YOU WILL ALSO NEED INNER TRANQUILITY TO ENDURE THAT WEIGHT.
IN OTHER WORDS, STRIKE A BALANCE BETWEEN STRENGTH AND TRANQUILITY OF YOUR HEART, OR YOUR GRAVITY WILL FALL TO DARKNESS.
NEVER FORGET.
THE FALL TO DARKNESS...
...IS THE FALL TO ZIGGY.
DON'T

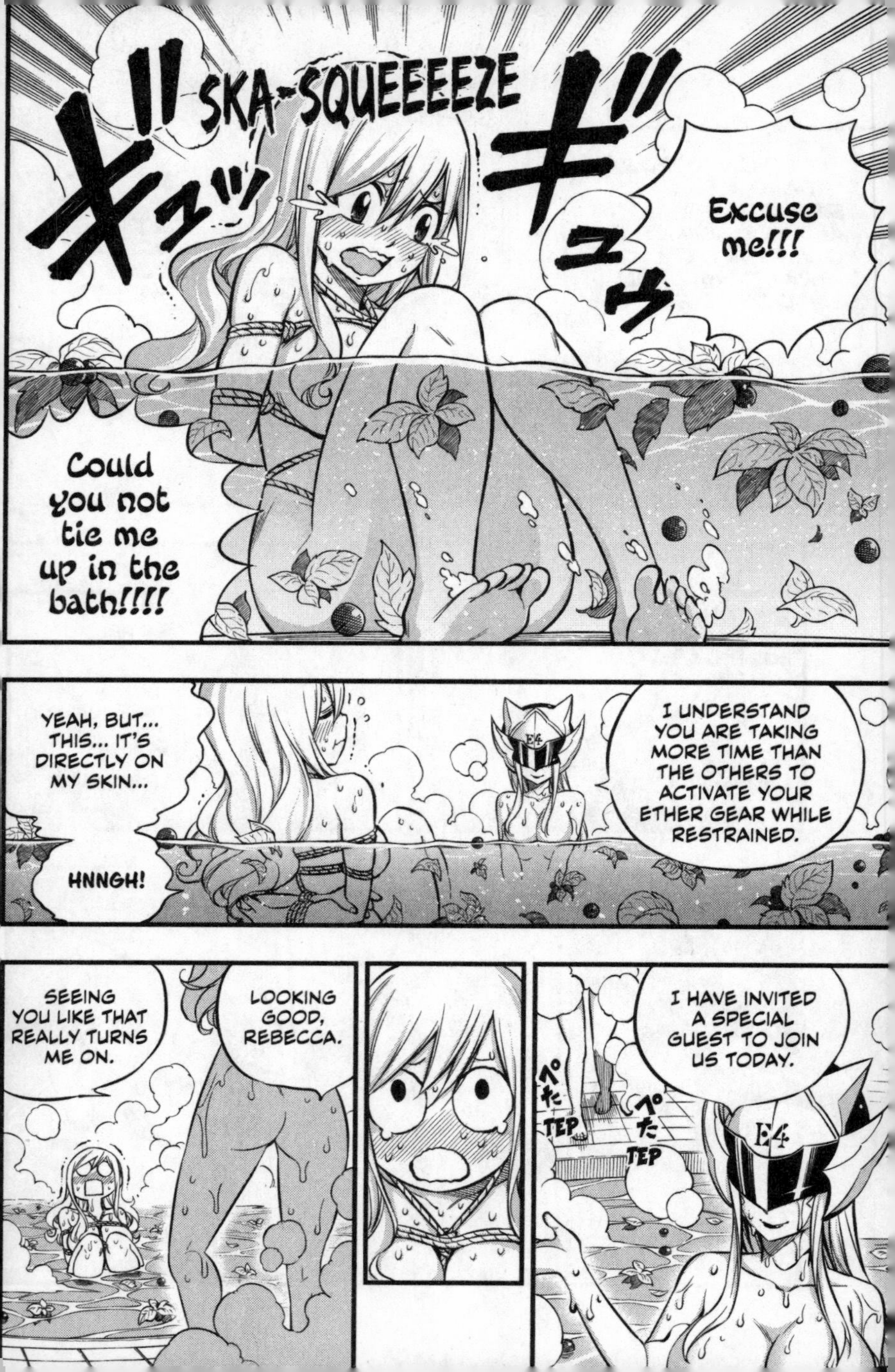
ギュッ
SKA-SQUEEEEZE
ギュウ
Excuse me!!!
Could you not tie me up in the bath!!!!
I UNDERSTAND YOU ARE TAKING MORE TIME THAN THE OTHERS TO ACTIVATE YOUR ETHER GEAR WHILE RESTRAINED.
YEAH, BUT... THIS... IT'S DIRECTLY ON MY SKIN...
HNNGH!
I HAVE INVITED A SPECIAL GUEST TO JOIN US TODAY.
ぺた TEP
ぺた TEP
LOOKING GOOD, REBECCA.
SEEING YOU LIKE THAT REALLY TURNS ME ON.

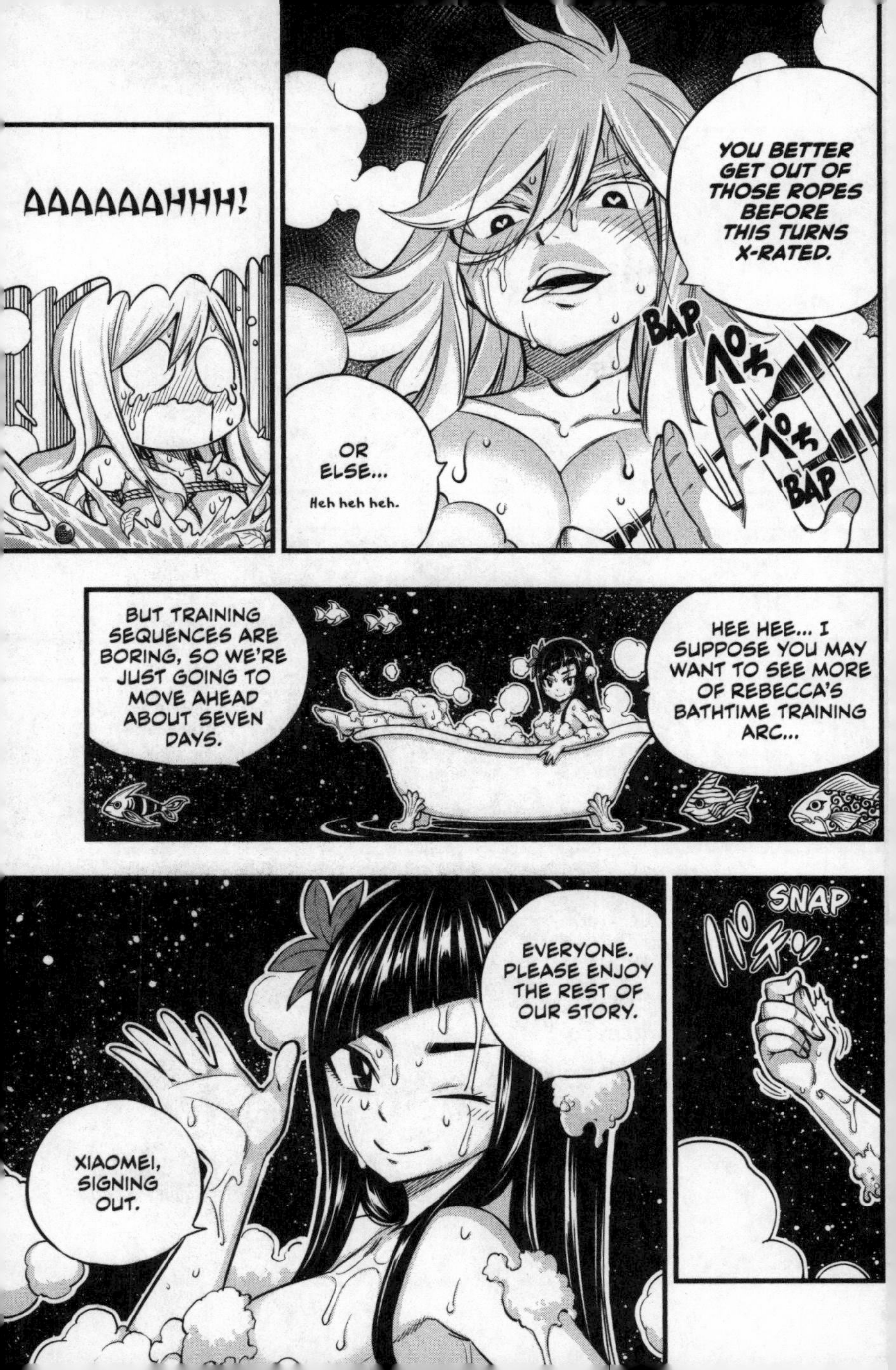
YOU BETTER GET OUT OF THOSE ROPES BEFORE THIS TURNS X-RATED.
BAP
BAP
OR ELSE...
Heh heh heh.
AAAAAAHHH!
HEE HEE... I SUPPOSE YOU MAY WANT TO SEE MORE OF REBECCA'S BATHTIME TRAINING ARC...
BUT TRAINING SEQUENCES ARE BORING, SO WE'RE JUST GOING TO MOVE AHEAD ABOUT SEVEN DAYS.
SNAP
EVERYONE. PLEASE ENJOY THE REST OF OUR STORY.
XIAOMEI, SIGNING OUT.

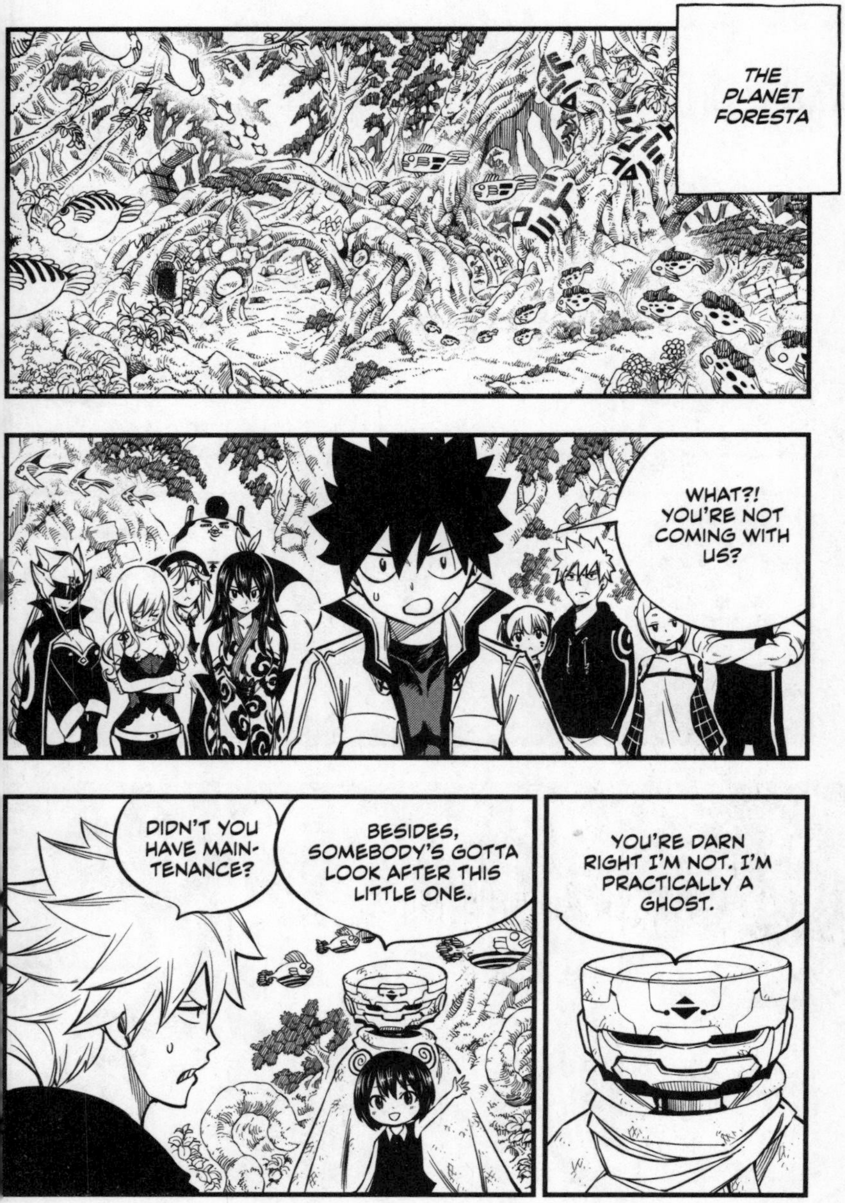
THE PLANET FORESTA
WHAT?! YOU'RE NOT COMING WITH US?
YOU'RE DARN RIGHT I'M NOT. I'M PRACTICALLY A GHOST.
BESIDES, SOMEBODY'S GOTTA LOOK AFTER THIS LITTLE ONE.
DIDN'T YOU HAVE MAIN-TENANCE?

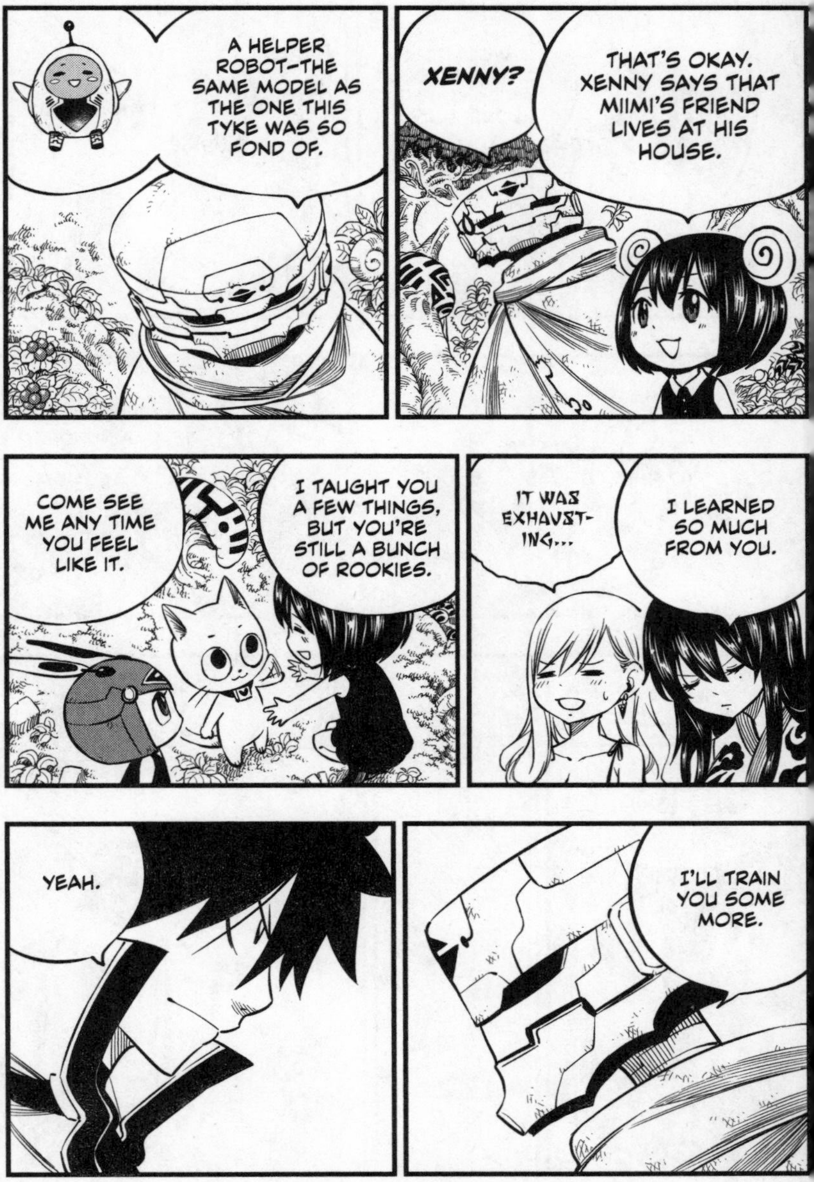
THAT'S OKAY. XENNY SAYS THAT MIIMI'S FRIEND LIVES AT HIS HOUSE.
XENNY?
A HELPER ROBOT—THE SAME MODEL AS THE ONE THIS TYKE WAS SO FOND OF.
I LEARNED SO MUCH FROM YOU.
IT WAS EXHAUSTING...
I TAUGHT YOU A FEW THINGS, BUT YOU'RE STILL A BUNCH OF ROOKIES.
COME SEE ME ANY TIME YOU FEEL LIKE IT.
I'LL TRAIN YOU SOME MORE.
YEAH.

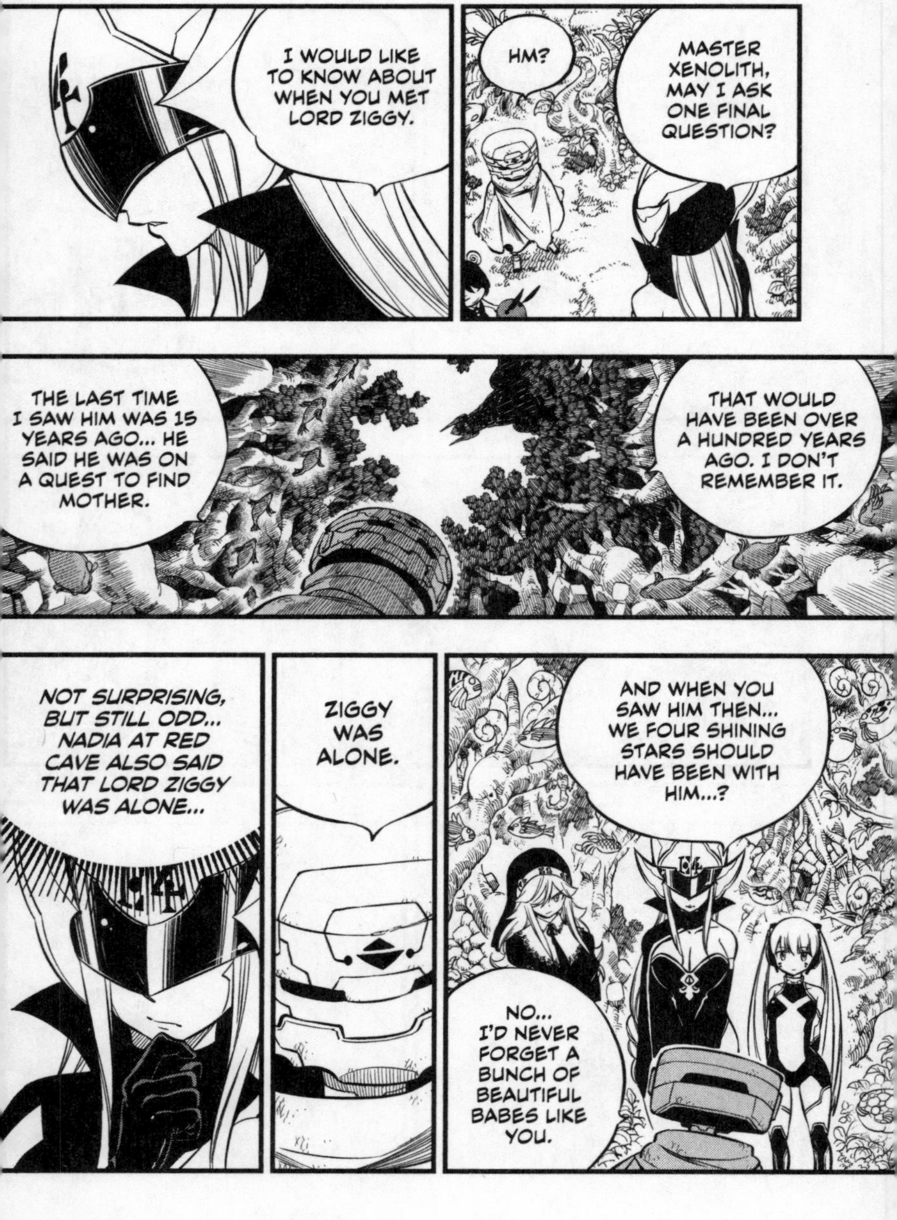
MASTER XENOLITH, MAY I ASK ONE FINAL QUESTION?
HM?
I WOULD LIKE TO KNOW ABOUT WHEN YOU MET LORD ZIGGY.
THAT WOULD HAVE BEEN OVER A HUNDRED YEARS AGO. I DON'T REMEMBER IT.
THE LAST TIME I SAW HIM WAS 15 YEARS AGO... HE SAID HE WAS ON A QUEST TO FIND MOTHER.
AND WHEN YOU SAW HIM THEN... WE FOUR SHINING STARS SHOULD HAVE BEEN WITH HIM...?
NO... I'D NEVER FORGET A BUNCH OF BEAUTIFUL BABES LIKE YOU.
ZIGGY WAS ALONE.
NOT SURPRISING, BUT STILL ODD... NADIA AT RED CAVE ALSO SAID THAT LORD ZIGGY WAS ALONE...

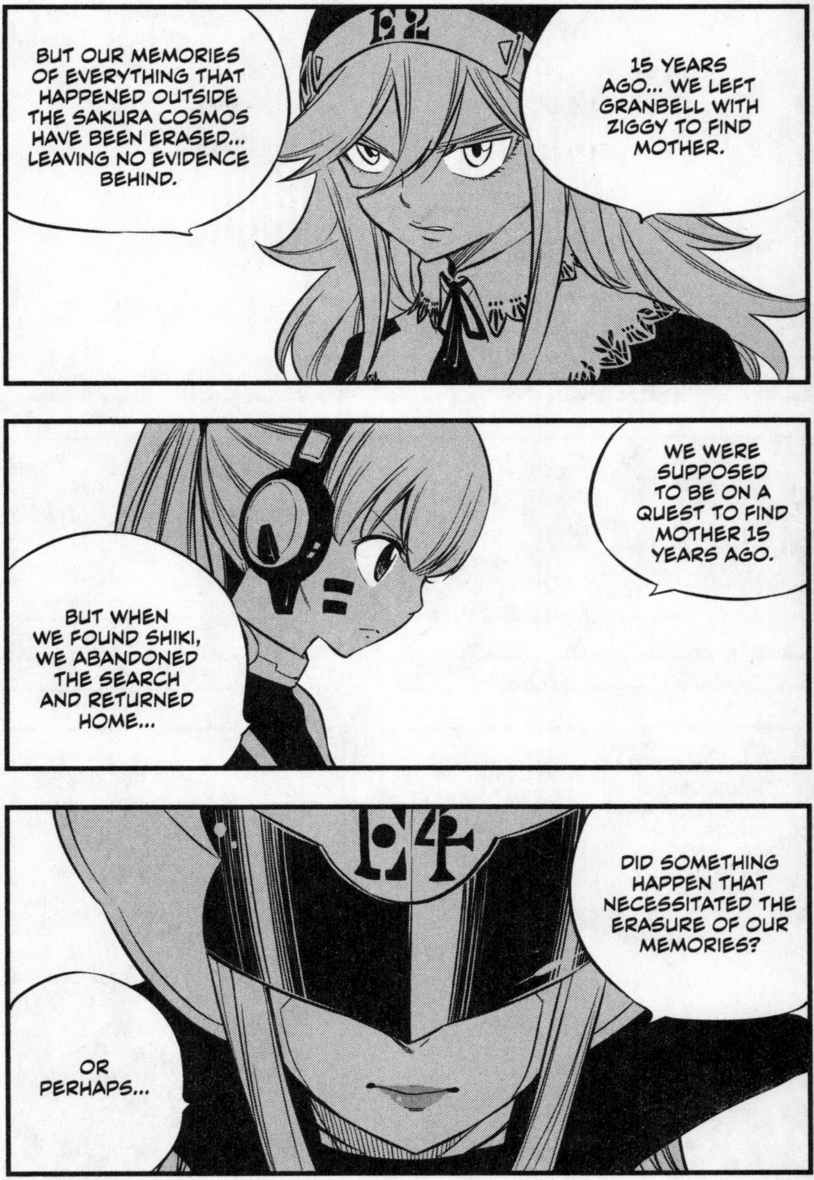
15 YEARS AGO... WE LEFT GRANBELL WITH ZIGGY TO FIND MOTHER.
BUT OUR MEMORIES OF EVERYTHING THAT HAPPENED OUTSIDE THE SAKURA COSMOS HAVE BEEN ERASED... LEAVING NO EVIDENCE BEHIND.
WE WERE SUPPOSED TO BE ON A QUEST TO FIND MOTHER 15 YEARS AGO.
BUT WHEN WE FOUND SHIKI, WE ABANDONED THE SEARCH AND RETURNED HOME...
DID SOMETHING HAPPEN THAT NECESSITATED THE ERASURE OF OUR MEMORIES?
OR PERHAPS...

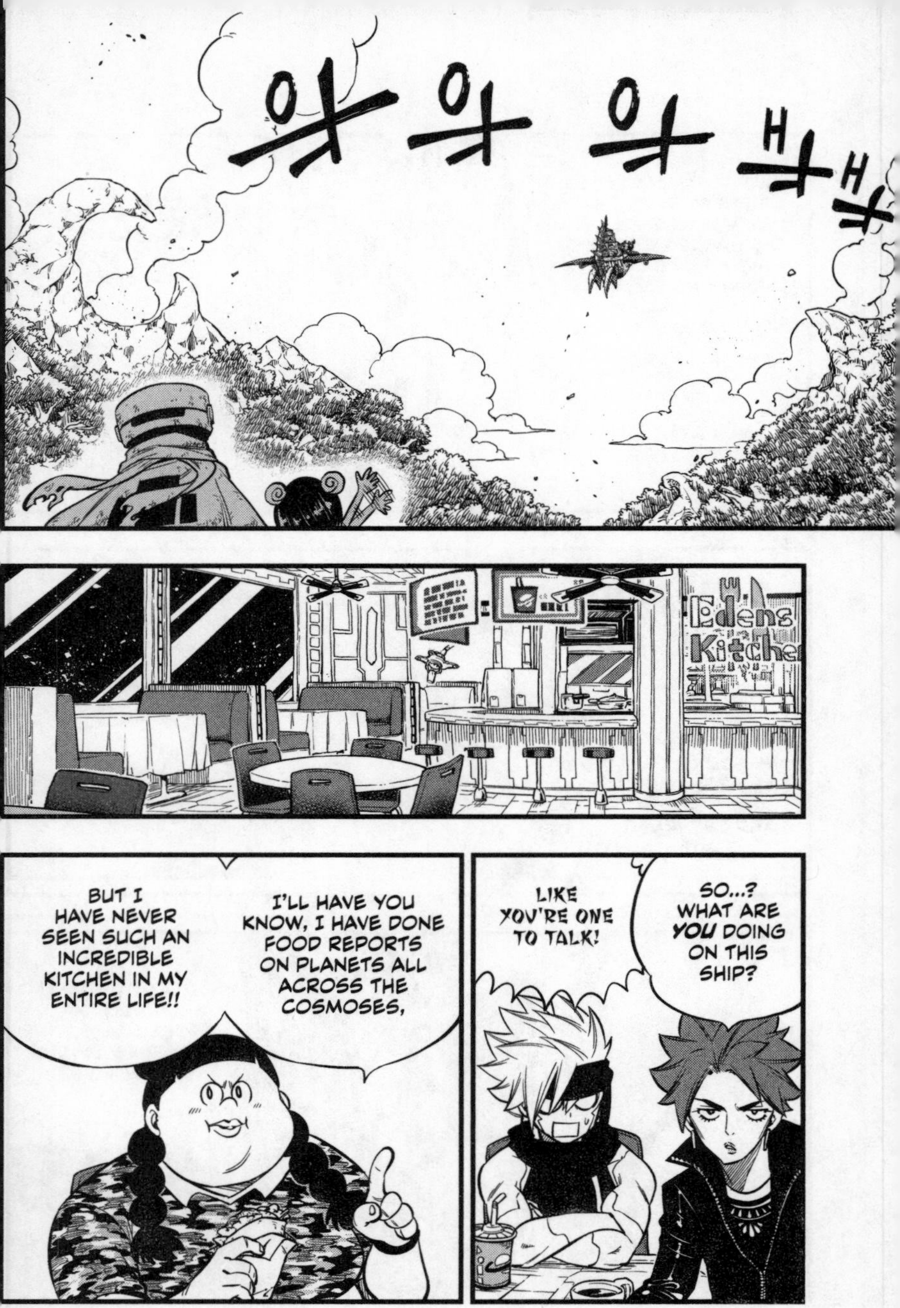
SO...? WHAT ARE *YOU* DOING ON THIS SHIP?
LIKE YOU'RE ONE TO TALK!
I'LL HAVE YOU KNOW, I HAVE DONE FOOD REPORTS ON PLANETS ALL ACROSS THE COSMOSES,
BUT I HAVE NEVER SEEN SUCH AN INCREDIBLE KITCHEN IN MY ENTIRE LIFE!!

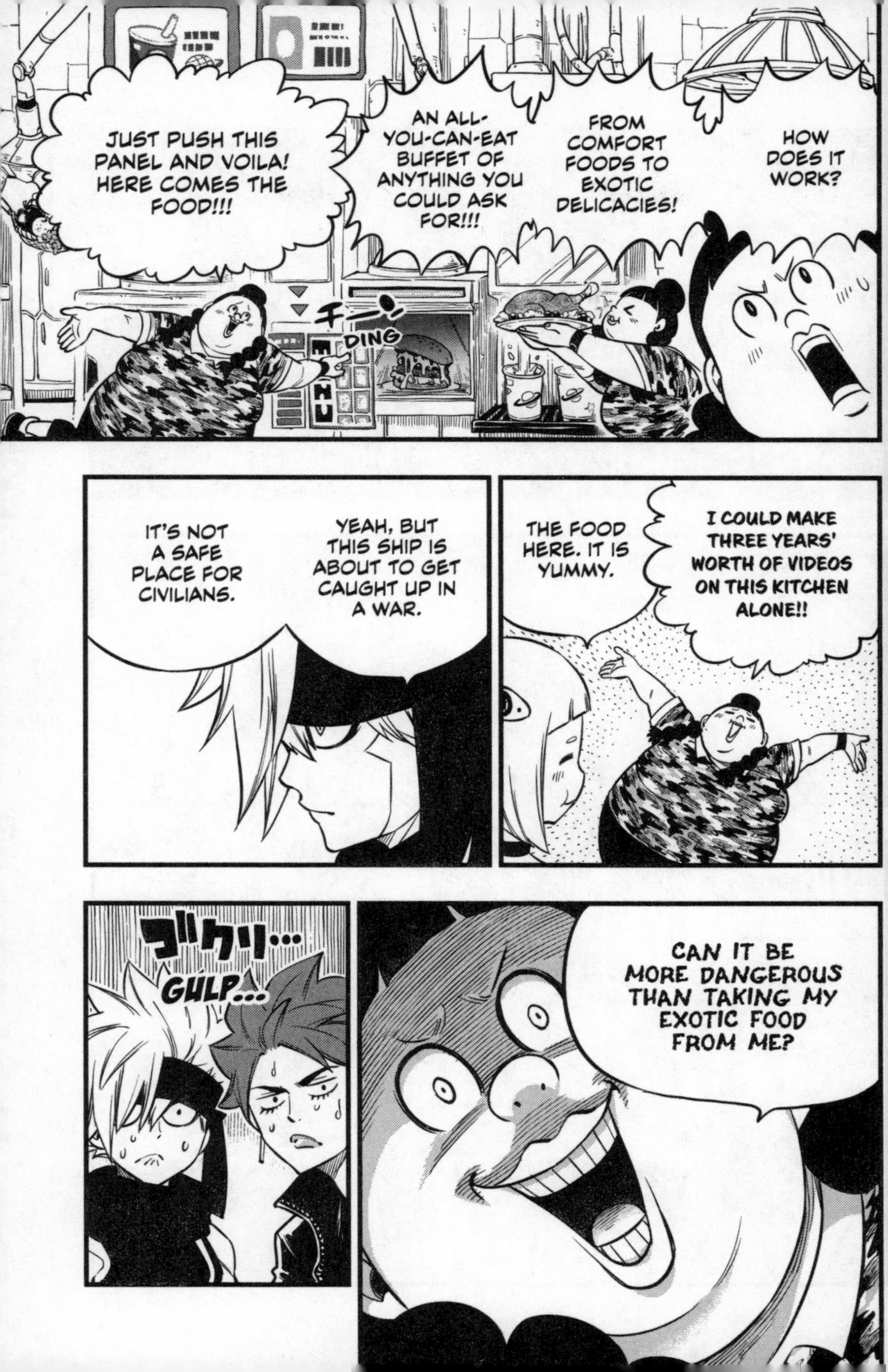
HOW DOES IT WORK?
FROM COMFORT FOODS TO EXOTIC DELICACIES!
AN ALL-YOU-CAN-EAT BUFFET OF ANYTHING YOU COULD ASK FOR!!!
JUST PUSH THIS PANEL AND VOILA! HERE COMES THE FOOD!!!
DING
I COULD MAKE THREE YEARS' WORTH OF VIDEOS ON THIS KITCHEN ALONE!!
THE FOOD HERE. IT IS YUMMY.
YEAH, BUT THIS SHIP IS ABOUT TO GET CAUGHT UP IN A WAR.
IT'S NOT A SAFE PLACE FOR CIVILIANS.
CAN IT BE MORE DANGEROUS THAN TAKING MY EXOTIC FOOD FROM ME?
GULP...

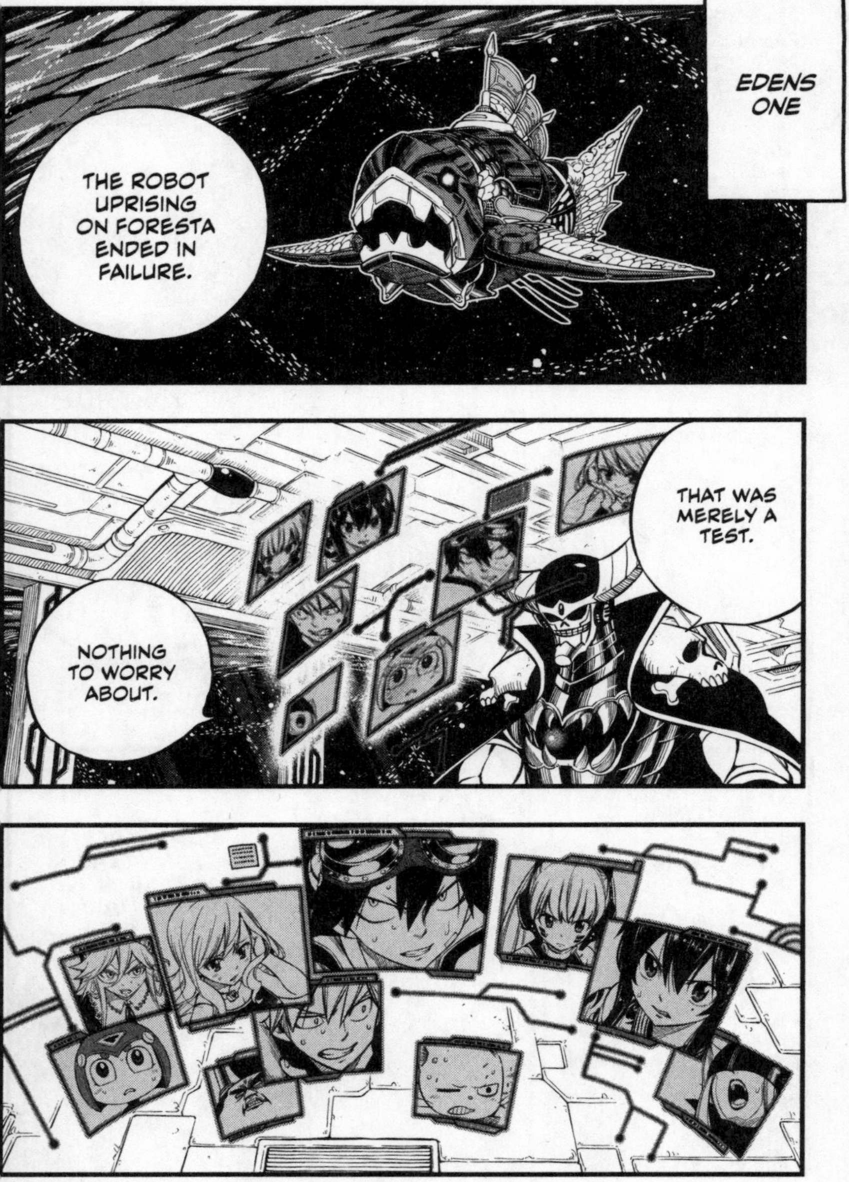
EDENS ONE
THE ROBOT UPRISING ON FORESTA ENDED IN FAILURE.
THAT WAS MERELY A TEST.
NOTHING TO WORRY ABOUT.

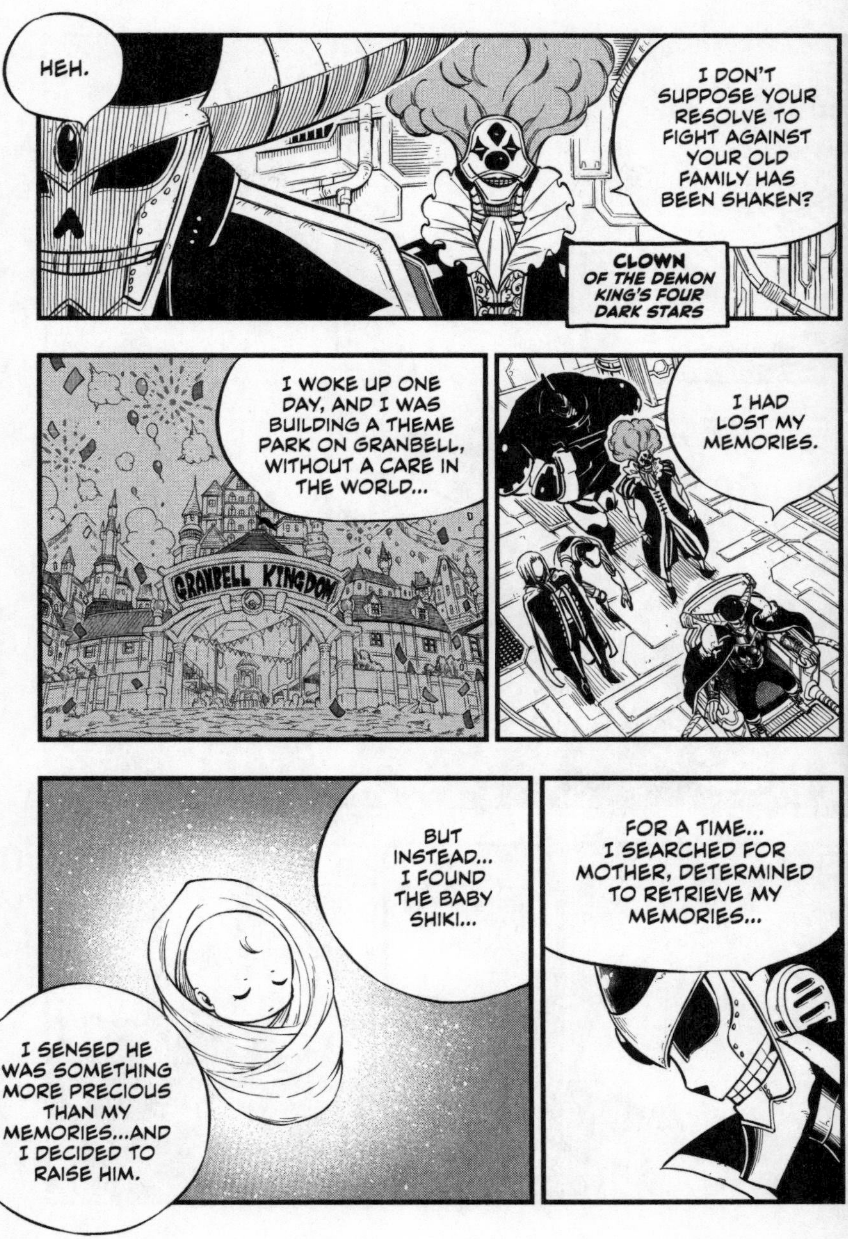
I DON'T SUPPOSE YOUR RESOLVE TO FIGHT AGAINST YOUR OLD FAMILY HAS BEEN SHAKEN?
HEH.
CLOWN OF THE DEMON KING'S FOUR DARK STARS
I HAD LOST MY MEMORIES.
I WOKE UP ONE DAY, AND I WAS BUILDING A THEME PARK ON GRANBELL, WITHOUT A CARE IN THE WORLD...
GRANBELL KINGDOM
FOR A TIME... I SEARCHED FOR MOTHER, DETERMINED TO RETRIEVE MY MEMORIES...
BUT INSTEAD... I FOUND THE BABY SHIKI...
I SENSED HE WAS SOMETHING MORE PRECIOUS THAN MY MEMORIES...AND I DECIDED TO RAISE HIM.

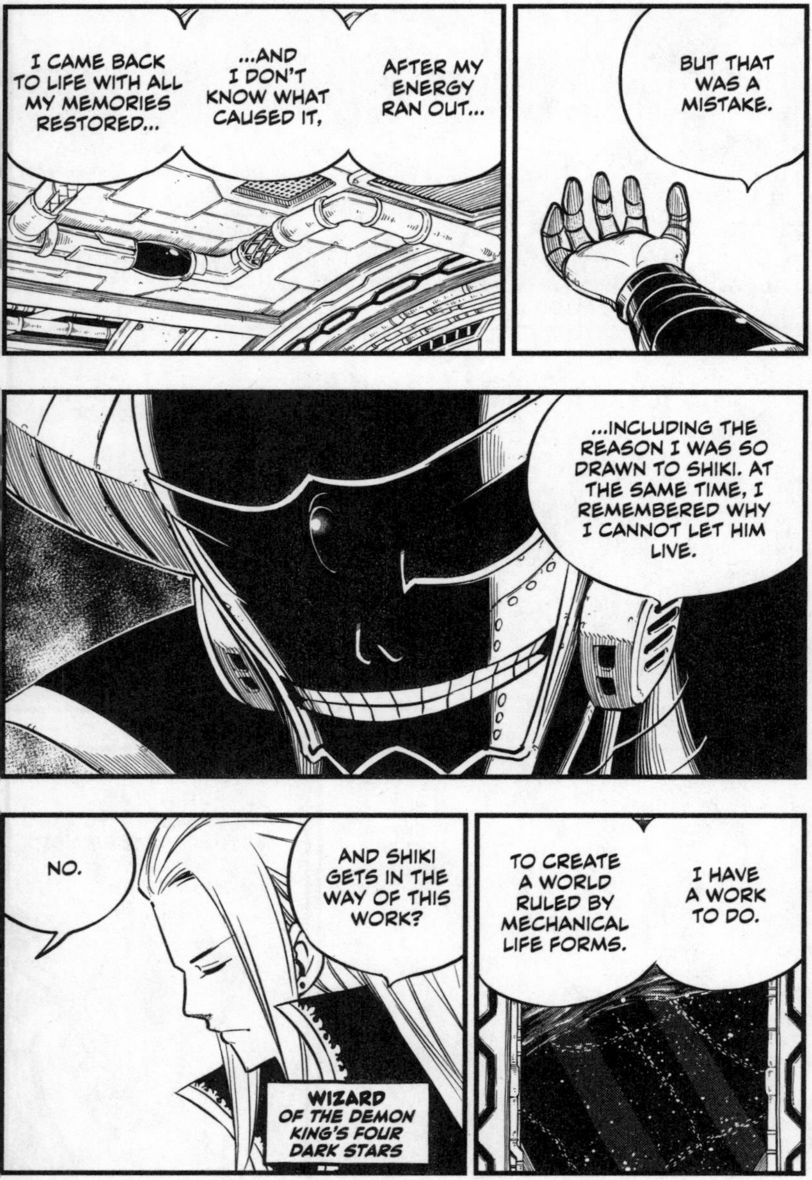
BUT THAT WAS A MISTAKE.
AFTER MY ENERGY RAN OUT...
...AND I DON'T KNOW WHAT CAUSED IT,
I CAME BACK TO LIFE WITH ALL MY MEMORIES RESTORED...
...INCLUDING THE REASON I WAS SO DRAWN TO SHIKI. AT THE SAME TIME, I REMEMBERED WHY I CANNOT LET HIM LIVE.
I HAVE A WORK TO DO.
TO CREATE A WORLD RULED BY MECHANICAL LIFE FORMS.
AND SHIKI GETS IN THE WAY OF THIS WORK?
NO.
WIZARD OF THE DEMON KING'S FOUR DARK STARS

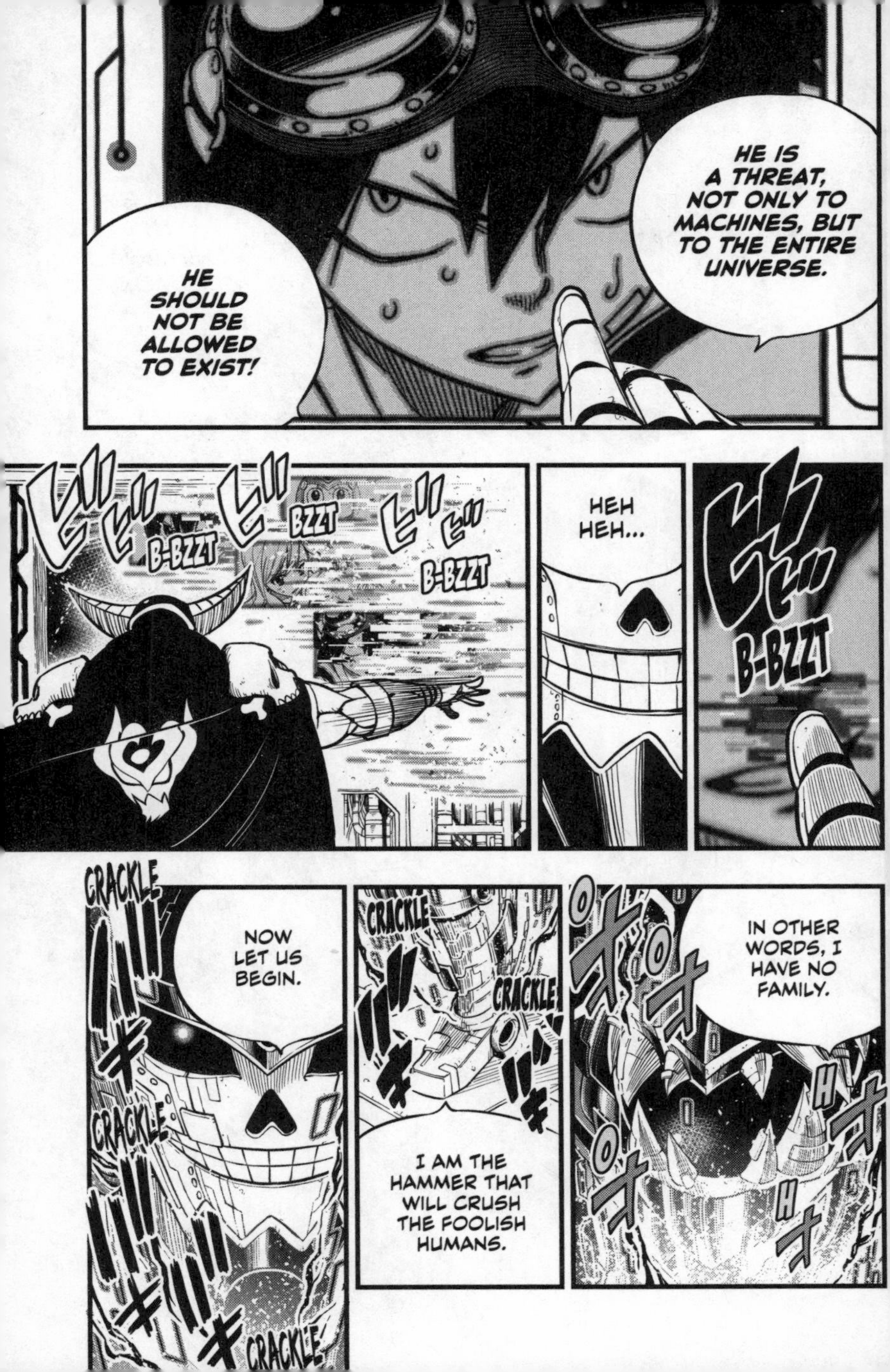
HE IS A THREAT, NOT ONLY TO MACHINES, BUT TO THE ENTIRE UNIVERSE.
HE SHOULD NOT BE ALLOWED TO EXIST!
B-BZZT
HEH HEH...
B-BZZT
BZZT
B-BZZT
IN OTHER WORDS, I HAVE NO FAMILY.
CRACKLE
CRACKLE
I AM THE HAMMER THAT WILL CRUSH THE FOOLISH HUMANS.
CRACKLE
NOW LET US BEGIN.
CRACKLE
CRACKLE

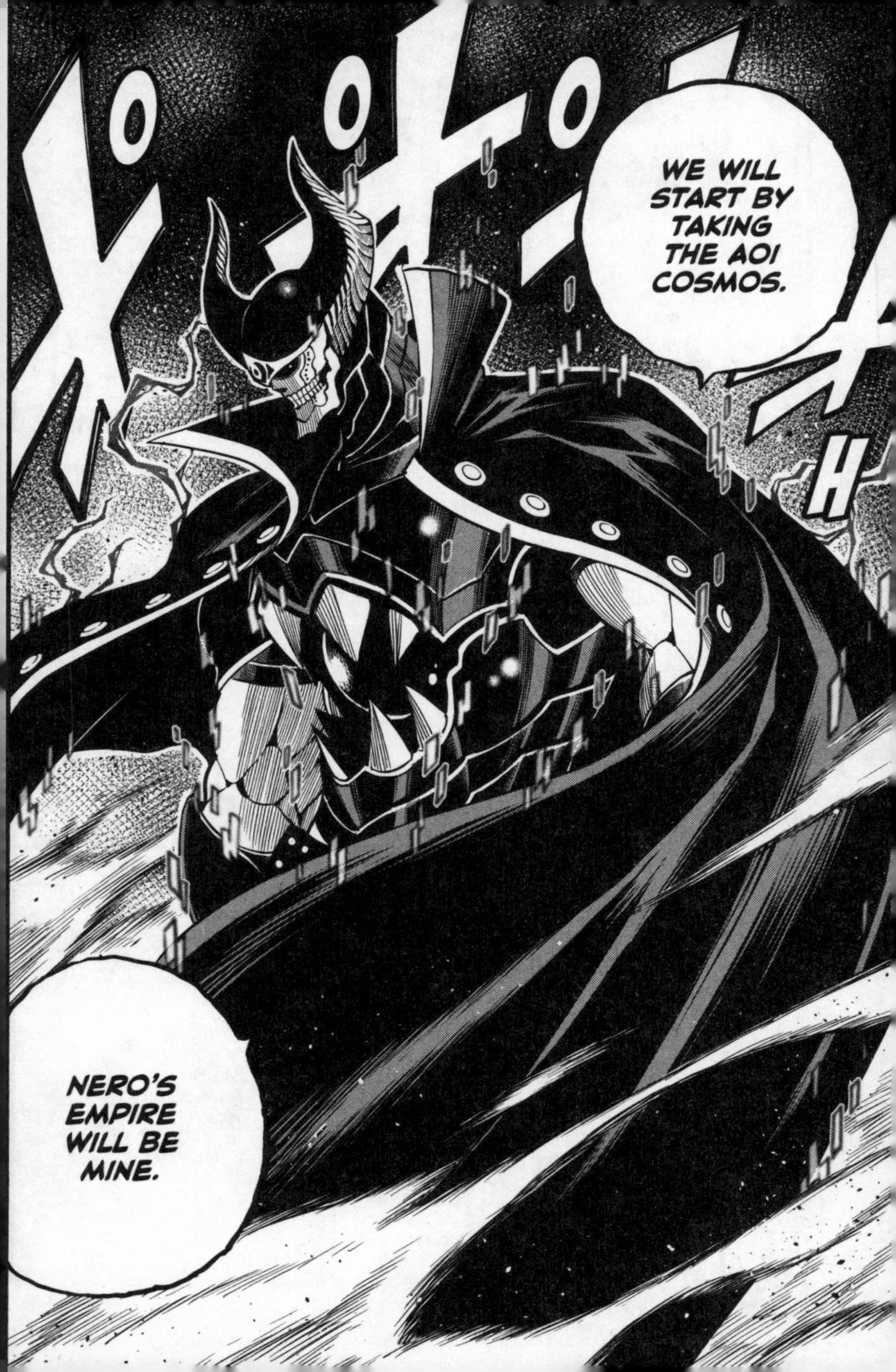
WE WILL START BY TAKING THE AOI COSMOS.
NERO'S EMPIRE WILL BE MINE.

EDENS ZERO

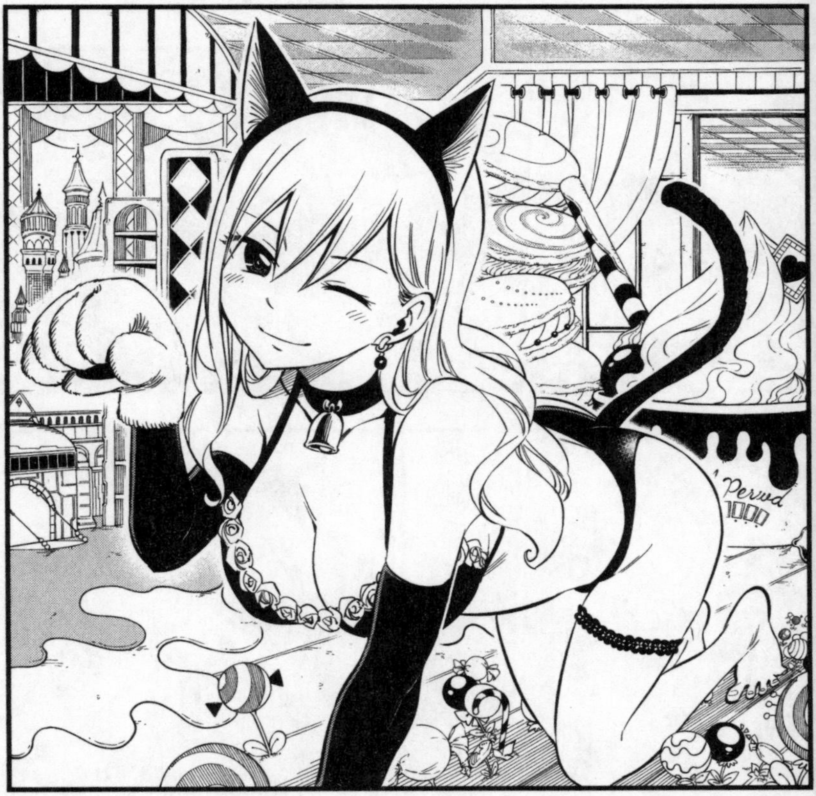

CHAPTER 134: JUDGMENT DAY

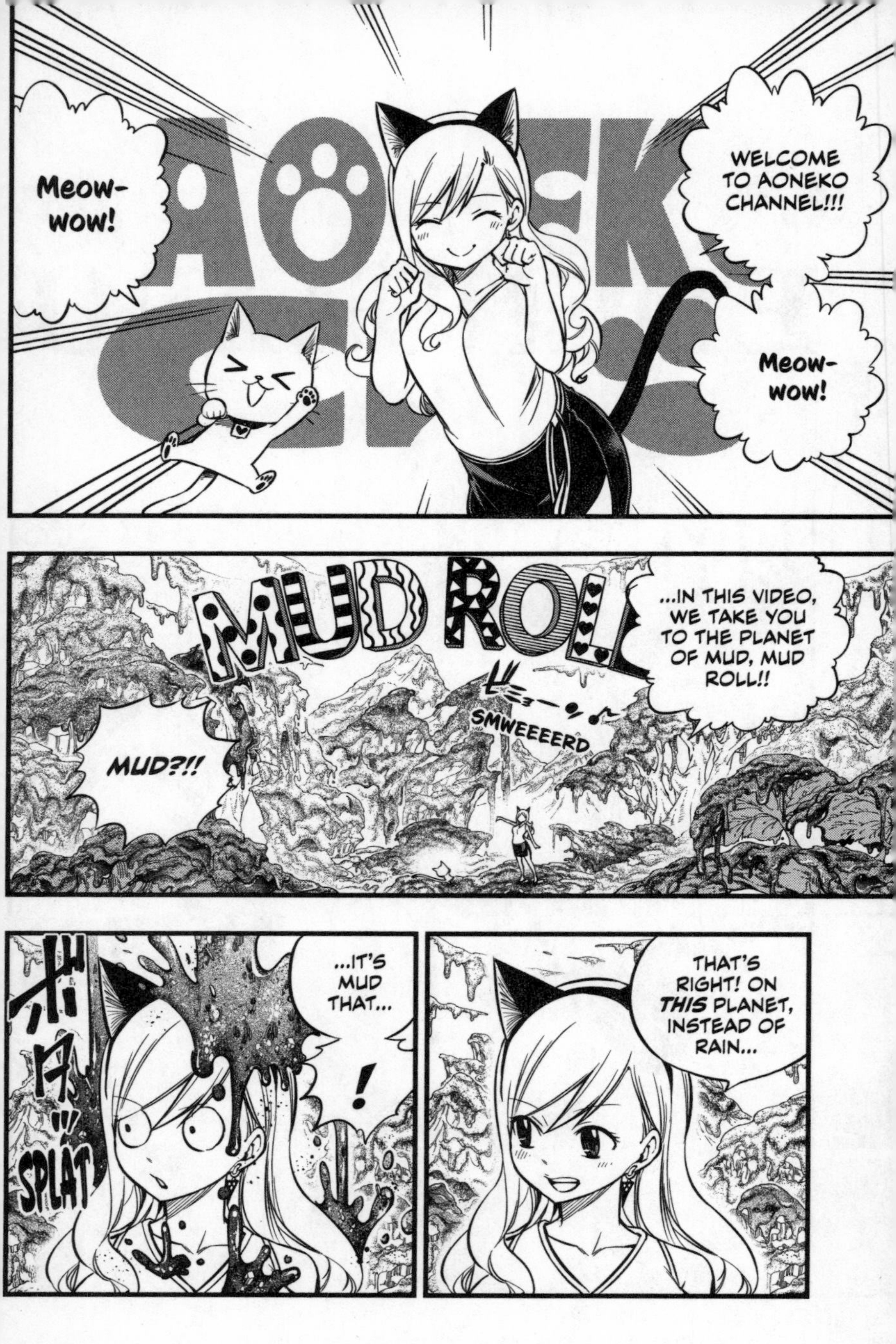
WELCOME TO AONEKO CHANNEL!!!
Meow-wow!
Meow-wow!
MUD ROLL
...IN THIS VIDEO, WE TAKE YOU TO THE PLANET OF MUD, MUD ROLL!!
SMWEEEERD
MUD?!!
THAT'S RIGHT! ON *THIS* PLANET, INSTEAD OF RAIN...
...IT'S MUD THAT...
!
SPLAT

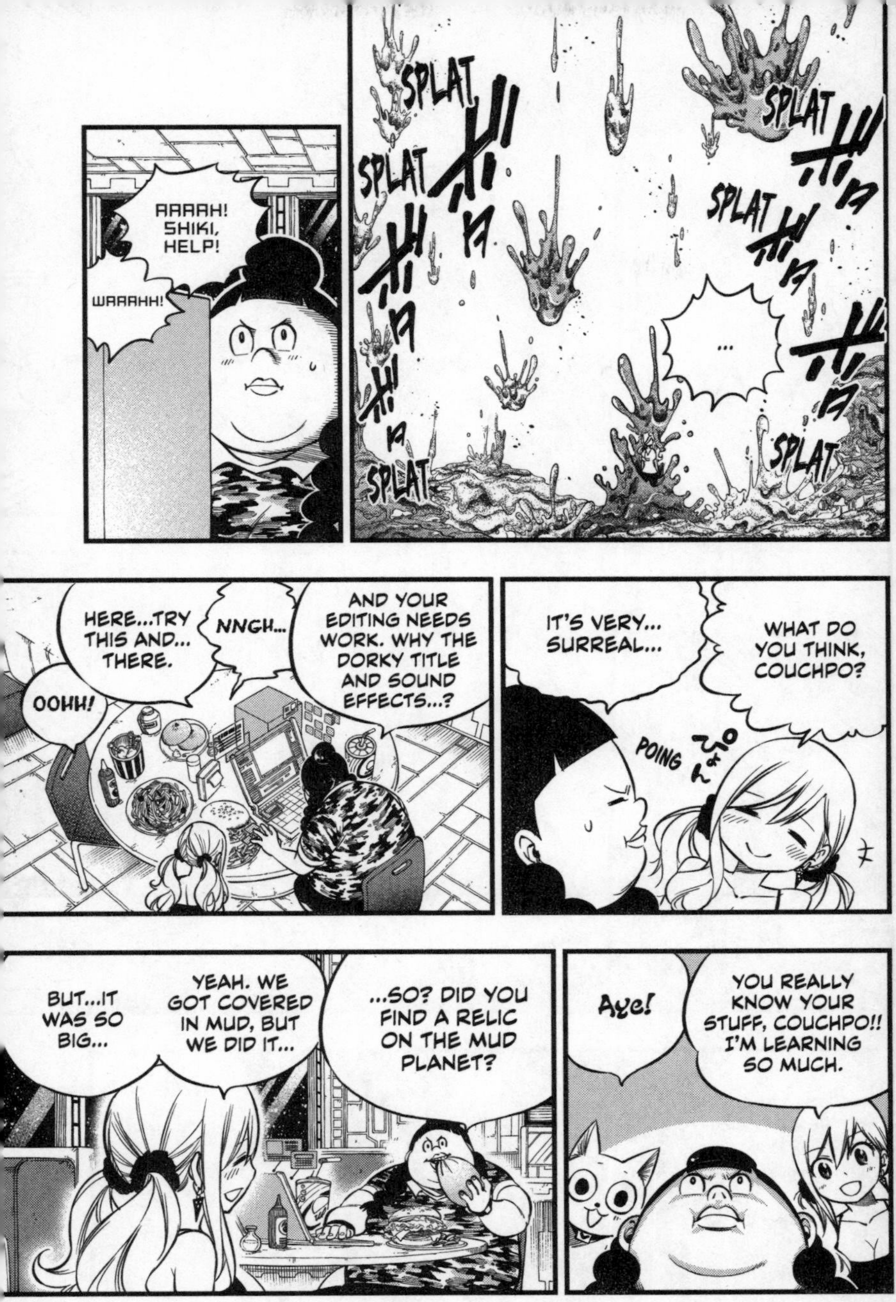
SPLAT
SPLAT
...
SPLAT
SPLAT
SPLAT
SPLAT
AAAAH! SHIKI, HELP!
WAAAHH!
WHAT DO YOU THINK, COUCHPO?
IT'S VERY... SURREAL...
POING
ぴょん
AND YOUR EDITING NEEDS WORK. WHY THE DORKY TITLE AND SOUND EFFECTS...?
NNGH...
HERE...TRY THIS AND... THERE.
OOHH!
YOU REALLY KNOW YOUR STUFF, COUCHPO!! I'M LEARNING SO MUCH.
Aye!
...SO? DID YOU FIND A RELIC ON THE MUD PLANET?
YEAH. WE GOT COVERED IN MUD, BUT WE DID IT...
BUT...IT WAS SO BIG...

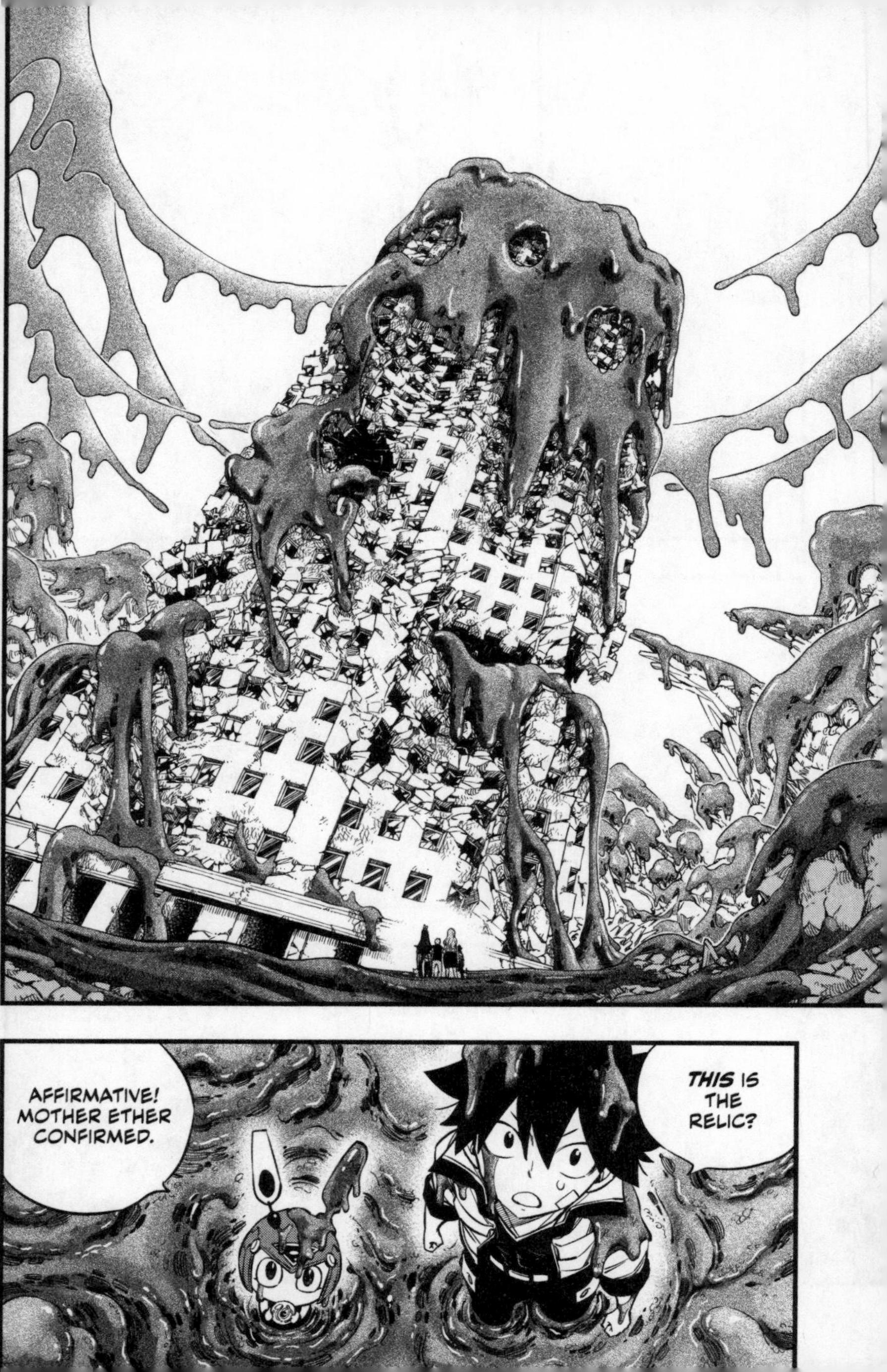
THIS IS THE RELIC?
AFFIRMATIVE! MOTHER ETHER CONFIRMED.

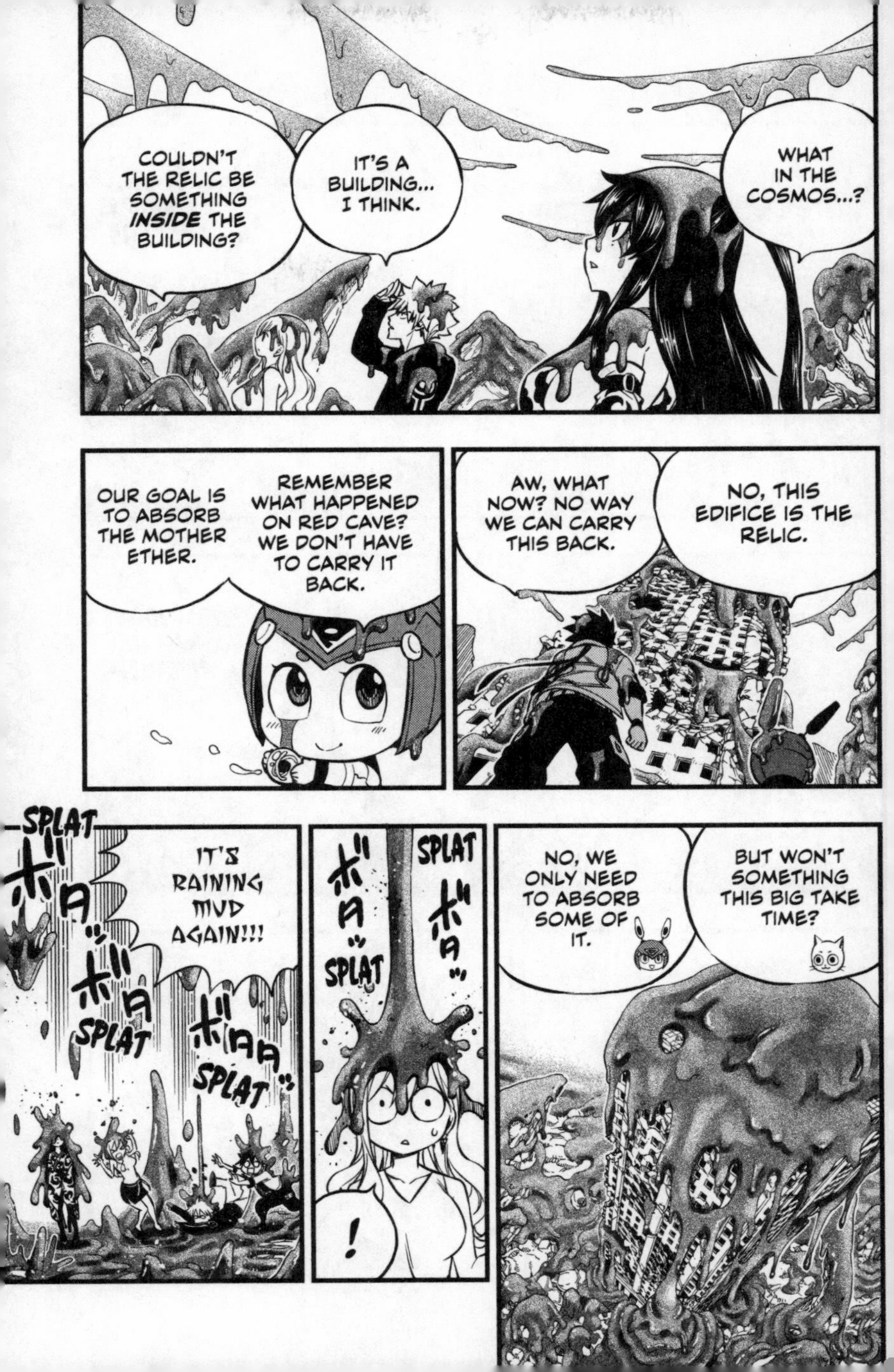

WHAT IN THE COSMOS...?
IT'S A BUILDING... I THINK.
COULDN'T THE RELIC BE SOMETHING *INSIDE* THE BUILDING?
NO, THIS EDIFICE IS THE RELIC.
AW, WHAT NOW? NO WAY WE CAN CARRY THIS BACK.
REMEMBER WHAT HAPPENED ON RED CAVE? WE DON'T HAVE TO CARRY IT BACK.
OUR GOAL IS TO ABSORB THE MOTHER ETHER.
BUT WON'T SOMETHING THIS BIG TAKE TIME?
NO, WE ONLY NEED TO ABSORB SOME OF IT.
SPLAT
SPLAT
!
SPLAT
IT'S RAINING MUD AGAIN!!!
SPLAT
SPLAT

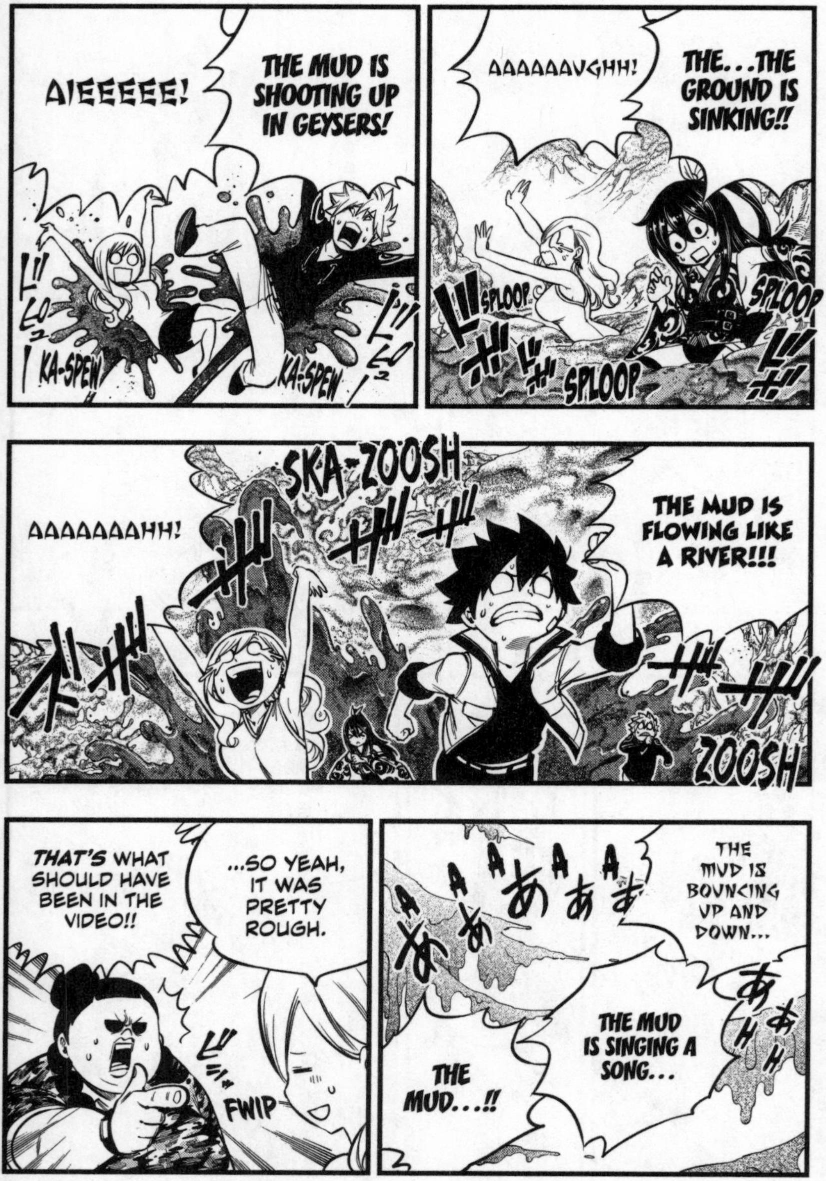
THE...THE GROUND IS SINKING!!
AAAAAAUGHH!
SPLOOP
SPLOOP
SPLOOP
THE MUD IS SHOOTING UP IN GEYSERS!
AIEEEEE!
KA-SPEW
KA-SPEW
THE MUD IS FLOWING LIKE A RIVER!!!
SKA-ZOOSH
AAAAAAAHH!
ZOOSH
THE MUD IS BOUNCING UP AND DOWN...
A A A A A
THE MUD IS SINGING A SONG...
THE MUD...!!
...SO YEAH, IT WAS PRETTY ROUGH.
THAT'S WHAT SHOULD HAVE BEEN IN THE VIDEO!!
FWIP

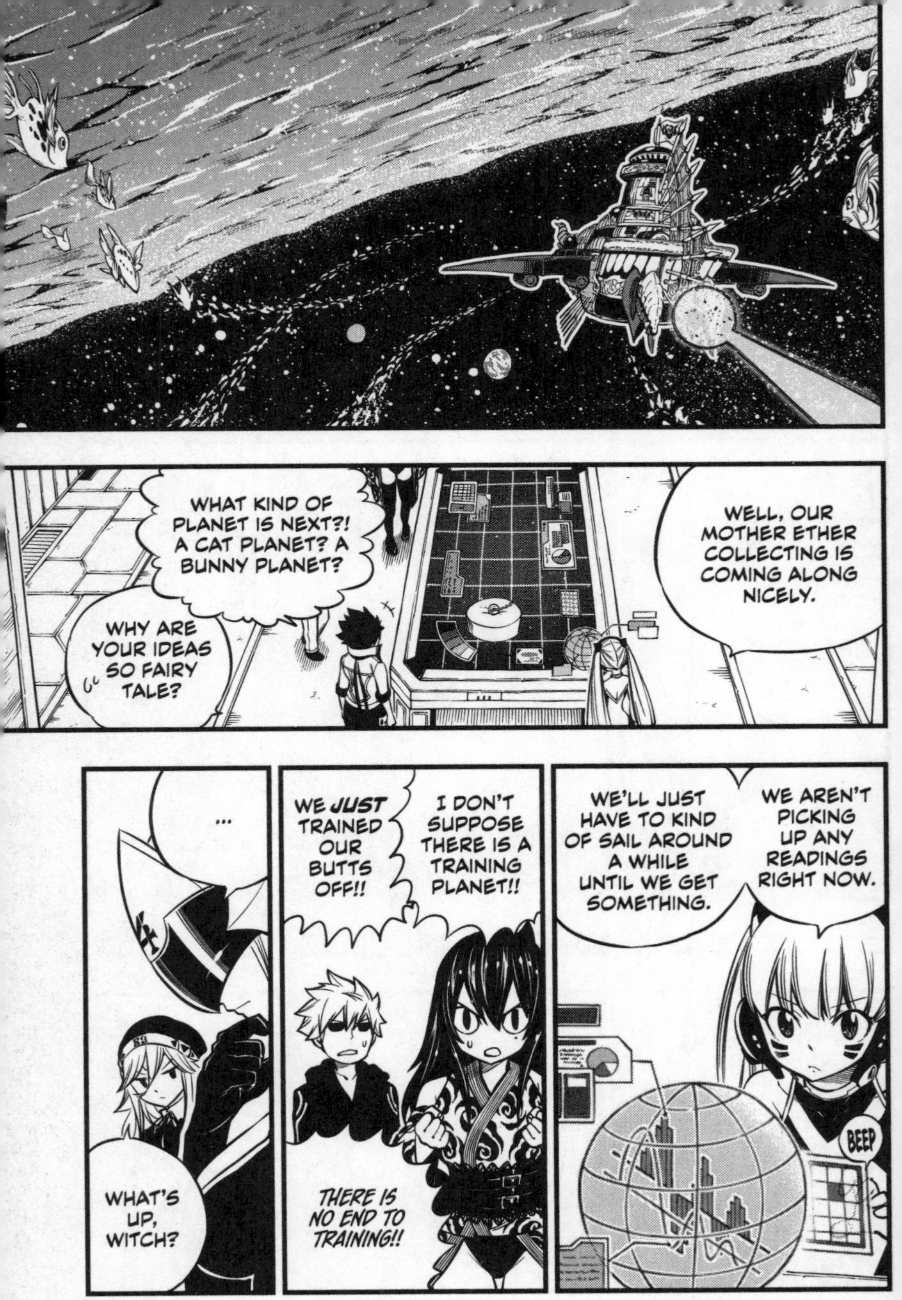
WELL, OUR MOTHER ETHER COLLECTING IS COMING ALONG NICELY.
WHAT KIND OF PLANET IS NEXT?! A CAT PLANET? A BUNNY PLANET?
WHY ARE YOUR IDEAS SO FAIRY TALE?
WE AREN'T PICKING UP ANY READINGS RIGHT NOW.
WE'LL JUST HAVE TO KIND OF SAIL AROUND A WHILE UNTIL WE GET SOMETHING.
BEEP
I DON'T SUPPOSE THERE IS A TRAINING PLANET!!
WE *JUST* TRAINED OUR BUTTS OFF!!
THERE IS NO END TO TRAINING!!
...
WHAT'S UP, WITCH?

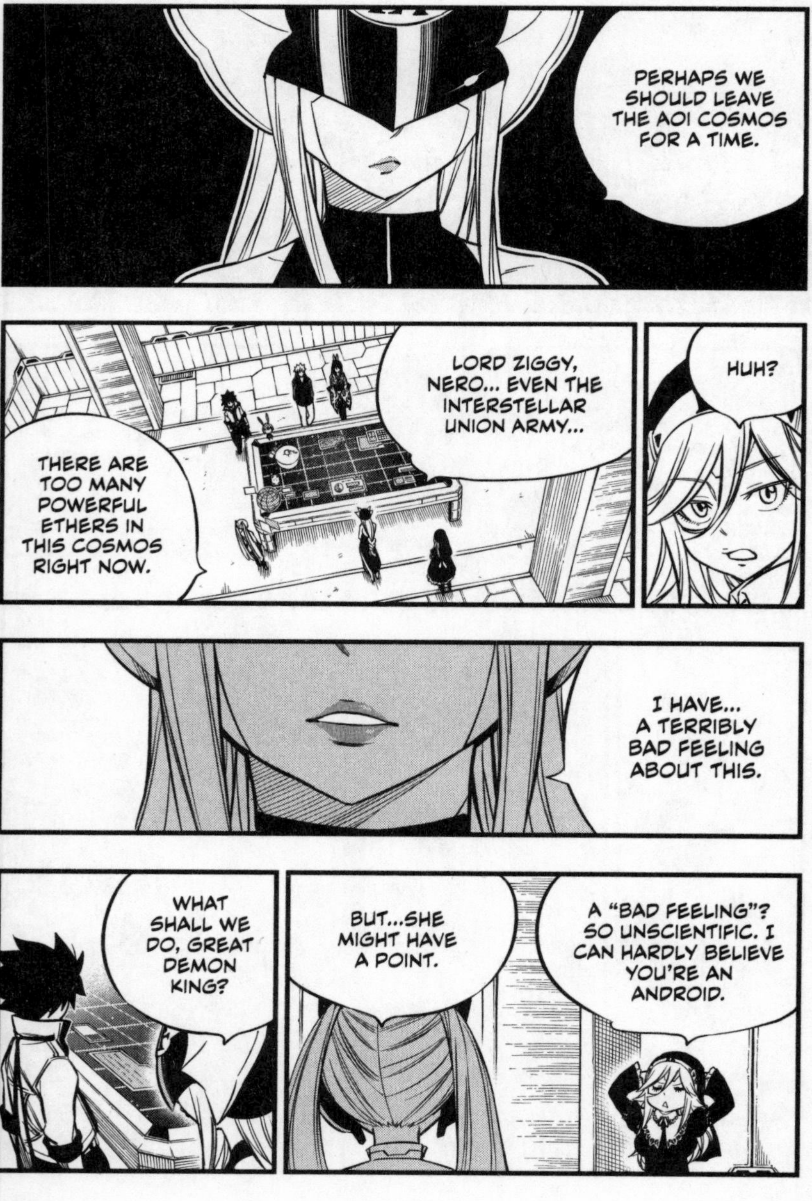
PERHAPS WE SHOULD LEAVE THE AOI COSMOS FOR A TIME.
HUH?
LORD ZIGGY, NERO... EVEN THE INTERSTELLAR UNION ARMY...
THERE ARE TOO MANY POWERFUL ETHERS IN THIS COSMOS RIGHT NOW.
I HAVE... A TERRIBLY BAD FEELING ABOUT THIS.
A "BAD FEELING"? SO UNSCIENTIFIC. I CAN HARDLY BELIEVE YOU'RE AN ANDROID.
BUT...SHE MIGHT HAVE A POINT.
WHAT SHALL WE DO, GREAT DEMON KING?

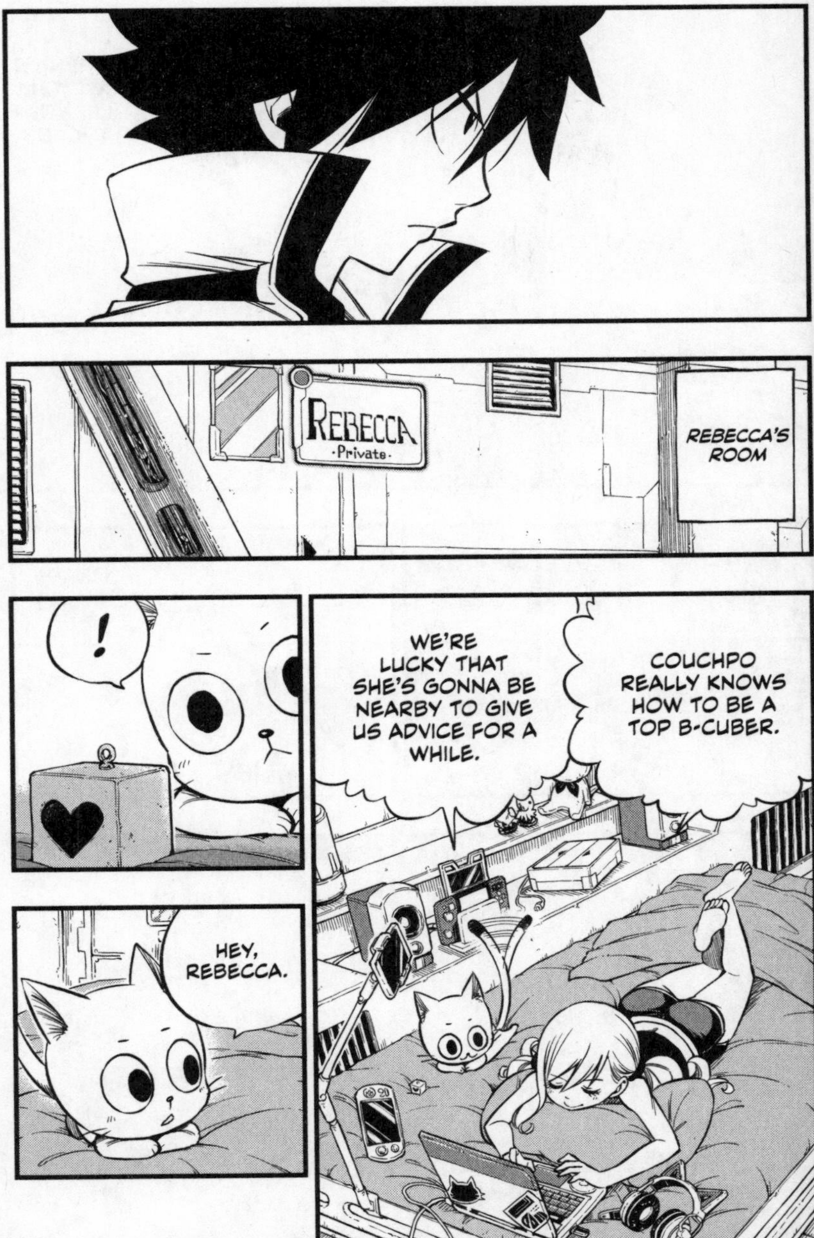
REBECCA'S ROOM
REBECCA
•Private•
COUCHPO REALLY KNOWS HOW TO BE A TOP B-CUBER.
WE'RE LUCKY THAT SHE'S GONNA BE NEARBY TO GIVE US ADVICE FOR A WHILE.
!
HEY, REBECCA.

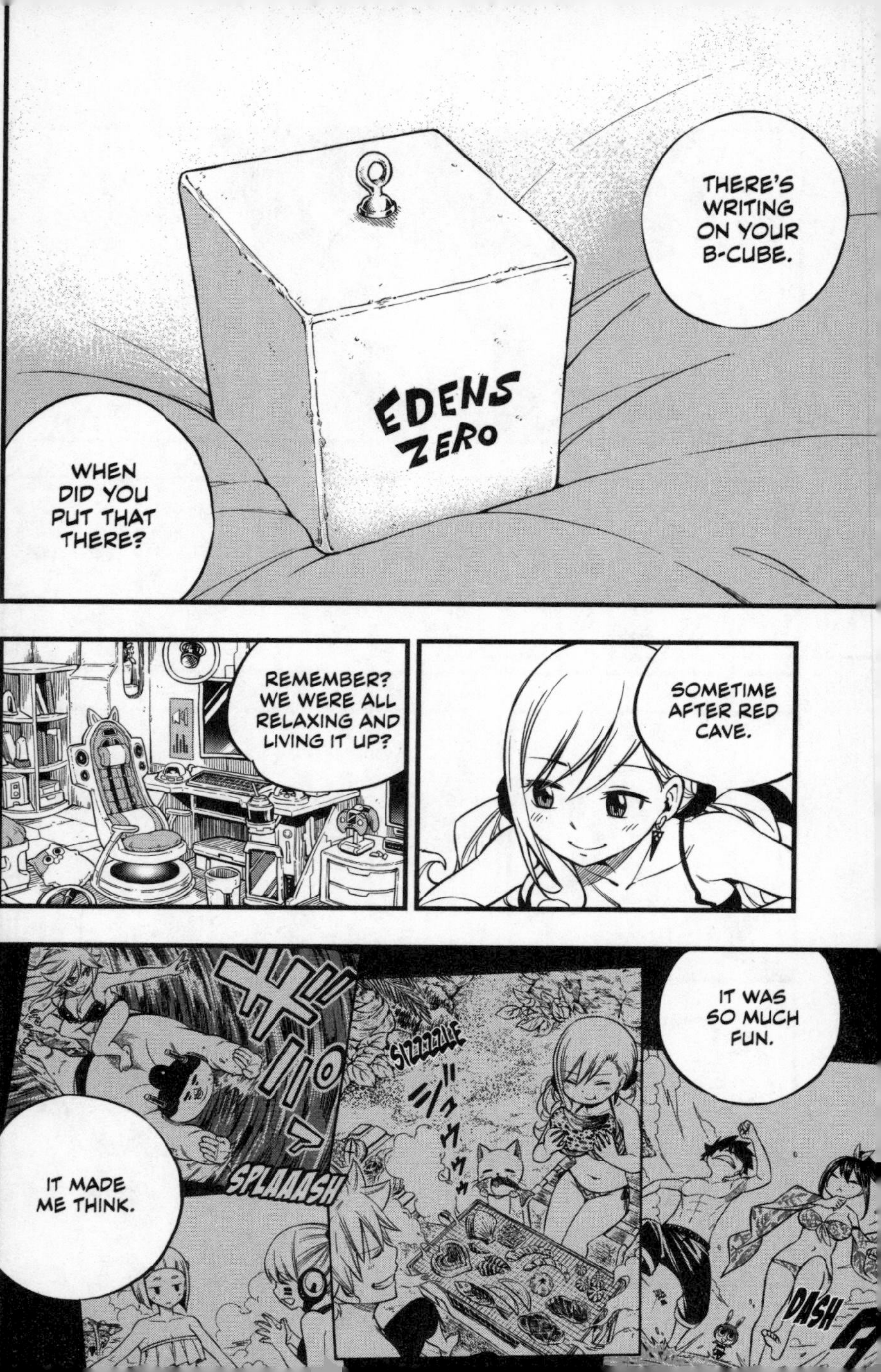

THERE'S WRITING ON YOUR B-CUBE.
EDENS ZERO
WHEN DID YOU PUT THAT THERE?
SOMETIME AFTER RED CAVE.
REMEMBER? WE WERE ALL RELAXING AND LIVING IT UP?
IT WAS SO MUCH FUN.
DASH
SPLAAASH
IT MADE ME THINK.

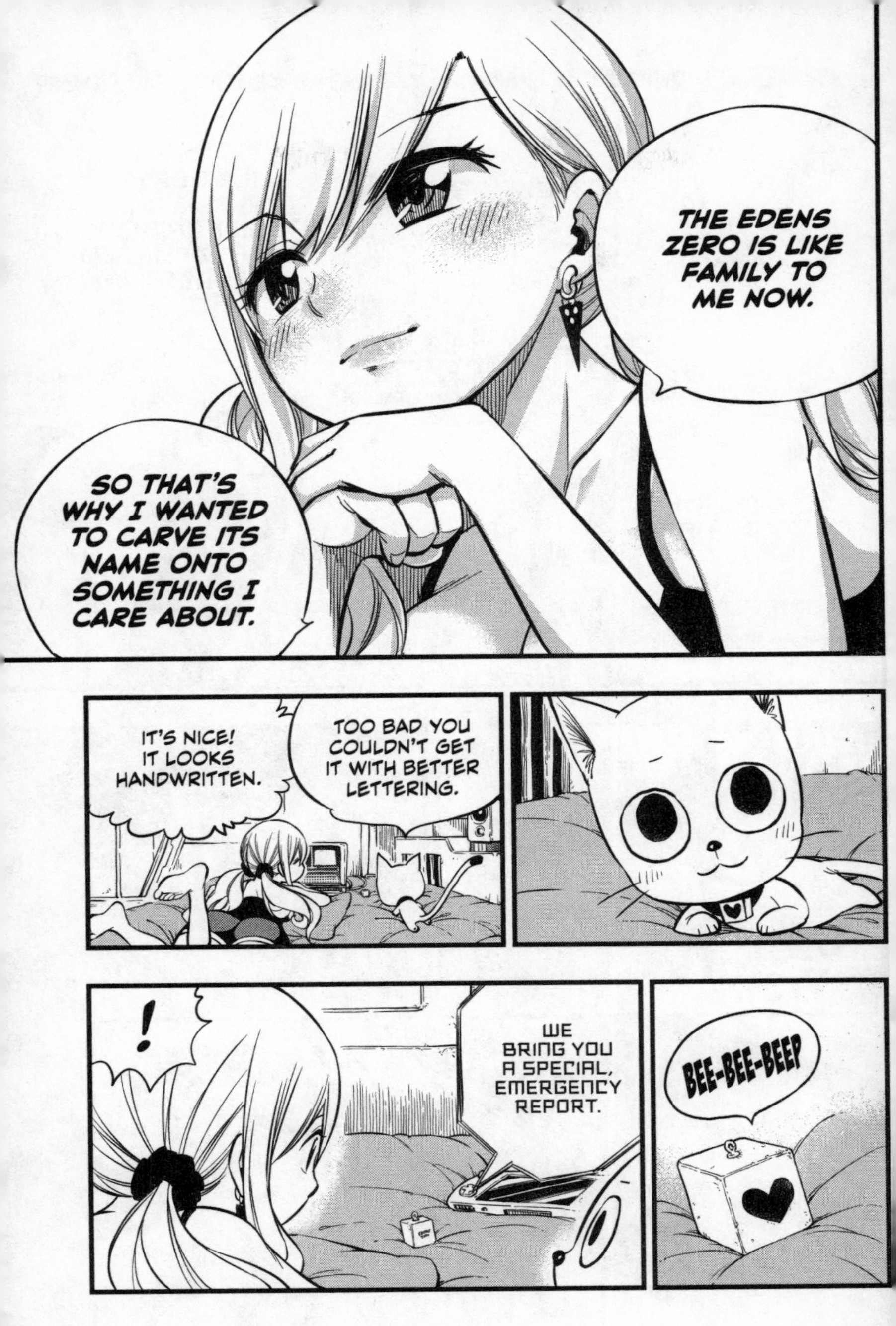
THE EDENS ZERO IS LIKE FAMILY TO ME NOW.
SO THAT'S WHY I WANTED TO CARVE ITS NAME ONTO SOMETHING I CARE ABOUT.
TOO BAD YOU COULDN'T GET IT WITH BETTER LETTERING.
IT'S NICE! IT LOOKS HANDWRITTEN.
BEE-BEE-BEEP
WE BRING YOU A SPECIAL, EMERGENCY REPORT.
!

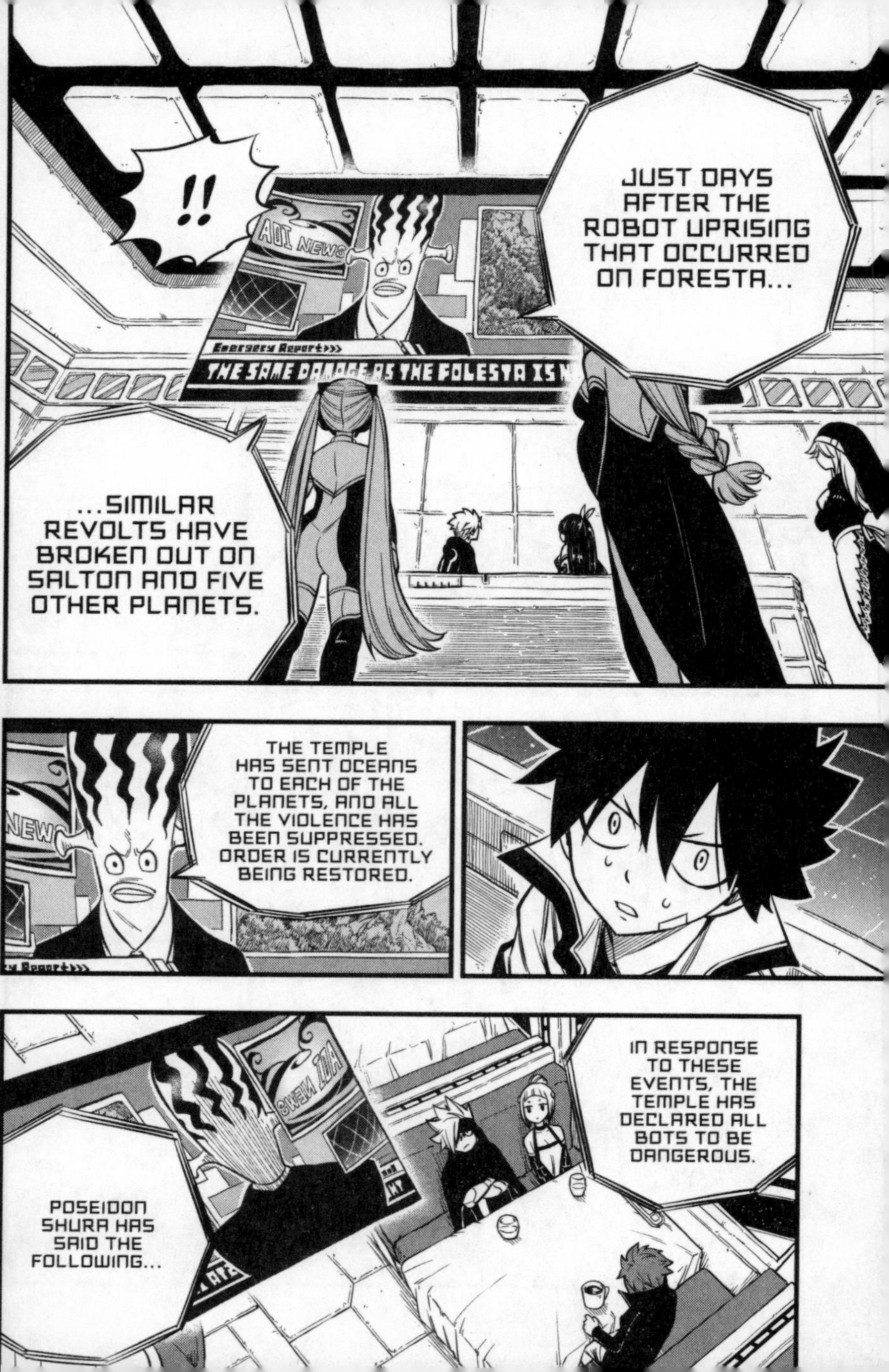
JUST DAYS AFTER THE ROBOT UPRISING THAT OCCURRED ON FORESTA...
!!
...SIMILAR REVOLTS HAVE BROKEN OUT ON SALTON AND FIVE OTHER PLANETS.
THE TEMPLE HAS SENT OCEANS TO EACH OF THE PLANETS, AND ALL THE VIOLENCE HAS BEEN SUPPRESSED. ORDER IS CURRENTLY BEING RESTORED.
IN RESPONSE TO THESE EVENTS, THE TEMPLE HAS DECLARED ALL BOTS TO BE DANGEROUS.
POSEIDON SHURA HAS SAID THE FOLLOWING...

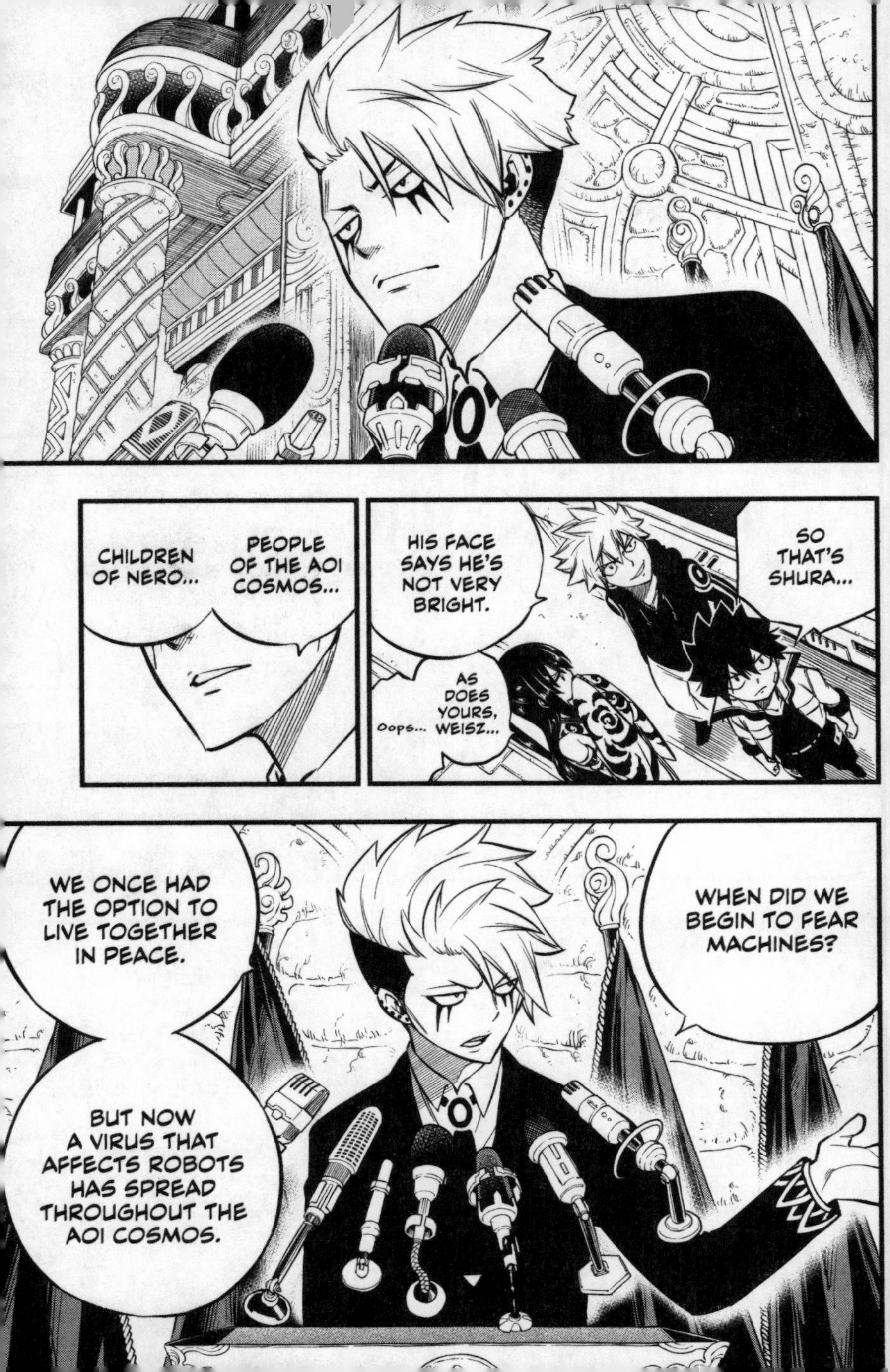
SO THAT'S SHURA...
HIS FACE SAYS HE'S NOT VERY BRIGHT.
AS DOES YOURS, WEISZ...
Oops...
PEOPLE OF THE AOI COSMOS...
CHILDREN OF NERO...
WHEN DID WE BEGIN TO FEAR MACHINES?
WE ONCE HAD THE OPTION TO LIVE TOGETHER IN PEACE.
BUT NOW A VIRUS THAT AFFECTS ROBOTS HAS SPREAD THROUGHOUT THE AOI COSMOS.

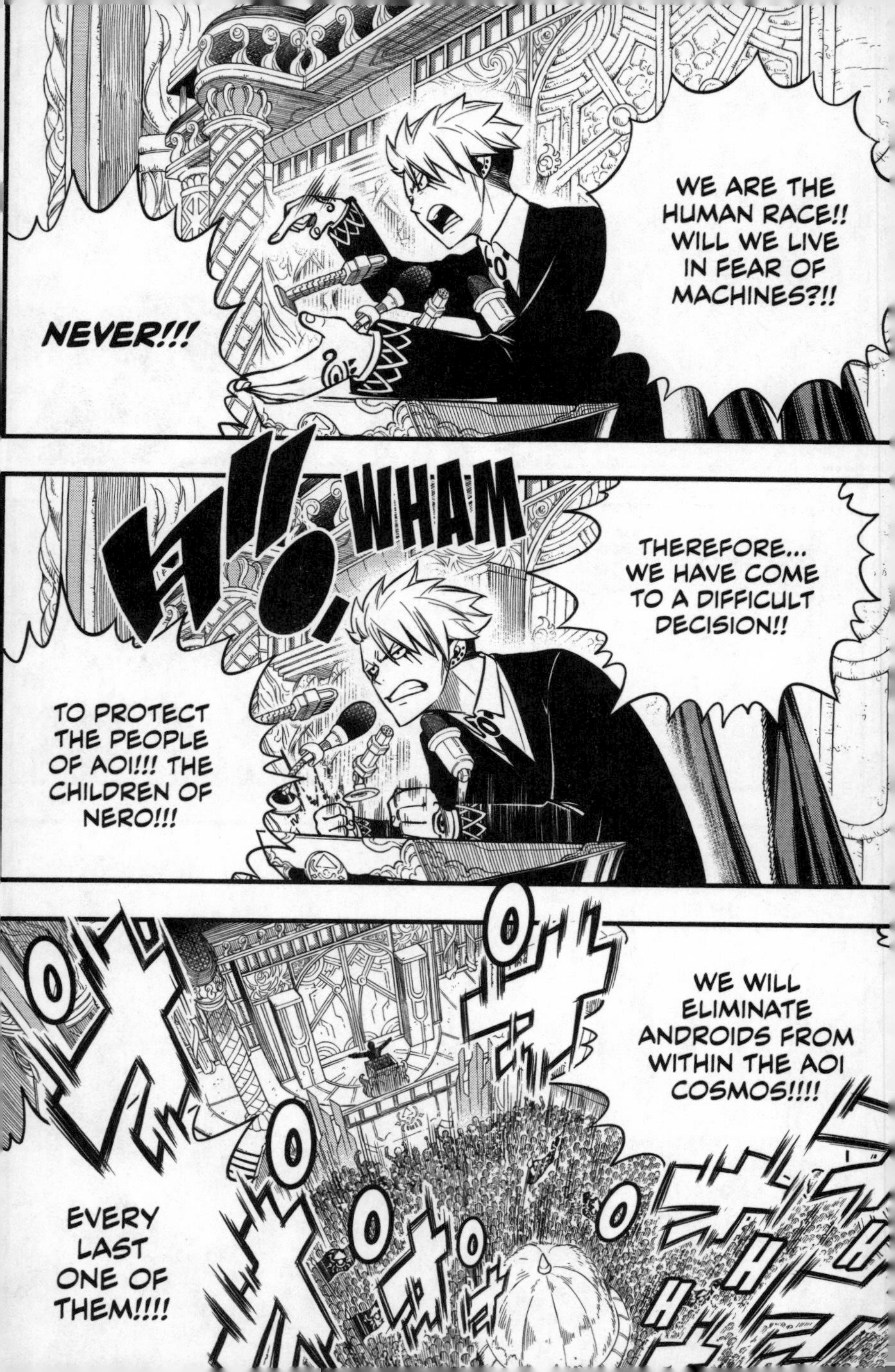
WE ARE THE HUMAN RACE!! WILL WE LIVE IN FEAR OF MACHINES?!!
NEVER!!!
THEREFORE... WE HAVE COME TO A DIFFICULT DECISION!!
WHAM
TO PROTECT THE PEOPLE OF AOI!!! THE CHILDREN OF NERO!!!
WE WILL ELIMINATE ANDROIDS FROM WITHIN THE AOI COSMOS!!!!
EVERY LAST ONE OF THEM!!!!

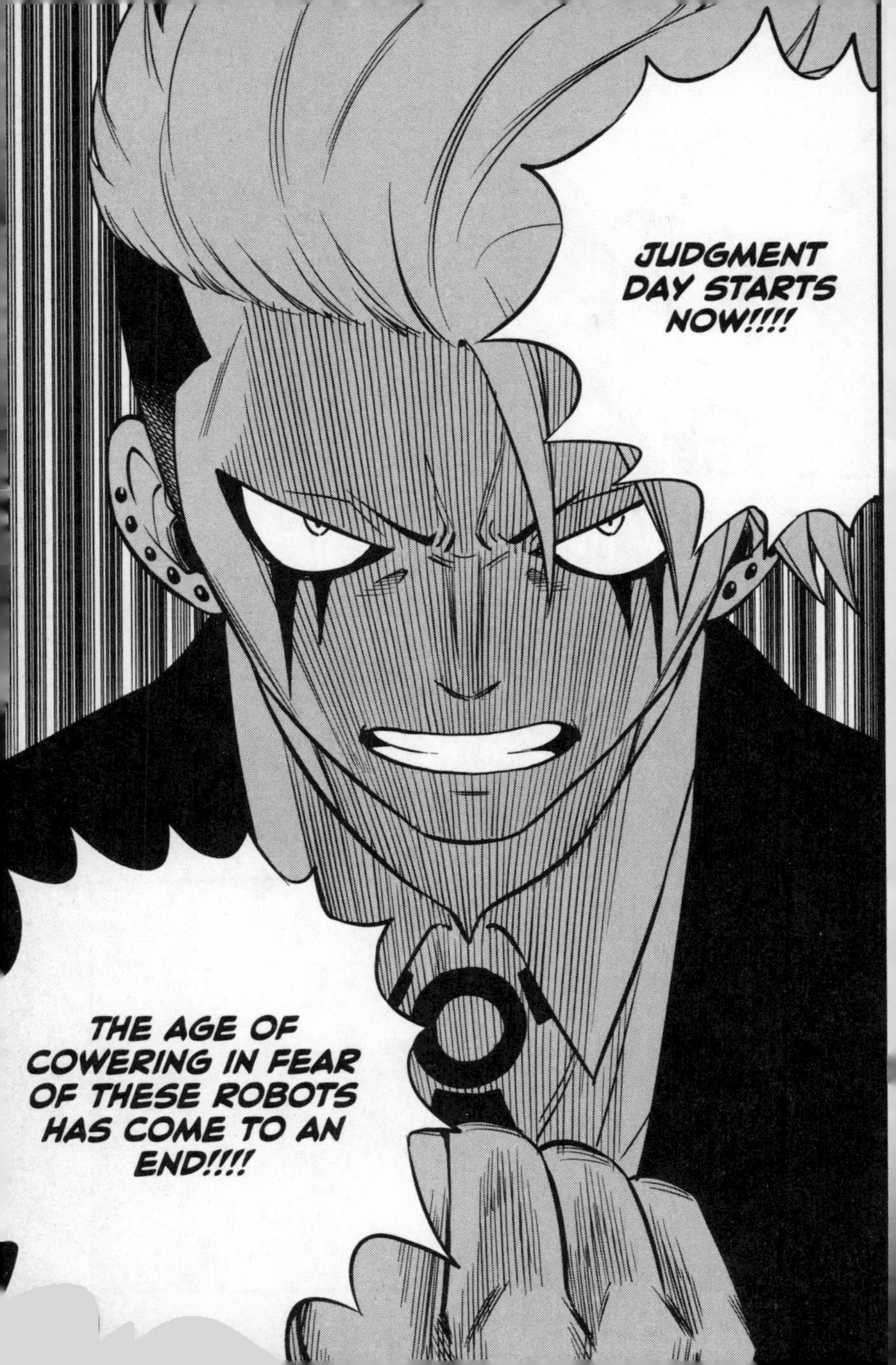
JUDGMENT DAY STARTS NOW!!!!
THE AGE OF COWERING IN FEAR OF THESE ROBOTS HAS COME TO AN END!!!!

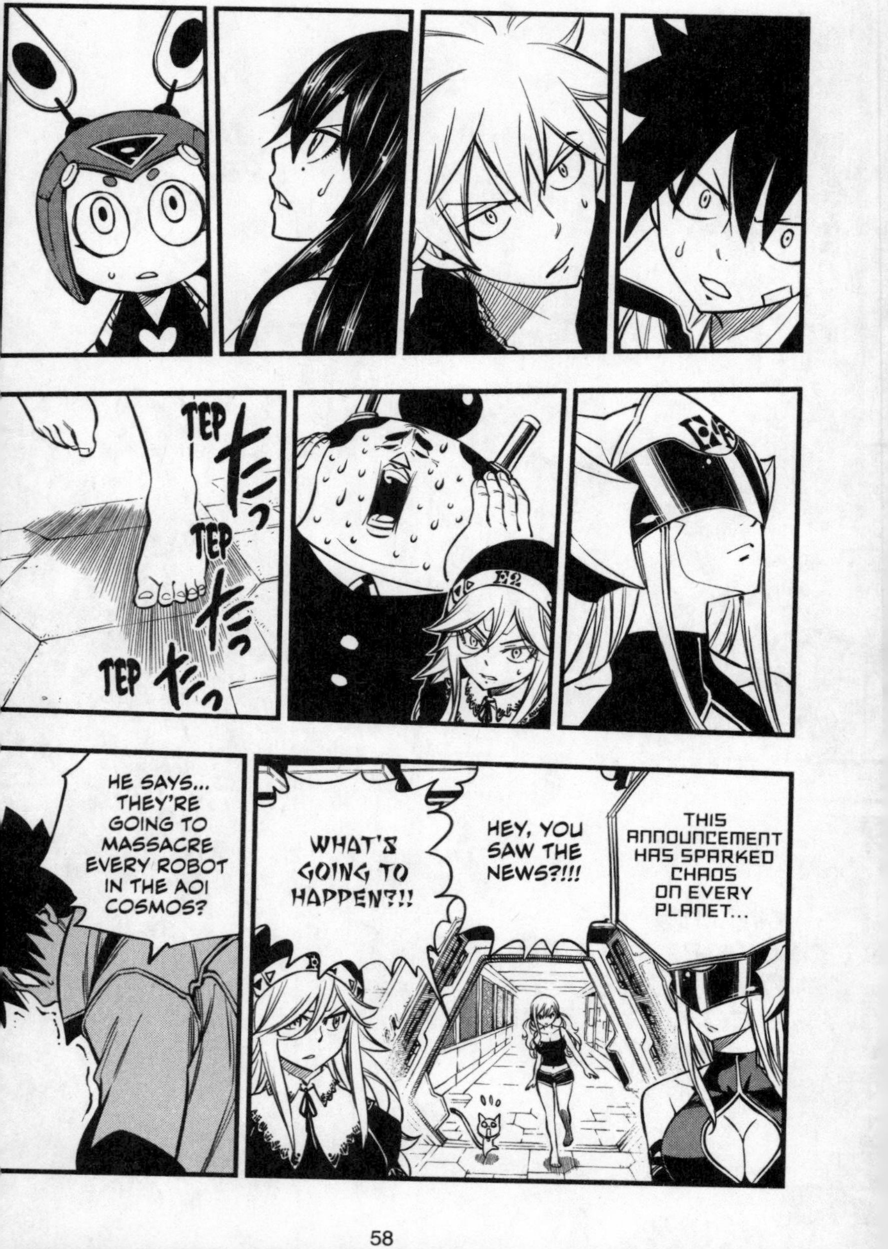
TEP
たっ
TEP
たっ
TEP
たっ
THIS ANNOUNCEMENT HAS SPARKED CHAOS ON EVERY PLANET...
HEY, YOU SAW THE NEWS?!!!
WHAT'S GOING TO HAPPEN?!!
HE SAYS... THEY'RE GOING TO MASSACRE EVERY ROBOT IN THE AOI COSMOS?

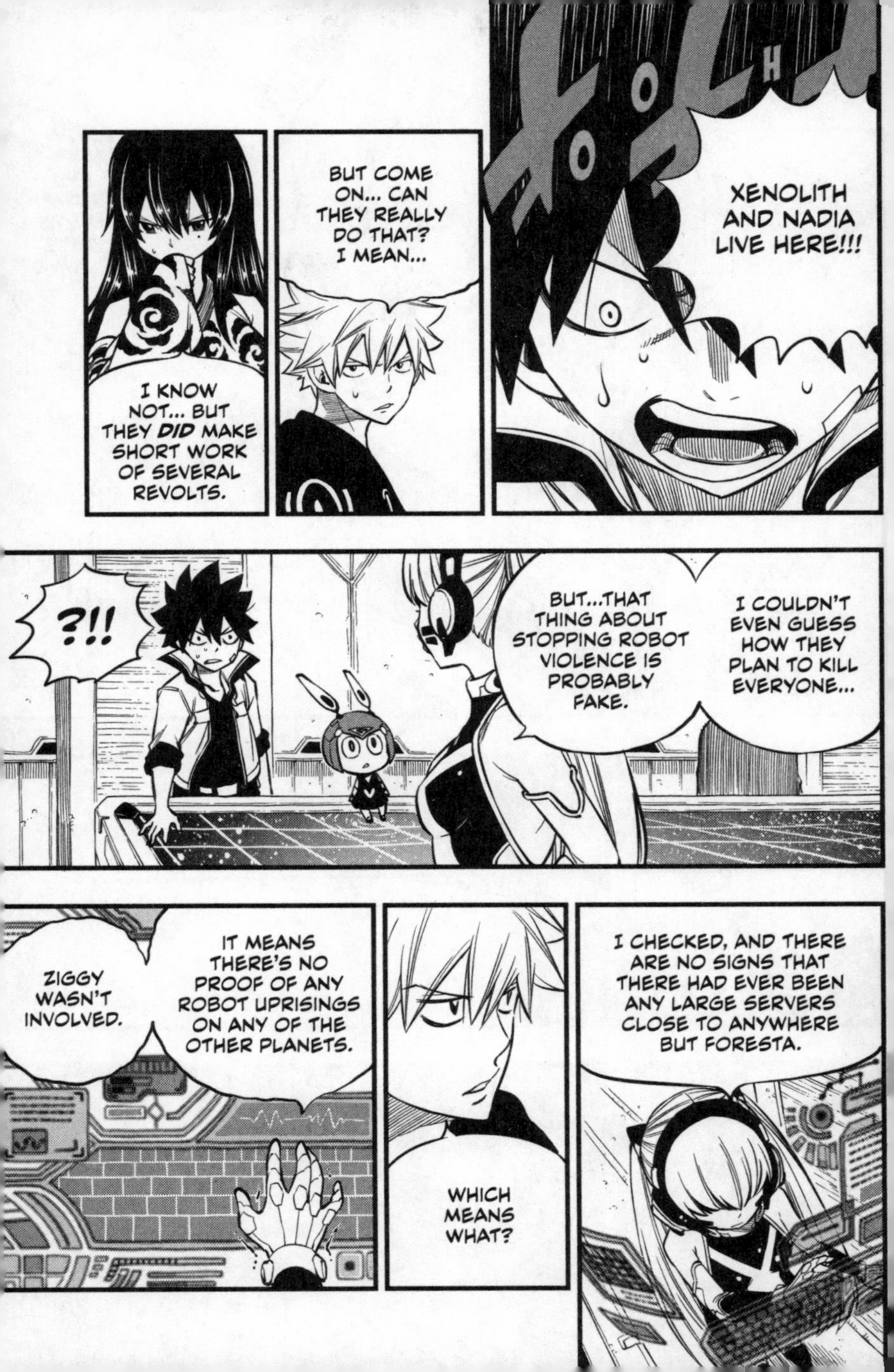
XENOLITH AND NADIA LIVE HERE!!!
BUT COME ON... CAN THEY REALLY DO THAT? I MEAN...
I KNOW NOT... BUT THEY *DID* MAKE SHORT WORK OF SEVERAL REVOLTS.
I COULDN'T EVEN GUESS HOW THEY PLAN TO KILL EVERYONE...
BUT...THAT THING ABOUT STOPPING ROBOT VIOLENCE IS PROBABLY FAKE.
?!!
I CHECKED, AND THERE ARE NO SIGNS THAT THERE HAD EVER BEEN ANY LARGE SERVERS CLOSE TO ANYWHERE BUT FORESTA.
WHICH MEANS WHAT?
IT MEANS THERE'S NO PROOF OF ANY ROBOT UPRISINGS ON ANY OF THE OTHER PLANETS.
ZIGGY WASN'T INVOLVED.

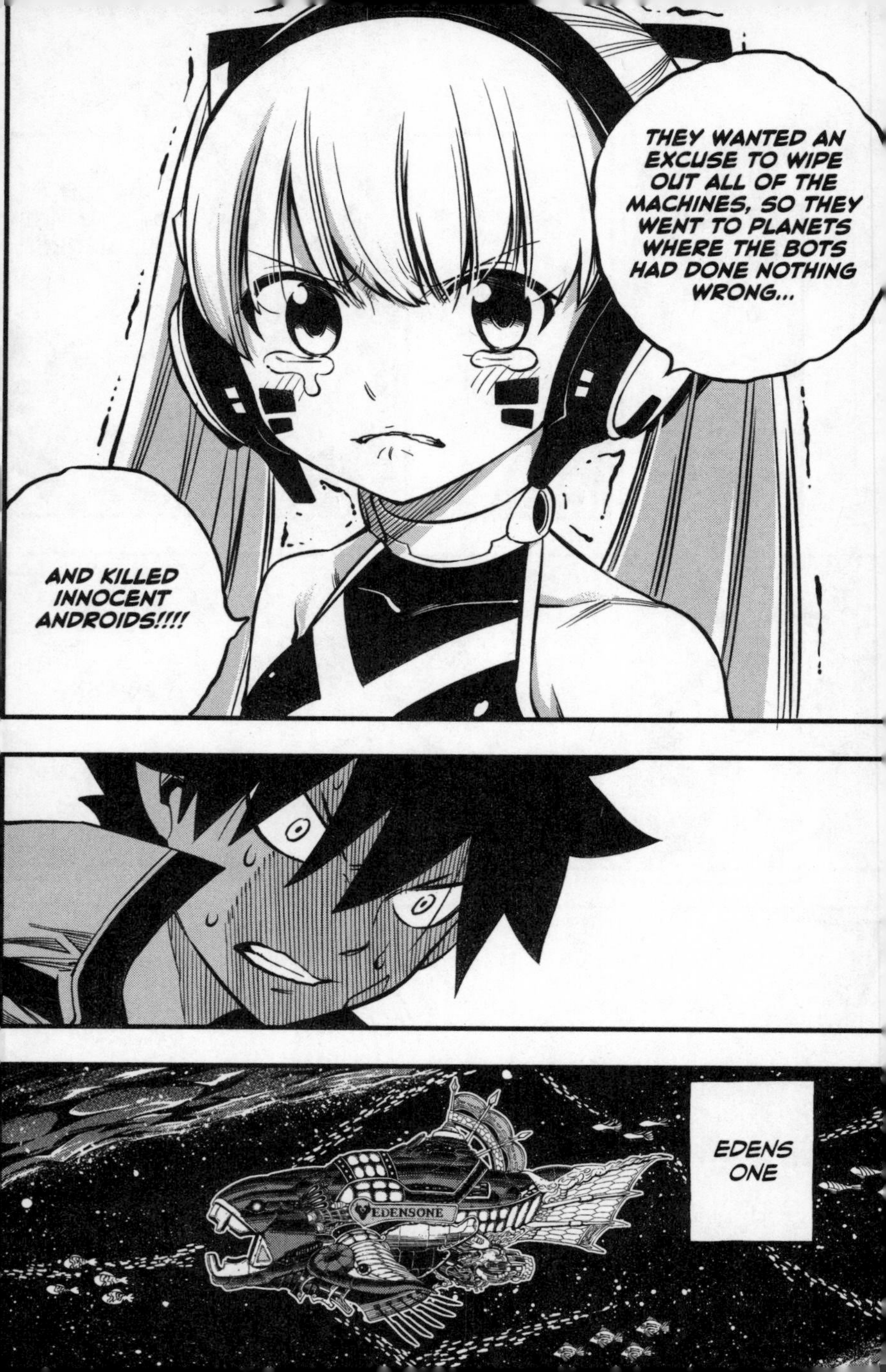
THEY WANTED AN EXCUSE TO WIPE OUT ALL OF THE MACHINES, SO THEY WENT TO PLANETS WHERE THE BOTS HAD DONE NOTHING WRONG...
AND KILLED INNOCENT ANDROIDS!!!!
EDENS ONE
EDENSONE

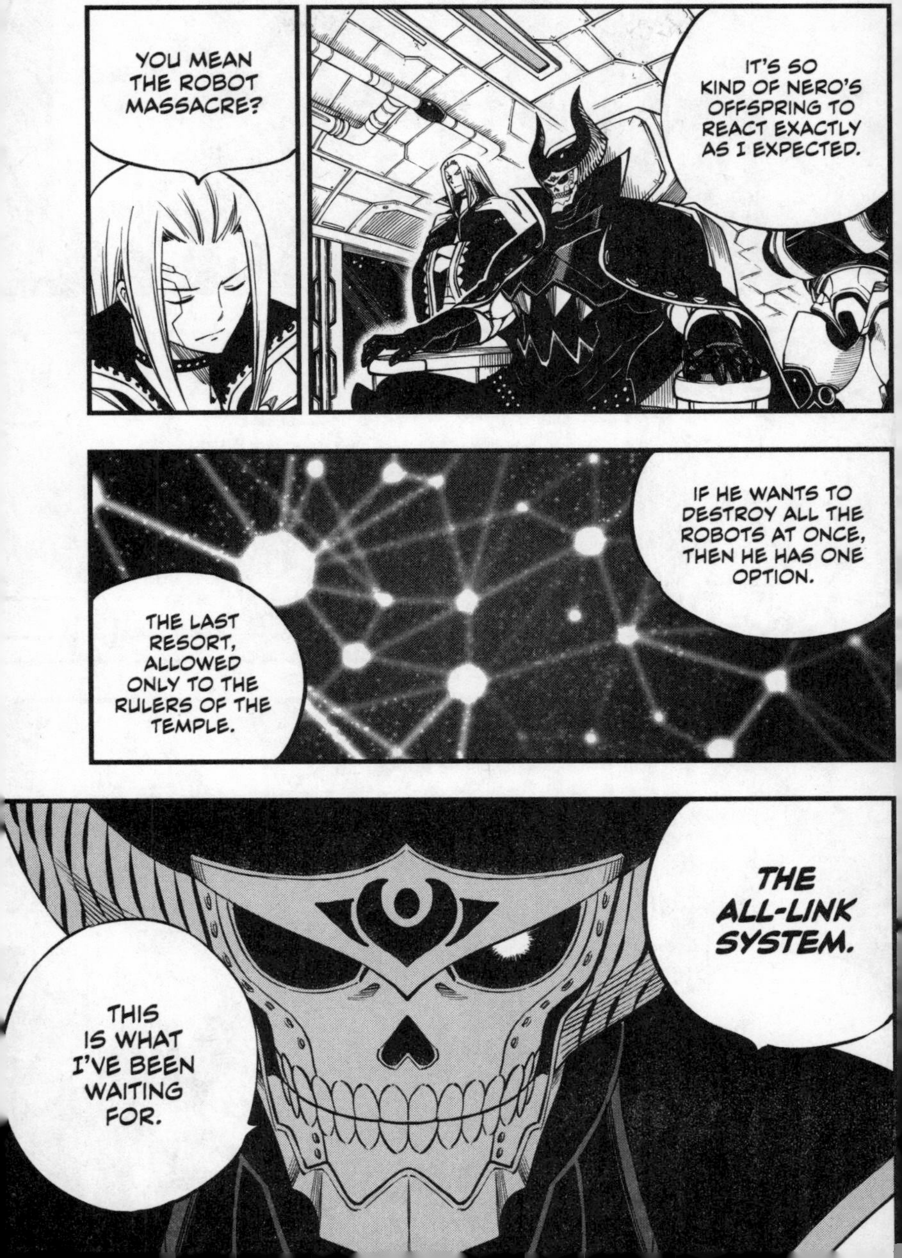

IT'S SO KIND OF NERO'S OFFSPRING TO REACT EXACTLY AS I EXPECTED.
YOU MEAN THE ROBOT MASSACRE?
IF HE WANTS TO DESTROY ALL THE ROBOTS AT ONCE, THEN HE HAS ONE OPTION.
THE LAST RESORT, ALLOWED ONLY TO THE RULERS OF THE TEMPLE.
THE ALL-LINK SYSTEM.
THIS IS WHAT I'VE BEEN WAITING FOR.

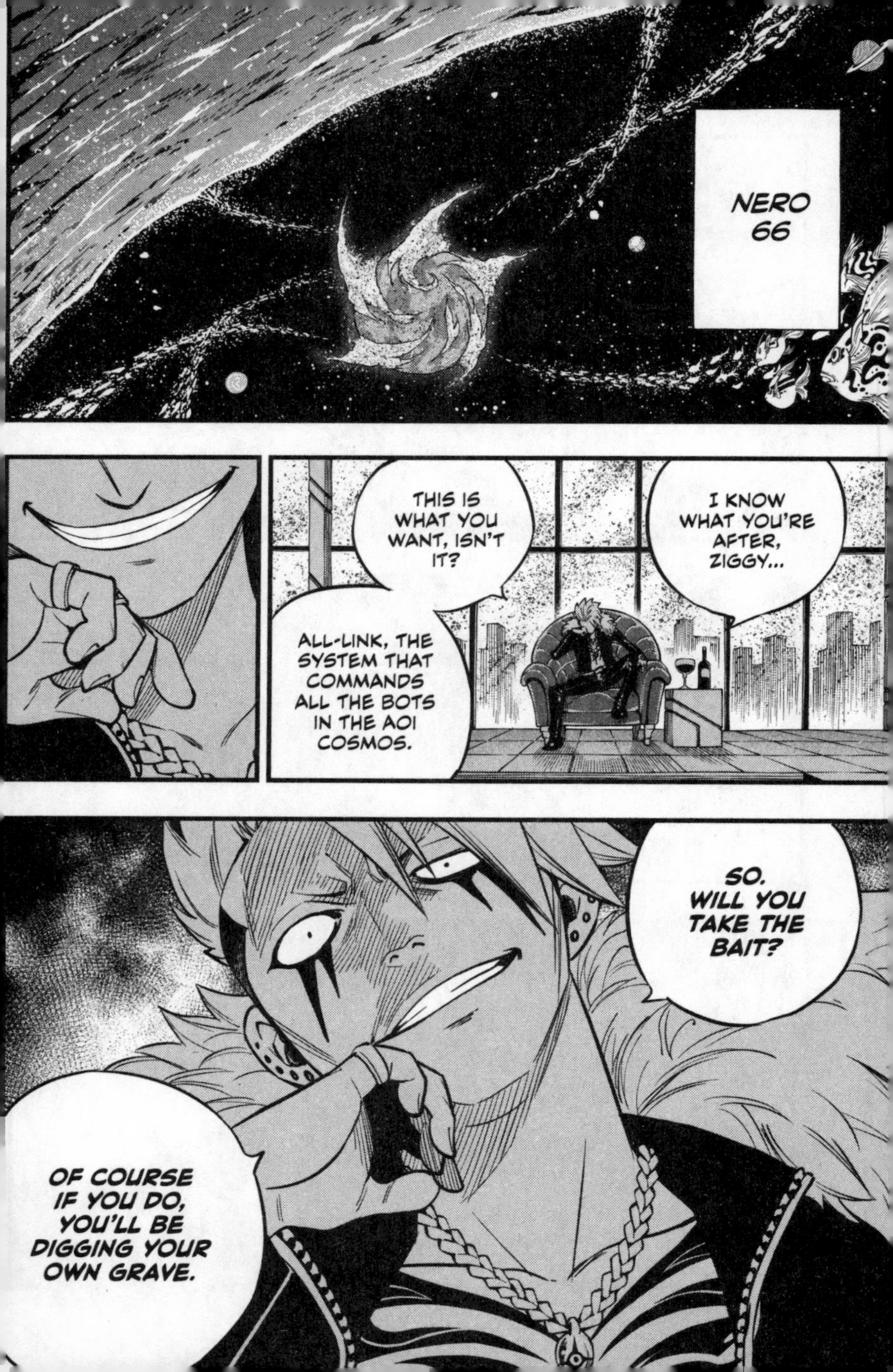
NERO 66
I KNOW WHAT YOU'RE AFTER, ZIGGY...
THIS IS WHAT YOU WANT, ISN'T IT?
ALL-LINK, THE SYSTEM THAT COMMANDS ALL THE BOTS IN THE AOI COSMOS.
SO. WILL YOU TAKE THE BAIT?
OF COURSE IF YOU DO, YOU'LL BE DIGGING YOUR OWN GRAVE.

EDENS ZERO

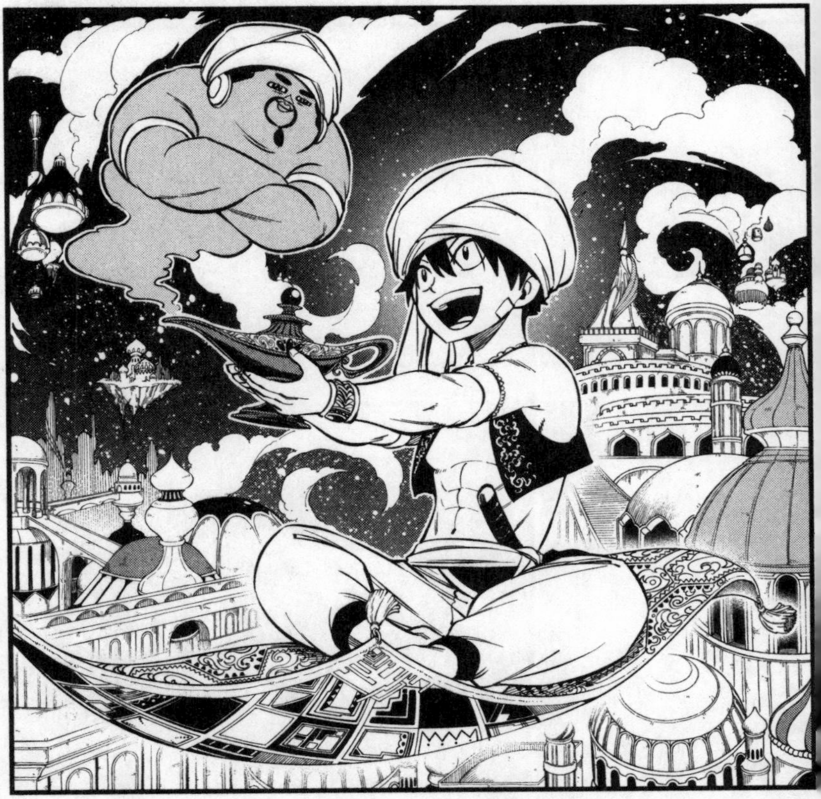

CHAPTER 135: DESERT OASIS

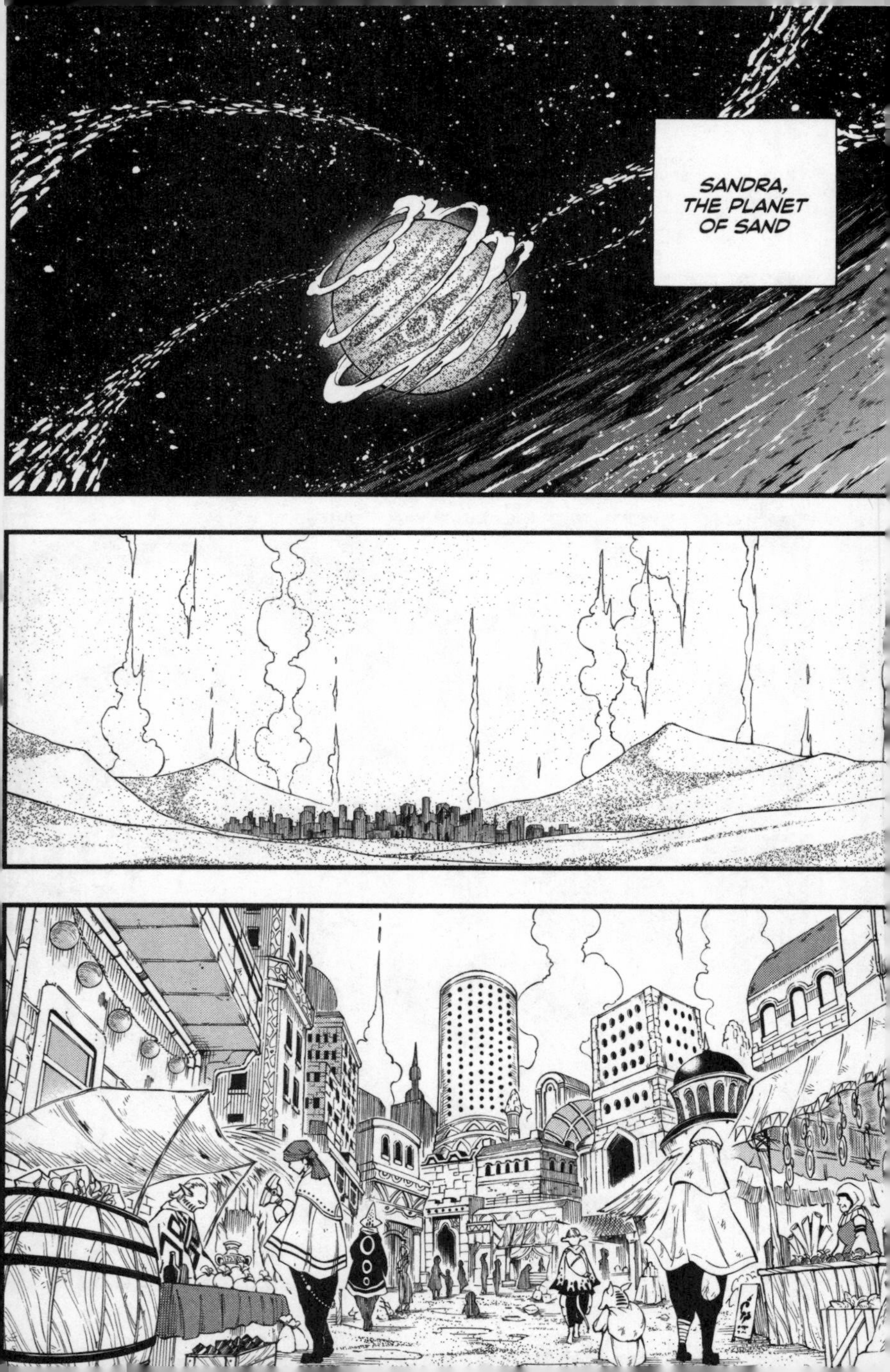
SANDRA, THE PLANET OF SAND

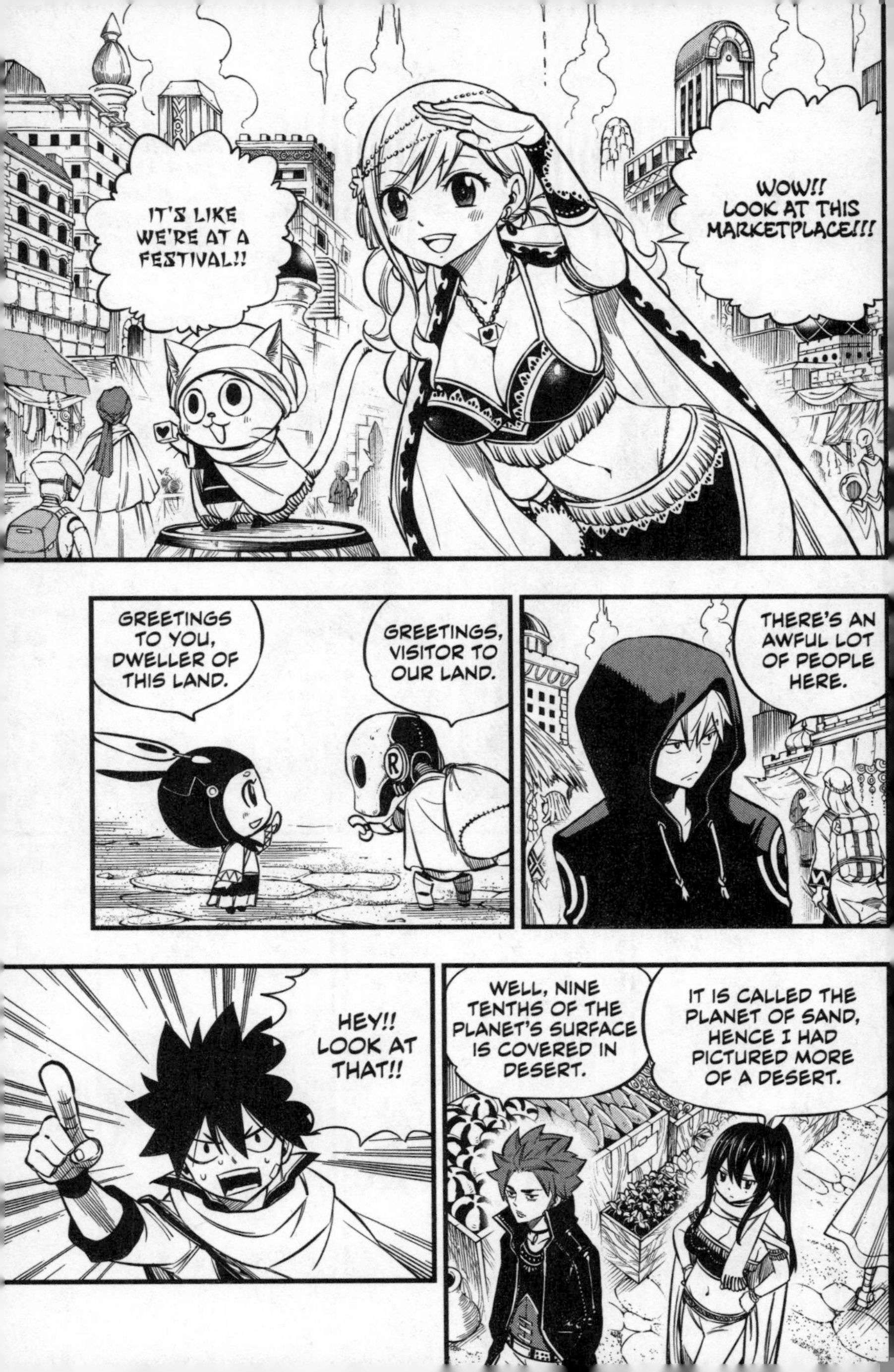
WOW!! LOOK AT THIS MARKETPLACE!!!
IT'S LIKE WE'RE AT A FESTIVAL!!
THERE'S AN AWFUL LOT OF PEOPLE HERE.
GREETINGS, VISITOR TO OUR LAND.
GREETINGS TO YOU, DWELLER OF THIS LAND.
IT IS CALLED THE PLANET OF SAND, HENCE I HAD PICTURED MORE OF A DESERT.
WELL, NINE TENTHS OF THE PLANET'S SURFACE IS COVERED IN DESERT.
HEY!! LOOK AT THAT!!

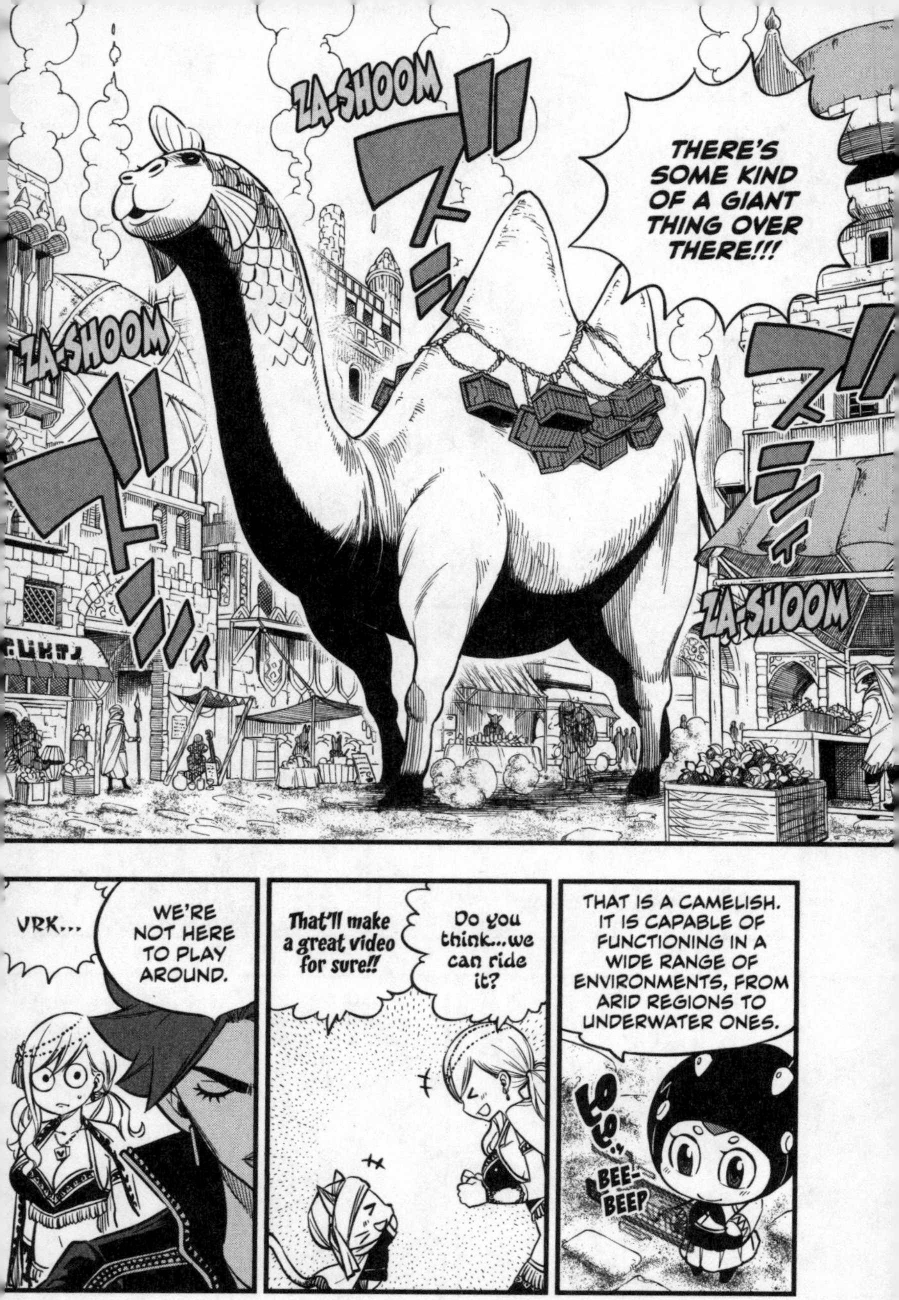
ZA-SHOOM
THERE'S SOME KIND OF A GIANT THING OVER THERE!!!
ZA-SHOOM
ZA-SHOOM
THAT IS A CAMELISH. IT IS CAPABLE OF FUNCTIONING IN A WIDE RANGE OF ENVIRONMENTS, FROM ARID REGIONS TO UNDERWATER ONES.
BEE-BEEP
Do you think...we can ride it?
That'll make a great video for sure!!
WE'RE NOT HERE TO PLAY AROUND.
VRK...

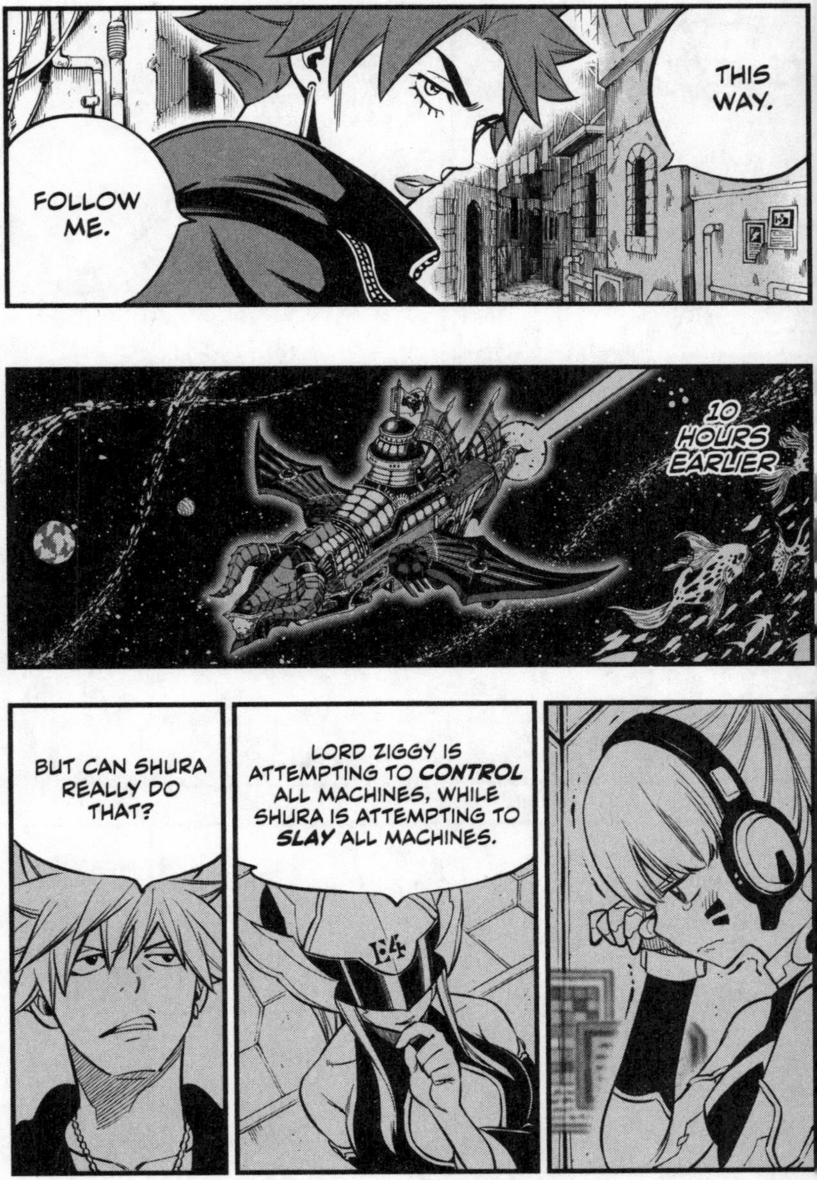
THIS WAY.
FOLLOW ME.
10 HOURS EARLIER
LORD ZIGGY IS ATTEMPTING TO CONTROL ALL MACHINES, WHILE SHURA IS ATTEMPTING TO SLAY ALL MACHINES.
BUT CAN SHURA REALLY DO THAT?

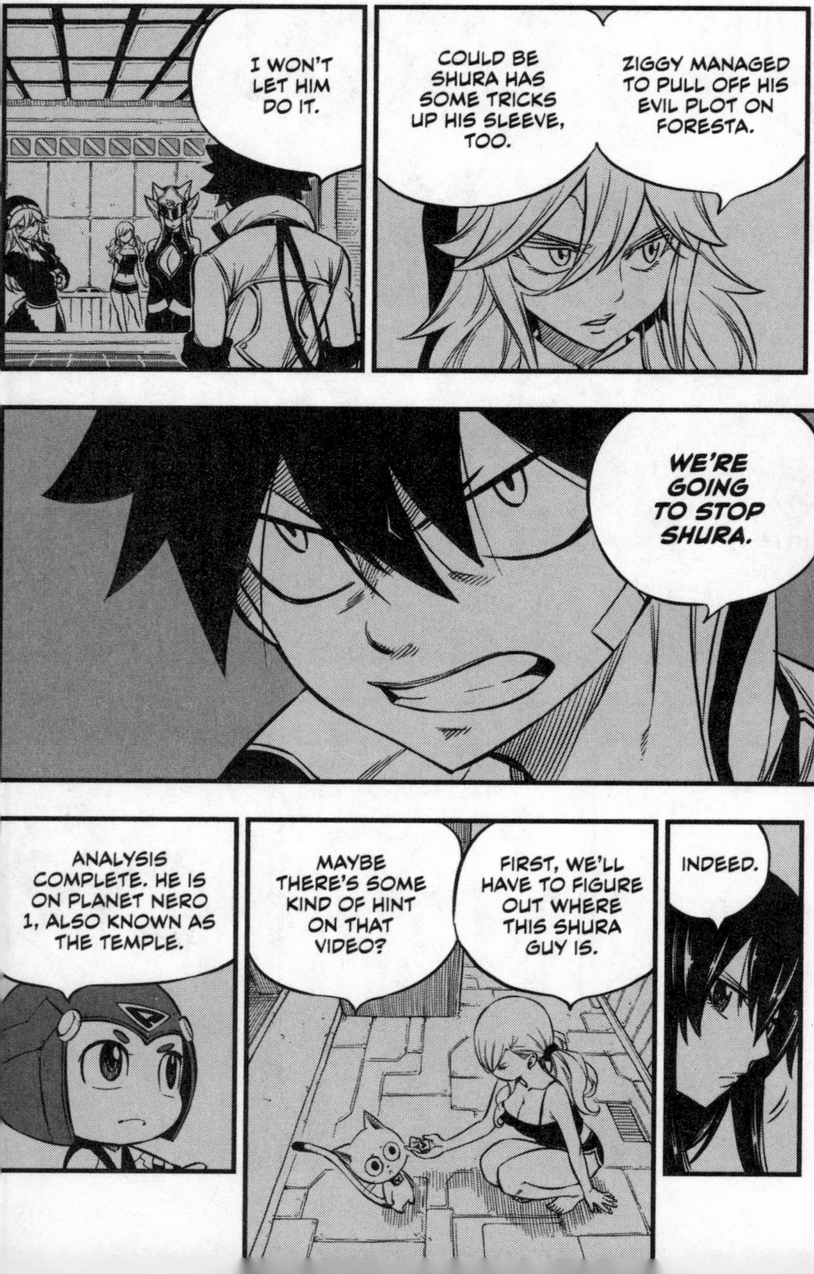
ZIGGY MANAGED TO PULL OFF HIS EVIL PLOT ON FORESTA.
COULD BE SHURA HAS SOME TRICKS UP HIS SLEEVE, TOO.
I WON'T LET HIM DO IT.
WE'RE GOING TO STOP SHURA.
INDEED.
FIRST, WE'LL HAVE TO FIGURE OUT WHERE THIS SHURA GUY IS.
MAYBE THERE'S SOME KIND OF HINT ON THAT VIDEO?
ANALYSIS COMPLETE. HE IS ON PLANET NERO 1, ALSO KNOWN AS THE TEMPLE.

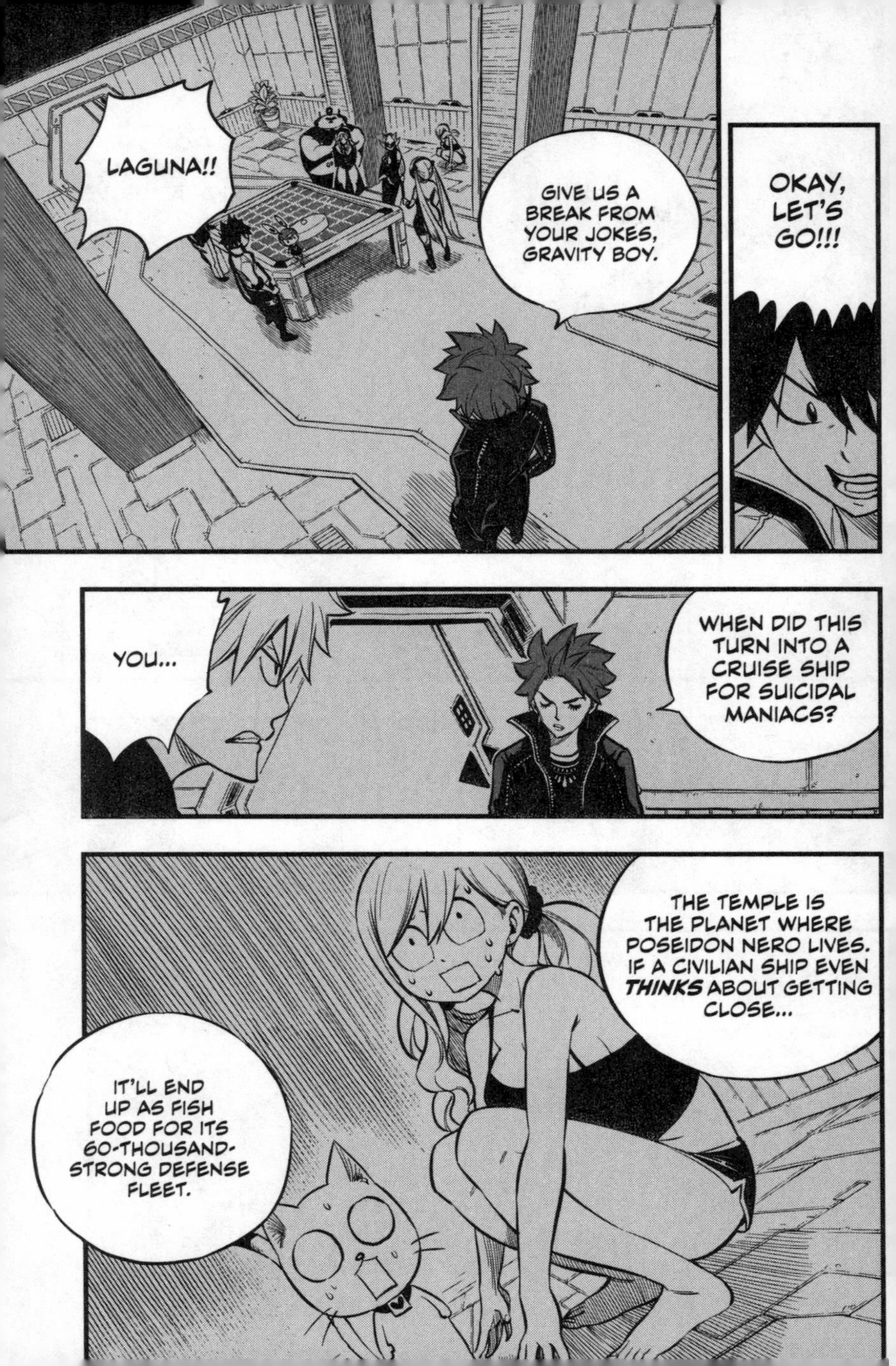
OKAY, LET'S GO!!!
LAGUNA!!
GIVE US A BREAK FROM YOUR JOKES, GRAVITY BOY.
WHEN DID THIS TURN INTO A CRUISE SHIP FOR SUICIDAL MANIACS?
YOU...
THE TEMPLE IS THE PLANET WHERE POSEIDON NERO LIVES. IF A CIVILIAN SHIP EVEN *THINKS* ABOUT GETTING CLOSE...
IT'LL END UP AS FISH FOOD FOR ITS 60-THOUSAND-STRONG DEFENSE FLEET.

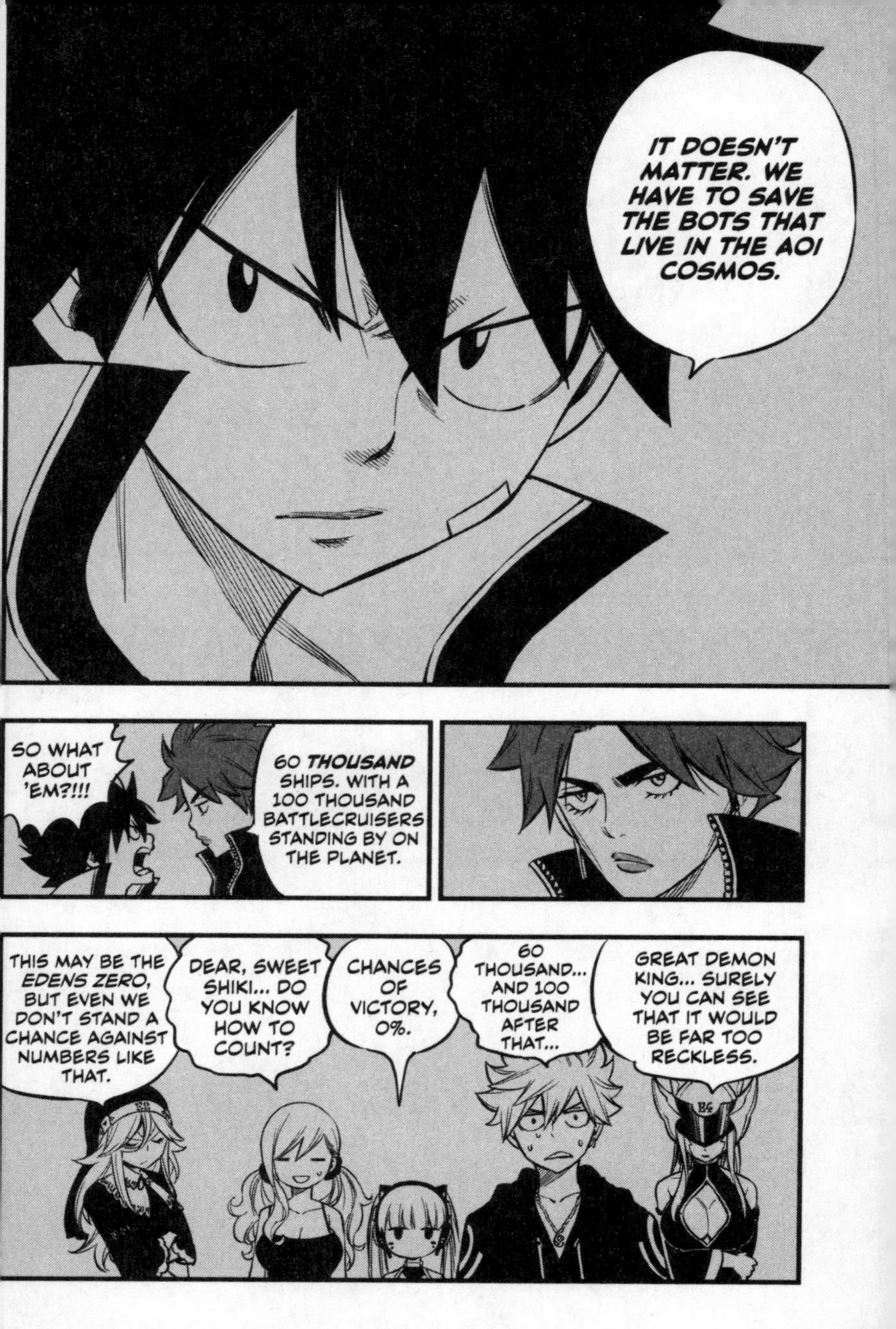

IT DOESN'T MATTER. WE HAVE TO SAVE THE BOTS THAT LIVE IN THE AOI COSMOS.
60 *THOUSAND* SHIPS. WITH A 100 THOUSAND BATTLECRUISERS STANDING BY ON THE PLANET.
SO WHAT ABOUT 'EM?!!!
GREAT DEMON KING... SURELY YOU CAN SEE THAT IT WOULD BE FAR TOO RECKLESS.
60 THOUSAND... AND 100 THOUSAND AFTER THAT...
CHANCES OF VICTORY, 0%.
DEAR, SWEET SHIKI... DO YOU KNOW HOW TO COUNT?
THIS MAY BE THE *EDENS ZERO*, BUT EVEN WE DON'T STAND A CHANCE AGAINST NUMBERS LIKE THAT.

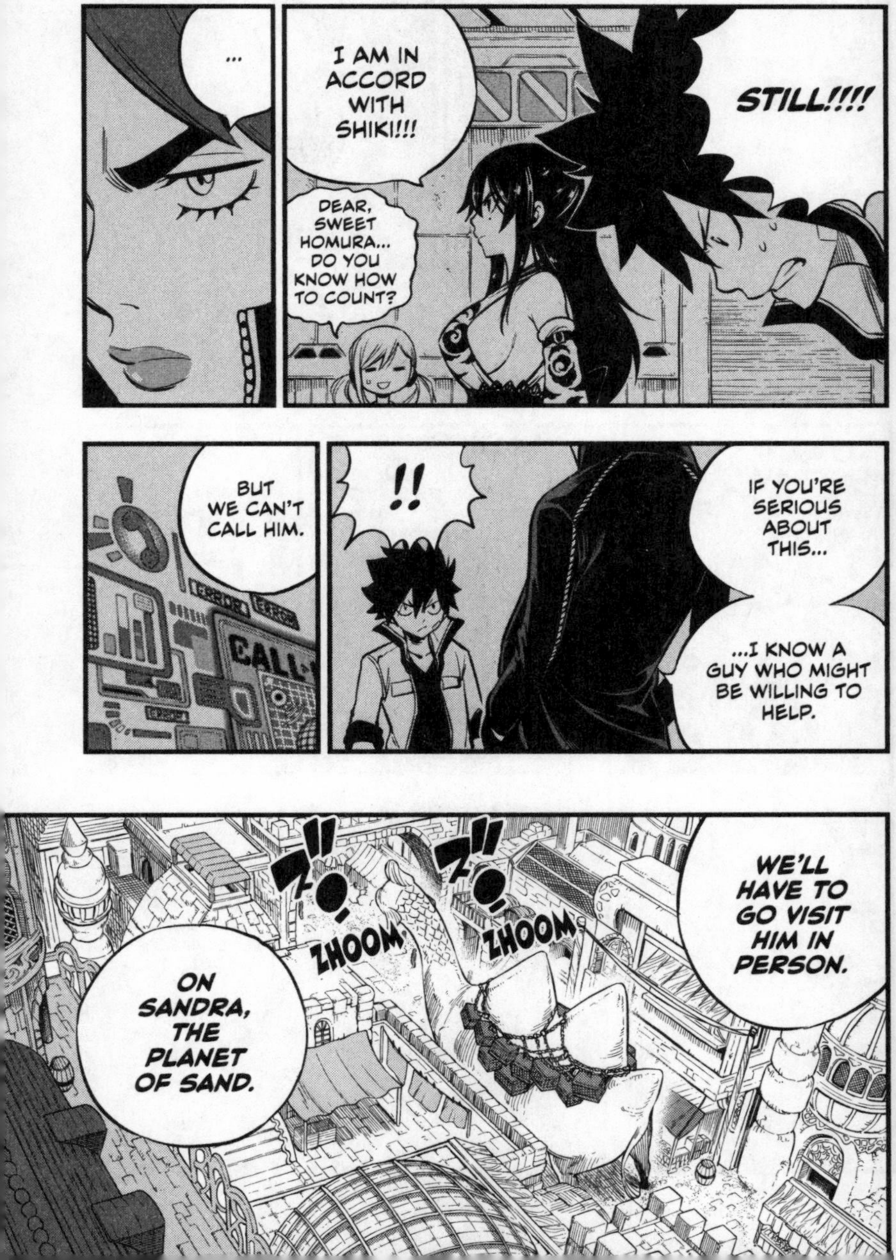
STILL!!!!
I AM IN ACCORD WITH SHIKI!!!
DEAR, SWEET HOMURA... DO YOU KNOW HOW TO COUNT?
...
IF YOU'RE SERIOUS ABOUT THIS...
!!
...I KNOW A GUY WHO MIGHT BE WILLING TO HELP.
BUT WE CAN'T CALL HIM.
WE'LL HAVE TO GO VISIT HIM IN PERSON.
ZHOOM
ZHOOM
ON SANDRA, THE PLANET OF SAND.

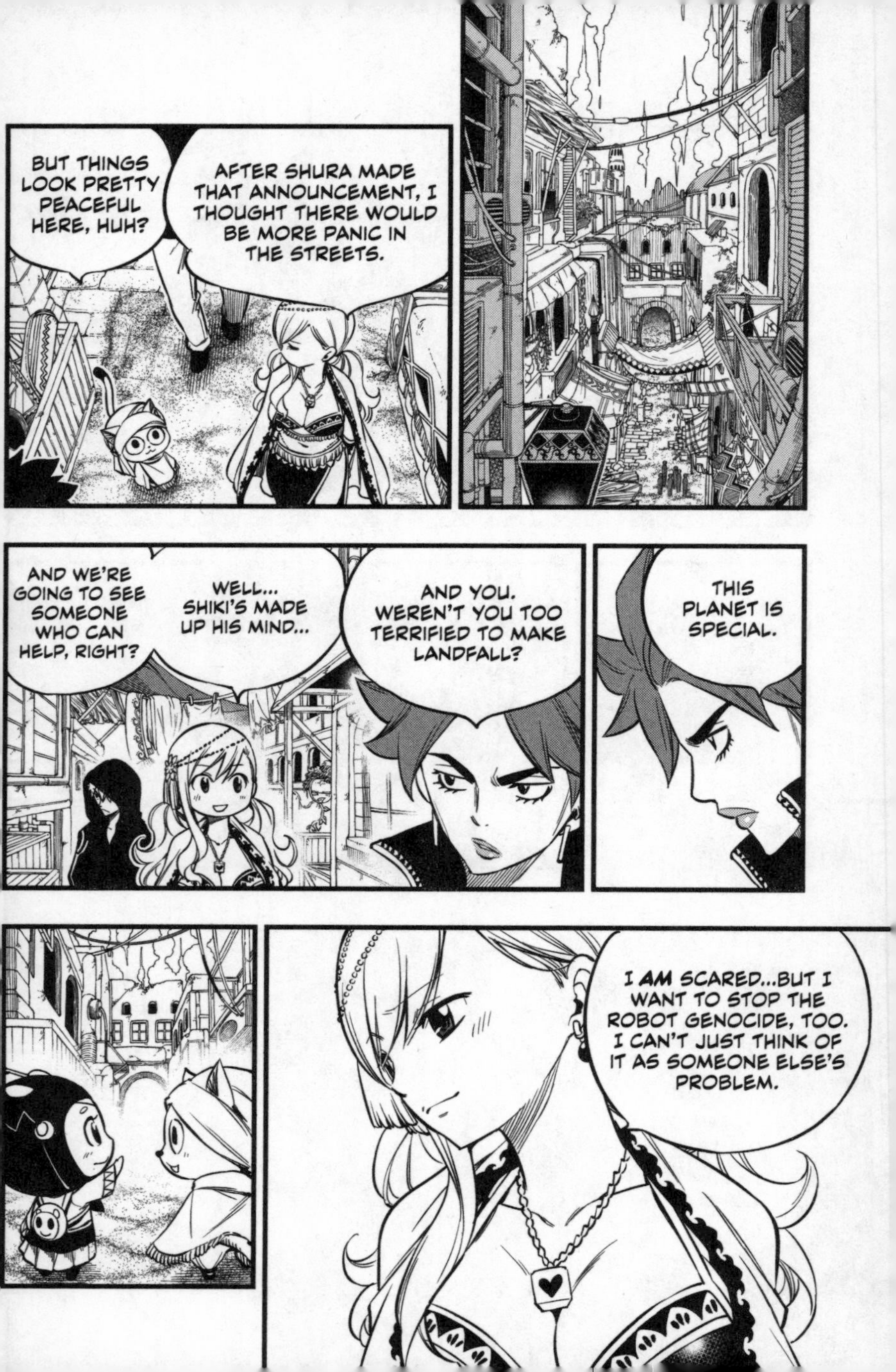
AFTER SHURA MADE THAT ANNOUNCEMENT, I THOUGHT THERE WOULD BE MORE PANIC IN THE STREETS.
BUT THINGS LOOK PRETTY PEACEFUL HERE, HUH?
THIS PLANET IS SPECIAL.
AND YOU. WEREN'T YOU TOO TERRIFIED TO MAKE LANDFALL?
WELL... SHIKI'S MADE UP HIS MIND...
AND WE'RE GOING TO SEE SOMEONE WHO CAN HELP, RIGHT?
I AM SCARED...BUT I WANT TO STOP THE ROBOT GENOCIDE, TOO. I CAN'T JUST THINK OF IT AS SOMEONE ELSE'S PROBLEM.

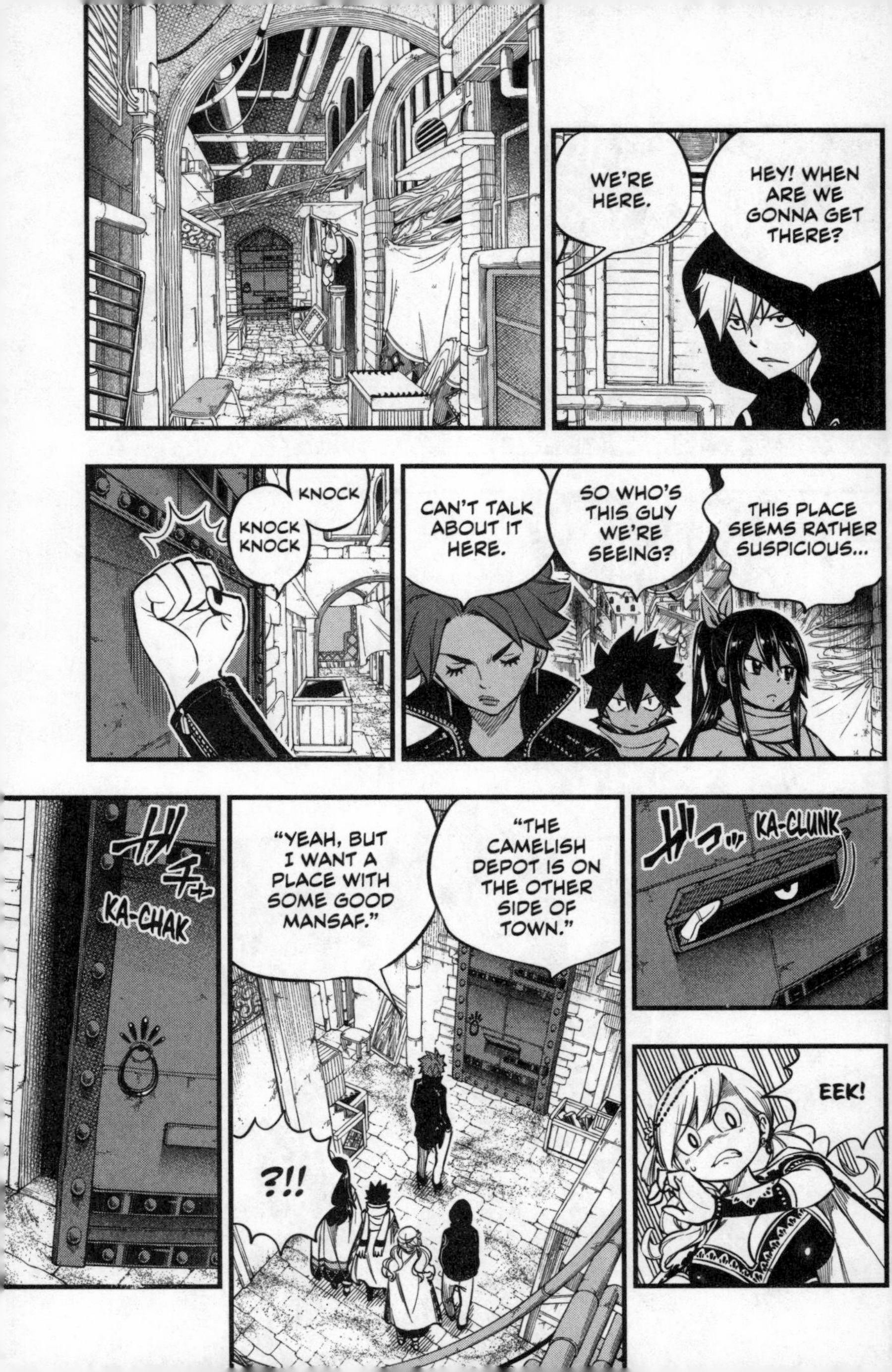
HEY! WHEN ARE WE GONNA GET THERE?
WE'RE HERE.
THIS PLACE SEEMS RATHER SUSPICIOUS...
SO WHO'S THIS GUY WE'RE SEEING?
CAN'T TALK ABOUT IT HERE.
KNOCK
KNOCK KNOCK
KA-CLUNK
EEK!
"THE CAMELISH DEPOT IS ON THE OTHER SIDE OF TOWN."
"YEAH, BUT I WANT A PLACE WITH SOME GOOD MANSAF."
?!!
KA-CHAK

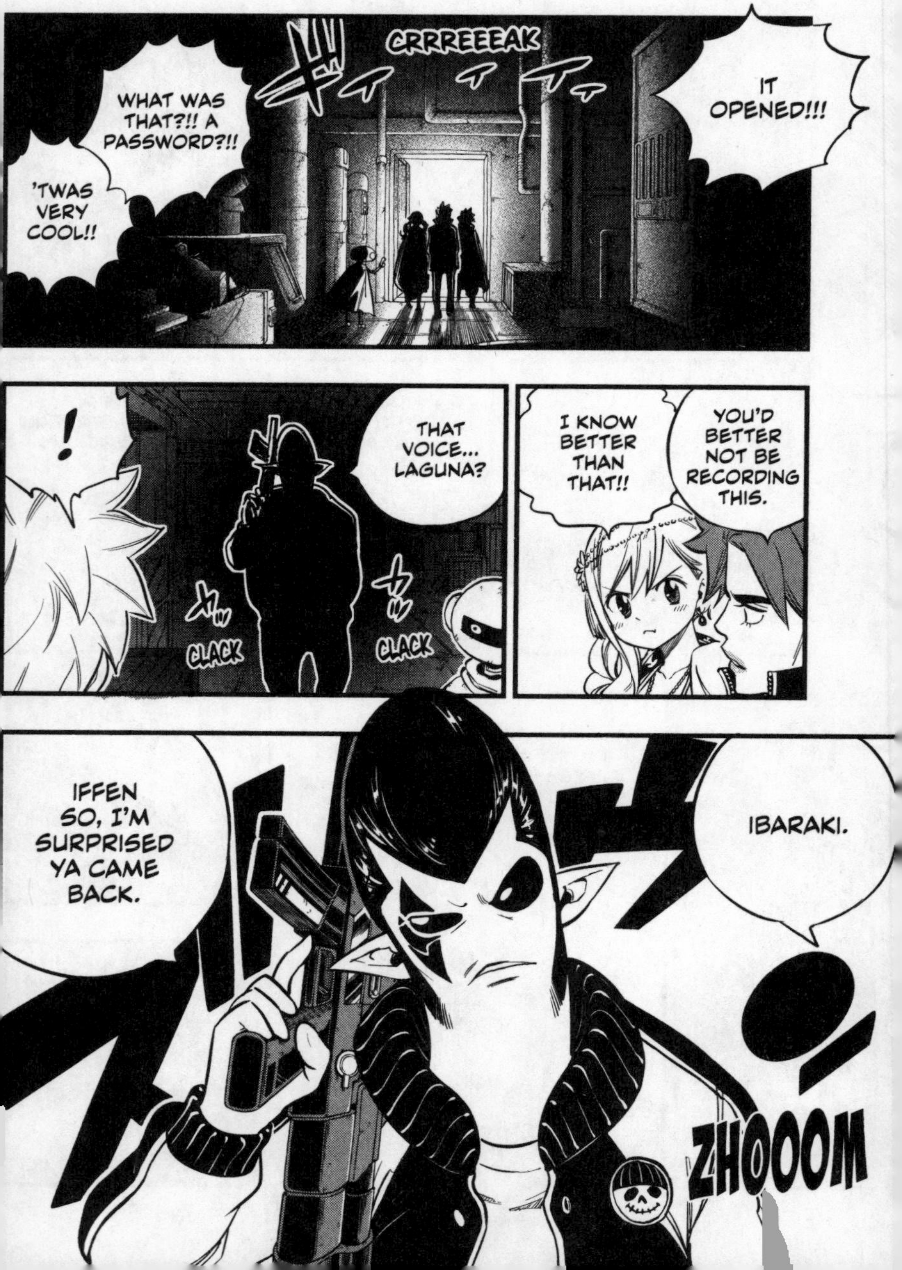
IT OPENED!!!
CRRREEEAK
WHAT WAS THAT?!! A PASSWORD?!!
'TWAS VERY COOL!!
YOU'D BETTER NOT BE RECORDING THIS.
I KNOW BETTER THAN THAT!!
THAT VOICE... LAGUNA?
CLACK
CLACK
!
IBARAKI.
IFFEN SO, I'M SURPRISED YA CAME BACK.
ZHOOOM

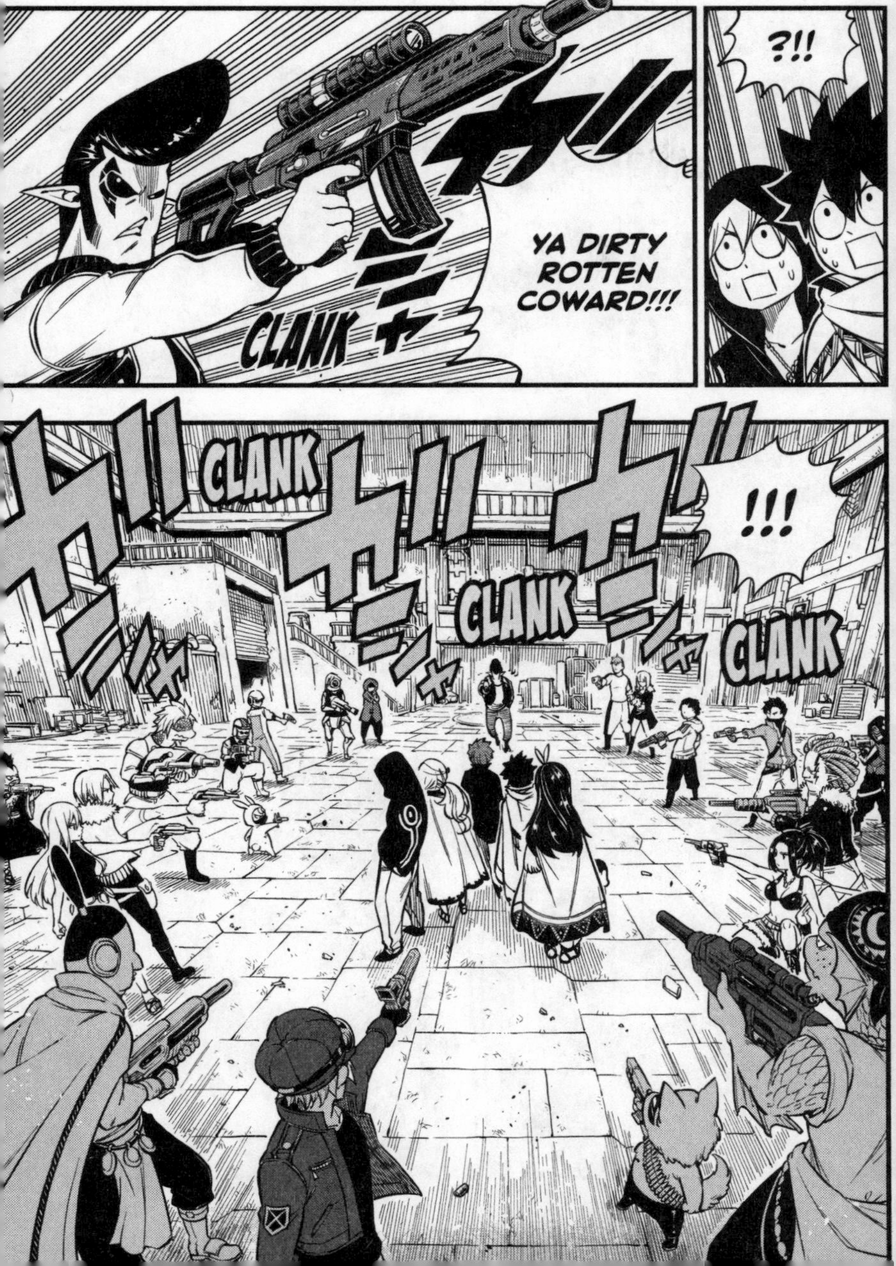
?!!
YA DIRTY ROTTEN COWARD!!!
CLANK
!!!
CLANK
CLANK
CLANK

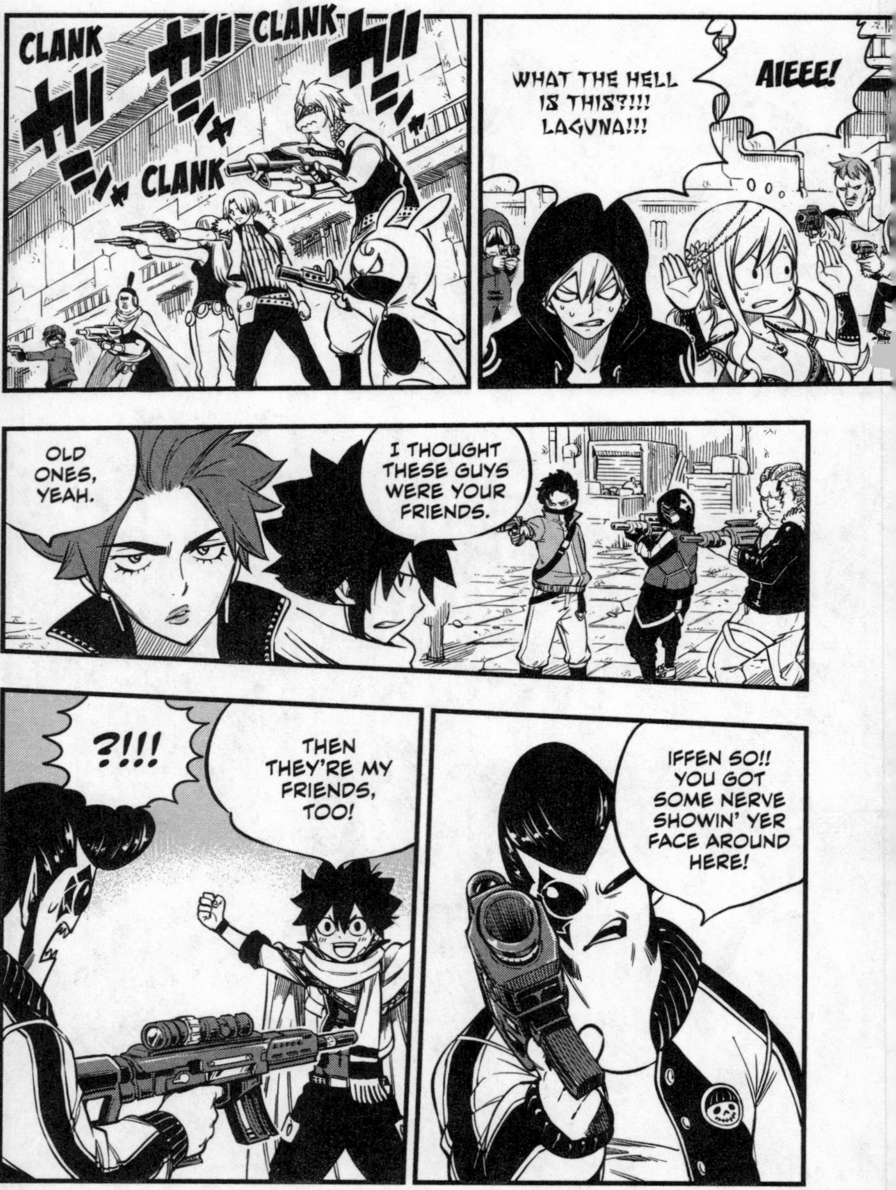
AIEEE!
WHAT THE HELL IS THIS?!!! LAGUNA!!!
CLANK
CLANK
CLANK
I THOUGHT THESE GUYS WERE YOUR FRIENDS.
OLD ONES, YEAH.
IFFEN SO!! YOU GOT SOME NERVE SHOWIN' YER FACE AROUND HERE!
THEN THEY'RE MY FRIENDS, TOO!
?!!!

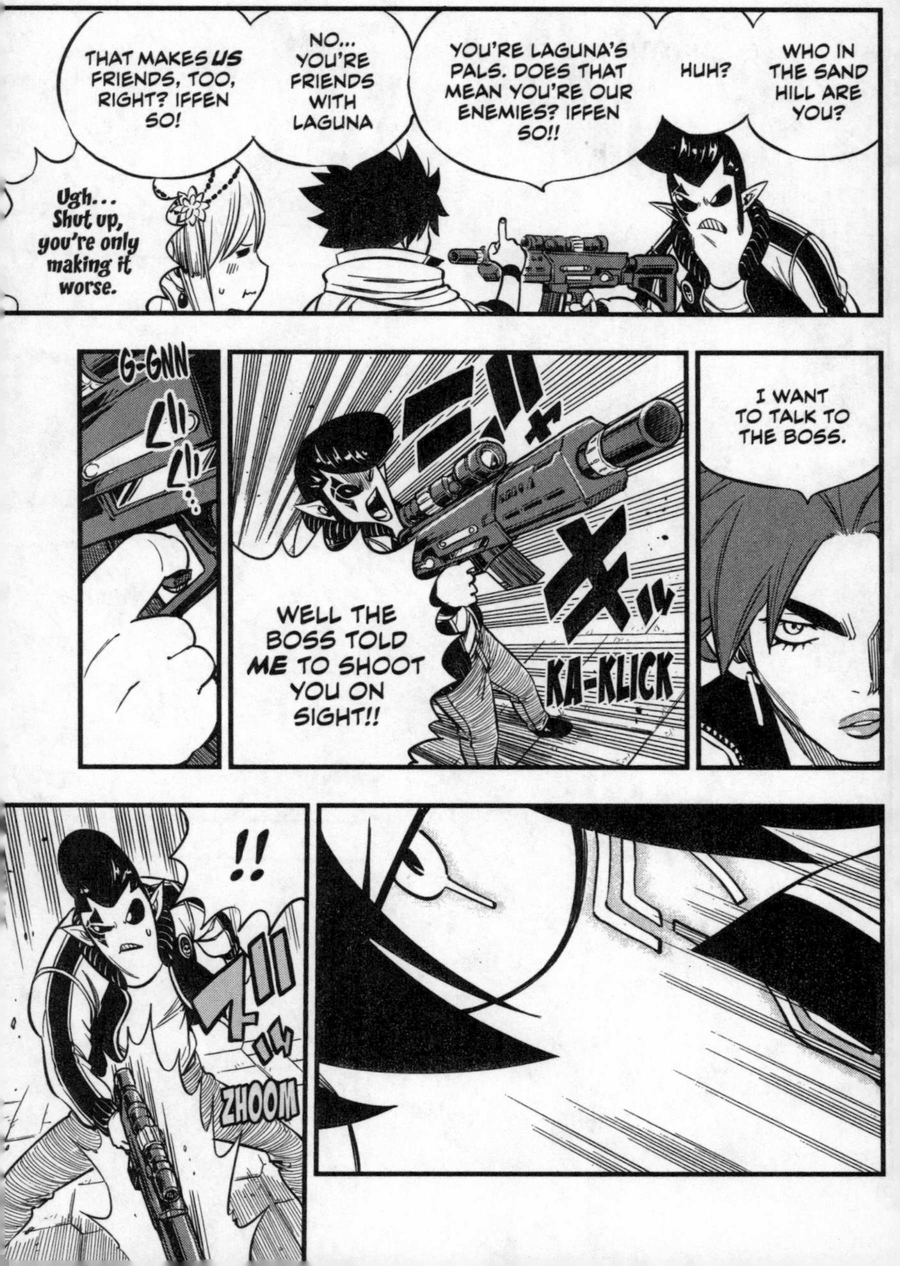
WHO IN THE SAND HILL ARE YOU?
HUH?
YOU'RE LAGUNA'S PALS. DOES THAT MEAN YOU'RE OUR ENEMIES? IFFEN SO!!
NO... YOU'RE FRIENDS WITH LAGUNA
THAT MAKES *US* FRIENDS, TOO, RIGHT? IFFEN SO!
Ugh... Shut up, you're only making it worse.
I WANT TO TALK TO THE BOSS.
WELL THE BOSS TOLD *ME* TO SHOOT YOU ON SIGHT!!
KA-KLICK
G-GNN
!!
ZHOOM

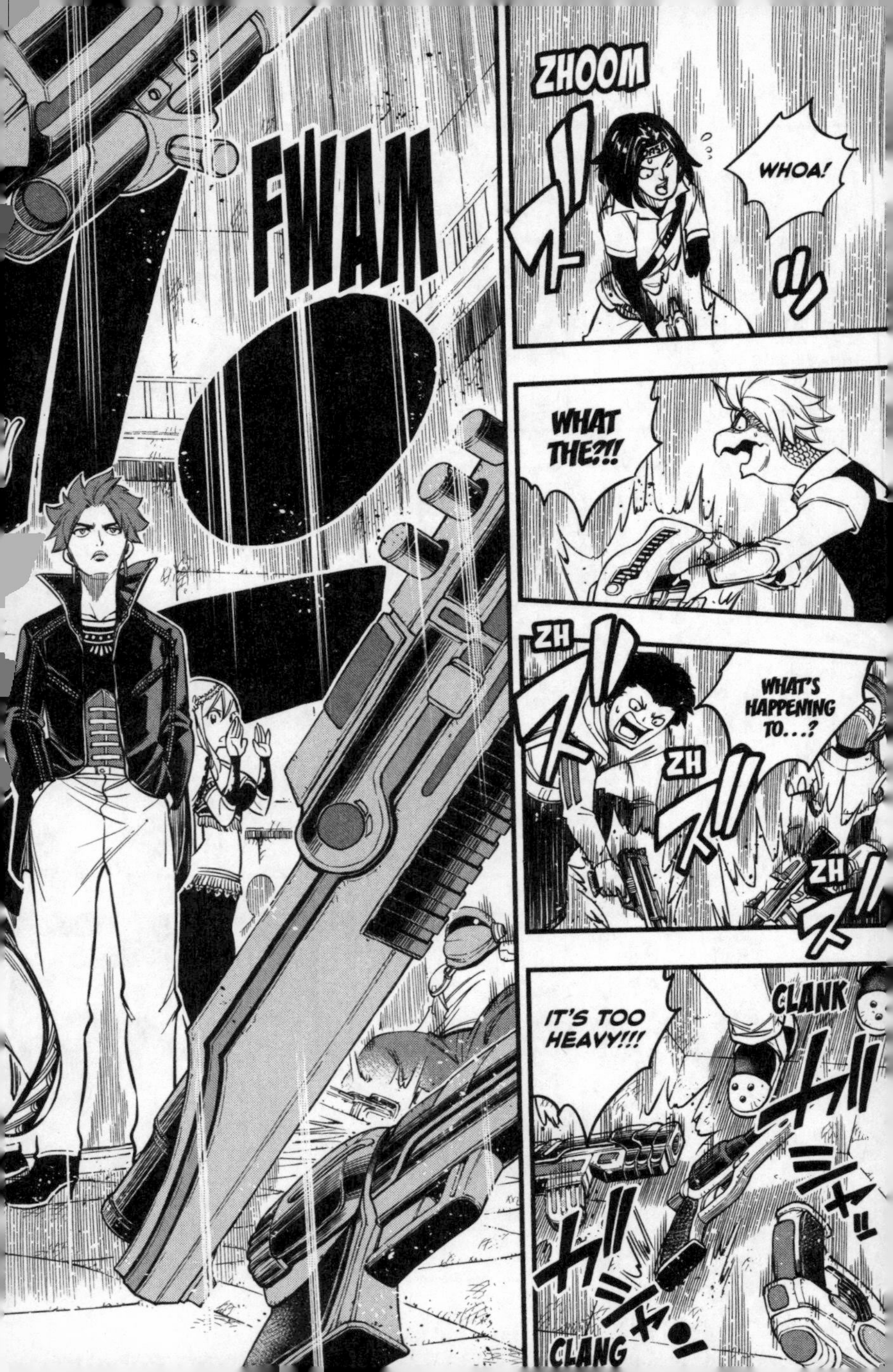
ZHOOM
WHOA!
WHAT THE?!!
ZH
WHAT'S HAPPENING TO...?
ZH
ZH
CLANK
IT'S TOO HEAVY!!!
CLANG
FWAM

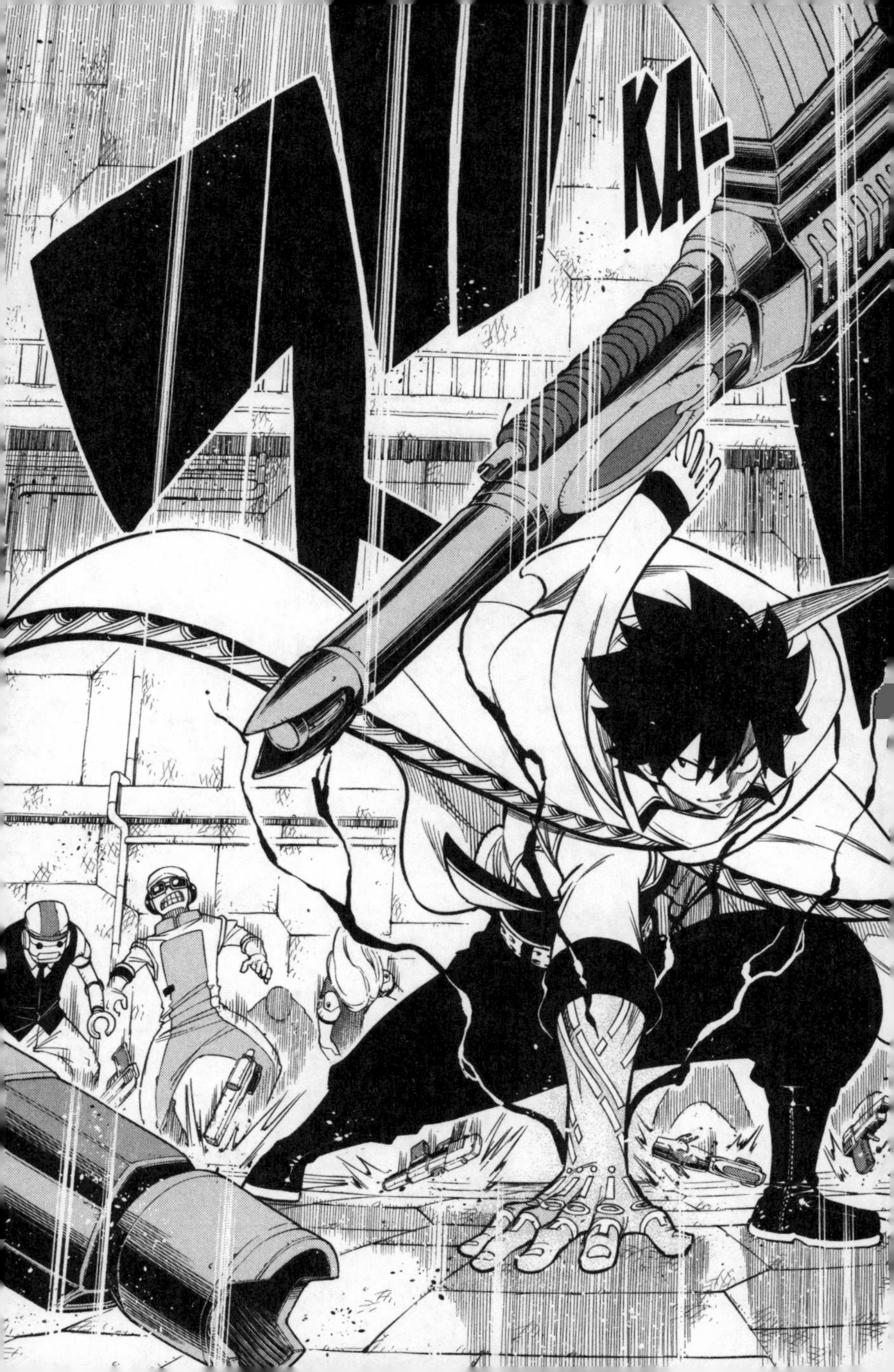
KA-

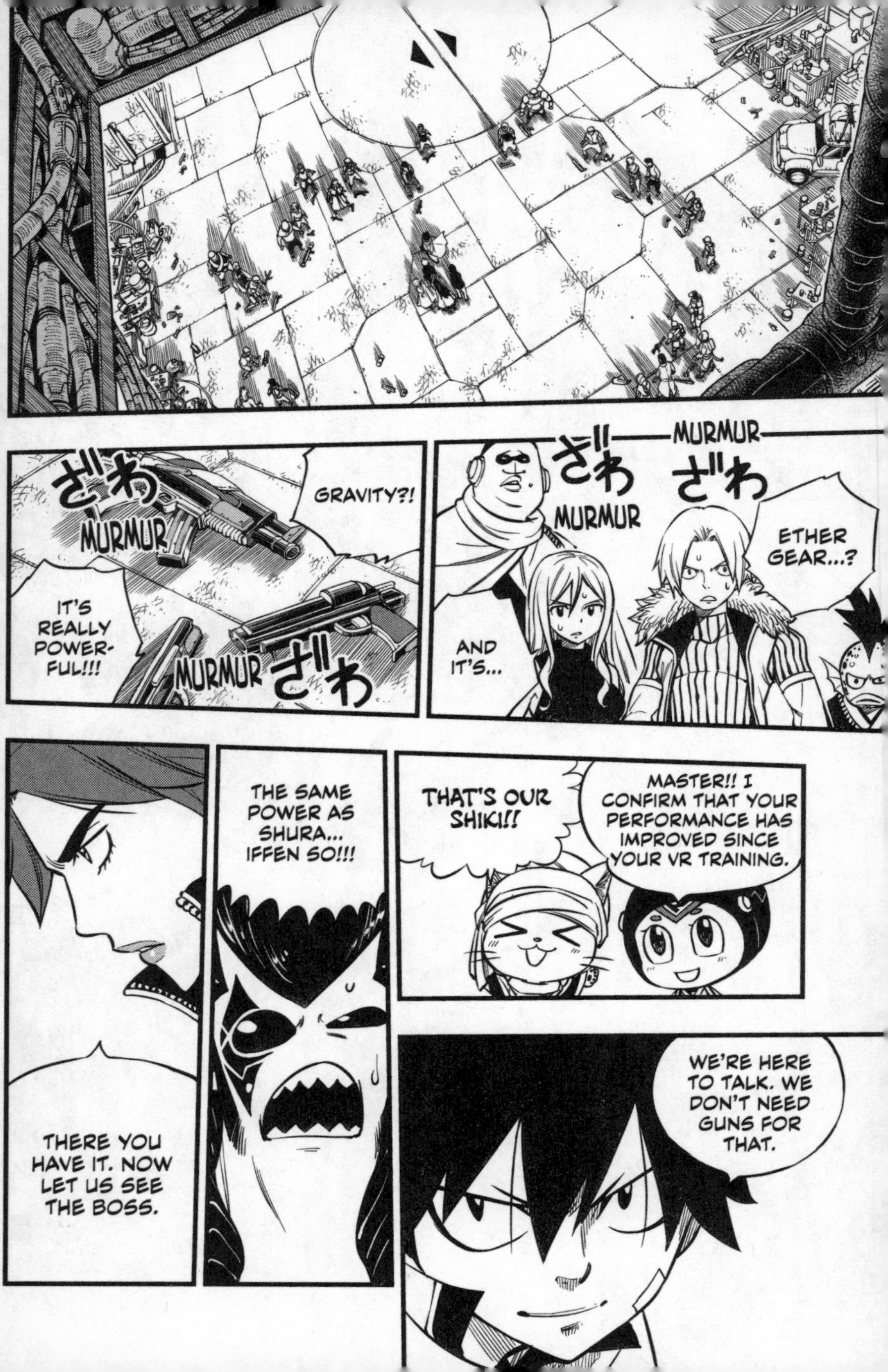

ざわ
MURMUR
ざわ
MURMUR
ETHER GEAR...?
AND IT'S...
GRAVITY?!
ざわ
MURMUR
IT'S REALLY POWER-FUL!!!
MURMUR
ざわ
MASTER!! I CONFIRM THAT YOUR PERFORMANCE HAS IMPROVED SINCE YOUR VR TRAINING.
THAT'S OUR SHIKI!!
WE'RE HERE TO TALK. WE DON'T NEED GUNS FOR THAT.
THE SAME POWER AS SHURA... IFFEN SO!!!
THERE YOU HAVE IT. NOW LET US SEE THE BOSS.

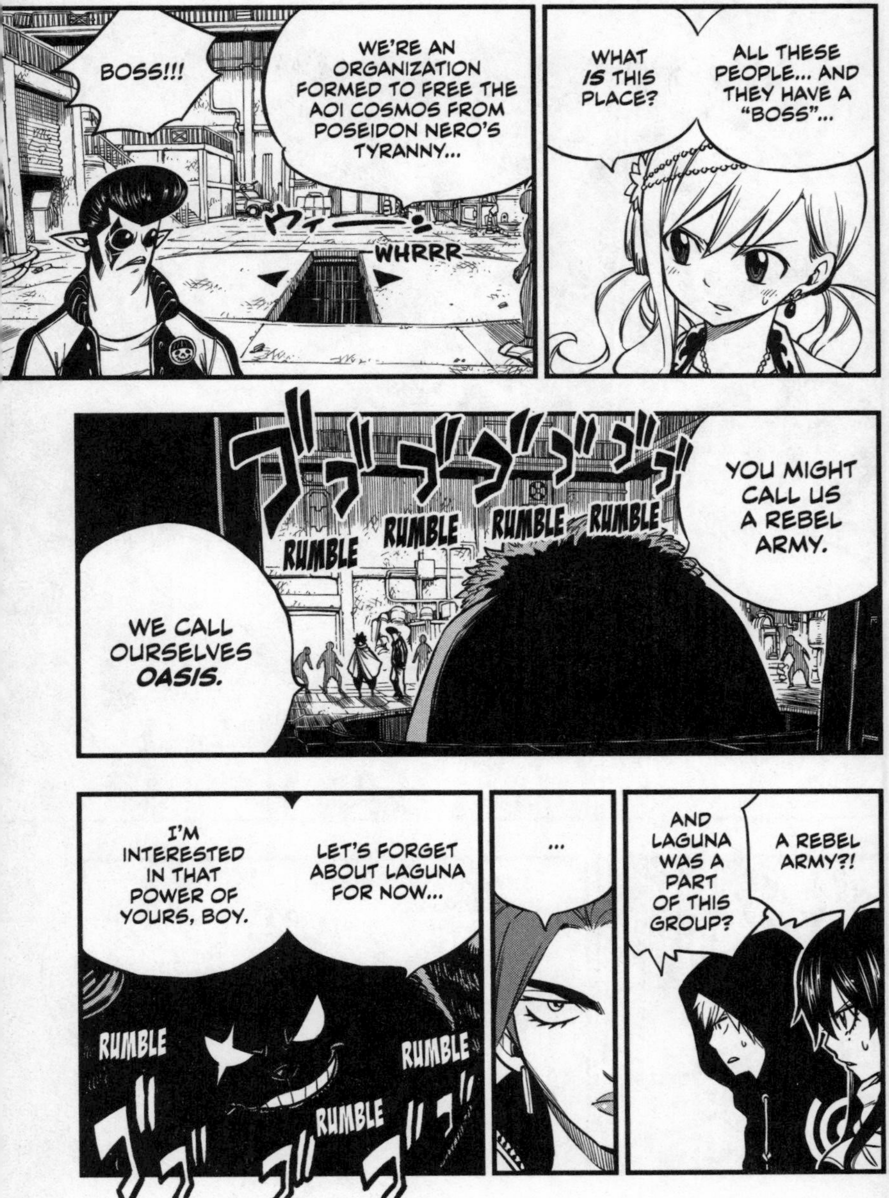
ALL THESE PEOPLE... AND THEY HAVE A "BOSS"...
WHAT *IS* THIS PLACE?
WE'RE AN ORGANIZATION FORMED TO FREE THE AOI COSMOS FROM POSEIDON NERO'S TYRANNY...
BOSS!!!
WHRRR
YOU MIGHT CALL US A REBEL ARMY.
RUMBLE
RUMBLE
RUMBLE
RUMBLE
WE CALL OURSELVES *OASIS.*
A REBEL ARMY?!
AND LAGUNA WAS A PART OF THIS GROUP?
...
LET'S FORGET ABOUT LAGUNA FOR NOW...
I'M INTERESTED IN THAT POWER OF YOURS, BOY.
RUMBLE
RUMBLE
RUMBLE

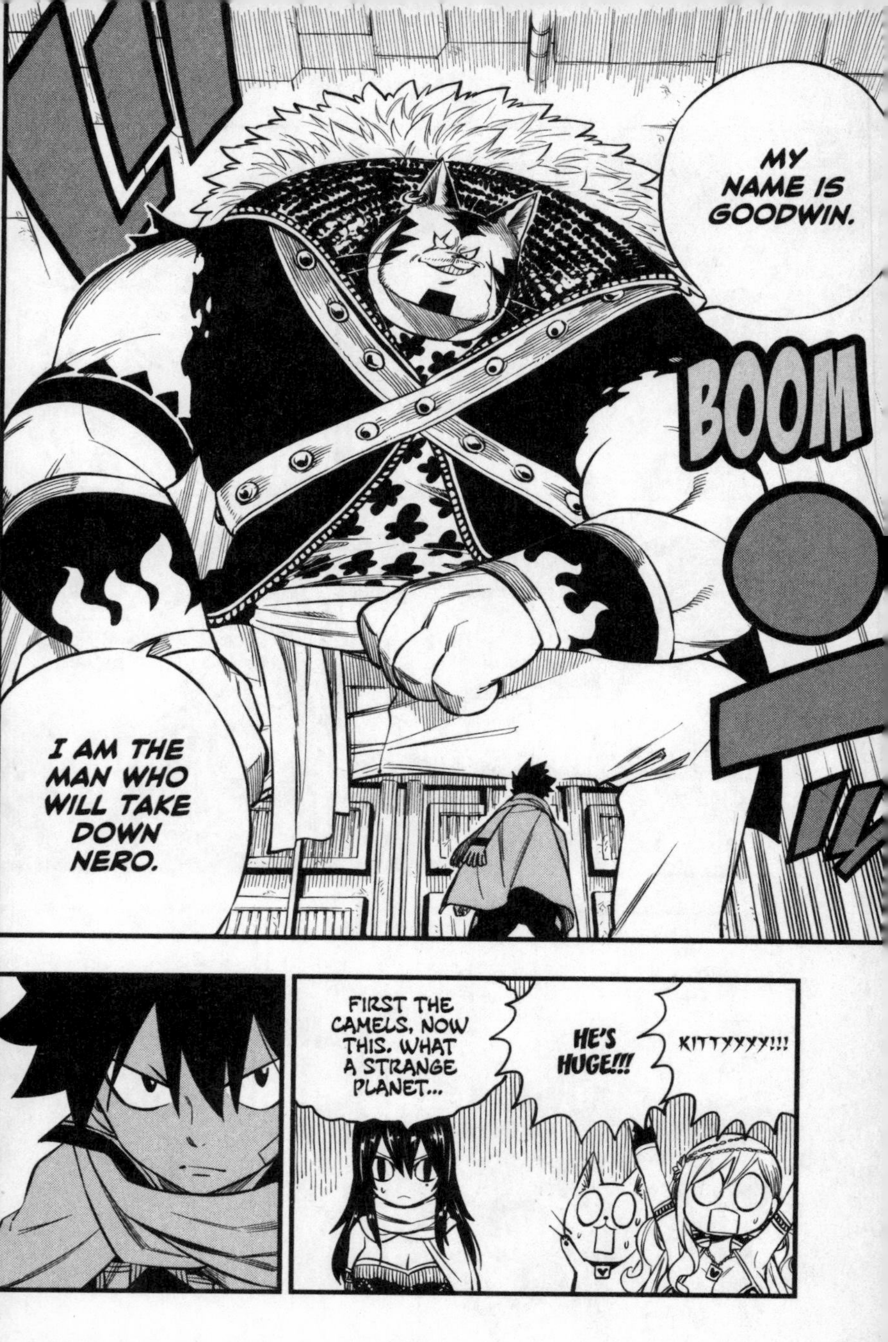
MY NAME IS GOODWIN.
BOOM
I AM THE MAN WHO WILL TAKE DOWN NERO.
KITTYYYY!!!
HE'S HUGE!!!
FIRST THE CAMELS, NOW THIS. WHAT A STRANGE PLANET...

EZ DRAWING

Your postcards are my greatest source of energy! EZ Drawing means it's easy to do, so we hope the fan art keeps coming! Everyone whose work is shown here received a special signed mini sketch!!

(MINT-SAN, OSAKA)

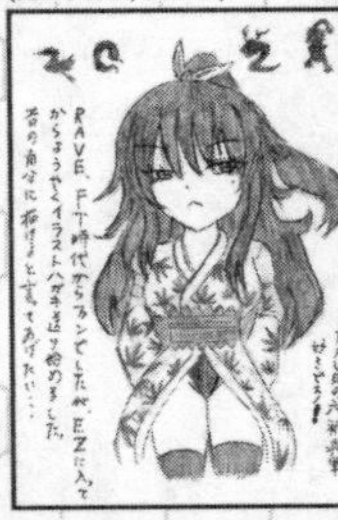
RAVE

▲YOU'VE BEEN READING SINCE RAVE MASTER? THANKS! I HOPE YOU'LL KEEP READING!!

(MAHO-SAN, SHIGA)

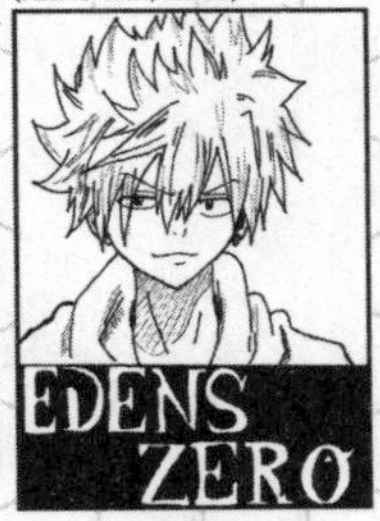
EDENS ZERO

▲IT'S SIMPLE AND EXUDES WEISZ'S DAUNTLESS SPIRIT. I LIKE IT!

(NEMUNOSUKE-SAN, NAGANO)

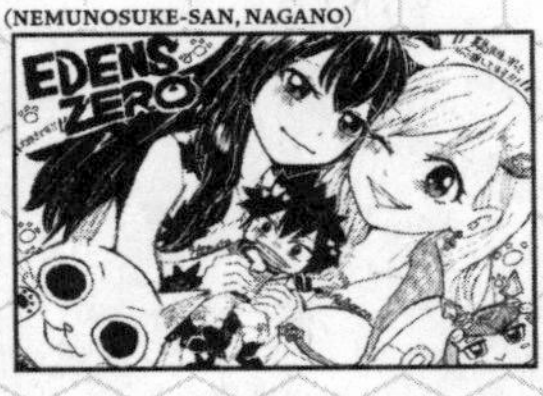
EDENS ZERO

▲THE CONTRAST BETWEEN REBECCA AND HOMURA IS IMPRESSIVE. IT'S SO CUTE!

(KOHARU-SAN, YAMAGATA)

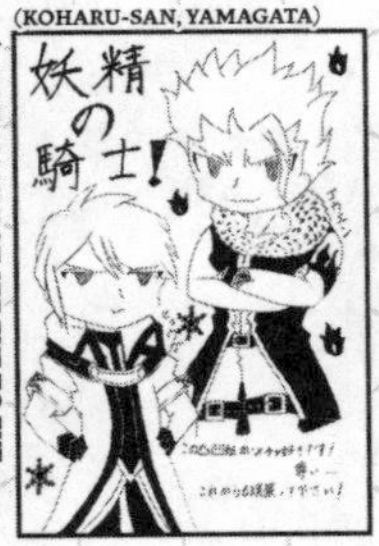
妖精の騎士!

▲THEY MAY NOT SEE EYE TO EYE, BUT AT LEAST WHEN IT COMES TO GUARDING THEIR PRINCESS, THEY'RE THE ULTIMATE BUDDIES!

(BANASHIN.-SAN, SHIZUOKA)

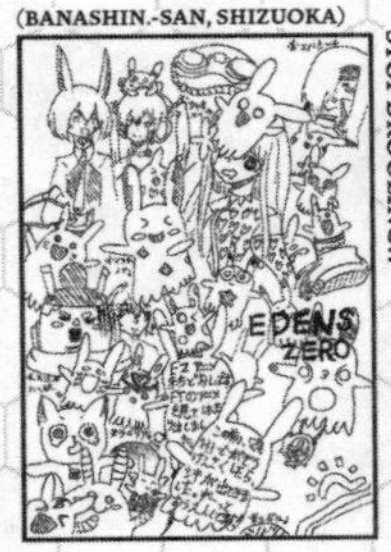
EDENS ZERO

▼IT'S JAM-PACKED WITH CUTE STUFF! AND I GUESS XIAO MEI CAN'T STOP DROOLING?!

MASHIMA'S ONE-HIT KO

(MOMO-SAN, TOYAMA)

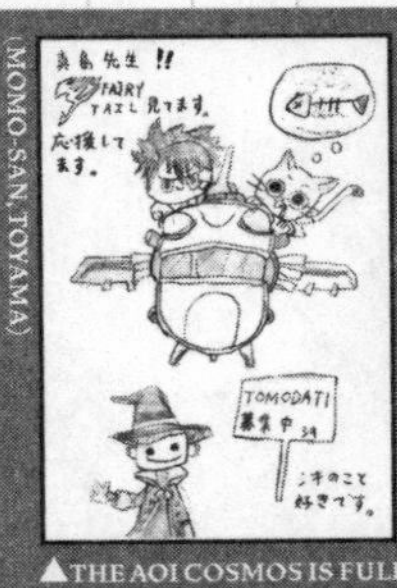
真島先生!!
FAIRY TAIL 見てます。
応援してます。
TOMODATI
募集中

▲THE AOI COSMOS IS FULL OF FISH! IT MUST BE HEAVEN FOR HAPPY!

(AONA GÔKE-SAN, MIYAGI)

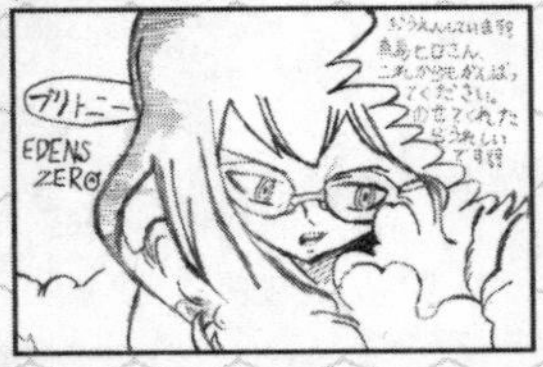
ブリトニー
EDENS ZERO

◀BRITNEY: DEFEATED BY GETTING SUCKED UP IN A VACUUM CLEANER. YOU SHOULDN'T CALL PEOPLE STUPID.

*Fan art submissions are limited to Japan-only.

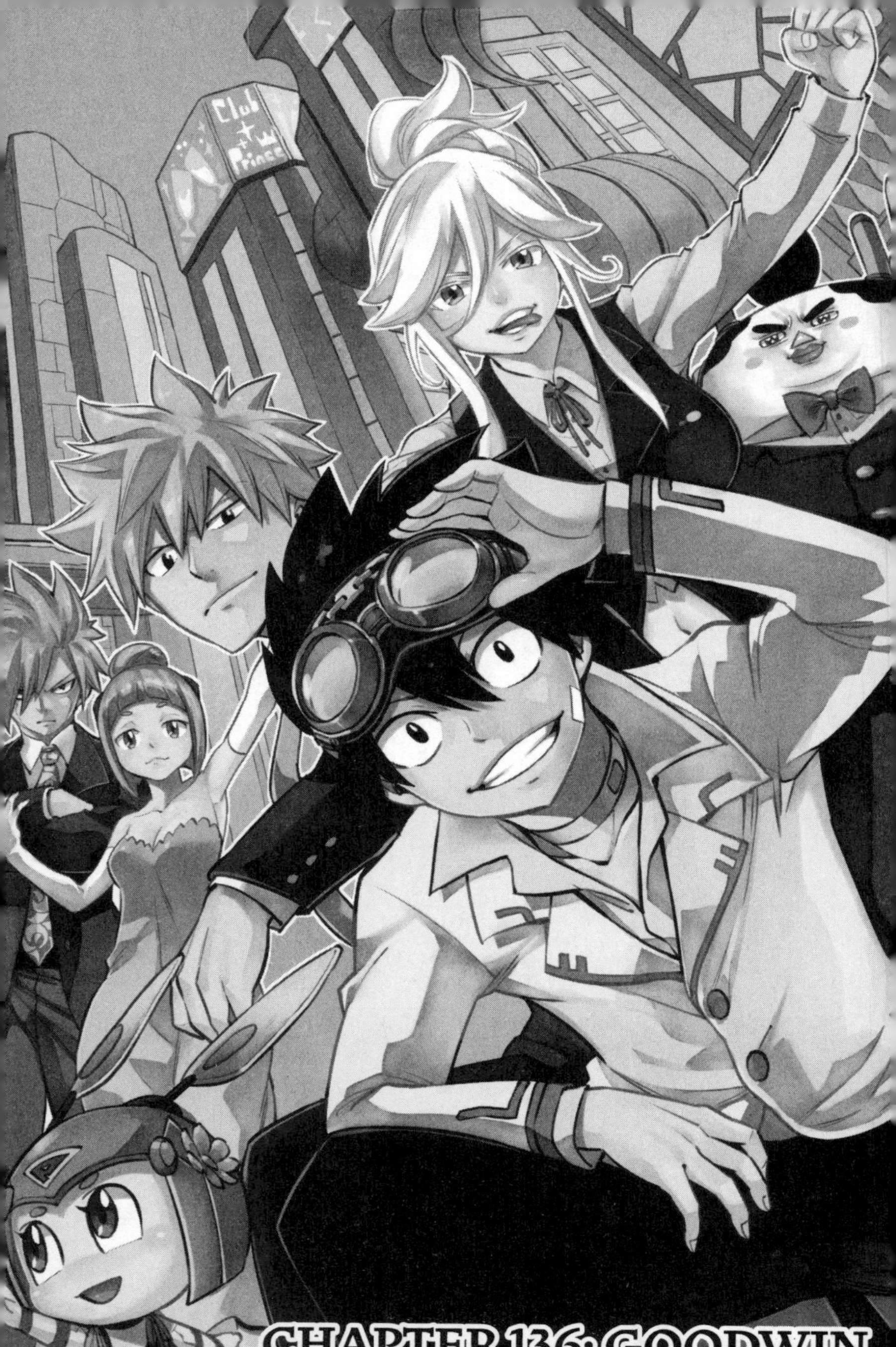
Club
Prince

CHAPTER 136: GOODWIN

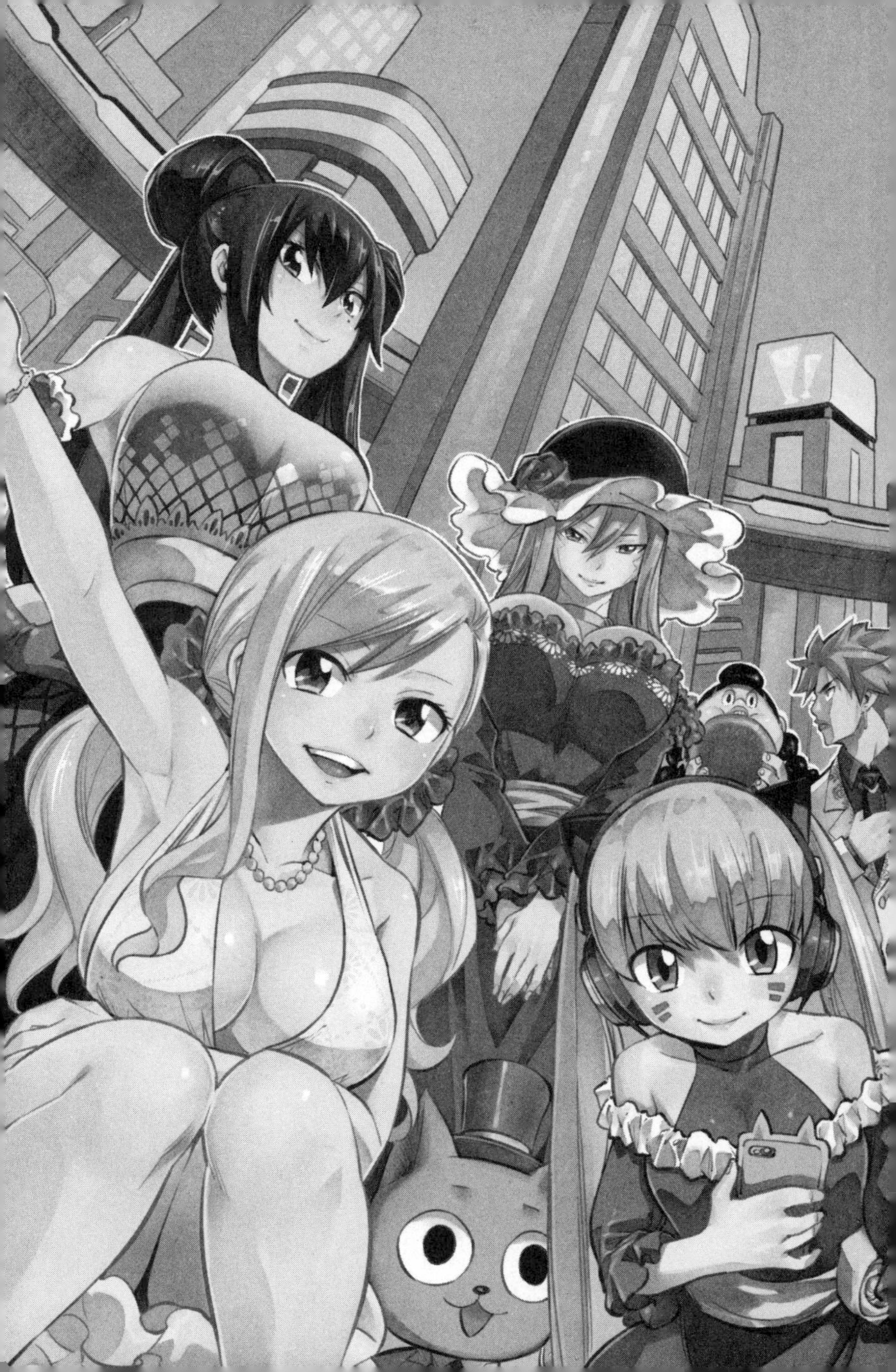

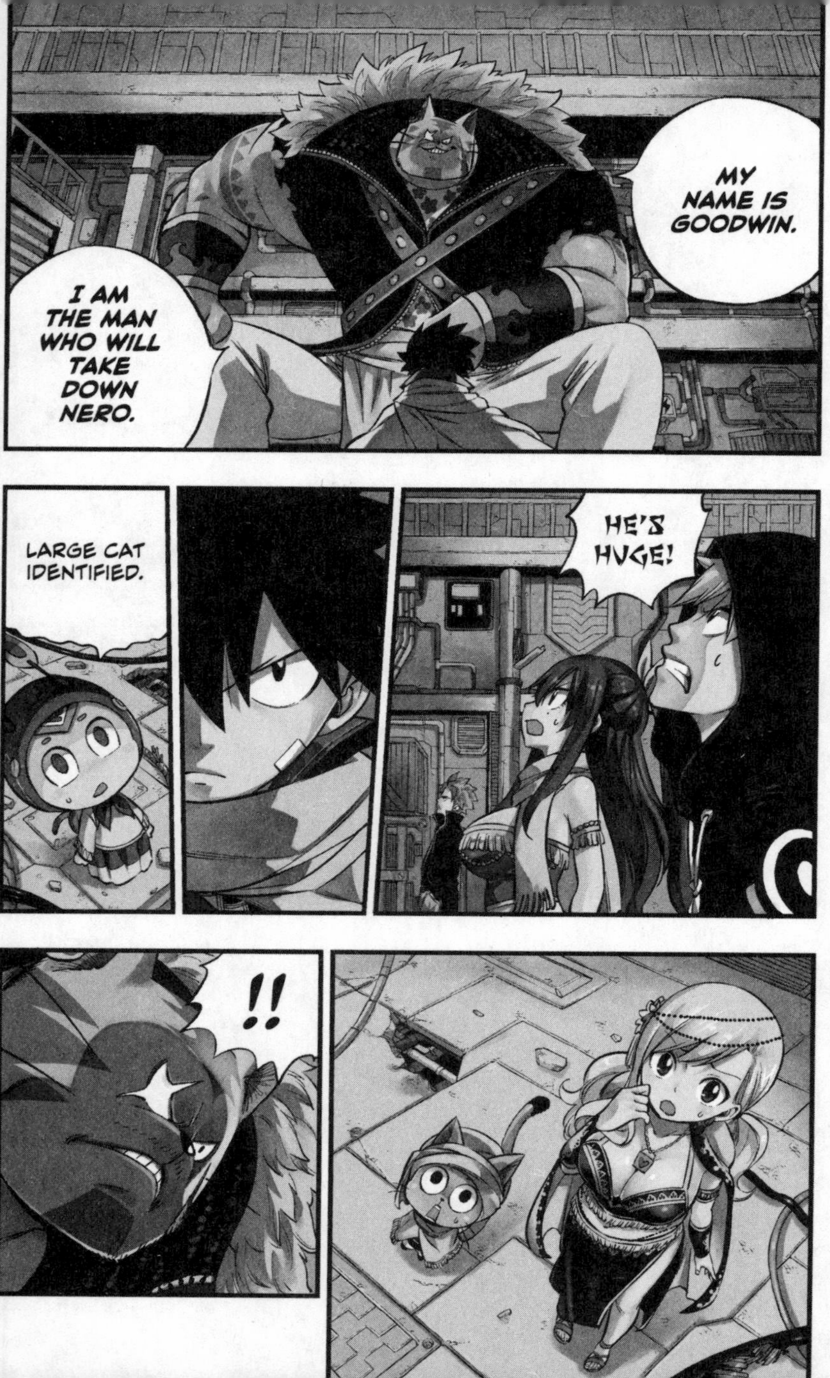
MY NAME IS GOODWIN.
I AM THE MAN WHO WILL TAKE DOWN NERO.
HE'S HUGE!
LARGE CAT IDENTIFIED.
!!

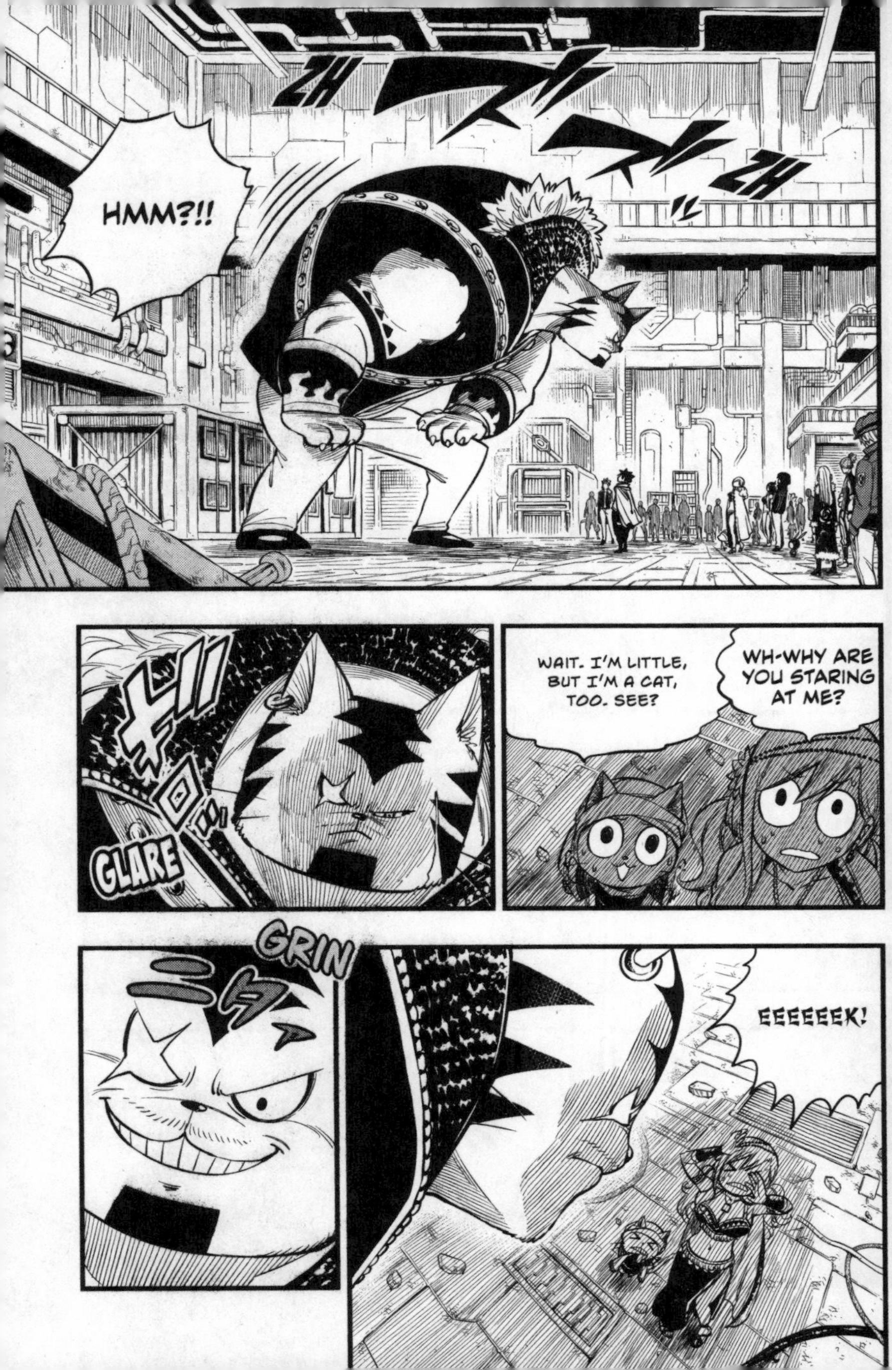
ZH
ZH
HMM?!!
WH-WHY ARE YOU STARING AT ME?
WAIT. I'M LITTLE, BUT I'M A CAT, TOO. SEE?
GLARE
EEEEEEK!
GRIN

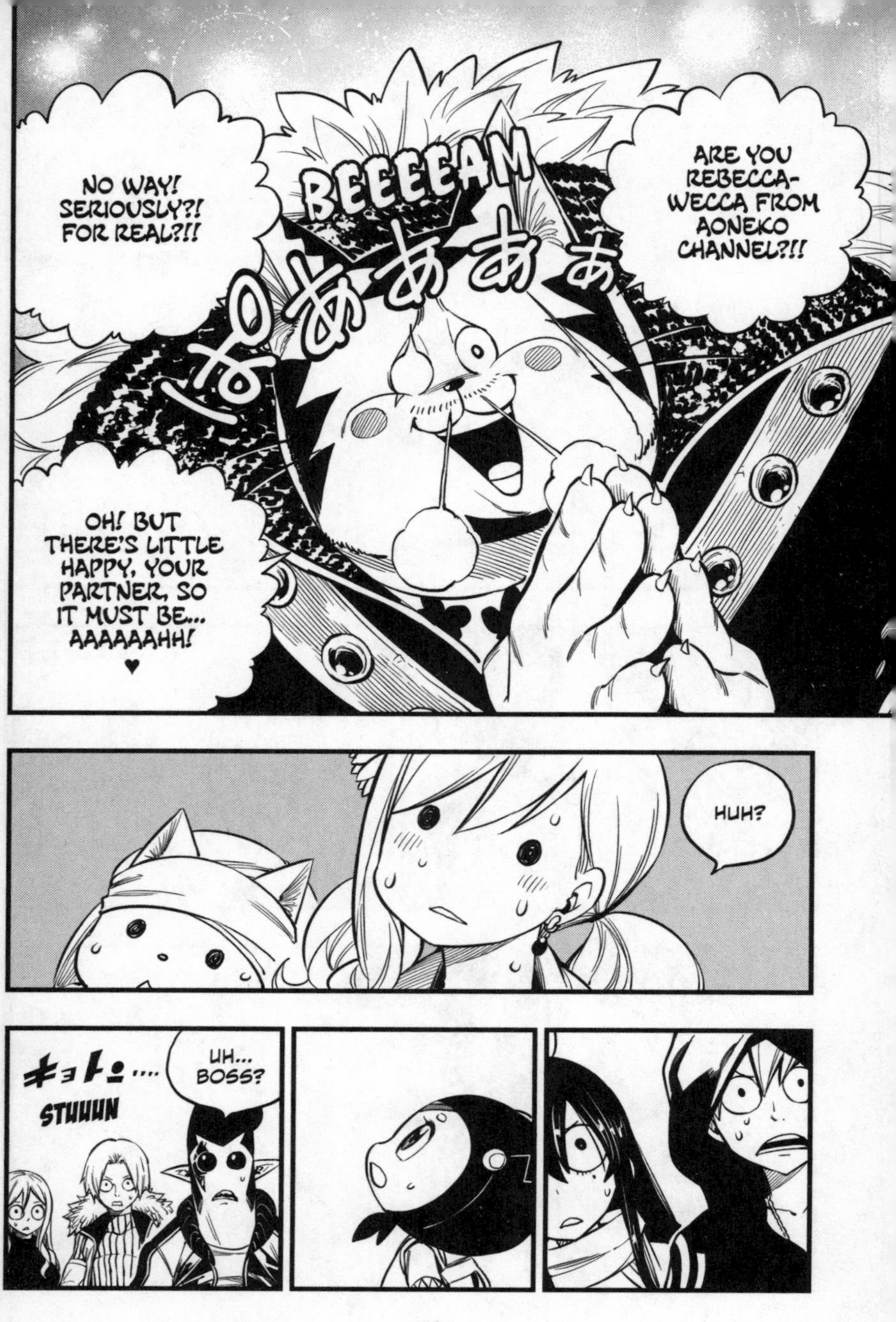
ARE YOU REBECCA-WECCA FROM AONEKO CHANNEL?!!
BEEEEAM
ぱあああぁ
NO WAY! SERIOUSLY?! FOR REAL?!!
OH! BUT THERE'S LITTLE HAPPY, YOUR PARTNER, SO IT MUST BE... AAAAAAHH! ♥
HUH?
UH... BOSS?
キョトン....
STUUUN

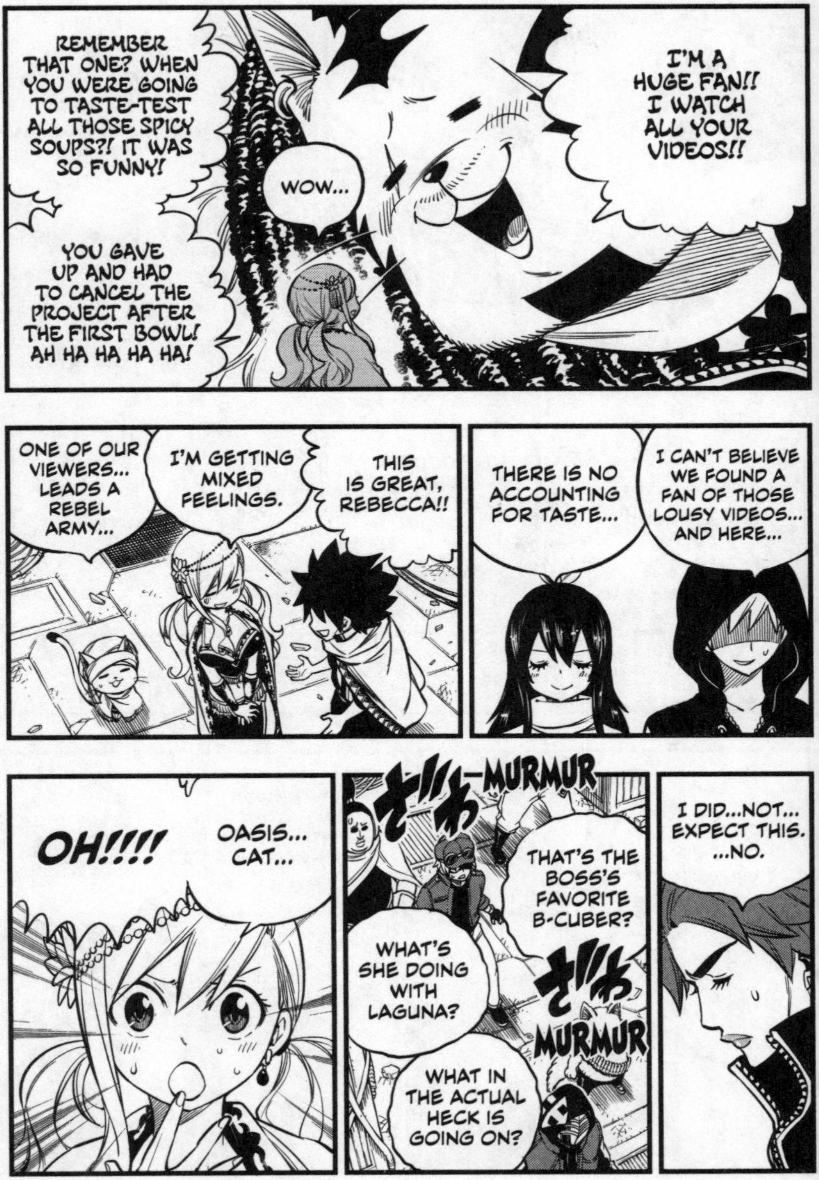
I'M A HUGE FAN!! I WATCH ALL YOUR VIDEOS!!
REMEMBER THAT ONE? WHEN YOU WERE GOING TO TASTE-TEST ALL THOSE SPICY SOUPS?! IT WAS SO FUNNY!
YOU GAVE UP AND HAD TO CANCEL THE PROJECT AFTER THE FIRST BOWL! AH HA HA HA HA!
WOW...
I CAN'T BELIEVE WE FOUND A FAN OF THOSE LOUSY VIDEOS... AND HERE...
THERE IS NO ACCOUNTING FOR TASTE...
THIS IS GREAT, REBECCA!!
I'M GETTING MIXED FEELINGS.
ONE OF OUR VIEWERS... LEADS A REBEL ARMY...
I DID...NOT... EXPECT THIS. ...NO.
MURMUR
THAT'S THE BOSS'S FAVORITE B-CUBER?
WHAT'S SHE DOING WITH LAGUNA?
MURMUR
WHAT IN THE ACTUAL HECK IS GOING ON?
OASIS... CAT...
OH!!!!

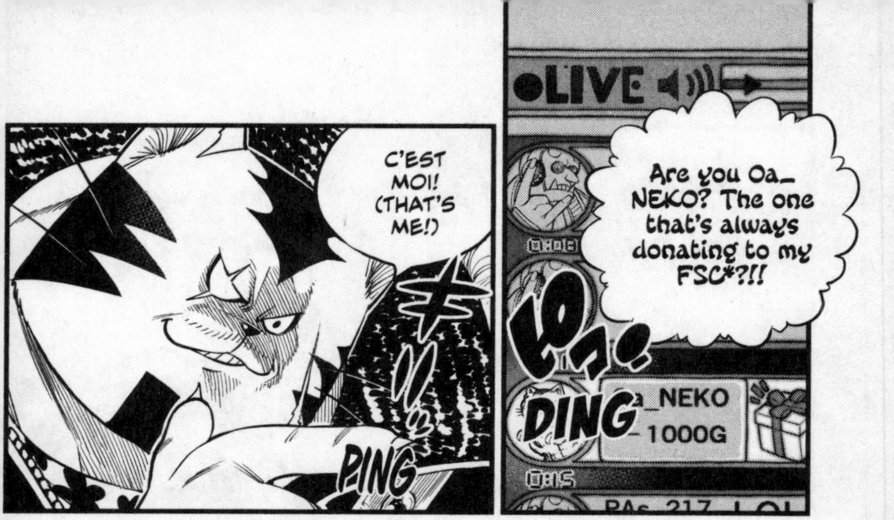
LIVE
Are you Oa_NEKO? The one that's always donating to my FSC*?!!
DING
1000G
C'EST MOI! (THAT'S ME!)
PING

*FSC: Financial Support Chat. A function that allows viewers to give gratuities to B-Cubers they want to support.

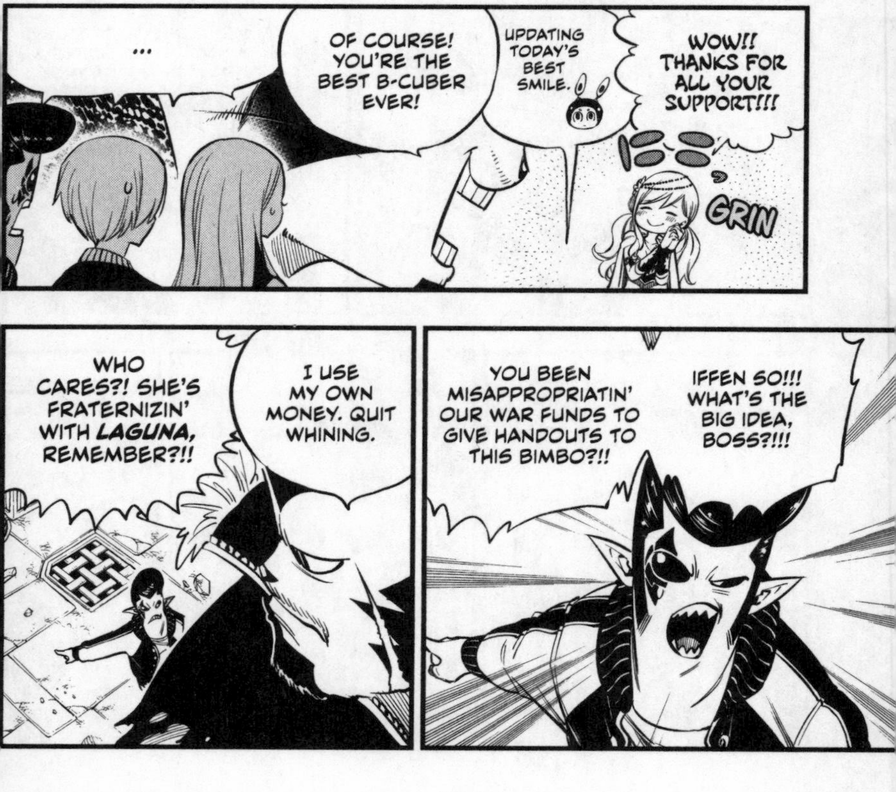
WOW!! THANKS FOR ALL YOUR SUPPORT!!!
UPDATING TODAY'S BEST SMILE.
GRIN
OF COURSE! YOU'RE THE BEST B-CUBER EVER!
...
IFFEN SO!!! WHAT'S THE BIG IDEA, BOSS?!!!
YOU BEEN MISAPPROPRIATIN' OUR WAR FUNDS TO GIVE HANDOUTS TO THIS BIMBO?!!
I USE MY OWN MONEY. QUIT WHINING.
WHO CARES?! SHE'S FRATERNIZIN' WITH *LAGUNA*, REMEMBER?!!

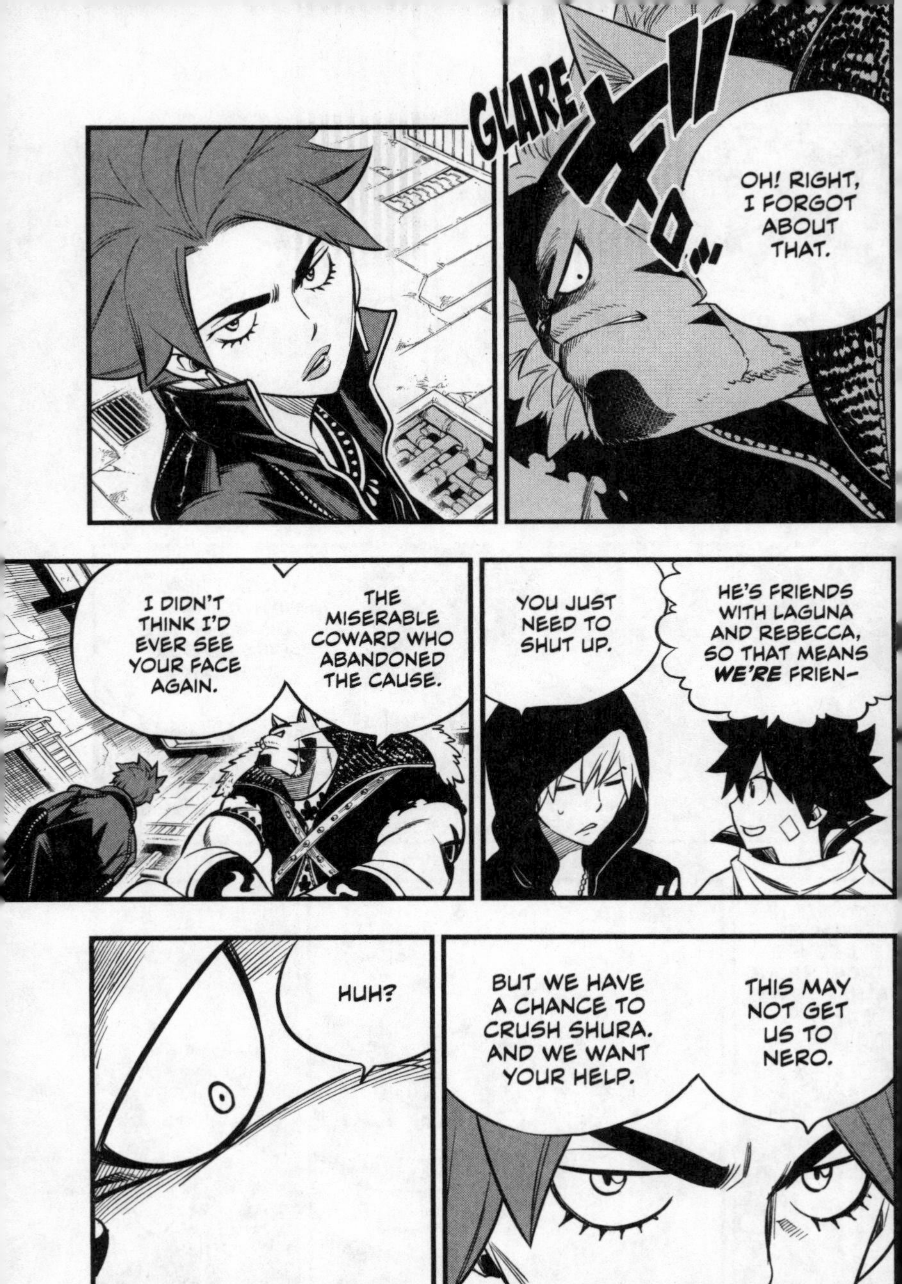
GLARE
OH! RIGHT, I FORGOT ABOUT THAT.
HE'S FRIENDS WITH LAGUNA AND REBECCA, SO THAT MEANS *WE'RE* FRIEN-
YOU JUST NEED TO SHUT UP.
THE MISERABLE COWARD WHO ABANDONED THE CAUSE.
I DIDN'T THINK I'D EVER SEE YOUR FACE AGAIN.
THIS MAY NOT GET US TO NERO.
BUT WE HAVE A CHANCE TO CRUSH SHURA. AND WE WANT YOUR HELP.
HUH?

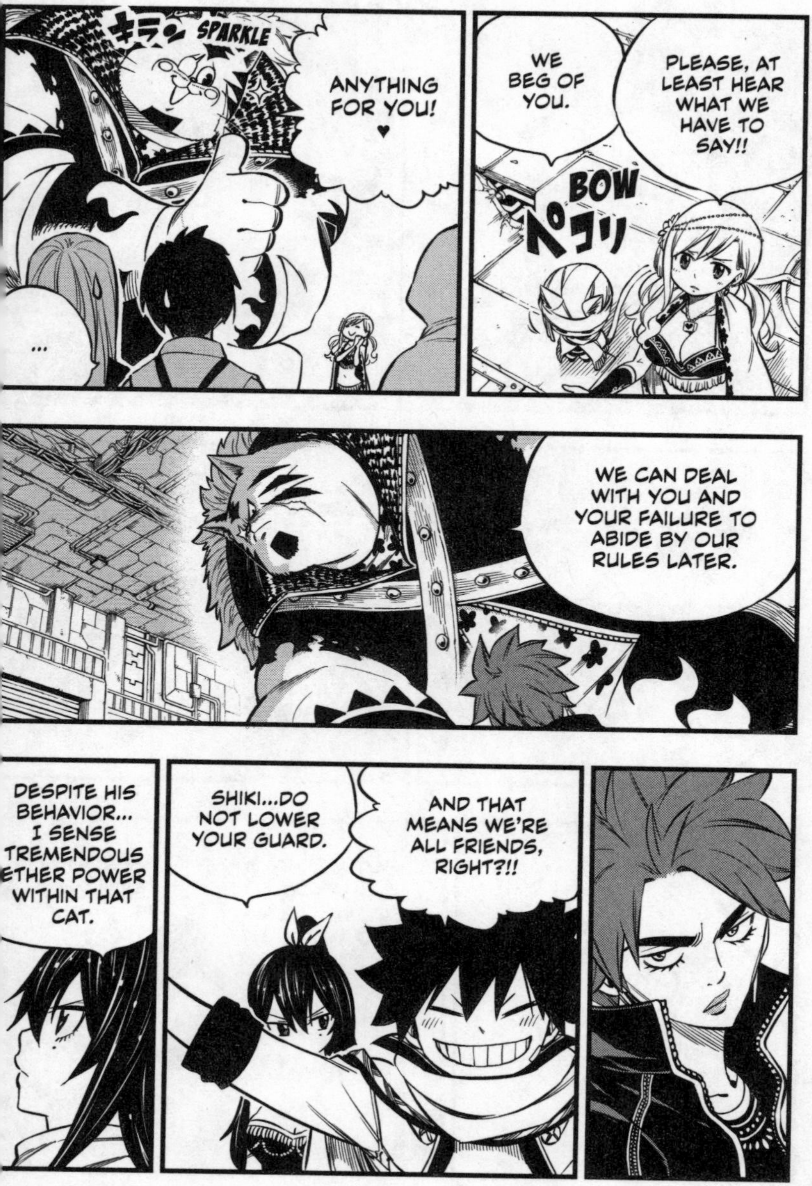
PLEASE, AT LEAST HEAR WHAT WE HAVE TO SAY!!
WE BEG OF YOU.
BOW
ペコリ
キラン
SPARKLE
ANYTHING FOR YOU! ♥
...
WE CAN DEAL WITH YOU AND YOUR FAILURE TO ABIDE BY OUR RULES LATER.
AND THAT MEANS WE'RE ALL FRIENDS, RIGHT?!!
SHIKI...DO NOT LOWER YOUR GUARD.
DESPITE HIS BEHAVIOR... I SENSE TREMENDOUS ETHER POWER WITHIN THAT CAT.

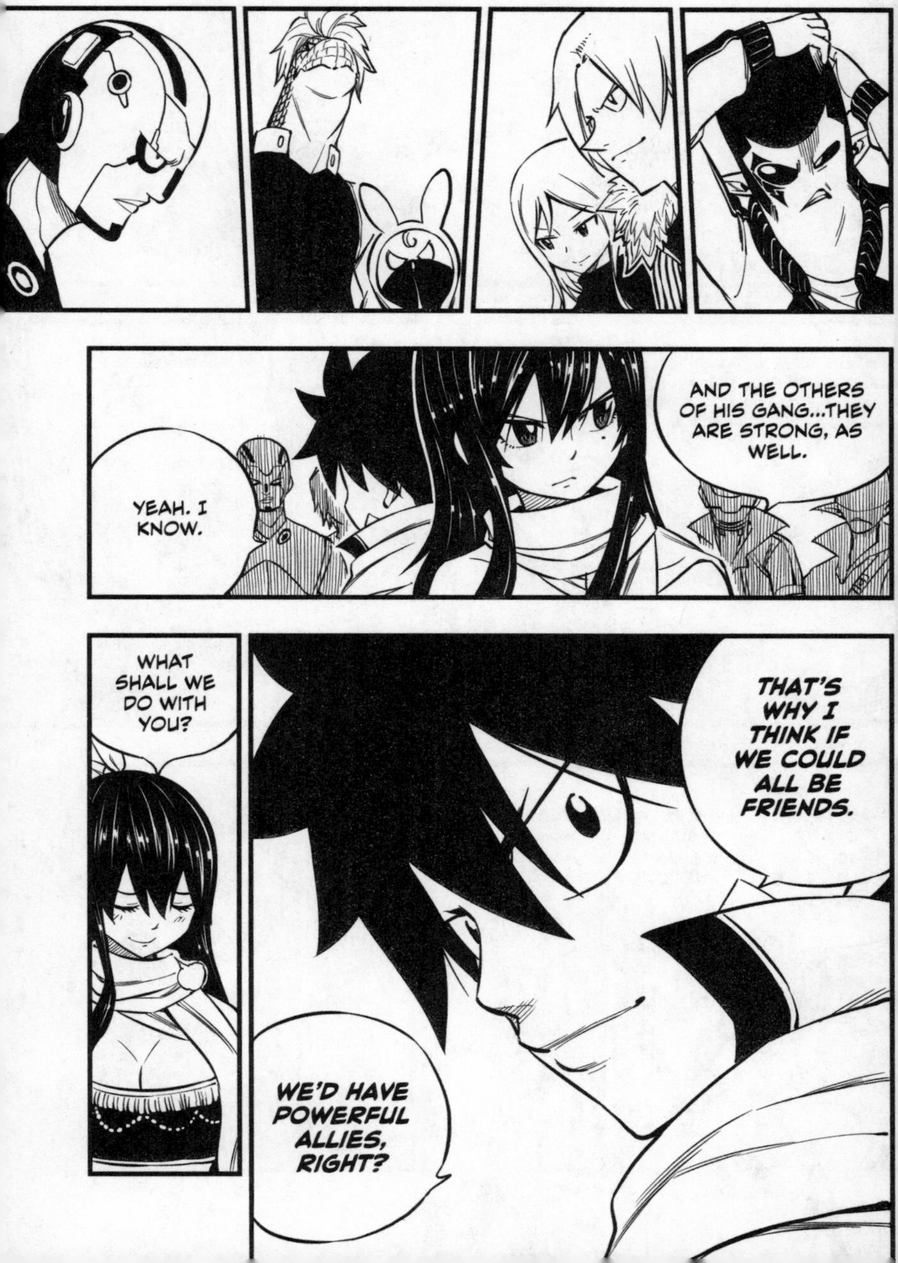
AND THE OTHERS OF HIS GANG...THEY ARE STRONG, AS WELL.
YEAH. I KNOW.
THAT'S WHY I THINK IF WE COULD ALL BE FRIENDS.
WE'D HAVE POWERFUL ALLIES, RIGHT?
WHAT SHALL WE DO WITH YOU?

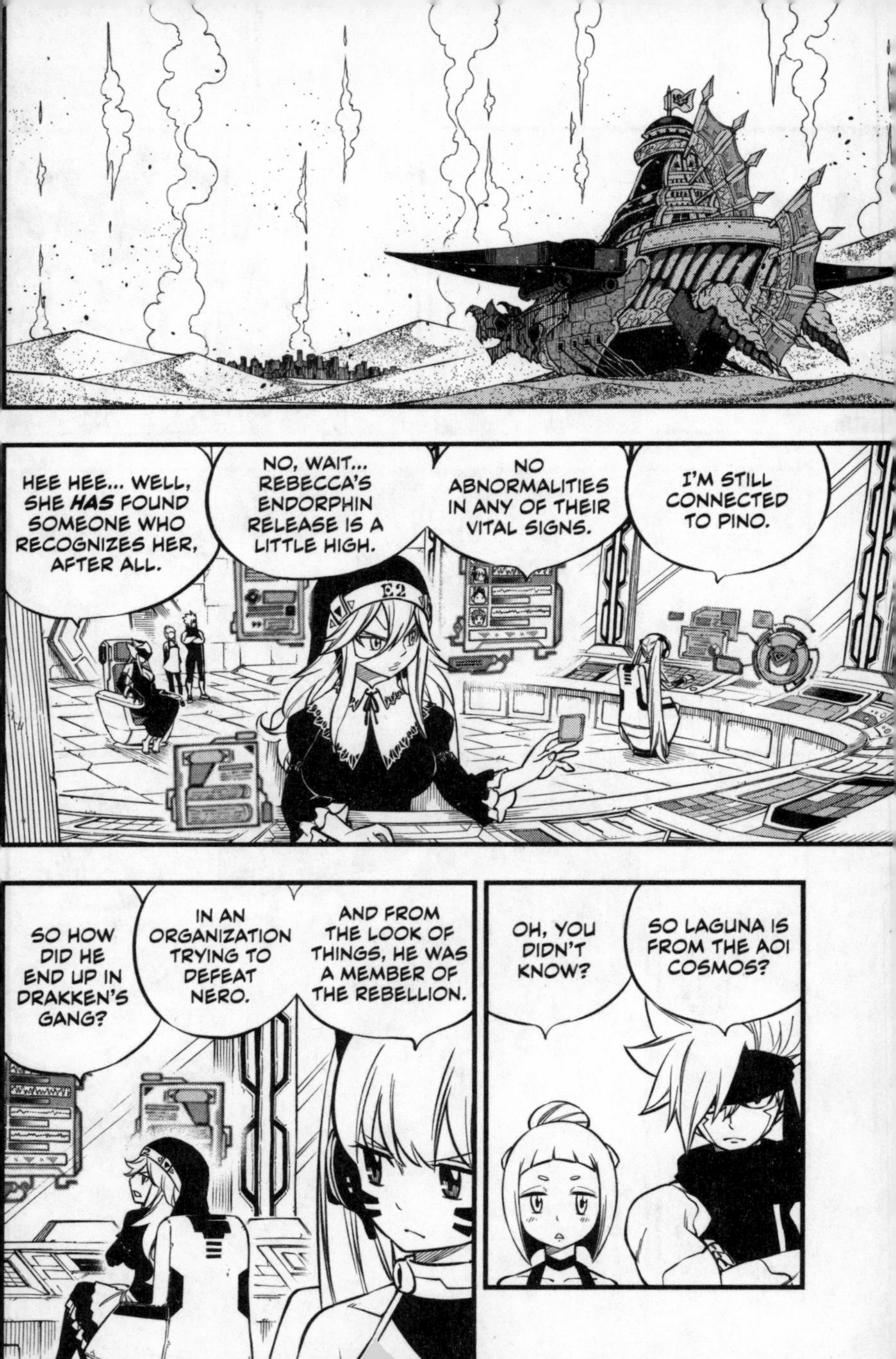
I'M STILL CONNECTED TO PINO.
NO ABNORMALITIES IN ANY OF THEIR VITAL SIGNS.
NO, WAIT... REBECCA'S ENDORPHIN RELEASE IS A LITTLE HIGH.
HEE HEE... WELL, SHE **HAS** FOUND SOMEONE WHO RECOGNIZES HER, AFTER ALL.
SO LAGUNA IS FROM THE AOI COSMOS?
OH, YOU DIDN'T KNOW?
AND FROM THE LOOK OF THINGS, HE WAS A MEMBER OF THE REBELLION.
IN AN ORGANIZATION TRYING TO DEFEAT NERO.
SO HOW DID HE END UP IN DRAKKEN'S GANG?

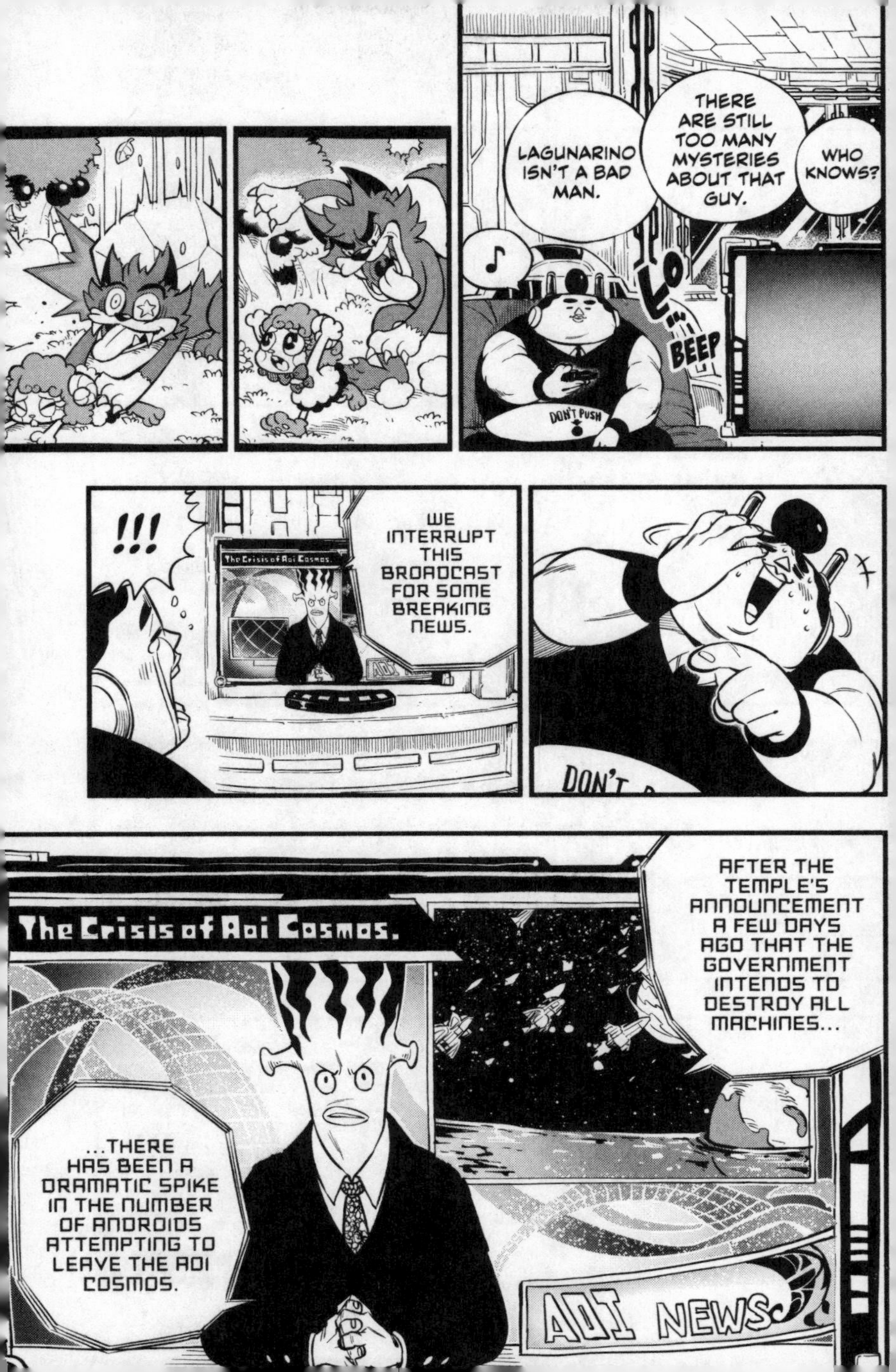
WHO KNOWS?
THERE ARE STILL TOO MANY MYSTERIES ABOUT THAT GUY.
LAGUNARINO ISN'T A BAD MAN.
BEEP
DON'T PUSH
DON'T
WE INTERRUPT THIS BROADCAST FOR SOME BREAKING NEWS.
The Crisis of Aoi Cosmos.
!!!
AFTER THE TEMPLE'S ANNOUNCEMENT A FEW DAYS AGO THAT THE GOVERNMENT INTENDS TO DESTROY ALL MACHINES...
The Crisis of Aoi Cosmos.
...THERE HAS BEEN A DRAMATIC SPIKE IN THE NUMBER OF ANDROIDS ATTEMPTING TO LEAVE THE AOI COSMOS.
AOI NEWS

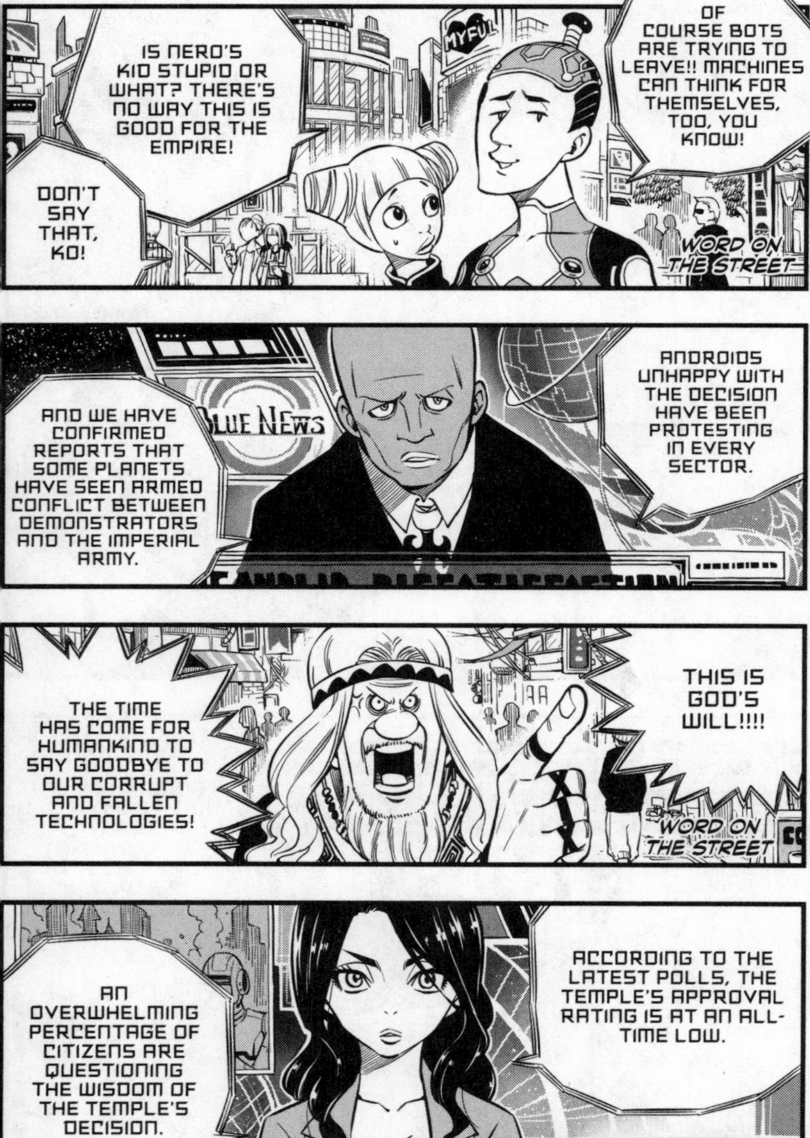
OF COURSE BOTS ARE TRYING TO LEAVE!! MACHINES CAN THINK FOR THEMSELVES, TOO, YOU KNOW!
MYFUL
IS NERO'S KID STUPID OR WHAT? THERE'S NO WAY THIS IS GOOD FOR THE EMPIRE!
DON'T SAY THAT, KO!
WORD ON THE STREET
ANDROIDS UNHAPPY WITH THE DECISION HAVE BEEN PROTESTING IN EVERY SECTOR.
AND WE HAVE CONFIRMED REPORTS THAT SOME PLANETS HAVE SEEN ARMED CONFLICT BETWEEN DEMONSTRATORS AND THE IMPERIAL ARMY.
THIS IS GOD'S WILL!!!!
THE TIME HAS COME FOR HUMANKIND TO SAY GOODBYE TO OUR CORRUPT AND FALLEN TECHNOLOGIES!
WORD ON THE STREET
ACCORDING TO THE LATEST POLLS, THE TEMPLE'S APPROVAL RATING IS AT AN ALL-TIME LOW.
AN OVERWHELMING PERCENTAGE OF CITIZENS ARE QUESTIONING THE WISDOM OF THE TEMPLE'S DECISION.

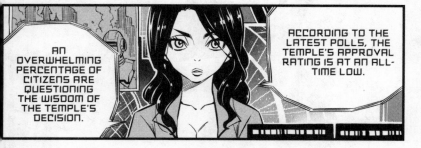

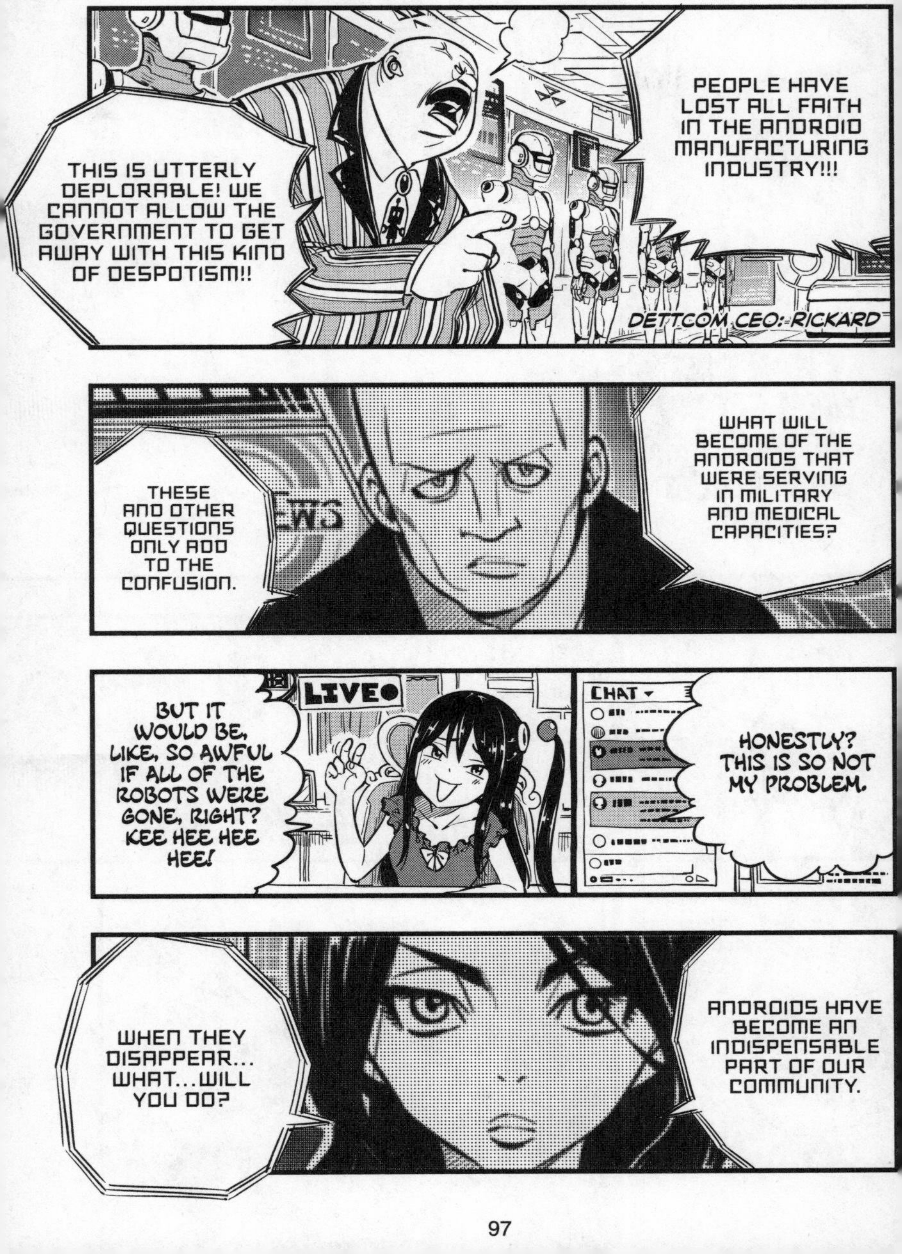
PEOPLE HAVE LOST ALL FAITH IN THE ANDROID MANUFACTURING INDUSTRY!!!
THIS IS UTTERLY DEPLORABLE! WE CANNOT ALLOW THE GOVERNMENT TO GET AWAY WITH THIS KIND OF DESPOTISM!!
DETTCOM CEO: RICKARD
WHAT WILL BECOME OF THE ANDROIDS THAT WERE SERVING IN MILITARY AND MEDICAL CAPACITIES?
THESE AND OTHER QUESTIONS ONLY ADD TO THE CONFUSION.
HONESTLY? THIS IS SO NOT MY PROBLEM.
CHAT
LIVE
BUT IT WOULD BE, LIKE, SO AWFUL IF ALL OF THE ROBOTS WERE GONE, RIGHT? KEE HEE HEE HEE!
ANDROIDS HAVE BECOME AN INDISPENSABLE PART OF OUR COMMUNITY.
WHEN THEY DISAPPEAR... WHAT...WILL YOU DO?

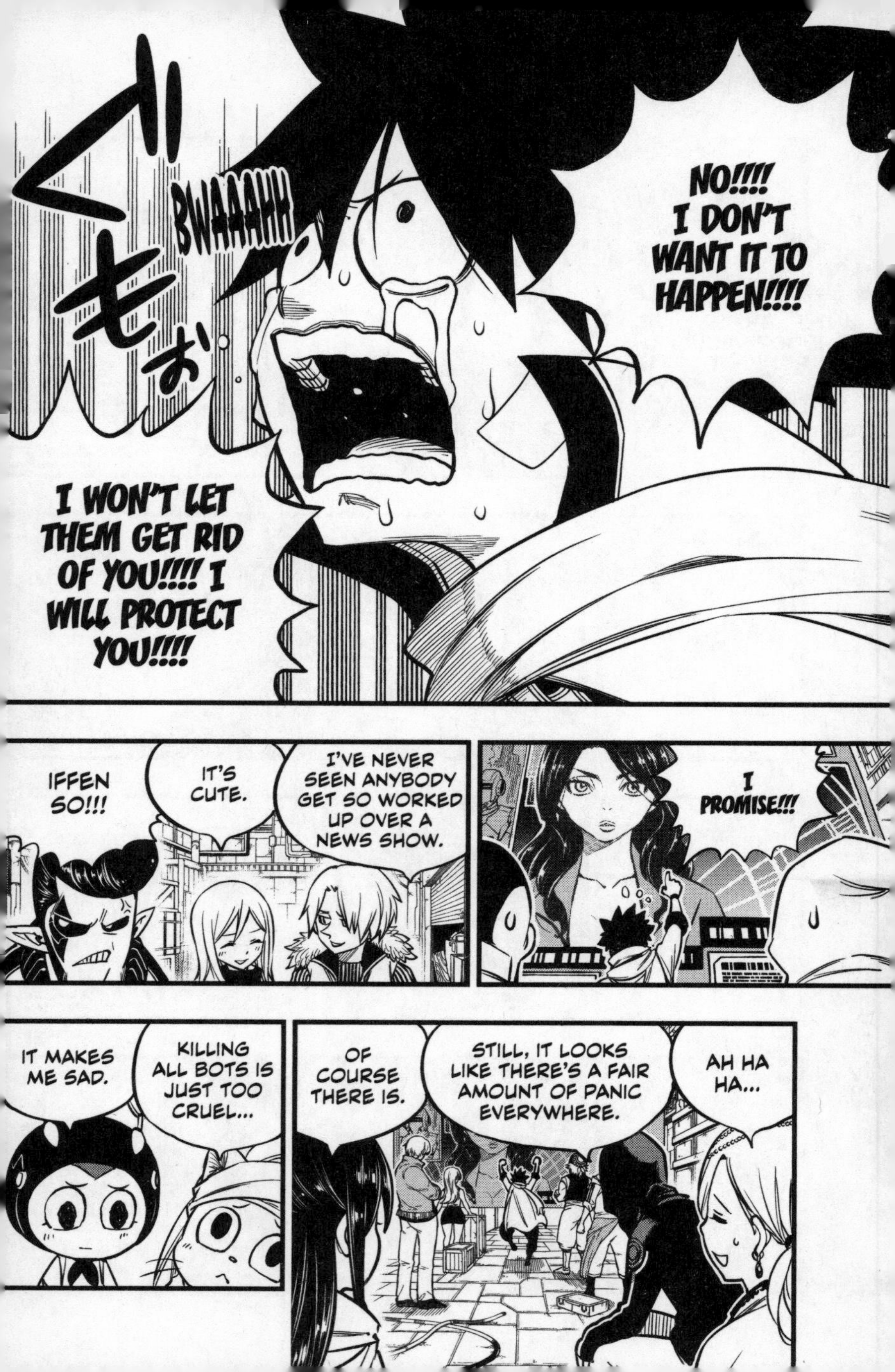
NO!!!! I DON'T WANT IT TO HAPPEN!!!!
BWAAAHH
ぐもぉ
I WON'T LET THEM GET RID OF YOU!!!! I WILL PROTECT YOU!!!!
I PROMISE!!!
I'VE NEVER SEEN ANYBODY GET SO WORKED UP OVER A NEWS SHOW.
IT'S CUTE.
IFFEN SO!!!
AH HA HA...
STILL, IT LOOKS LIKE THERE'S A FAIR AMOUNT OF PANIC EVERYWHERE.
OF COURSE THERE IS.
KILLING ALL BOTS IS JUST TOO CRUEL...
IT MAKES ME SAD.

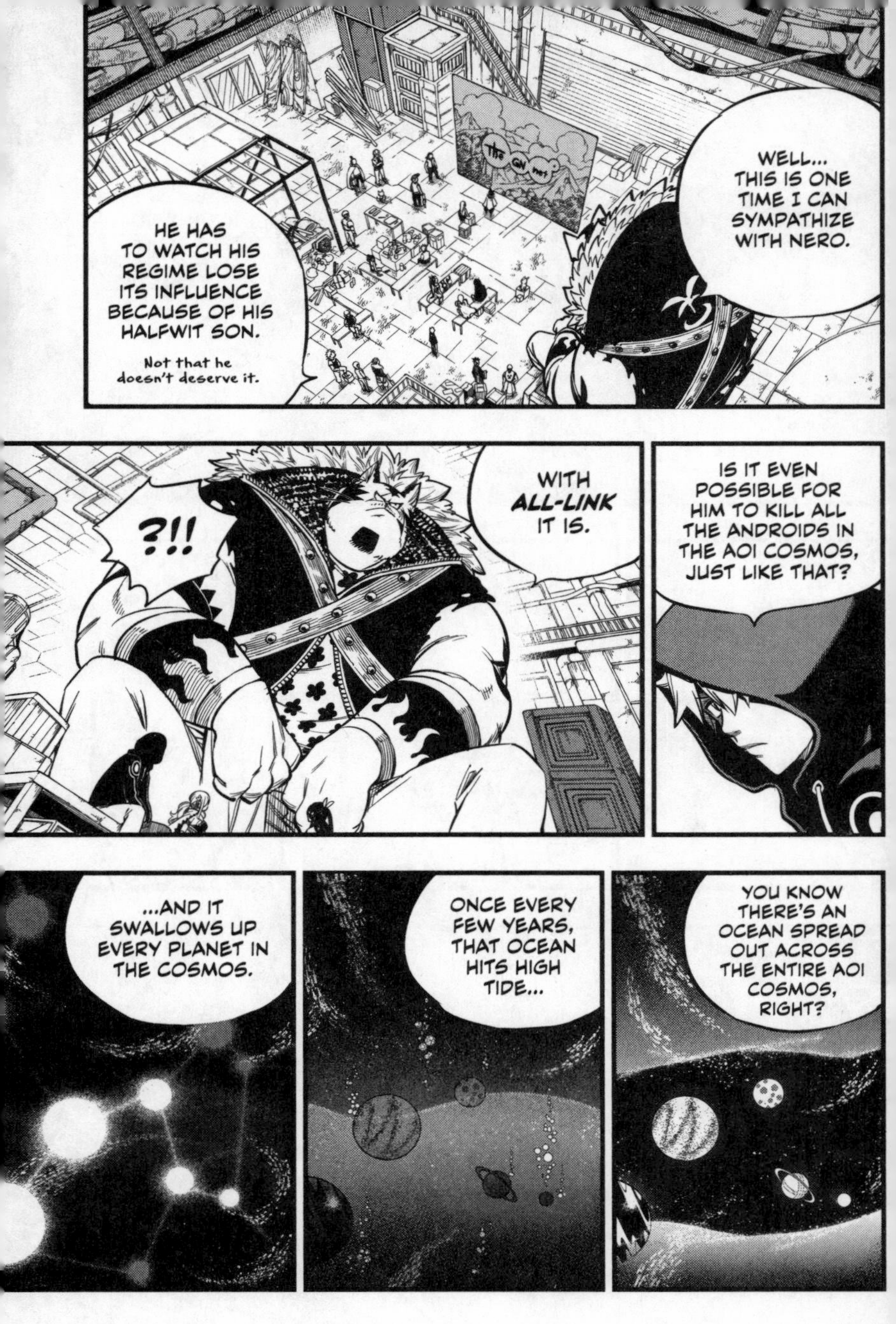
WELL... THIS IS ONE TIME I CAN SYMPATHIZE WITH NERO.
HE HAS TO WATCH HIS REGIME LOSE ITS INFLUENCE BECAUSE OF HIS HALFWIT SON.
Not that he doesn't deserve it.
IS IT EVEN POSSIBLE FOR HIM TO KILL ALL THE ANDROIDS IN THE AOI COSMOS, JUST LIKE THAT?
WITH **ALL-LINK** IT IS.
?!!
YOU KNOW THERE'S AN OCEAN SPREAD OUT ACROSS THE ENTIRE AOI COSMOS, RIGHT?
ONCE EVERY FEW YEARS, THAT OCEAN HITS HIGH TIDE...
...AND IT SWALLOWS UP EVERY PLANET IN THE COSMOS.

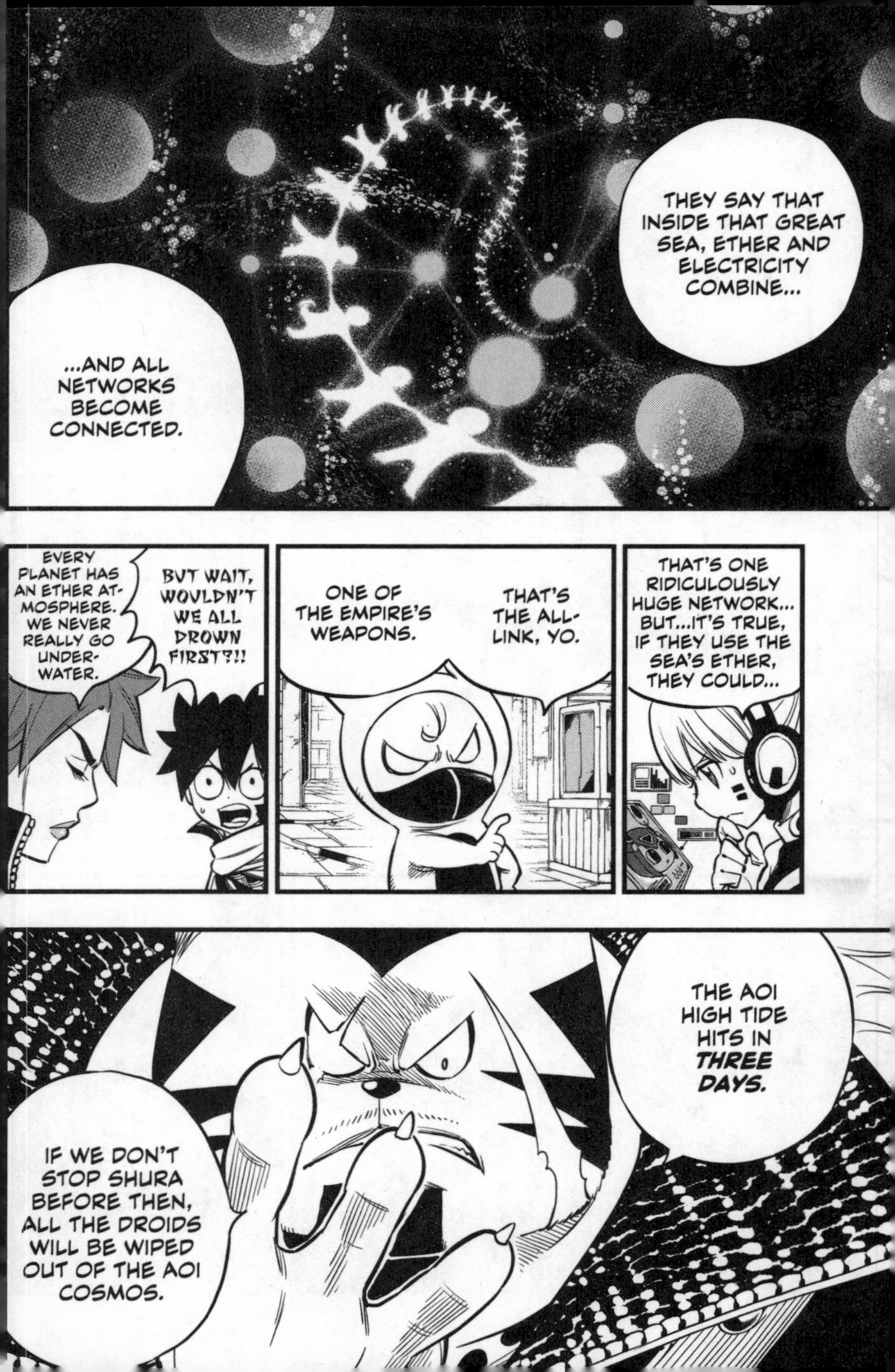
THEY SAY THAT INSIDE THAT GREAT SEA, ETHER AND ELECTRICITY COMBINE...
...AND ALL NETWORKS BECOME CONNECTED.
THAT'S ONE RIDICULOUSLY HUGE NETWORK... BUT...IT'S TRUE, IF THEY USE THE SEA'S ETHER, THEY COULD...
THAT'S THE ALL-LINK, YO.
ONE OF THE EMPIRE'S WEAPONS.
BUT WAIT, WOULDN'T WE ALL DROWN FIRST?!!
EVERY PLANET HAS AN ETHER ATMOSPHERE. WE NEVER REALLY GO UNDERWATER.
THE AOI HIGH TIDE HITS IN *THREE DAYS.*
IF WE DON'T STOP SHURA BEFORE THEN, ALL THE DROIDS WILL BE WIPED OUT OF THE AOI COSMOS.

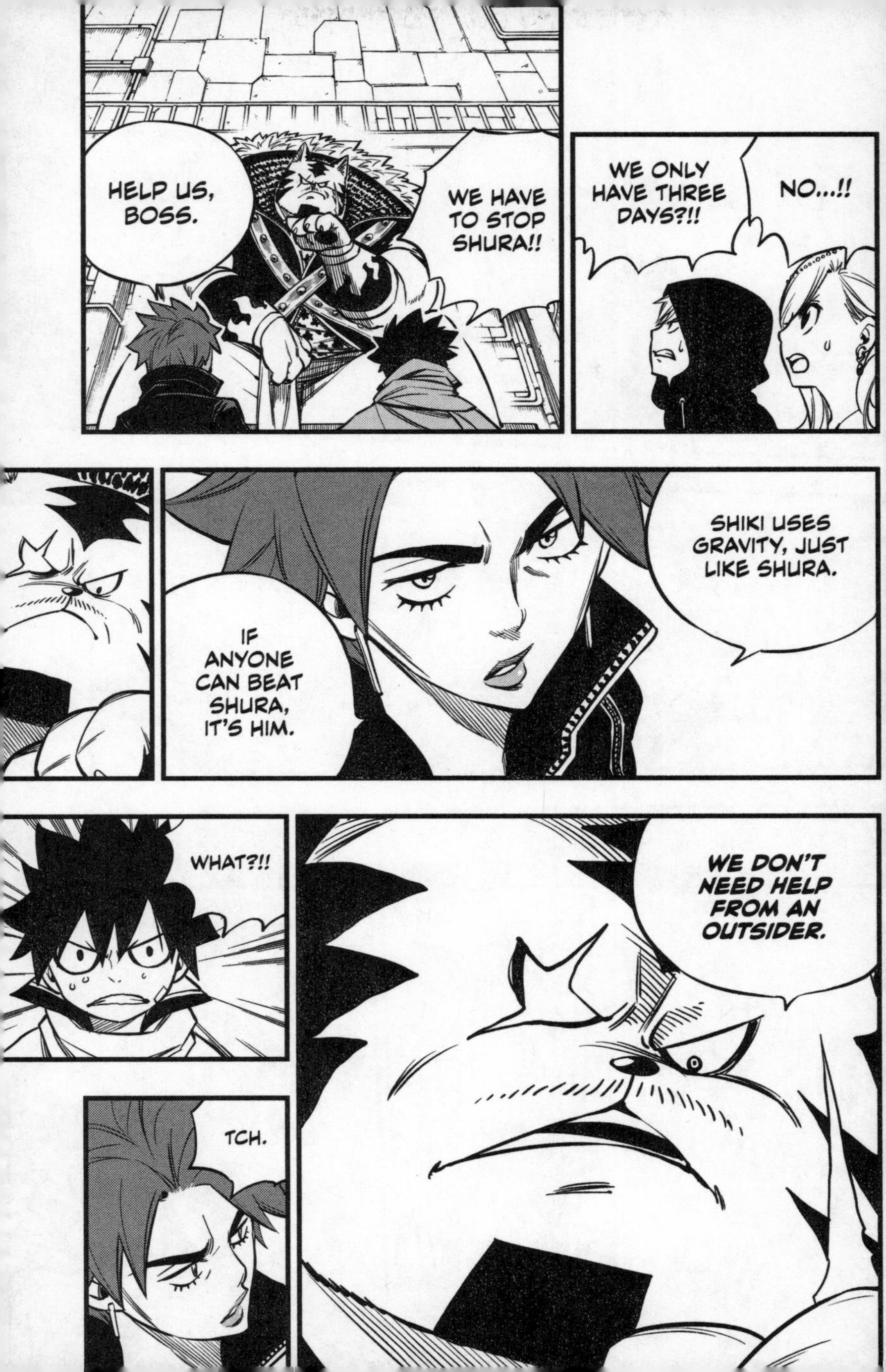
NO...!!
WE ONLY HAVE THREE DAYS?!!
WE HAVE TO STOP SHURA!!
HELP US, BOSS.
SHIKI USES GRAVITY, JUST LIKE SHURA.
IF ANYONE CAN BEAT SHURA, IT'S HIM.
WE DON'T NEED HELP FROM AN OUTSIDER.
WHAT?!!
TCH.

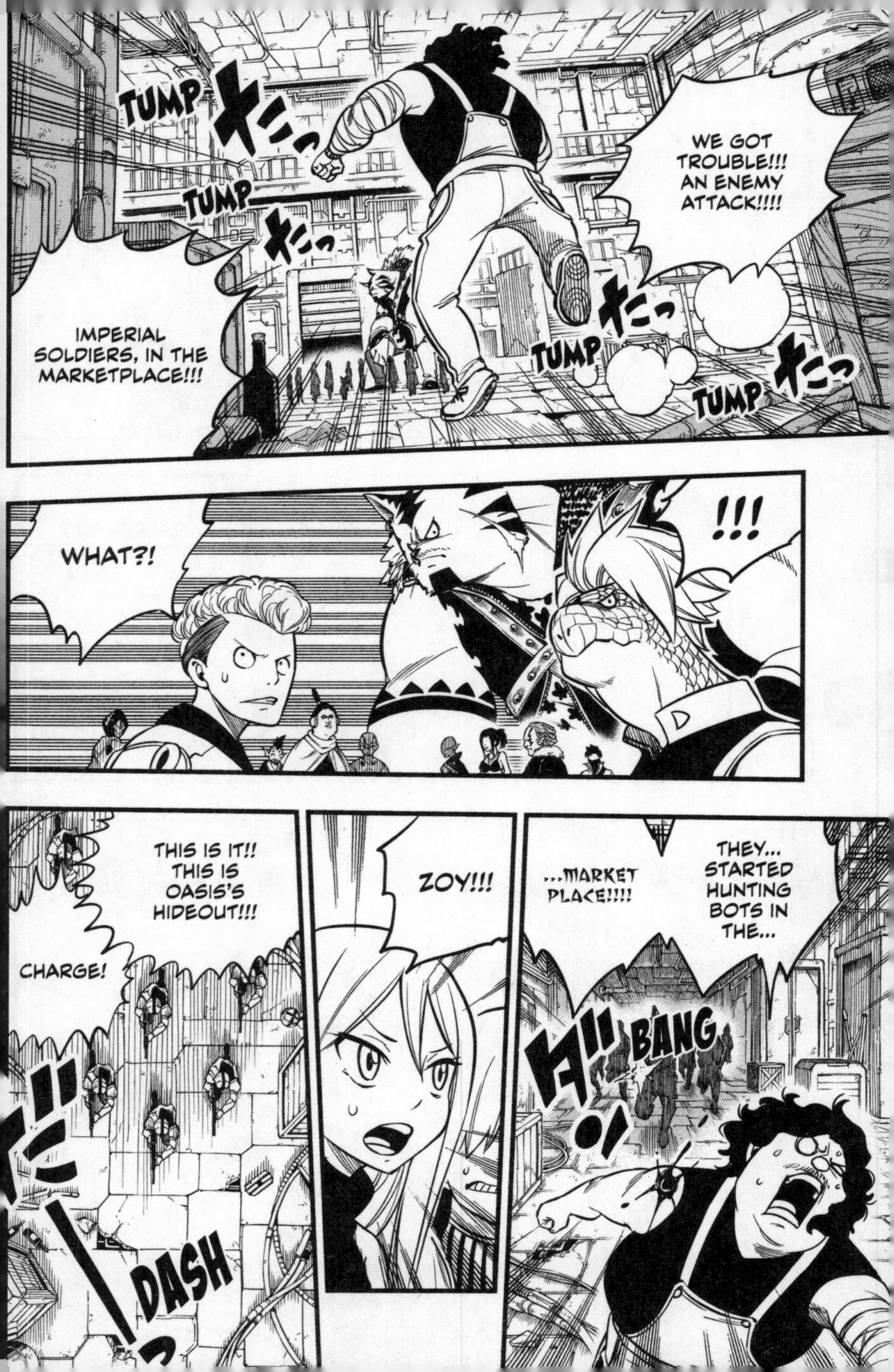
WE GOT TROUBLE!!! AN ENEMY ATTACK!!!!
TUMP
TUMP
TUMP
TUMP
IMPERIAL SOLDIERS, IN THE MARKETPLACE!!!
!!!
WHAT?!
THEY... STARTED HUNTING BOTS IN THE...
...MARKET PLACE!!!!
BANG
ZOY!!!
THIS IS IT!! THIS IS OASIS'S HIDEOUT!!!
CHARGE!
DASH

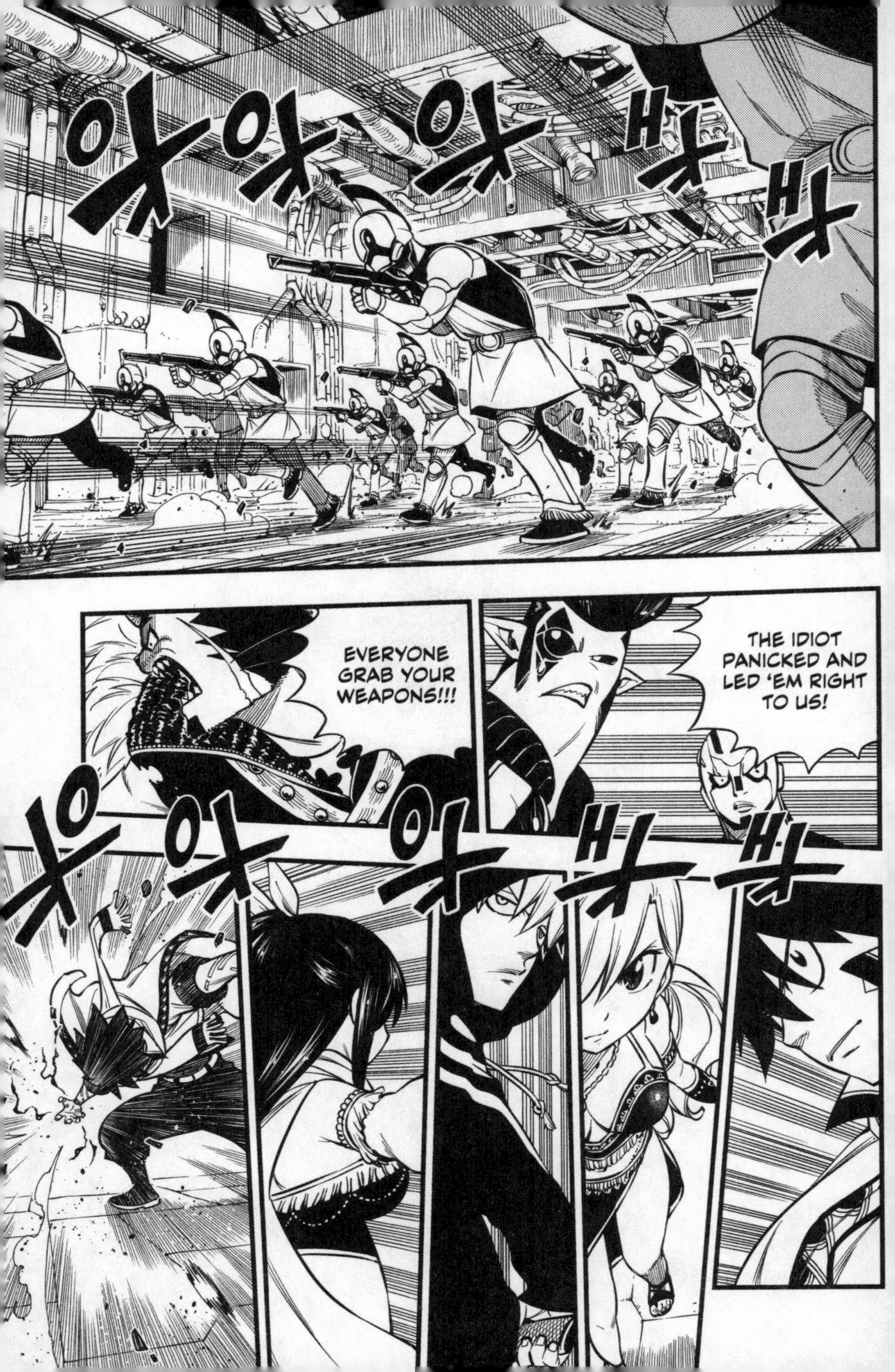
THE IDIOT PANICKED AND LED 'EM RIGHT TO US!
EVERYONE GRAB YOUR WEAPONS!!!

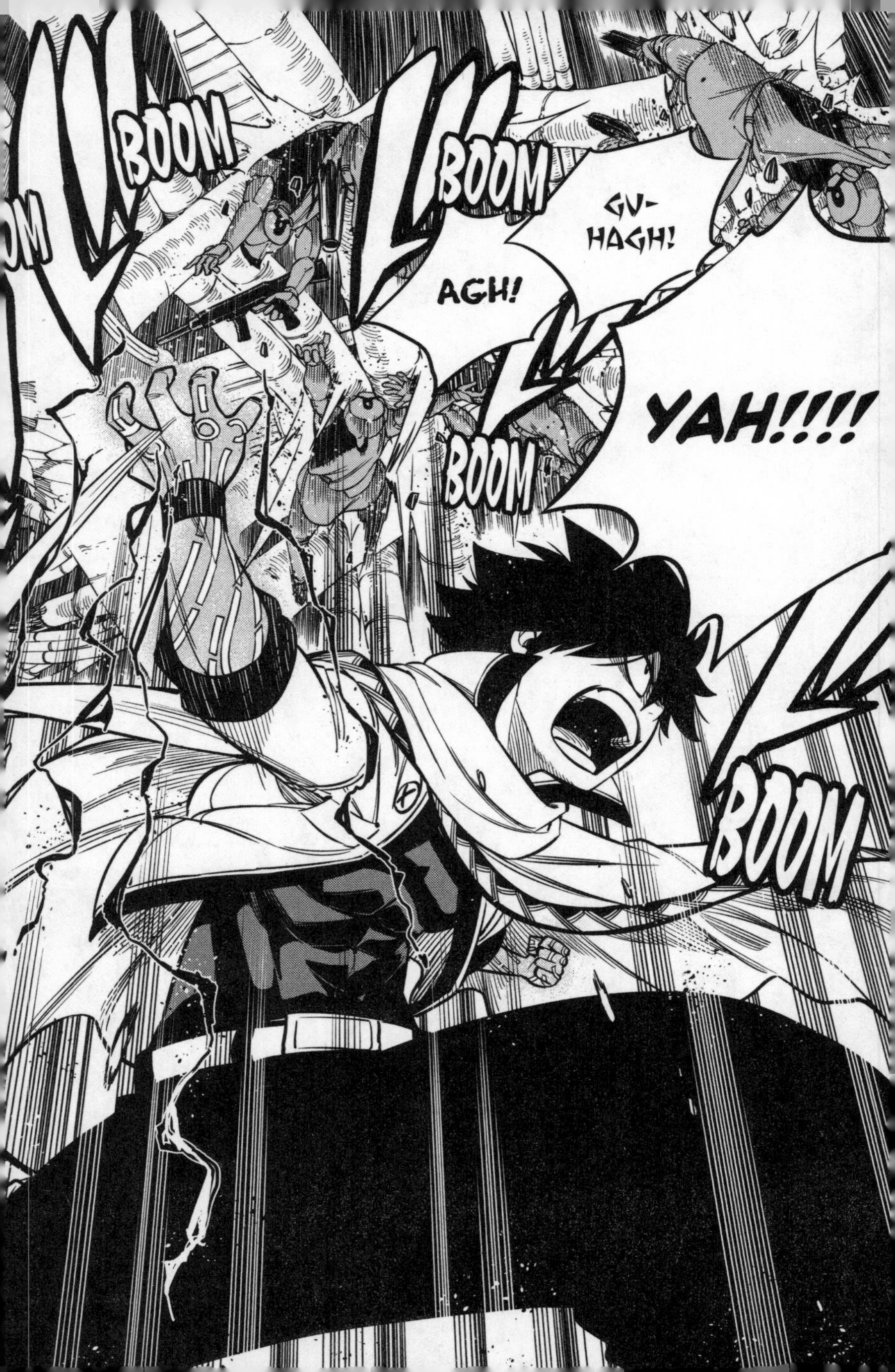
GU-HAGH!
BOOM
AGH!
BOOM
OM
YAH!!!!
BOOM
BOOM

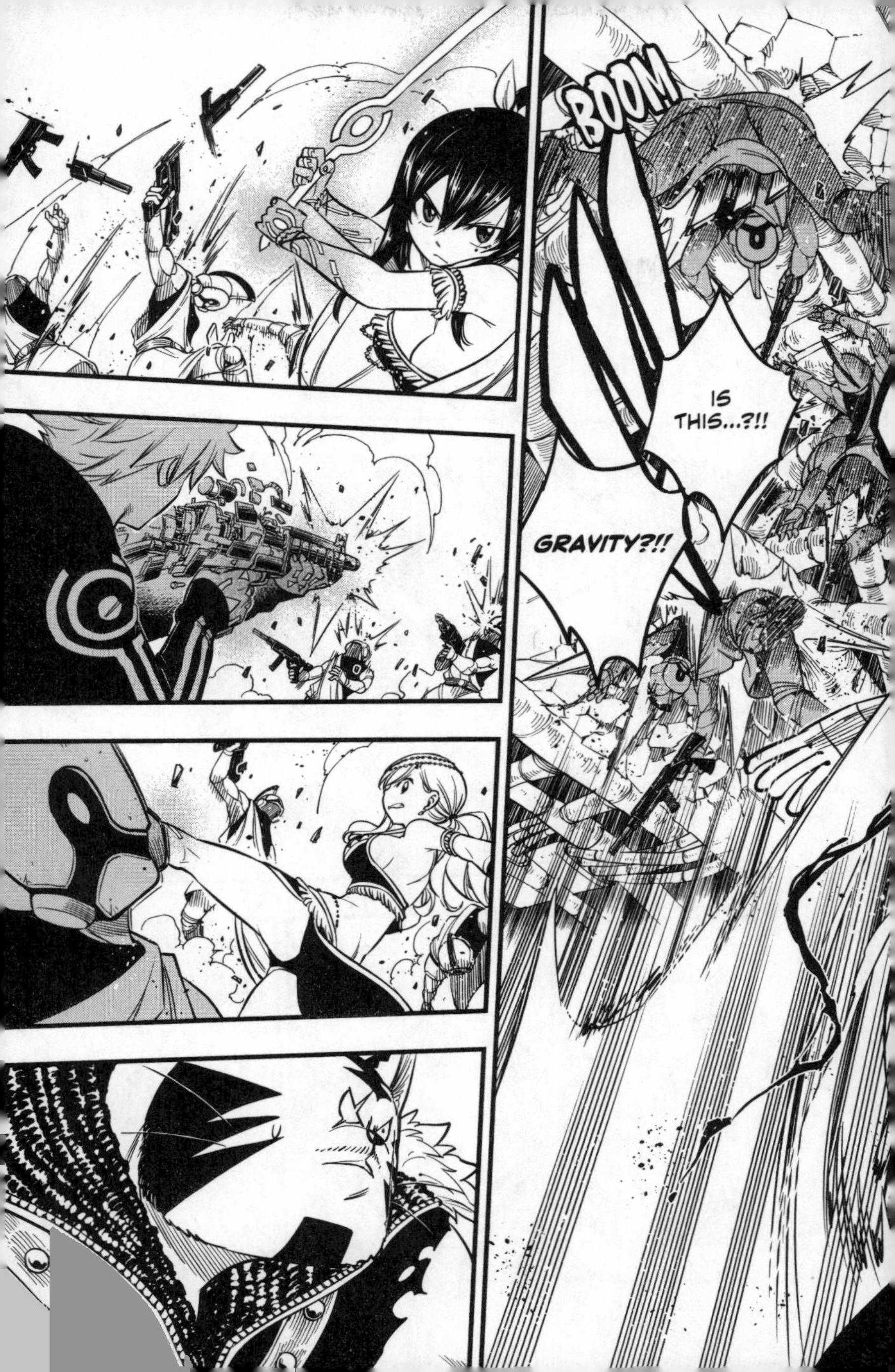
BOOM
IS THIS...?!!
GRAVITY?!!

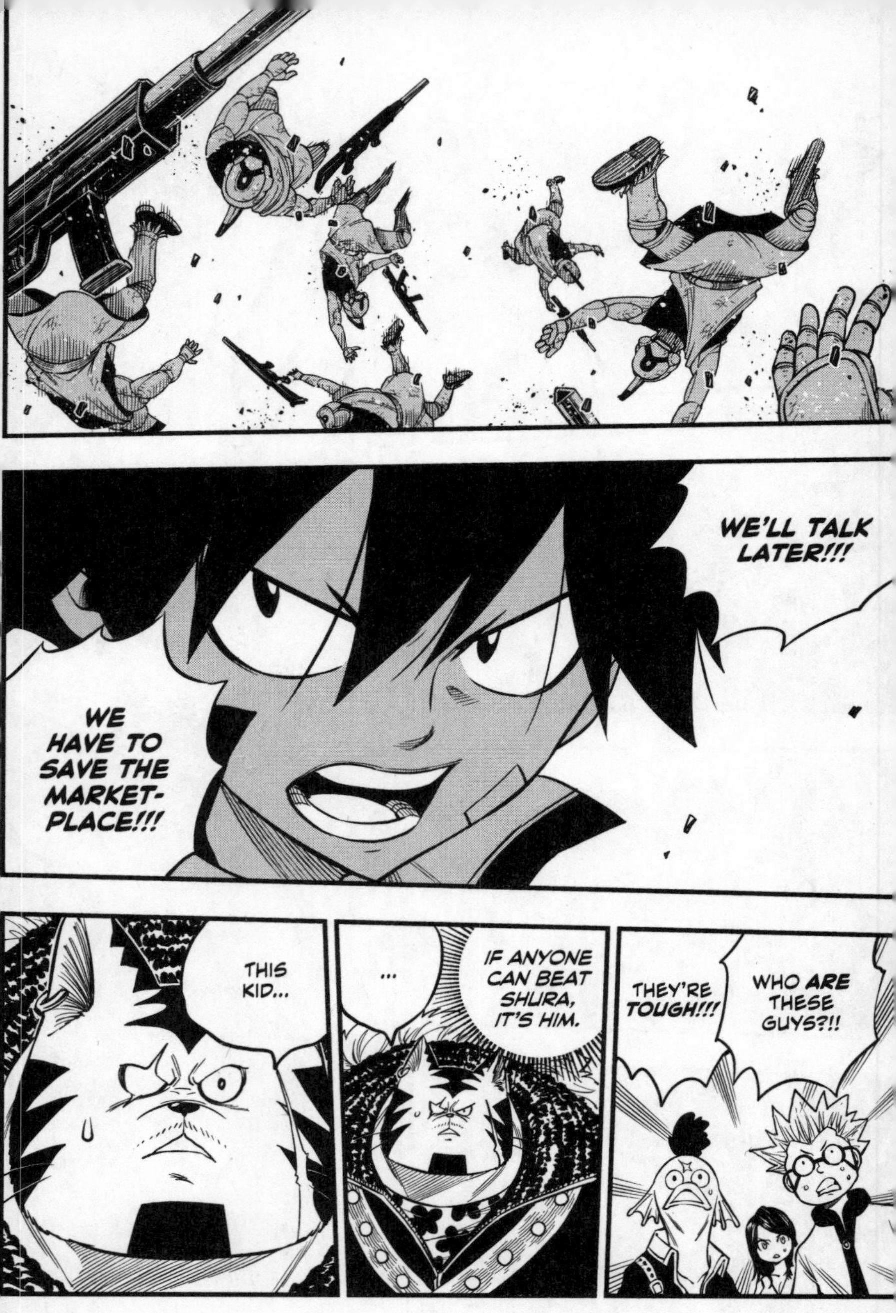
WE'LL TALK LATER!!!
WE HAVE TO SAVE THE MARKET-PLACE!!!
WHO ARE THESE GUYS?!!
THEY'RE TOUGH!!!
IF ANYONE CAN BEAT SHURA, IT'S HIM.
...
THIS KID...

CHAPTER 137: EMPIRE DICE

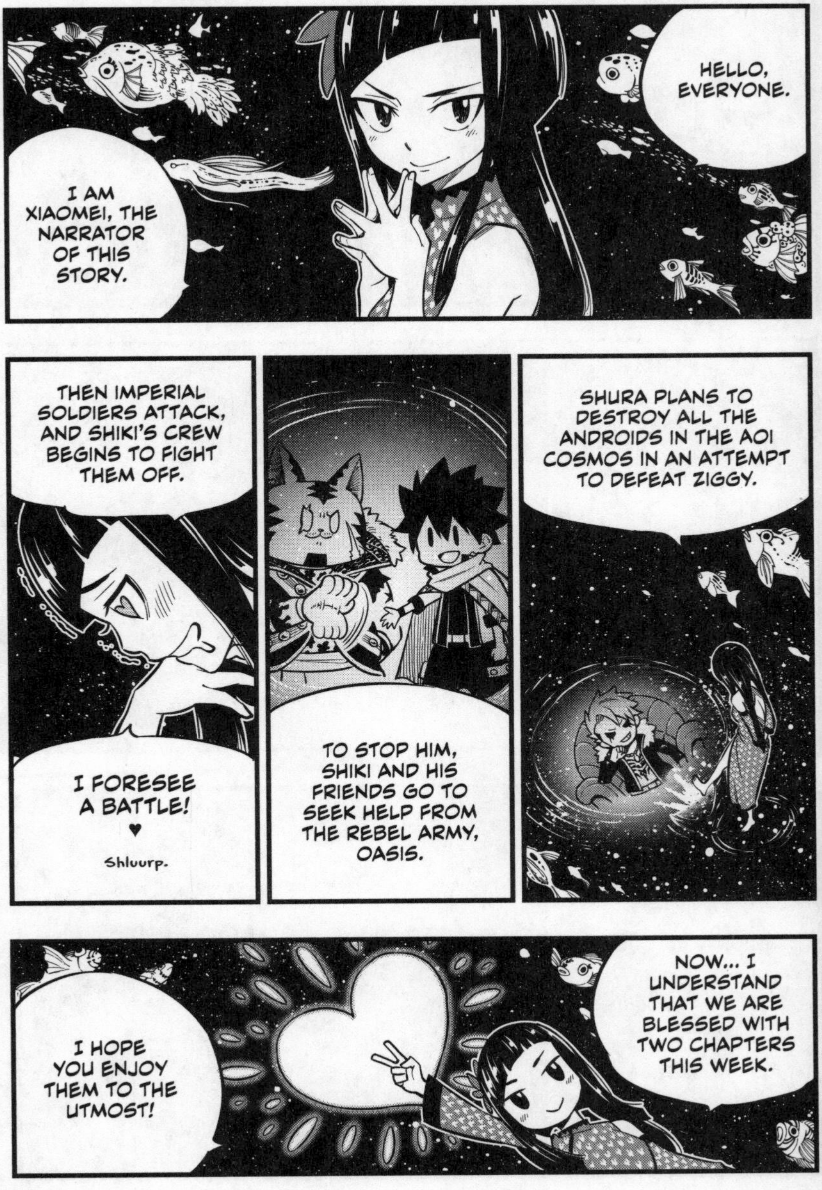
HELLO, EVERYONE.
I AM XIAOMEI, THE NARRATOR OF THIS STORY.
SHURA PLANS TO DESTROY ALL THE ANDROIDS IN THE AOI COSMOS IN AN ATTEMPT TO DEFEAT ZIGGY.
TO STOP HIM, SHIKI AND HIS FRIENDS GO TO SEEK HELP FROM THE REBEL ARMY, OASIS.
THEN IMPERIAL SOLDIERS ATTACK, AND SHIKI'S CREW BEGINS TO FIGHT THEM OFF.
I FORESEE A BATTLE! ♥
Shluurp.
NOW... I UNDERSTAND THAT WE ARE BLESSED WITH TWO CHAPTERS THIS WEEK.
I HOPE YOU ENJOY THEM TO THE UTMOST!

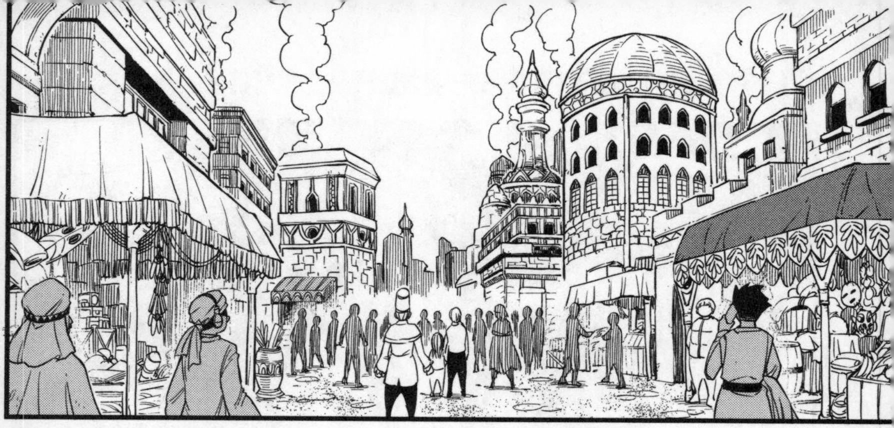

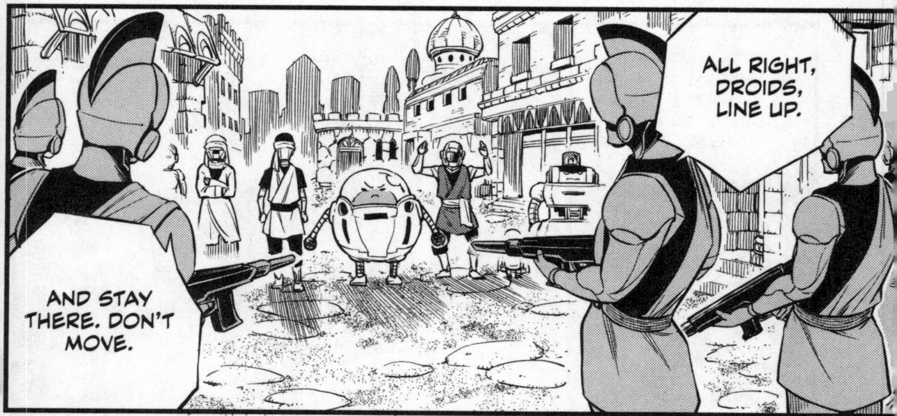
ALL RIGHT, DROIDS, LINE UP.
AND STAY THERE. DON'T MOVE.

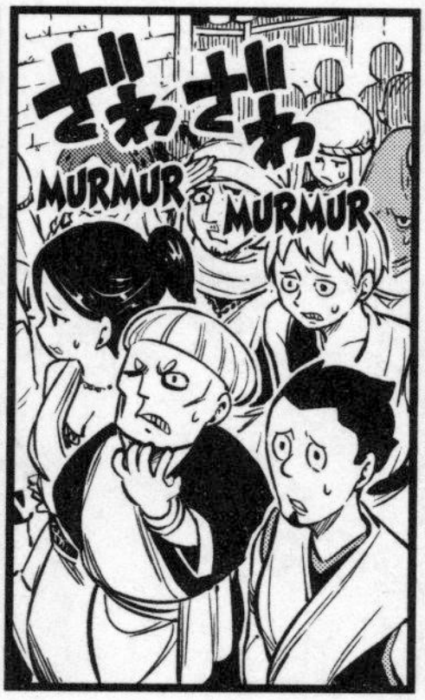
ざわざわ
MURMUR
MURMUR

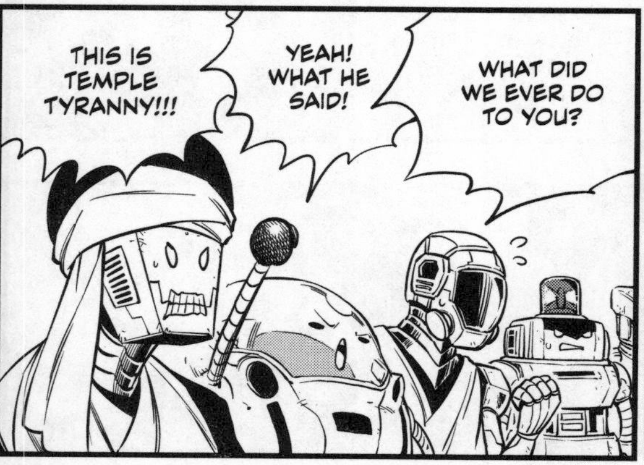
WHAT DID WE EVER DO TO YOU?
YEAH! WHAT HE SAID!
THIS IS TEMPLE TYRANNY!!!

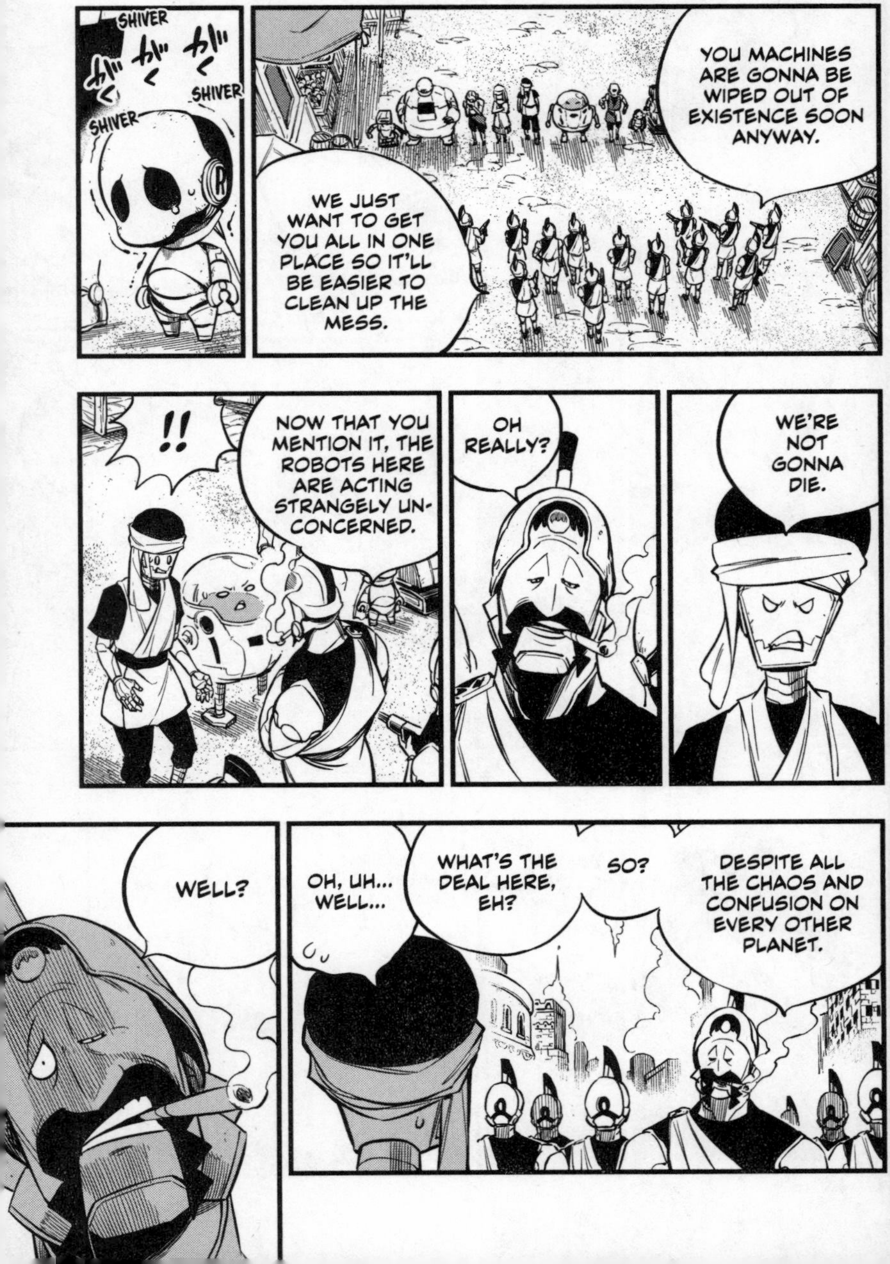
YOU MACHINES ARE GONNA BE WIPED OUT OF EXISTENCE SOON ANYWAY.
WE JUST WANT TO GET YOU ALL IN ONE PLACE SO IT'LL BE EASIER TO CLEAN UP THE MESS.
SHIVER
SHIVER
SHIVER
WE'RE NOT GONNA DIE.
OH REALLY?
NOW THAT YOU MENTION IT, THE ROBOTS HERE ARE ACTING STRANGELY UNCONCERNED.
!!
DESPITE ALL THE CHAOS AND CONFUSION ON EVERY OTHER PLANET.
SO?
WHAT'S THE DEAL HERE, EH?
OH, UH... WELL...
WELL?

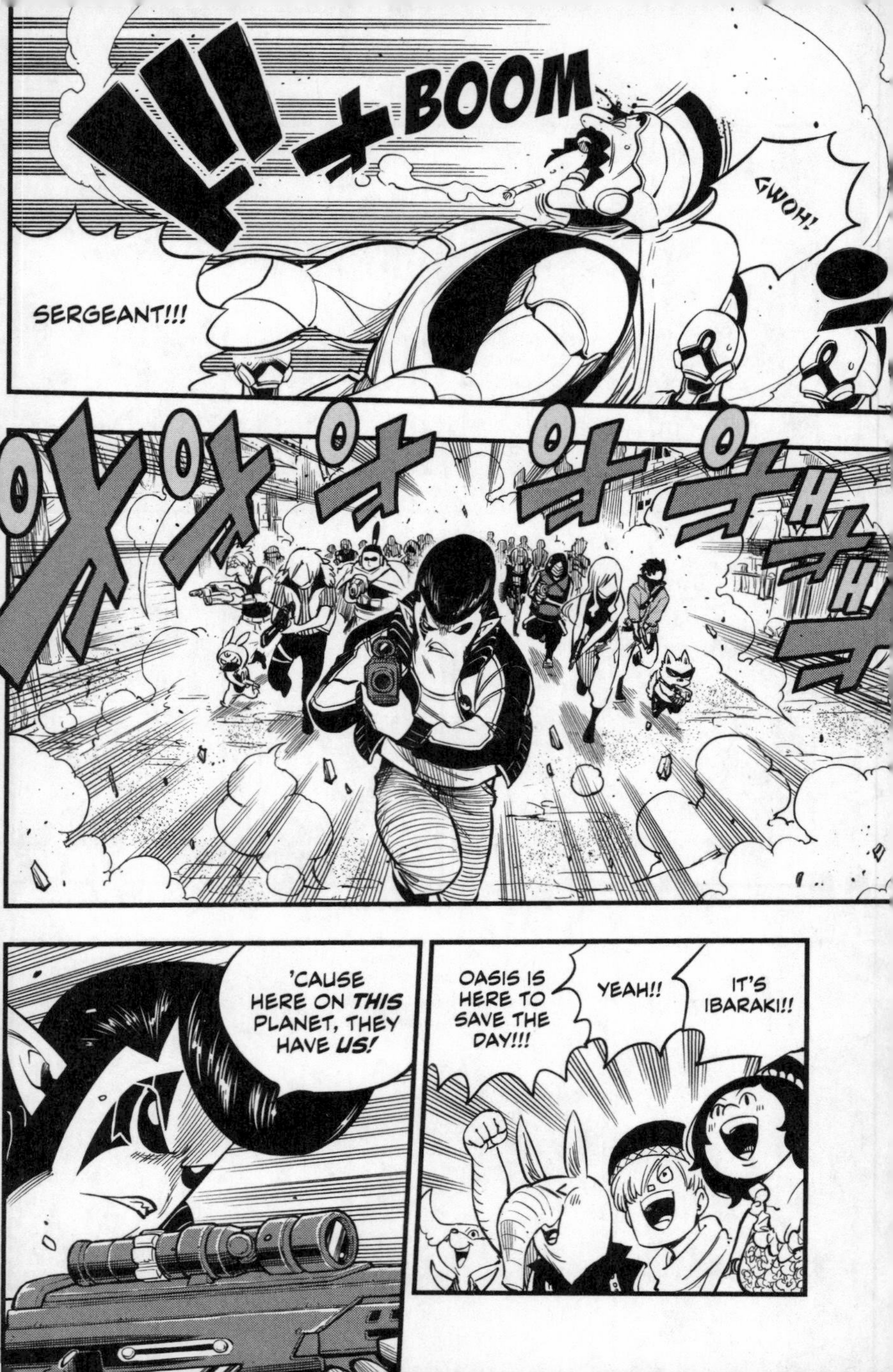
GWOH!
BOOM
SERGEANT!!!
IT'S IBARAKI!!
YEAH!!
OASIS IS HERE TO SAVE THE DAY!!!
'CAUSE HERE ON *THIS* PLANET, THEY HAVE *US!*

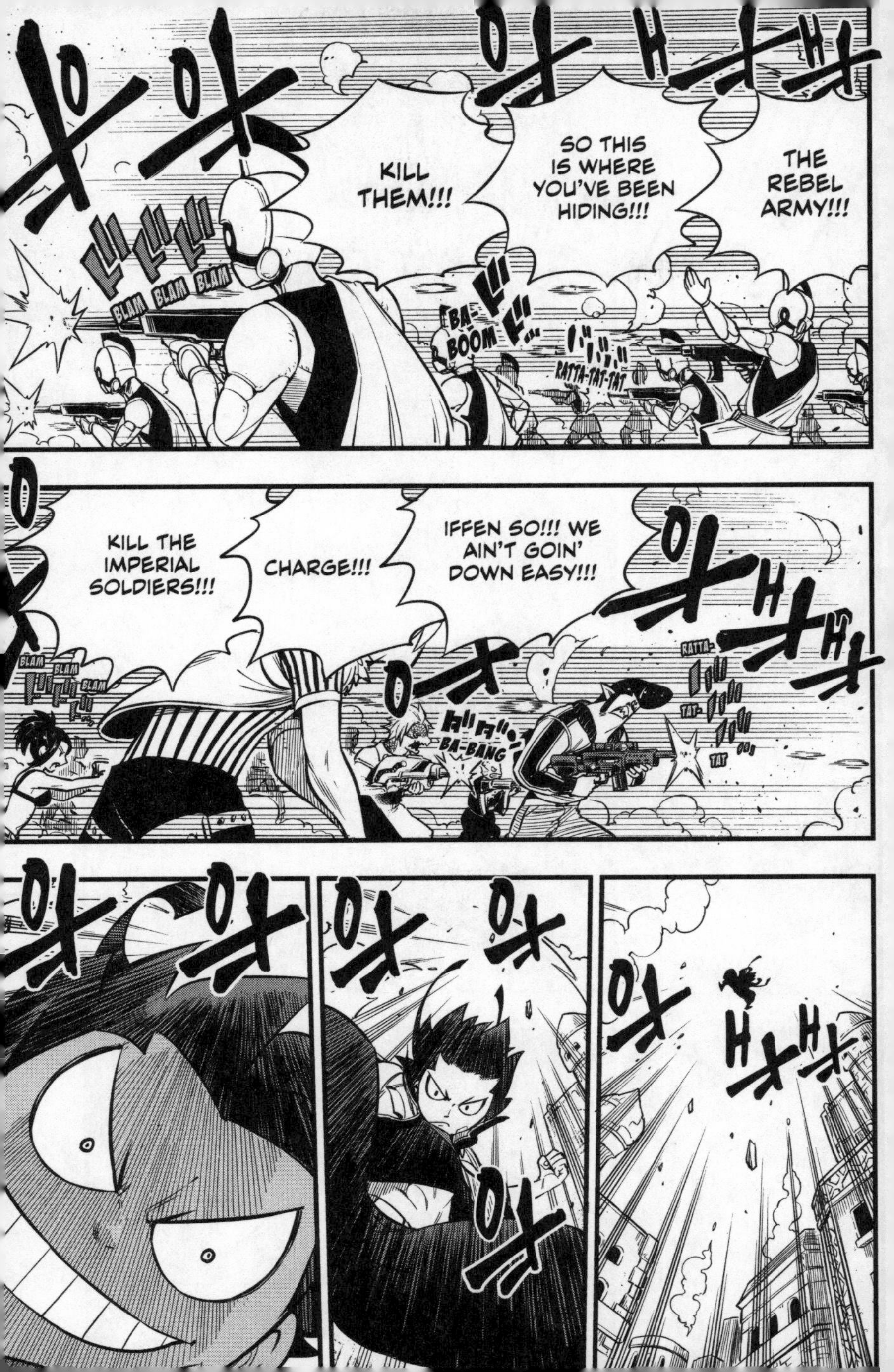
THE REBEL ARMY!!!
SO THIS IS WHERE YOU'VE BEEN HIDING!!!
KILL THEM!!!
RATTA-TAT-TAT
BA-BOOM
BLAM BLAM BLAM
IFFEN SO!!! WE AIN'T GOIN' DOWN EASY!!!
RATTA-TAT-TAT
BA-BANG
CHARGE!!!
KILL THE IMPERIAL SOLDIERS!!!
BLAM BLAM BLAM

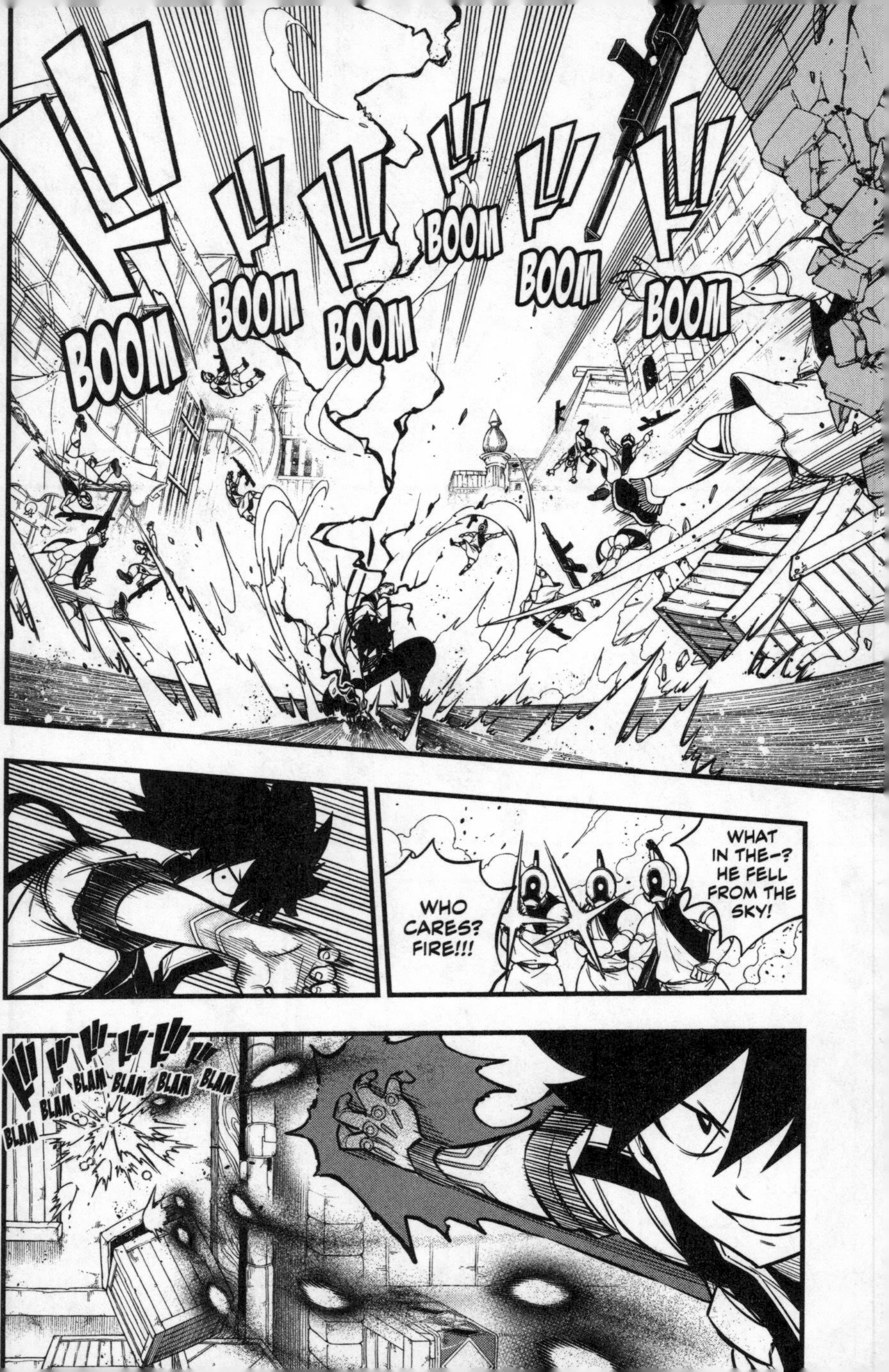
BOOM
BOOM
BOOM
BOOM
BOOM
BOOM
WHAT IN THE--? HE FELL FROM THE SKY!
WHO CARES? FIRE!!!
BLAM
BLAM
BLAM
BLAM
BLAM
BLAM

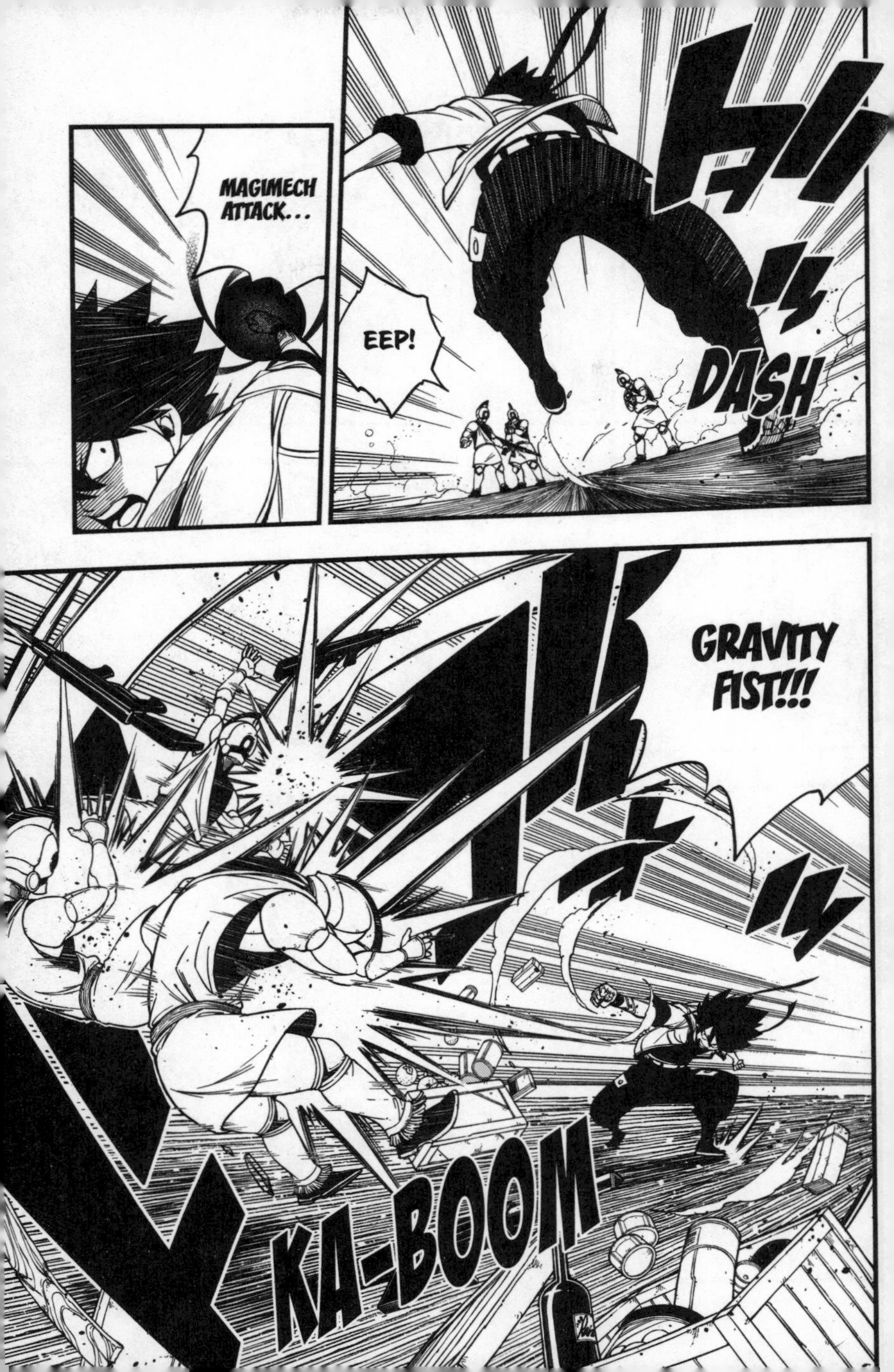
DASH
EEP!
MAGIMECH ATTACK...
GRAVITY FIST!!!
KA-BOOM

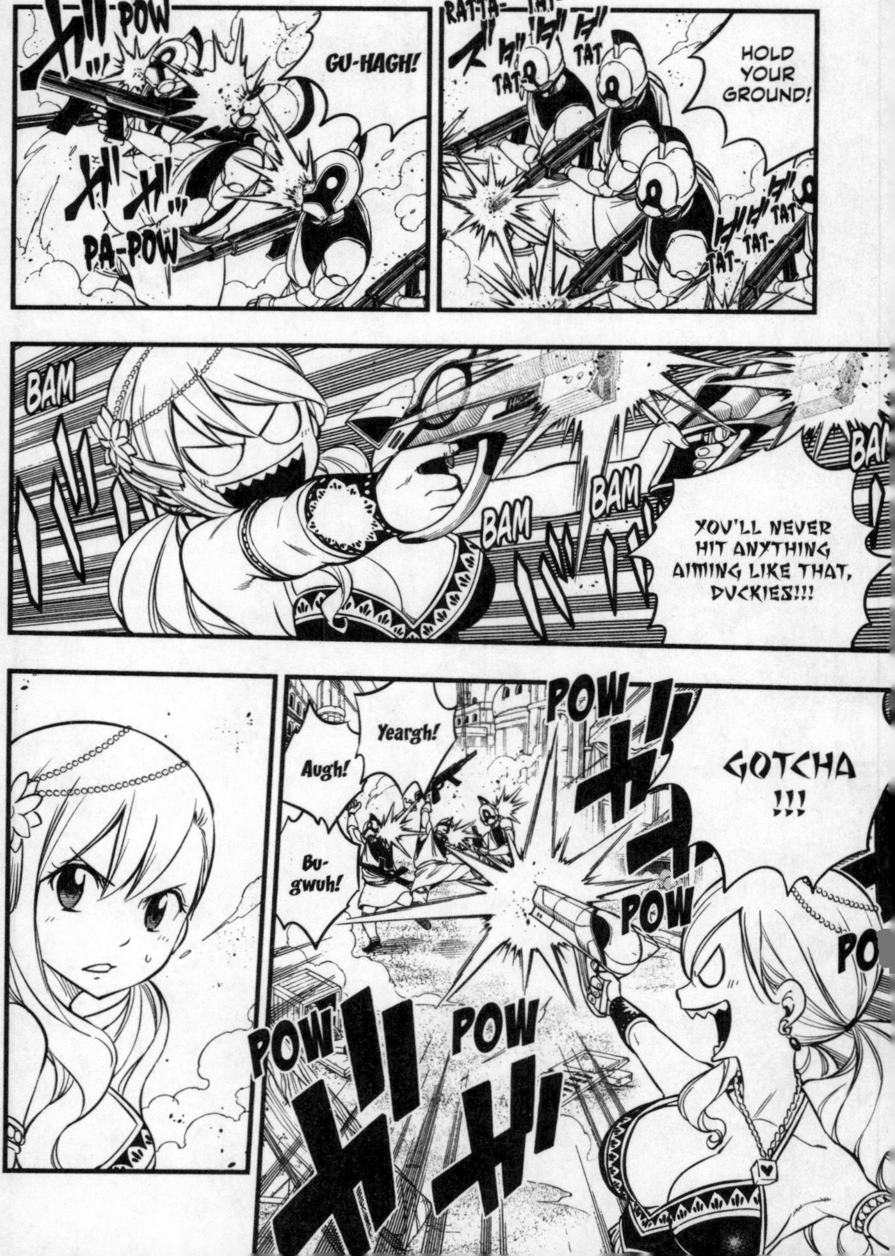
RAT-TA-TAT-TAT-TAT
TAT-TAT-TAT-
HOLD YOUR GROUND!
POW
GU-HAGH!
PA-POW
YOU'LL NEVER HIT ANYTHING AIMING LIKE THAT, DUCKIES!!!
BAM
BAM
BAM
POW
GOTCHA!!!
Yeargh!
Augh!
Bu-gwuh!
POW
POW
POW

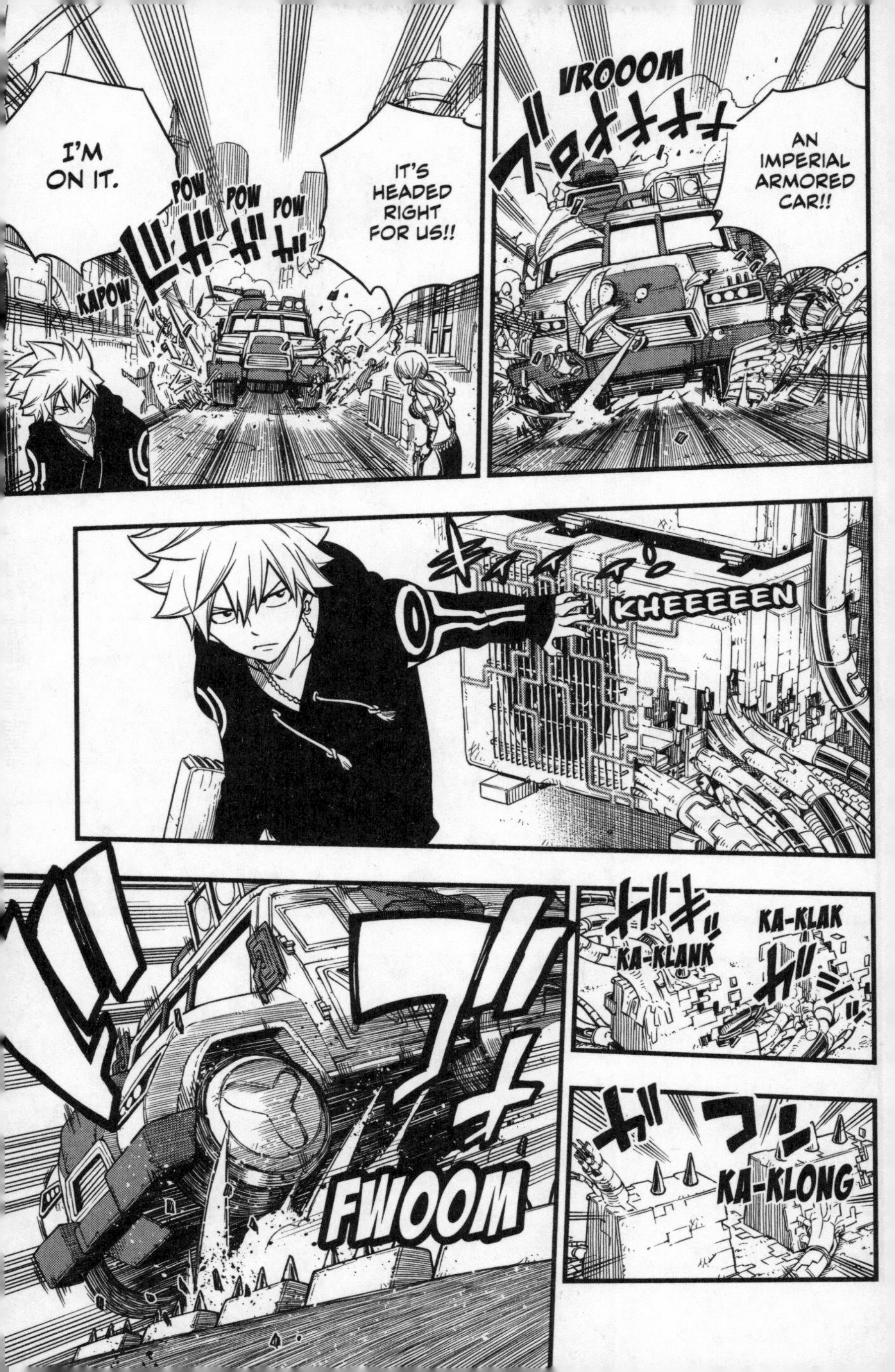
VROOOM
AN IMPERIAL ARMORED CAR!!
IT'S HEADED RIGHT FOR US!!
POW
POW
POW
KAPOW
I'M ON IT.
KHEEEEEEN
KA-KLAK
KA-KLANK
KA-KLONG
FWOOM

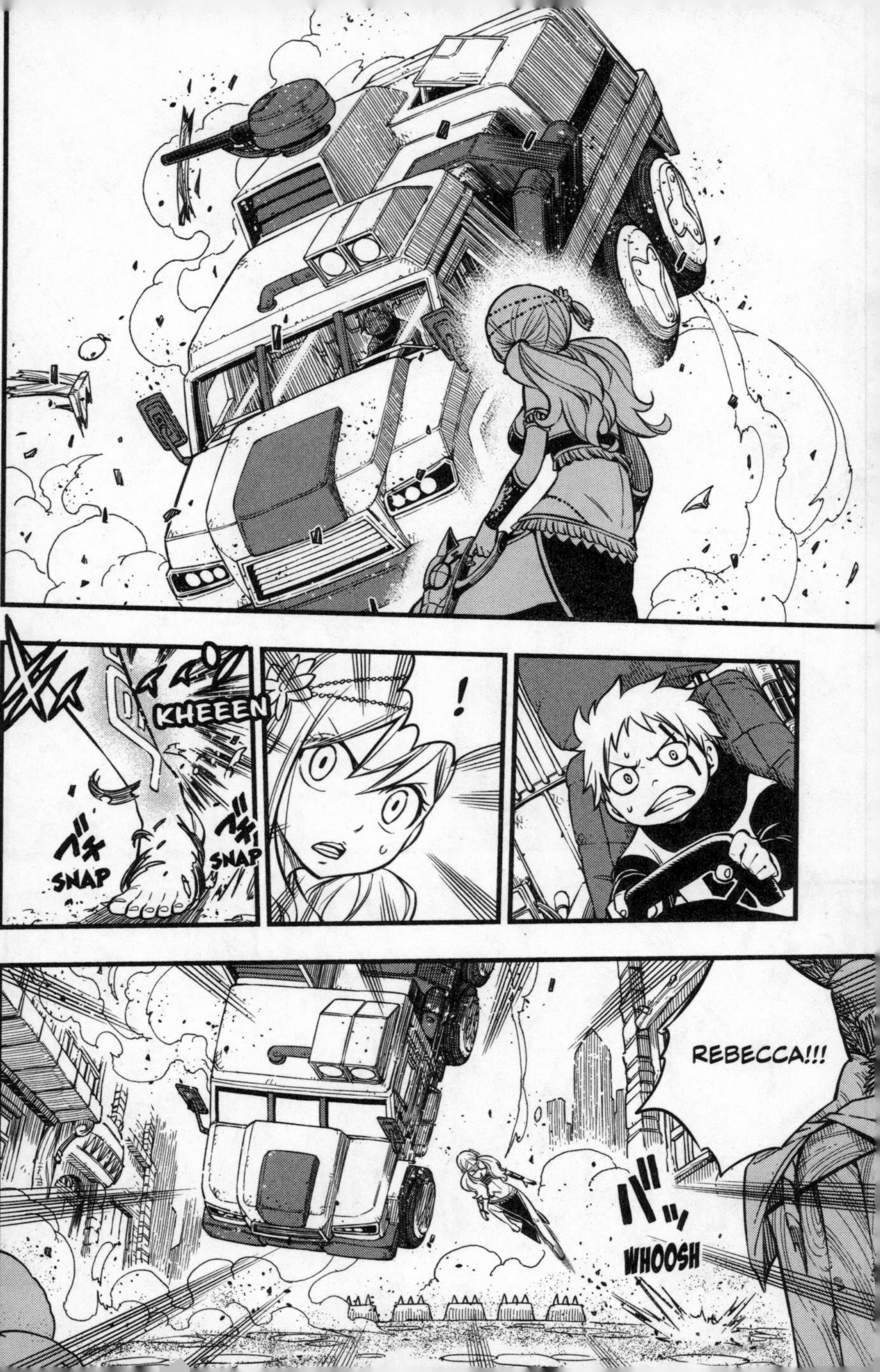
!
KHEEEN
SNAP
SNAP
REBECCA!!!
WHOOSH

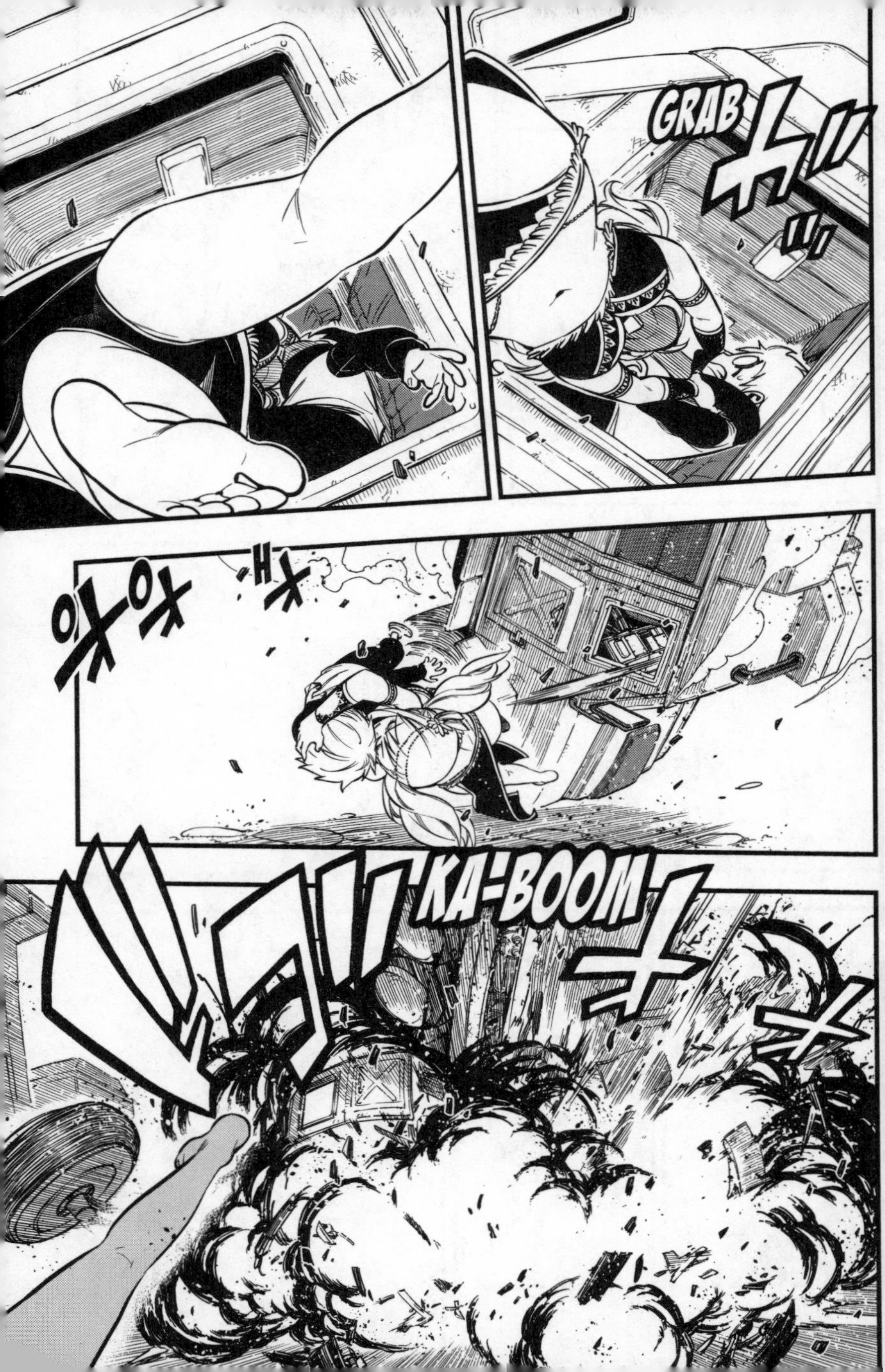
GRAB
KA-BOOM

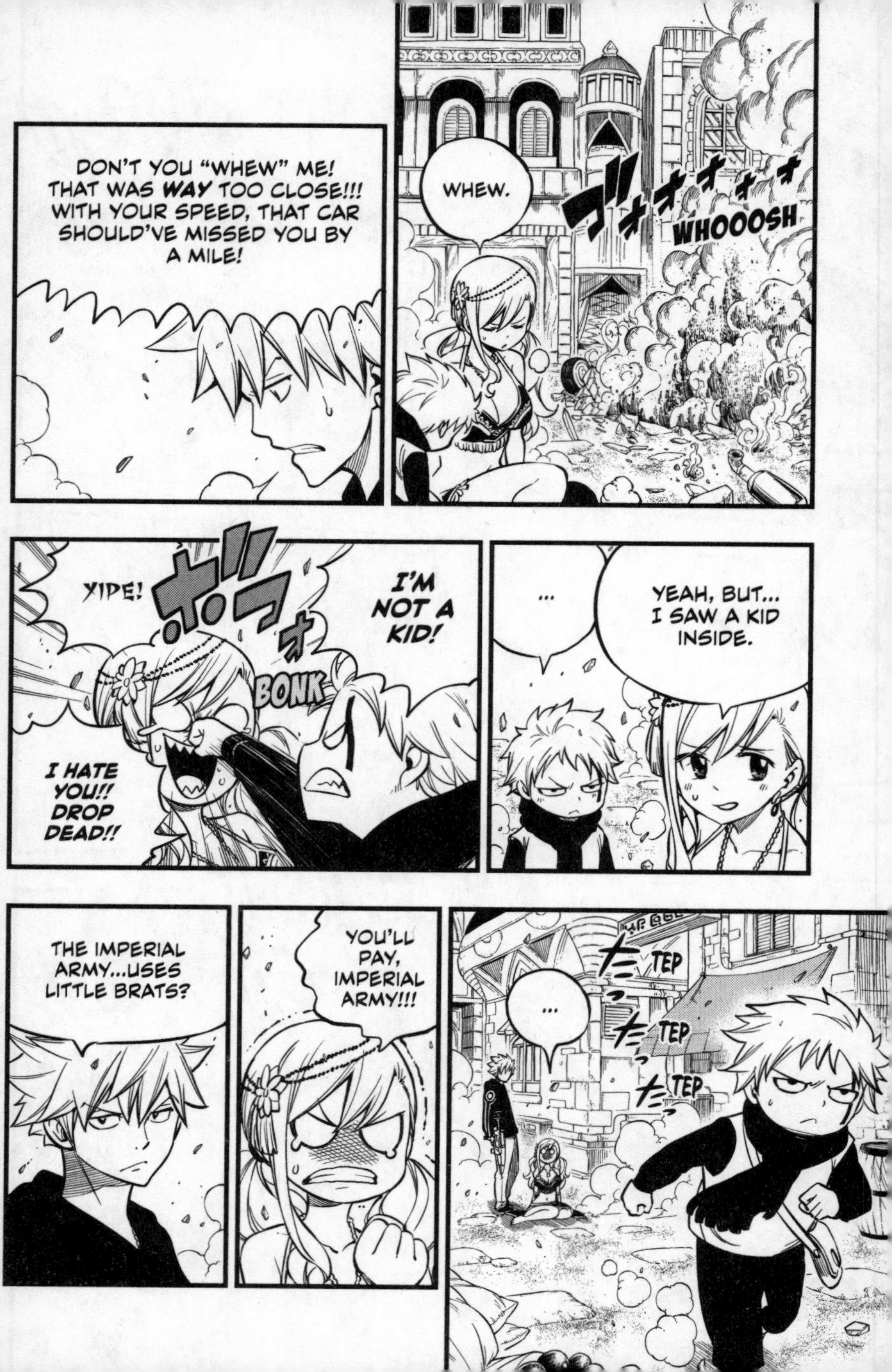

WHEW.
WHOOOSH
DON'T YOU "WHEW" ME! THAT WAS WAY TOO CLOSE!!! WITH YOUR SPEED, THAT CAR SHOULD'VE MISSED YOU BY A MILE!
YEAH, BUT... I SAW A KID INSIDE.
...
I'M NOT A KID!
BONK
YIPE!
I HATE YOU!! DROP DEAD!!
TEP
TEP
TEP
...
YOU'LL PAY, IMPERIAL ARMY!!!
THE IMPERIAL ARMY...USES LITTLE BRATS?

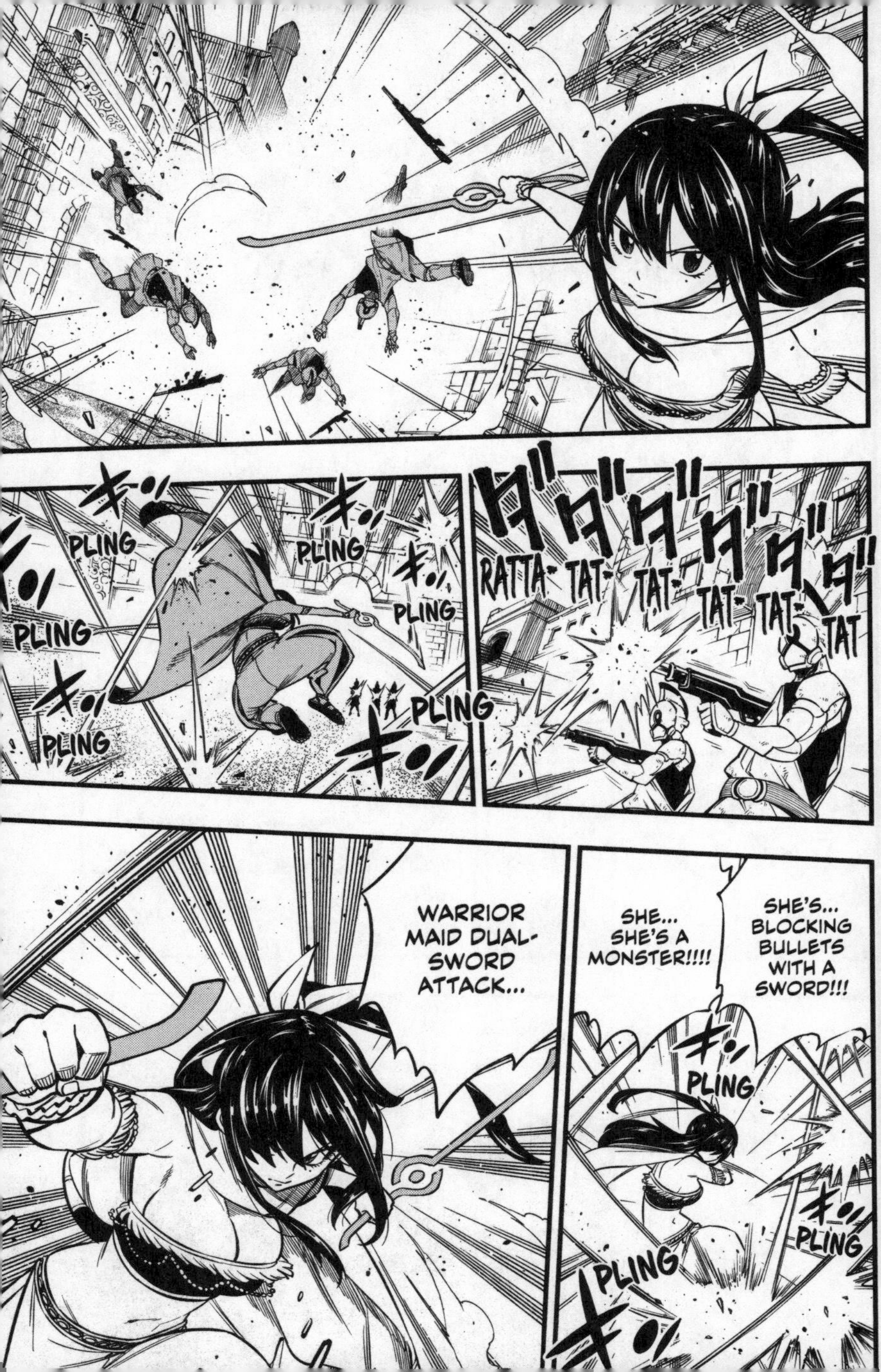
RATTA-TAT-TAT-TAT-TAT-TAT
PLING
PLING
PLING
PLING
PLING
PLING
SHE'S... BLOCKING BULLETS WITH A SWORD!!!
SHE... SHE'S A MONSTER!!!!
PLING
PLING
PLING
WARRIOR MAID DUAL-SWORD ATTACK...

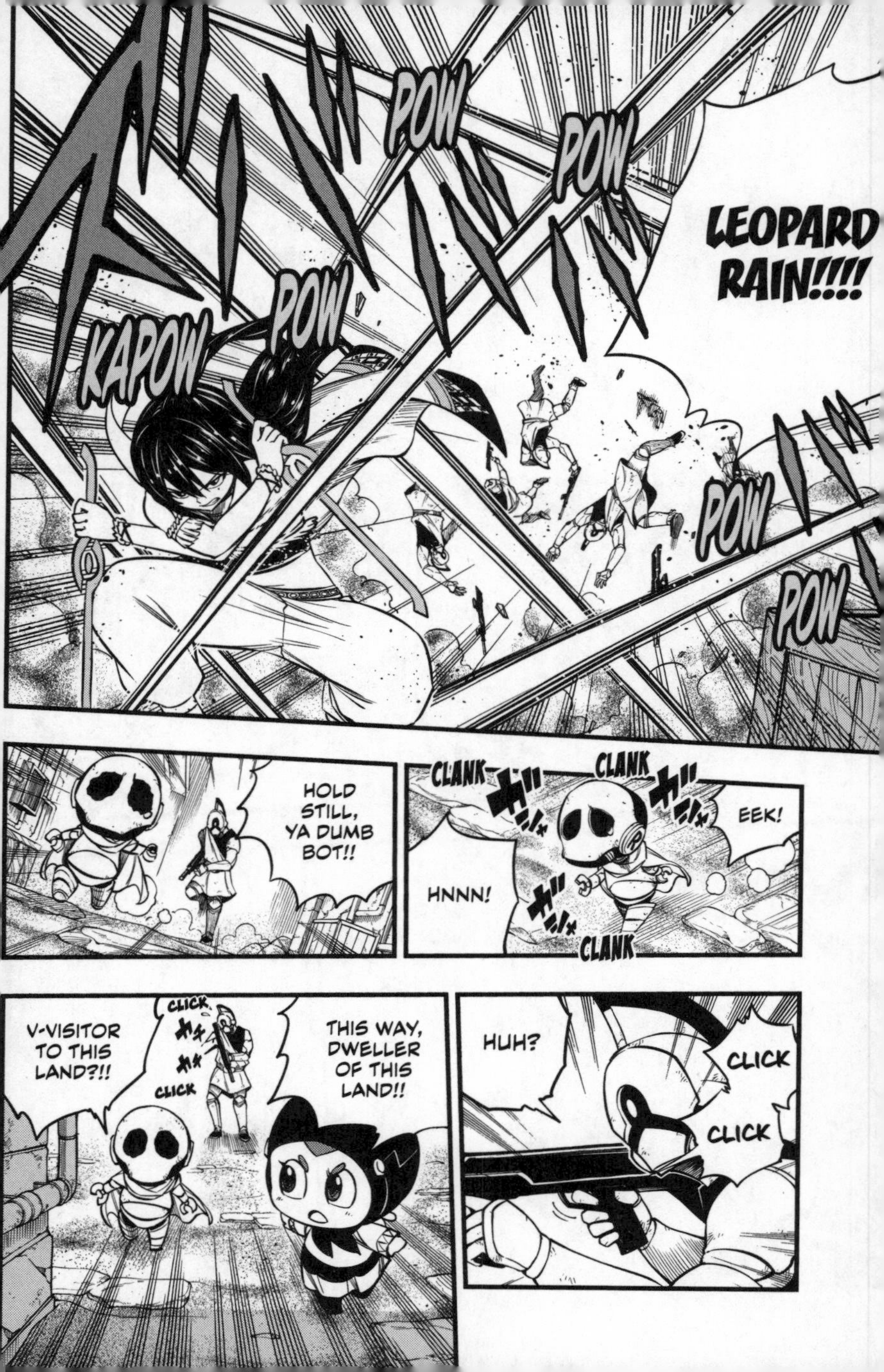
LEOPARD RAIN!!!!
POW
POW
POW
POW
POW
KAPOW
EEK!
CLANK
CLANK
HNNN!
CLANK
HOLD STILL, YA DUMB BOT!!
HUH?
CLICK
CLICK
THIS WAY, DWELLER OF THIS LAND!!
V-VISITOR TO THIS LAND?!!
CLICK
CLICK

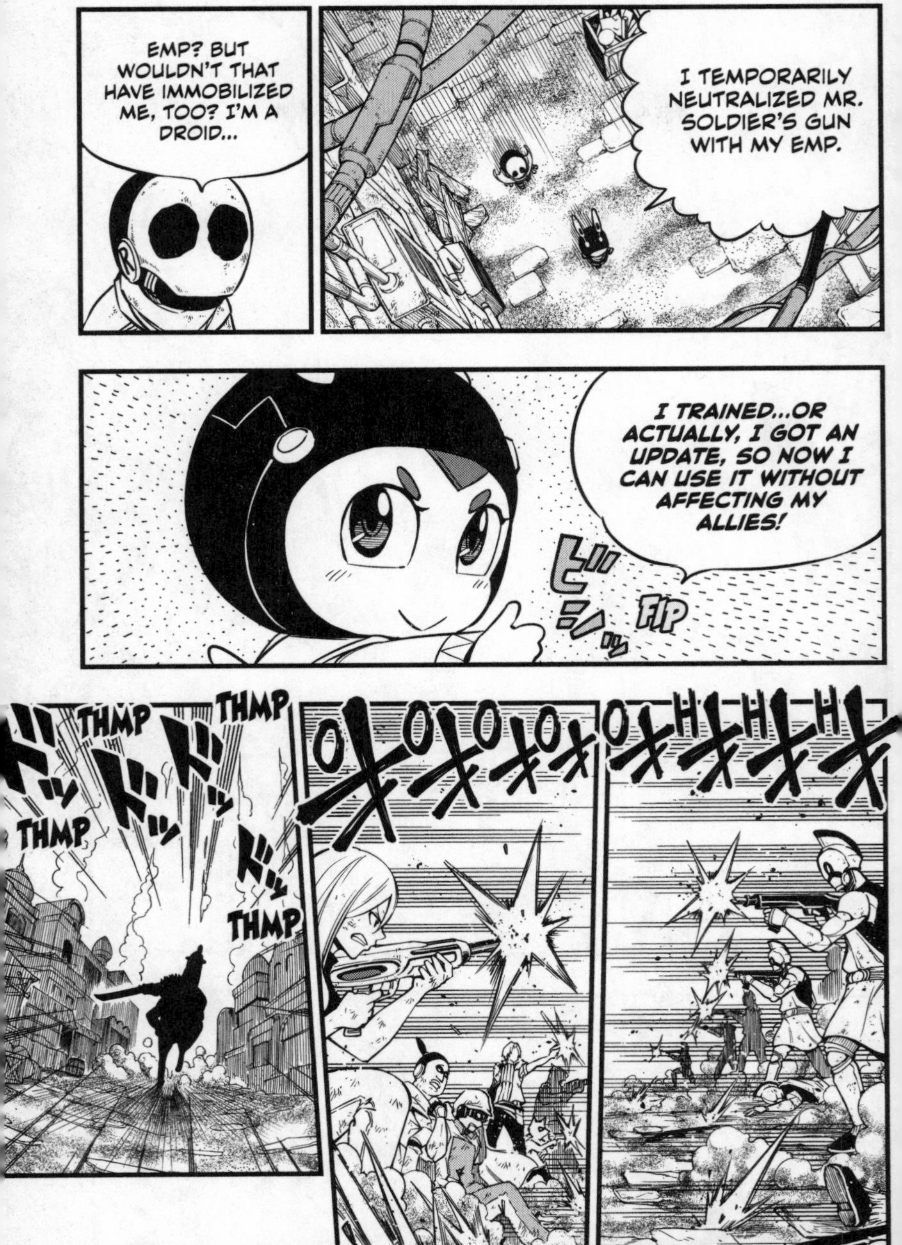
I TEMPORARILY NEUTRALIZED MR. SOLDIER'S GUN WITH MY EMP.
EMP? BUT WOULDN'T THAT HAVE IMMOBILIZED ME, TOO? I'M A DROID...
I TRAINED...OR ACTUALLY, I GOT AN UPDATE, SO NOW I CAN USE IT WITHOUT AFFECTING MY ALLIES!
FIP
OOOOOHHH
THMP
THMP
THMP
THMP

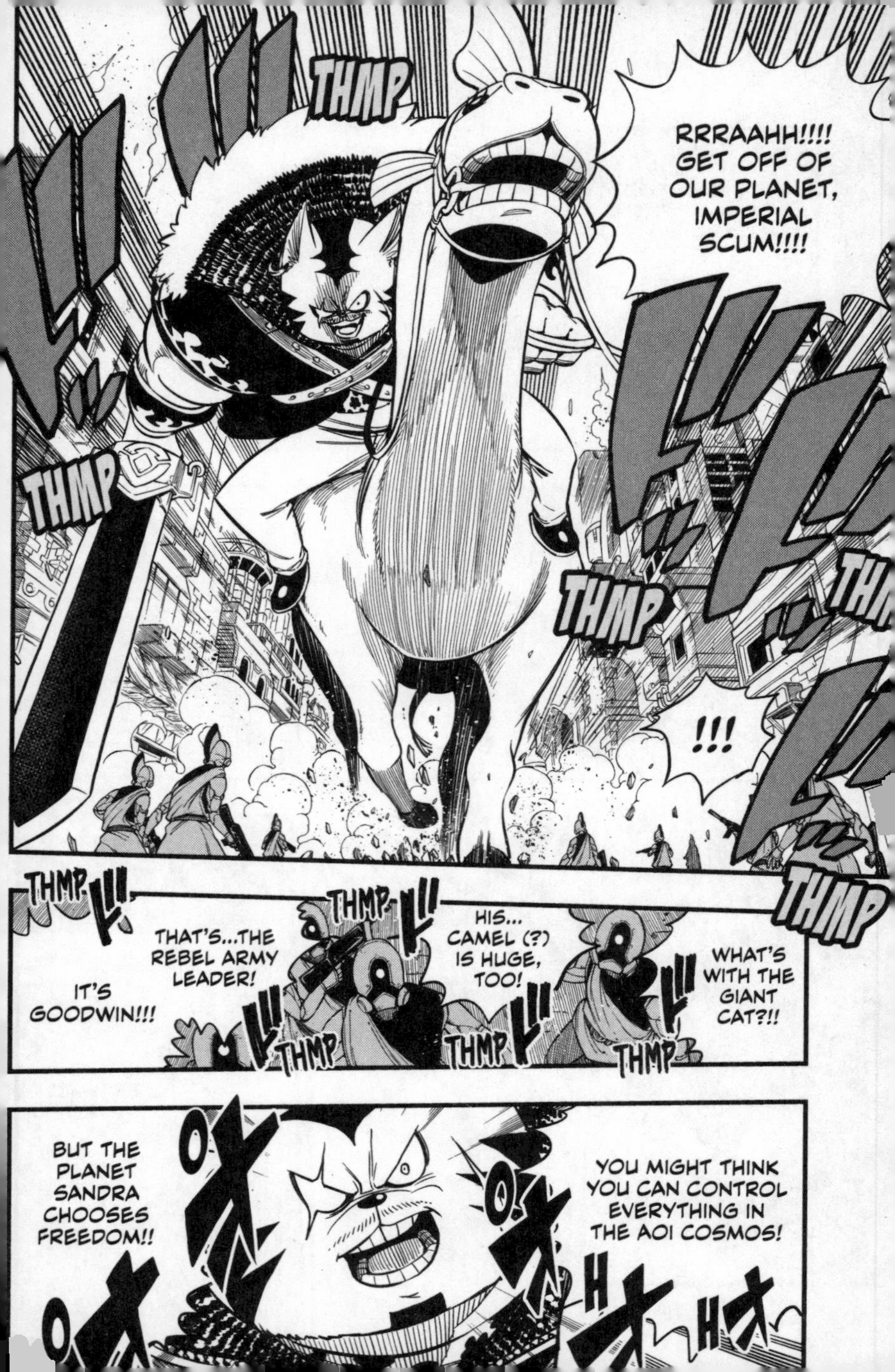
THMP
RRRAAHH!!!! GET OFF OF OUR PLANET, IMPERIAL SCUM!!!!
THMP
!!!
THMP
THMP
WHAT'S WITH THE GIANT CAT?!!
HIS... CAMEL (?) IS HUGE, TOO!
THMP
THAT'S...THE REBEL ARMY LEADER!
IT'S GOODWIN!!!
THMP
THMP
THMP
THMP
YOU MIGHT THINK YOU CAN CONTROL EVERYTHING IN THE AOI COSMOS!
BUT THE PLANET SANDRA CHOOSES FREEDOM!!

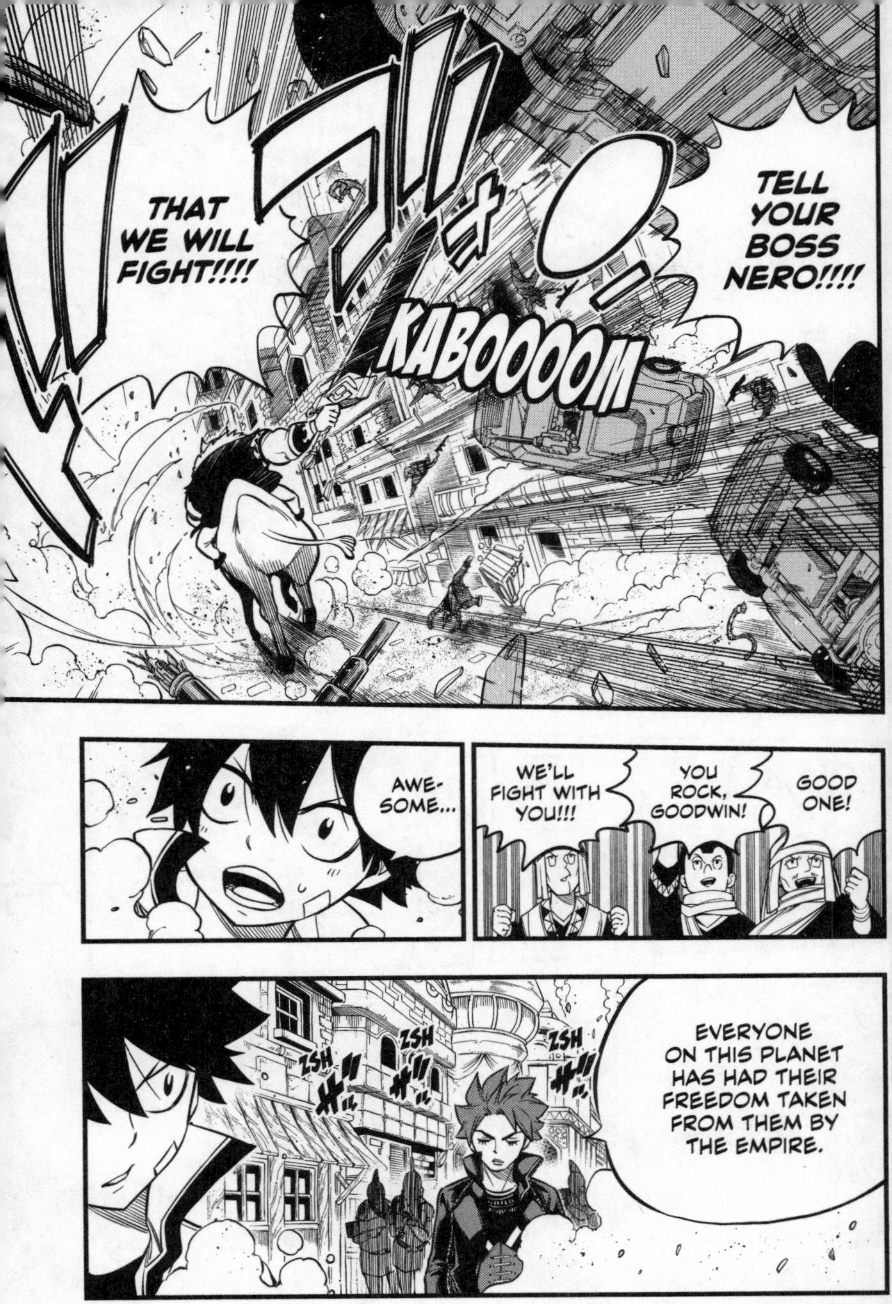
TELL YOUR BOSS NERO!!!!
THAT WE WILL FIGHT!!!!
KABOOOOM
GOOD ONE!
YOU ROCK, GOODWIN!
WE'LL FIGHT WITH YOU!!!
AWE-SOME...
EVERYONE ON THIS PLANET HAS HAD THEIR FREEDOM TAKEN FROM THEM BY THE EMPIRE.
ZSH
ZSH
ZSH

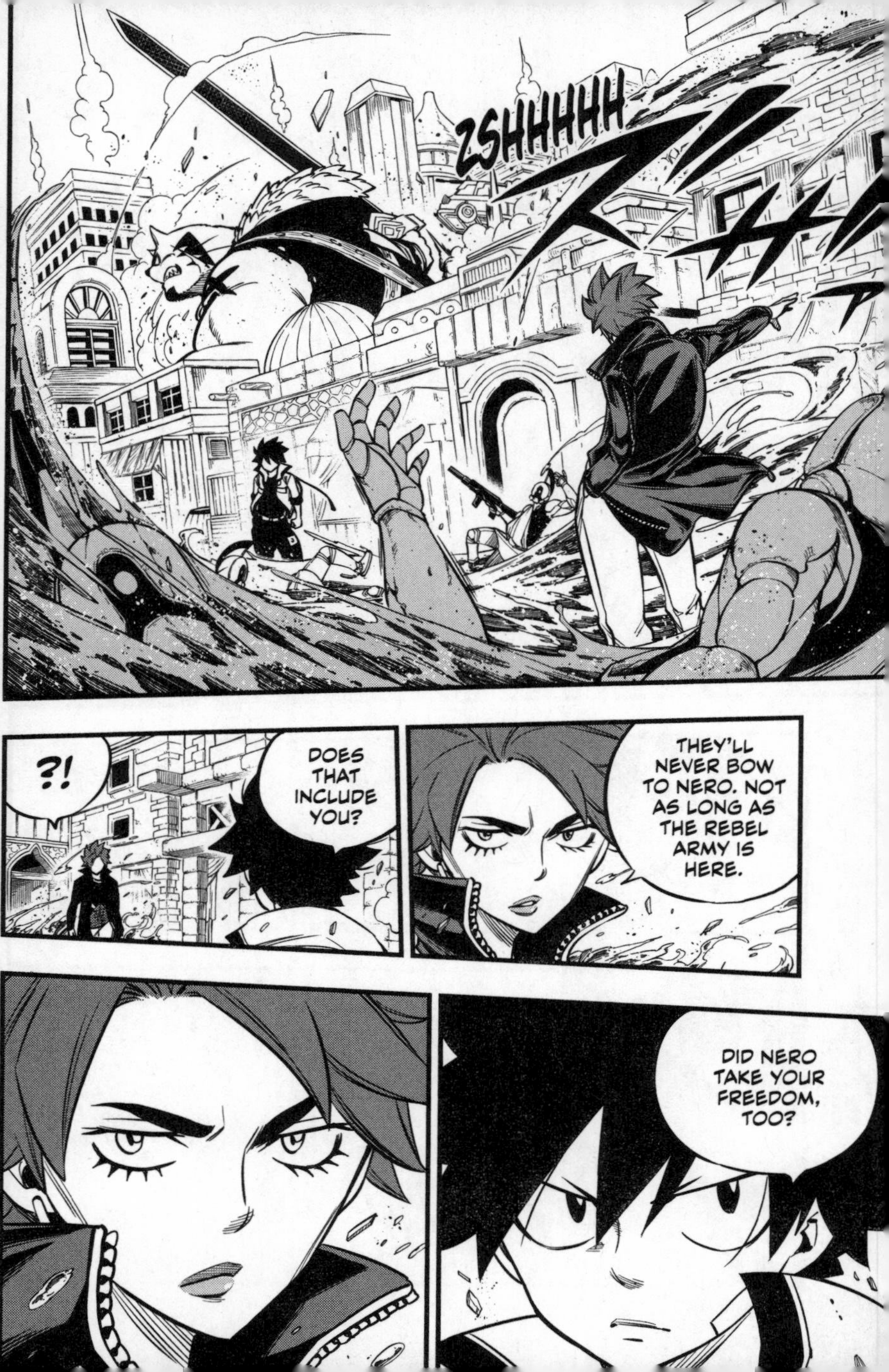
ZSHHHHH
THEY'LL NEVER BOW TO NERO. NOT AS LONG AS THE REBEL ARMY IS HERE.
DOES THAT INCLUDE YOU?
?!
DID NERO TAKE YOUR FREEDOM, TOO?

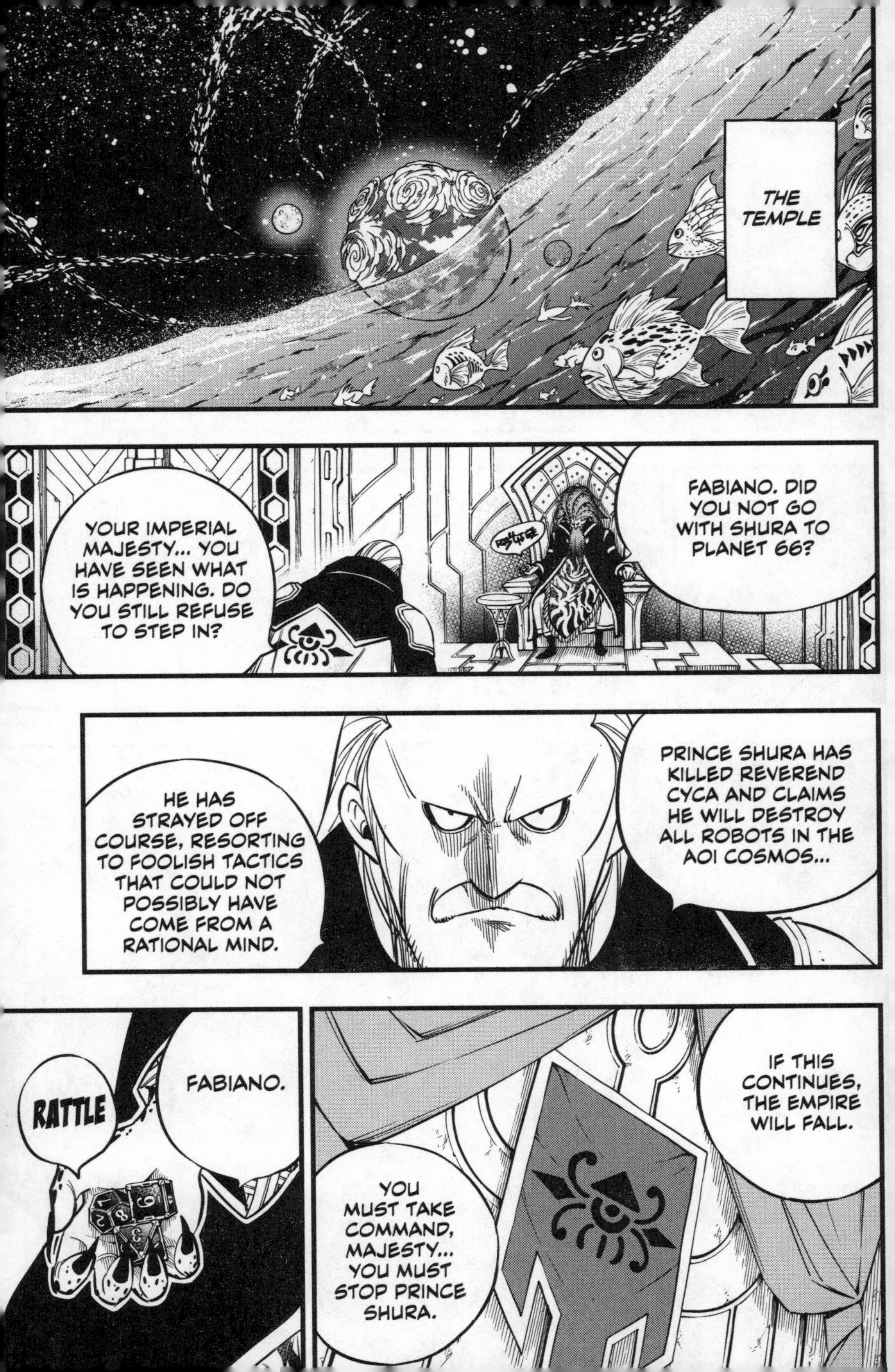
THE TEMPLE
FABIANO. DID YOU NOT GO WITH SHURA TO PLANET 66?
YOUR IMPERIAL MAJESTY... YOU HAVE SEEN WHAT IS HAPPENING. DO YOU STILL REFUSE TO STEP IN?
PRINCE SHURA HAS KILLED REVEREND CYCA AND CLAIMS HE WILL DESTROY ALL ROBOTS IN THE AOI COSMOS...
HE HAS STRAYED OFF COURSE, RESORTING TO FOOLISH TACTICS THAT COULD NOT POSSIBLY HAVE COME FROM A RATIONAL MIND.
IF THIS CONTINUES, THE EMPIRE WILL FALL.
YOU MUST TAKE COMMAND, MAJESTY... YOU MUST STOP PRINCE SHURA.
FABIANO.
RATTLE

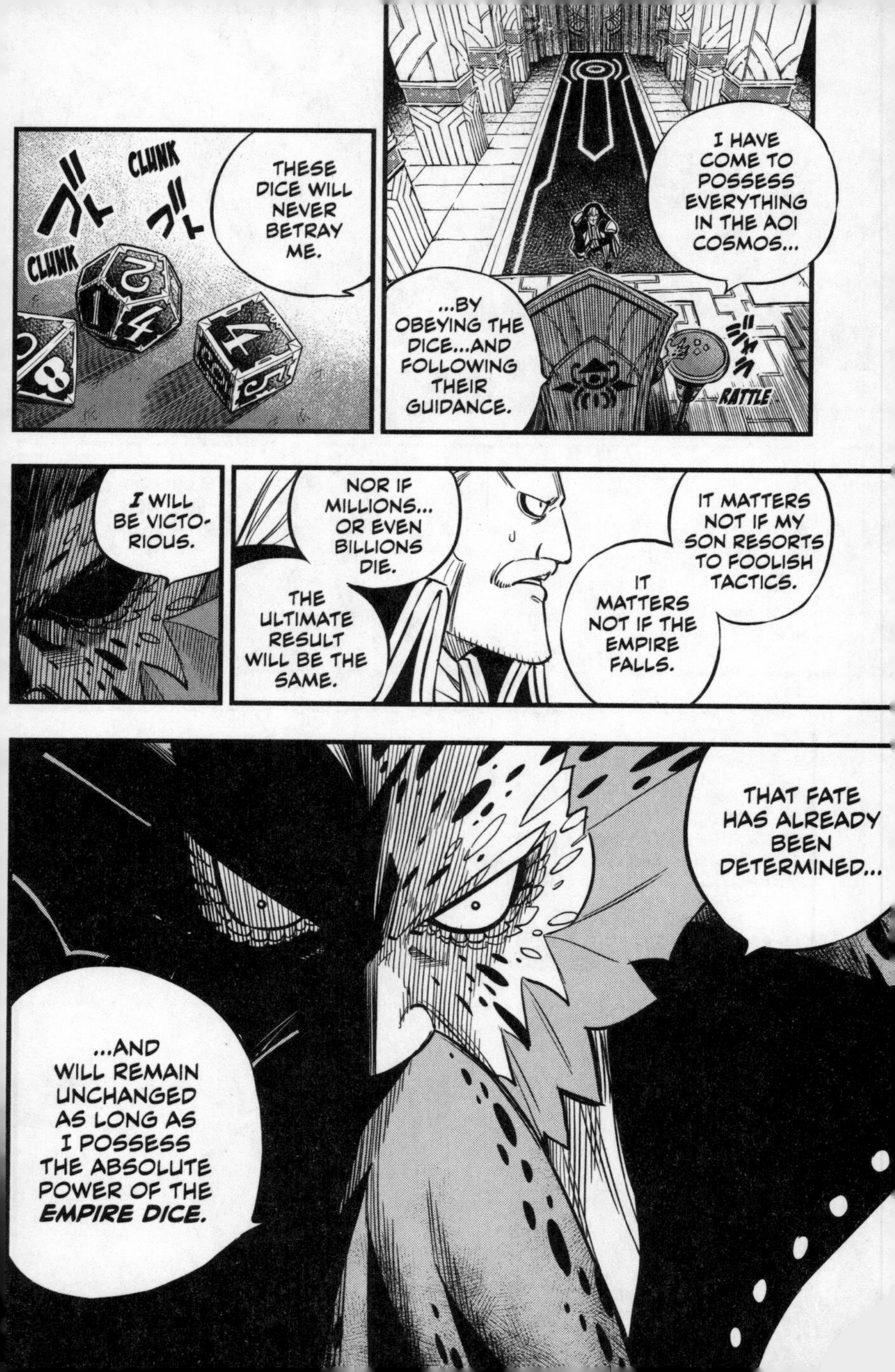
I HAVE COME TO POSSESS EVERYTHING IN THE AOI COSMOS...
...BY OBEYING THE DICE...AND FOLLOWING THEIR GUIDANCE.
RATTLE
CLUNK
CLUNK
THESE DICE WILL NEVER BETRAY ME.
IT MATTERS NOT IF MY SON RESORTS TO FOOLISH TACTICS.
IT MATTERS NOT IF THE EMPIRE FALLS.
NOR IF MILLIONS... OR EVEN BILLIONS DIE.
THE ULTIMATE RESULT WILL BE THE SAME.
I WILL BE VICTORIOUS.
THAT FATE HAS ALREADY BEEN DETERMINED...
...AND WILL REMAIN UNCHANGED AS LONG AS I POSSESS THE ABSOLUTE POWER OF THE *EMPIRE DICE.*

CHAPTER 138: PRELUDE TO THE AOI WAR

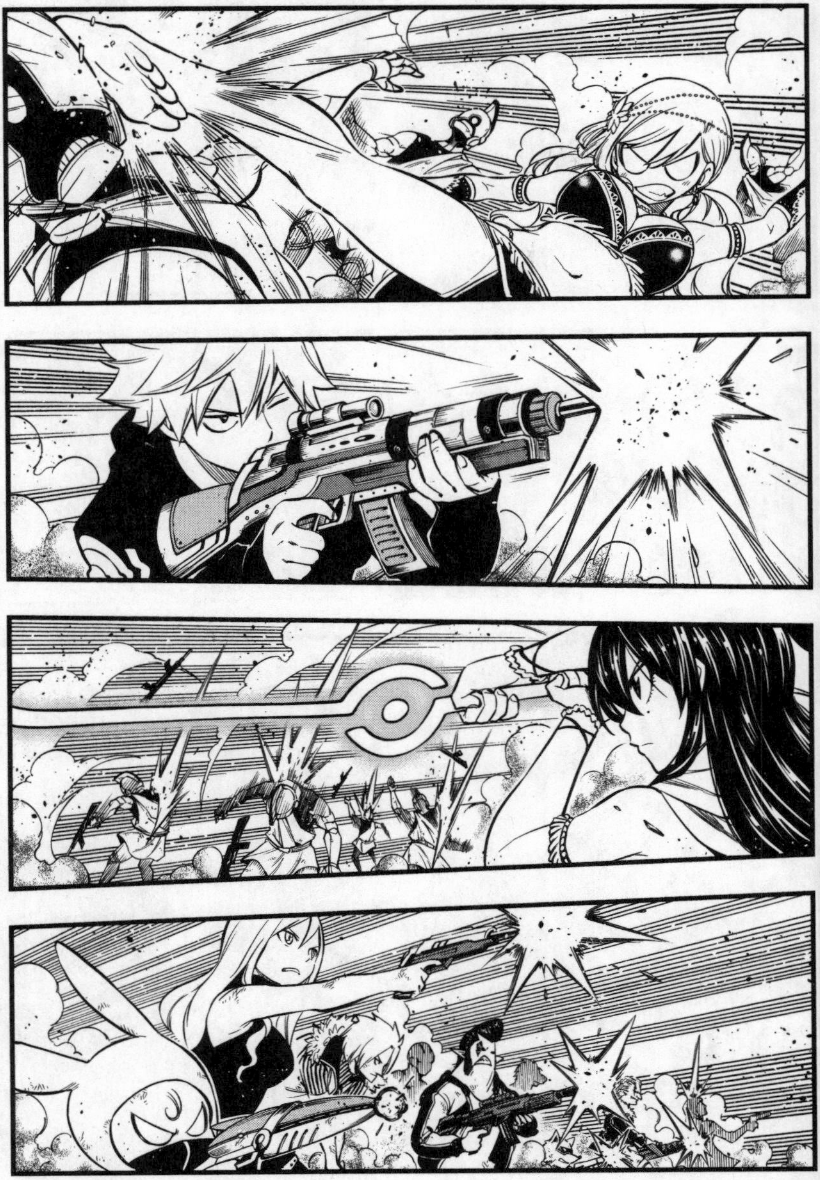

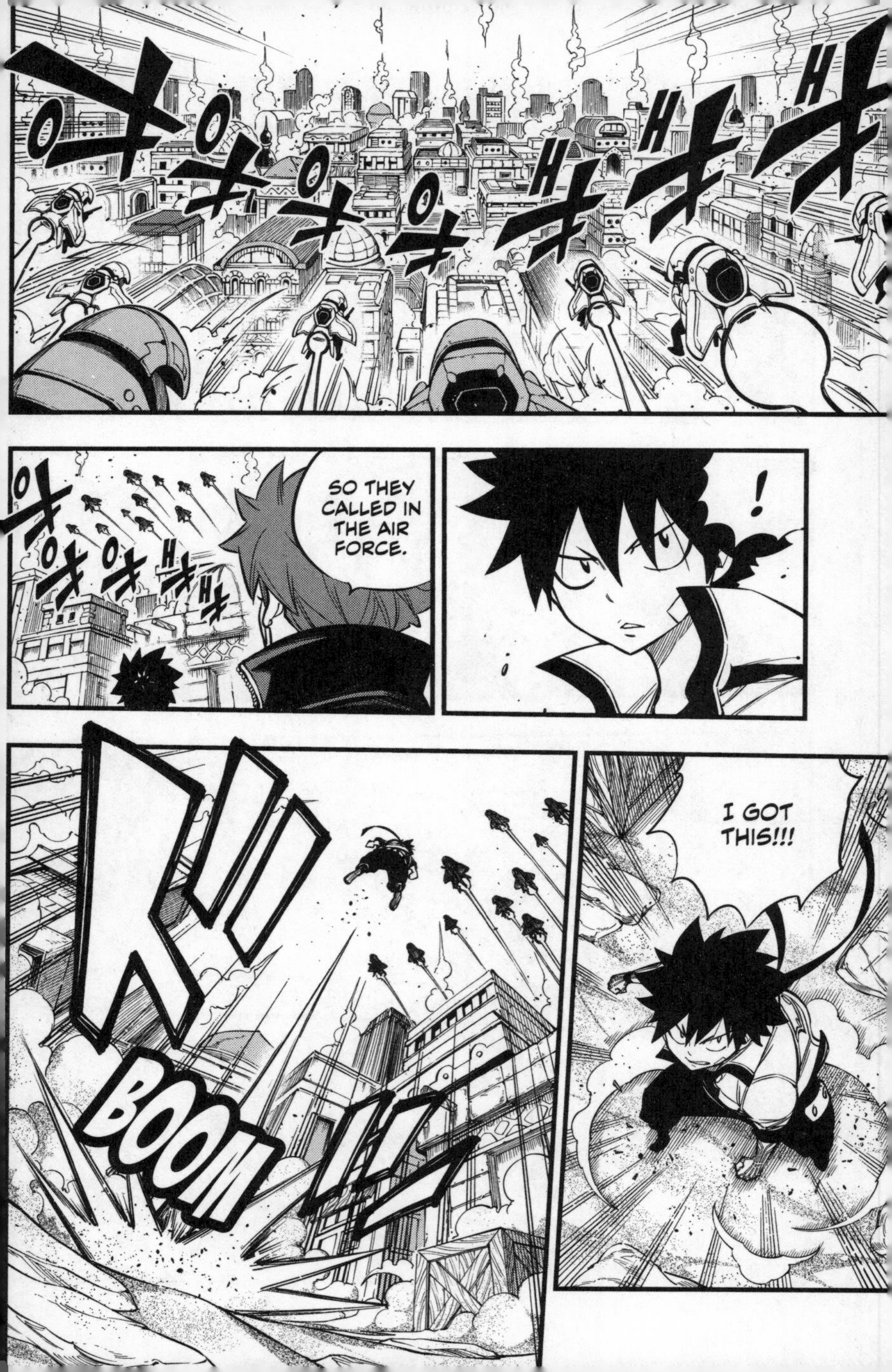
!
SO THEY CALLED IN THE AIR FORCE.
I GOT THIS!!!
BOOM

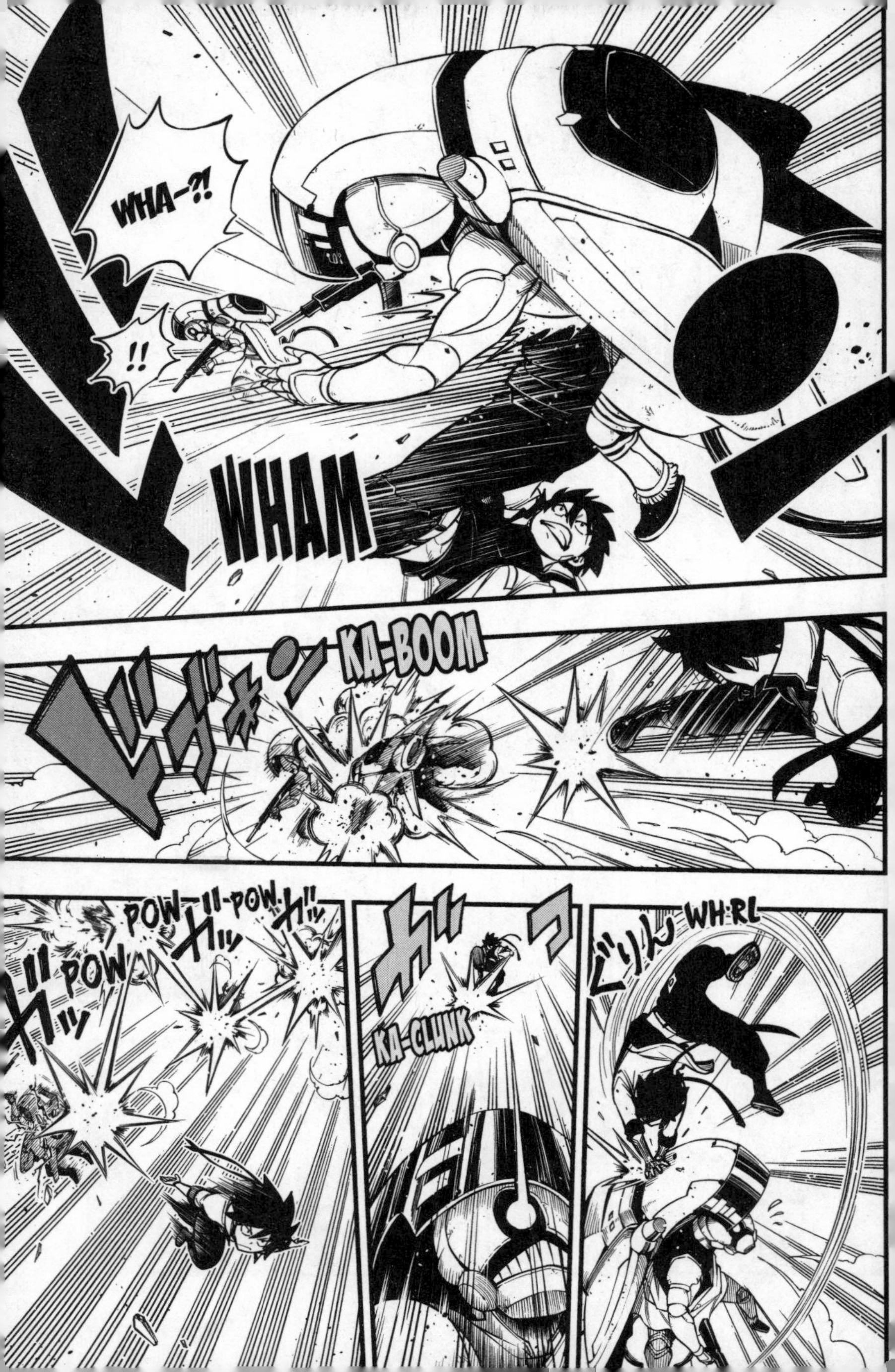
WHA-?!
!!
WHAM
KA-BOOM
WHIRL
KA-CLUNK
POW
POW
POW

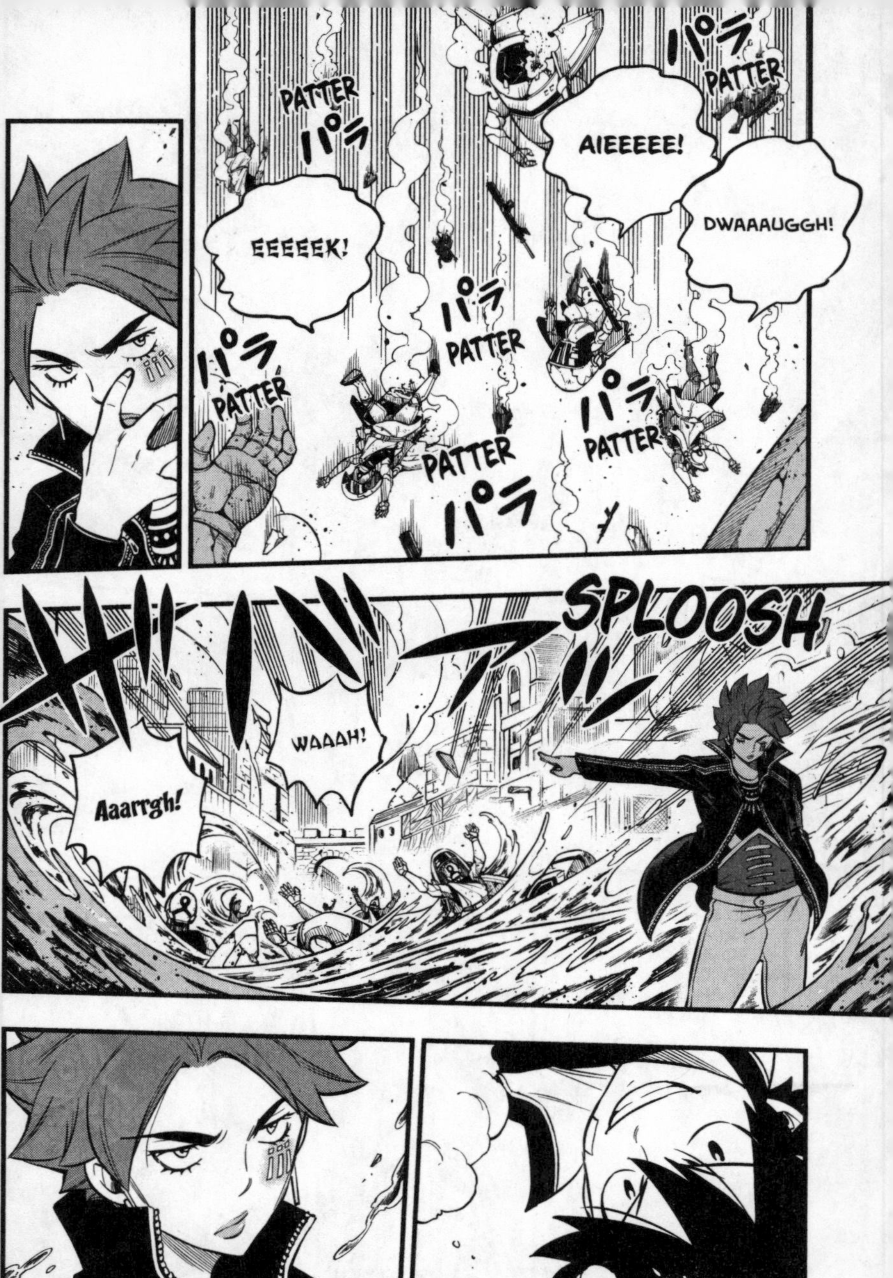
パラ
PATTER
AIEEEEE!
DWAAAUGGH!
PATTER
パラ
EEEEEK!
パラ
PATTER
パラ
PATTER
パラ
PATTER
PATTER
パラ
SPLOOSH
WAAAH!
Aaarrgh!

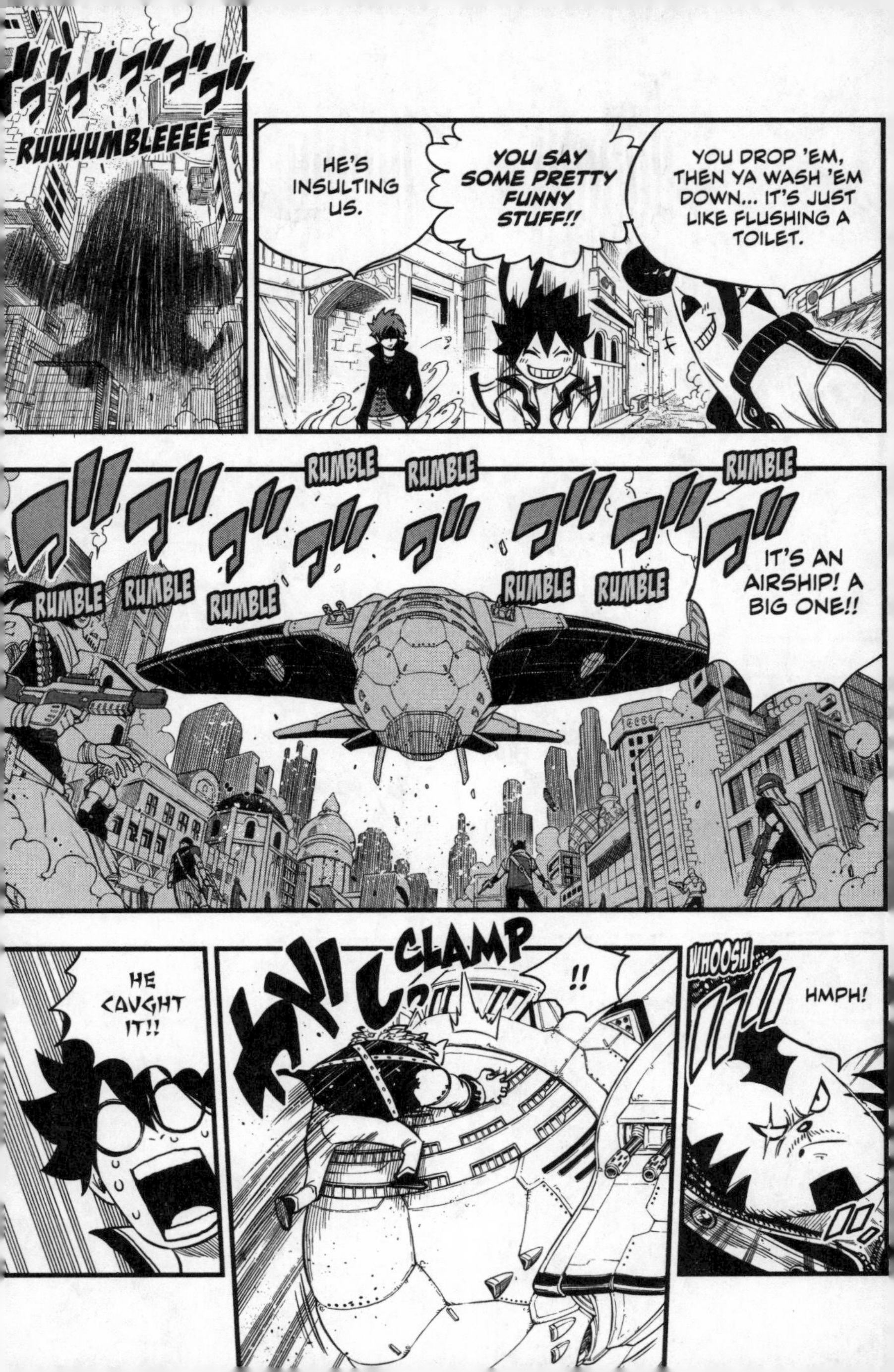
YOU DROP 'EM, THEN YA WASH 'EM DOWN... IT'S JUST LIKE FLUSHING A TOILET.
YOU SAY SOME PRETTY FUNNY STUFF!!
HE'S INSULTING US.
RUUUUMBLEEEE
RUMBLE
IT'S AN AIRSHIP! A BIG ONE!!
RUMBLE
RUMBLE
RUMBLE
RUMBLE
RUMBLE
RUMBLE
RUMBLE
RUMBLE
WHOOSH
HMPH!
!!
CLAMP
HE CAUGHT IT!!

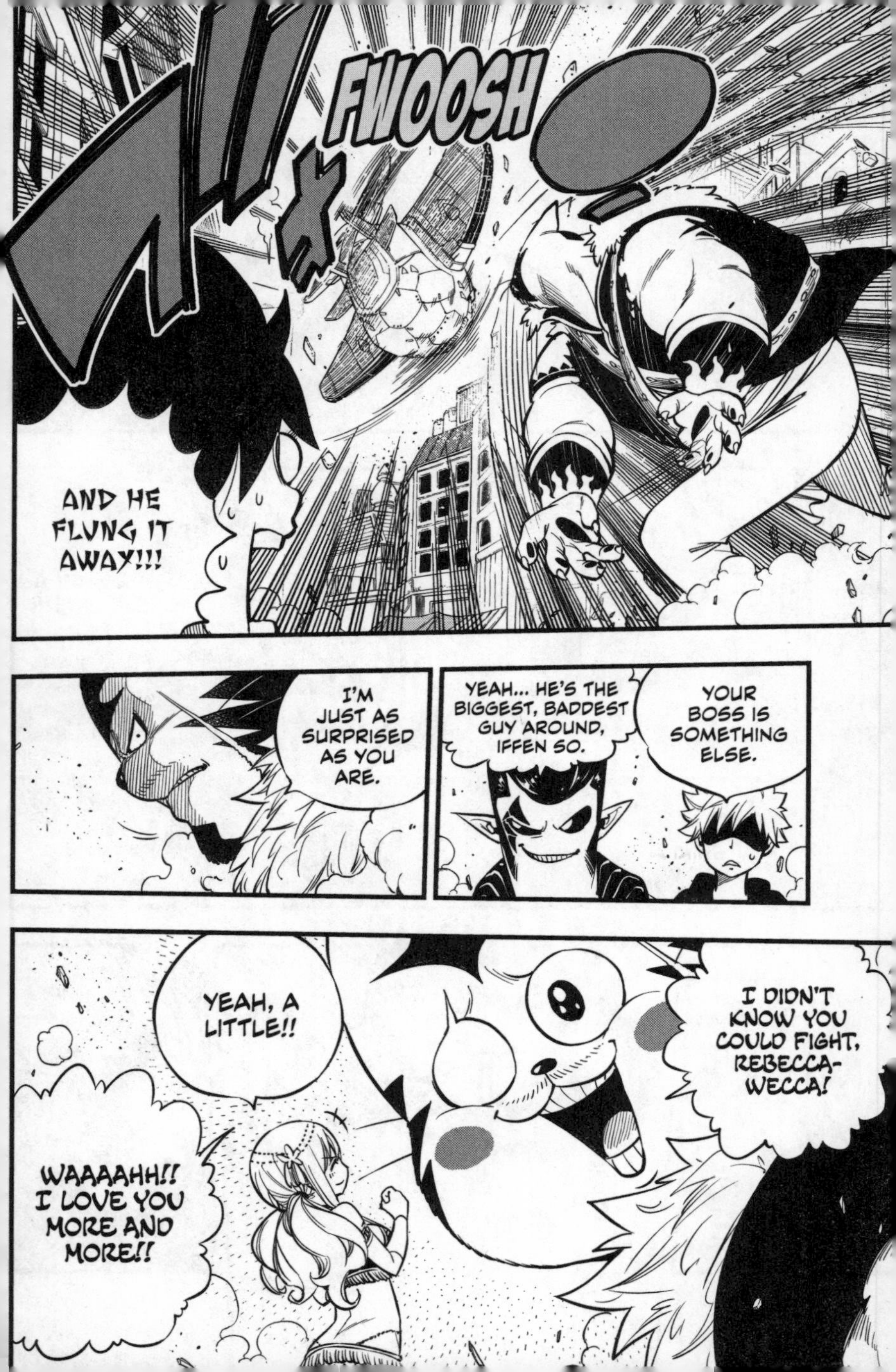
FWOOSH
AND HE FLUNG IT AWAY!!!
YOUR BOSS IS SOMETHING ELSE.
YEAH... HE'S THE BIGGEST, BADDEST GUY AROUND, IFFEN SO.
I'M JUST AS SURPRISED AS YOU ARE.
I DIDN'T KNOW YOU COULD FIGHT, REBECCA-WECCA!
YEAH, A LITTLE!!
WAAAAHH!! I LOVE YOU MORE AND MORE!!

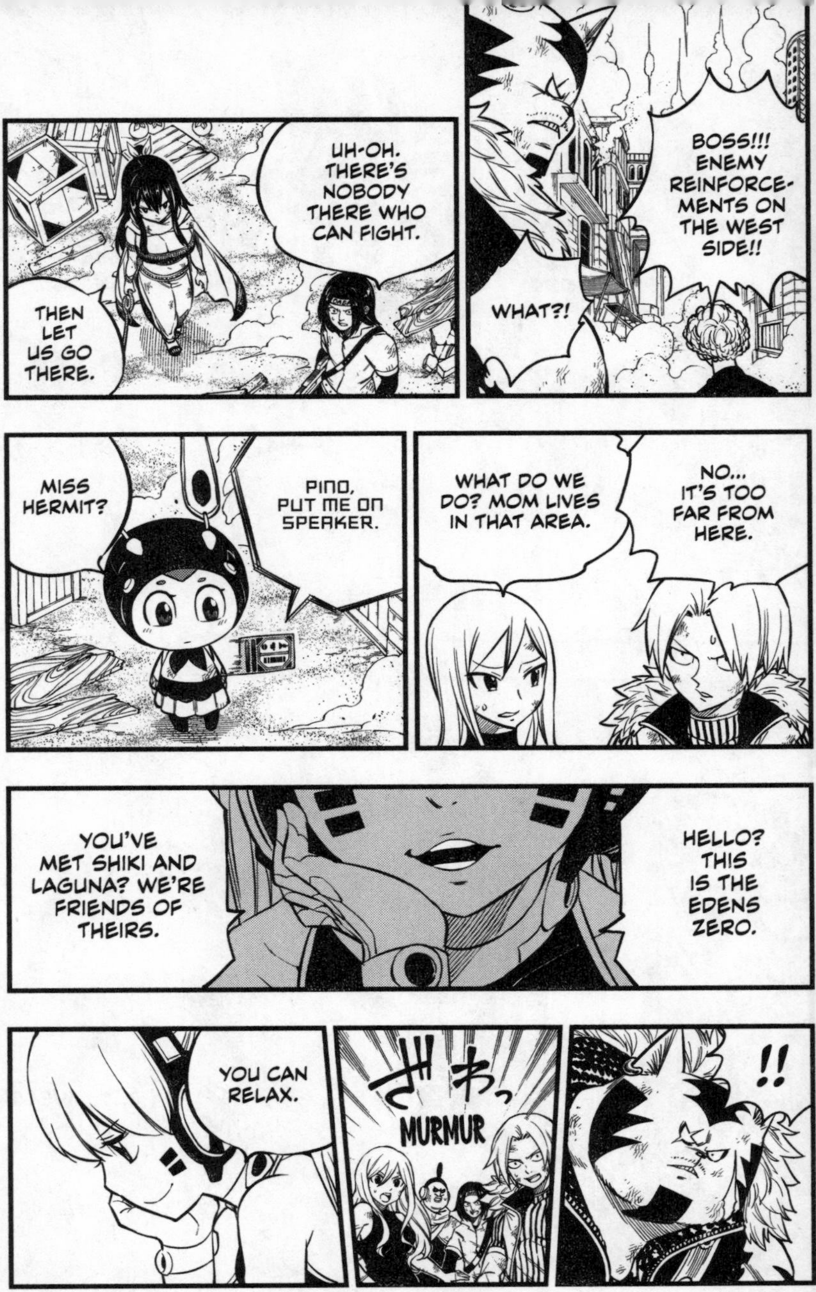
BOSS!!! ENEMY REINFORCEMENTS ON THE WEST SIDE!!
WHAT?!
UH-OH. THERE'S NOBODY THERE WHO CAN FIGHT.
THEN LET US GO THERE.
WHAT DO WE DO? MOM LIVES IN THAT AREA.
NO... IT'S TOO FAR FROM HERE.
PINO, PUT ME ON SPEAKER.
MISS HERMIT?
HELLO? THIS IS THE EDENS ZERO.
YOU'VE MET SHIKI AND LAGUNA? WE'RE FRIENDS OF THEIRS.
!!
ざわっ
MURMUR
YOU CAN RELAX.

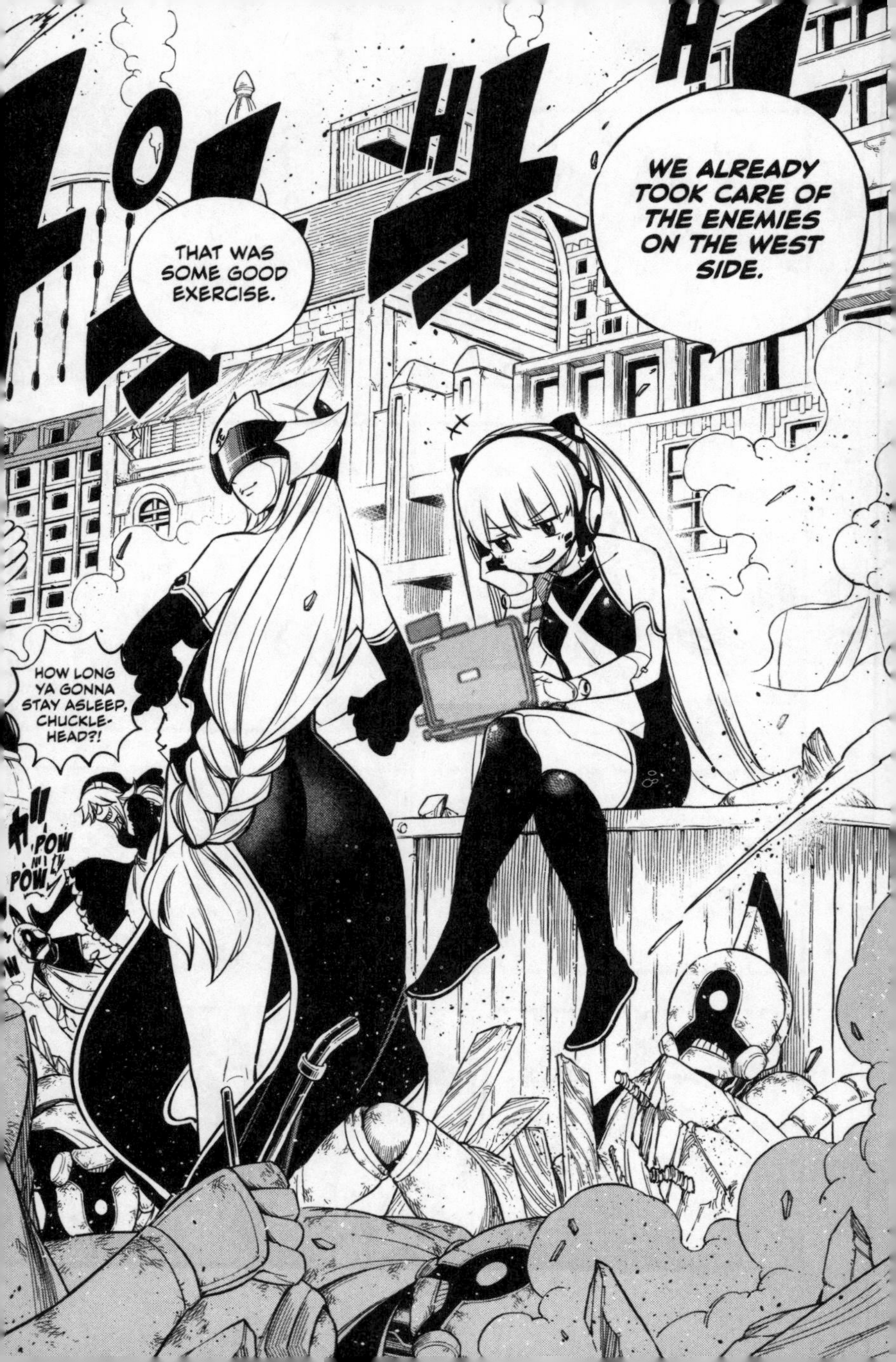
WE ALREADY TOOK CARE OF THE ENEMIES ON THE WEST SIDE.
THAT WAS SOME GOOD EXERCISE.
HOW LONG YA GONNA STAY ASLEEP, CHUCKLE-HEAD?!
POW
POW

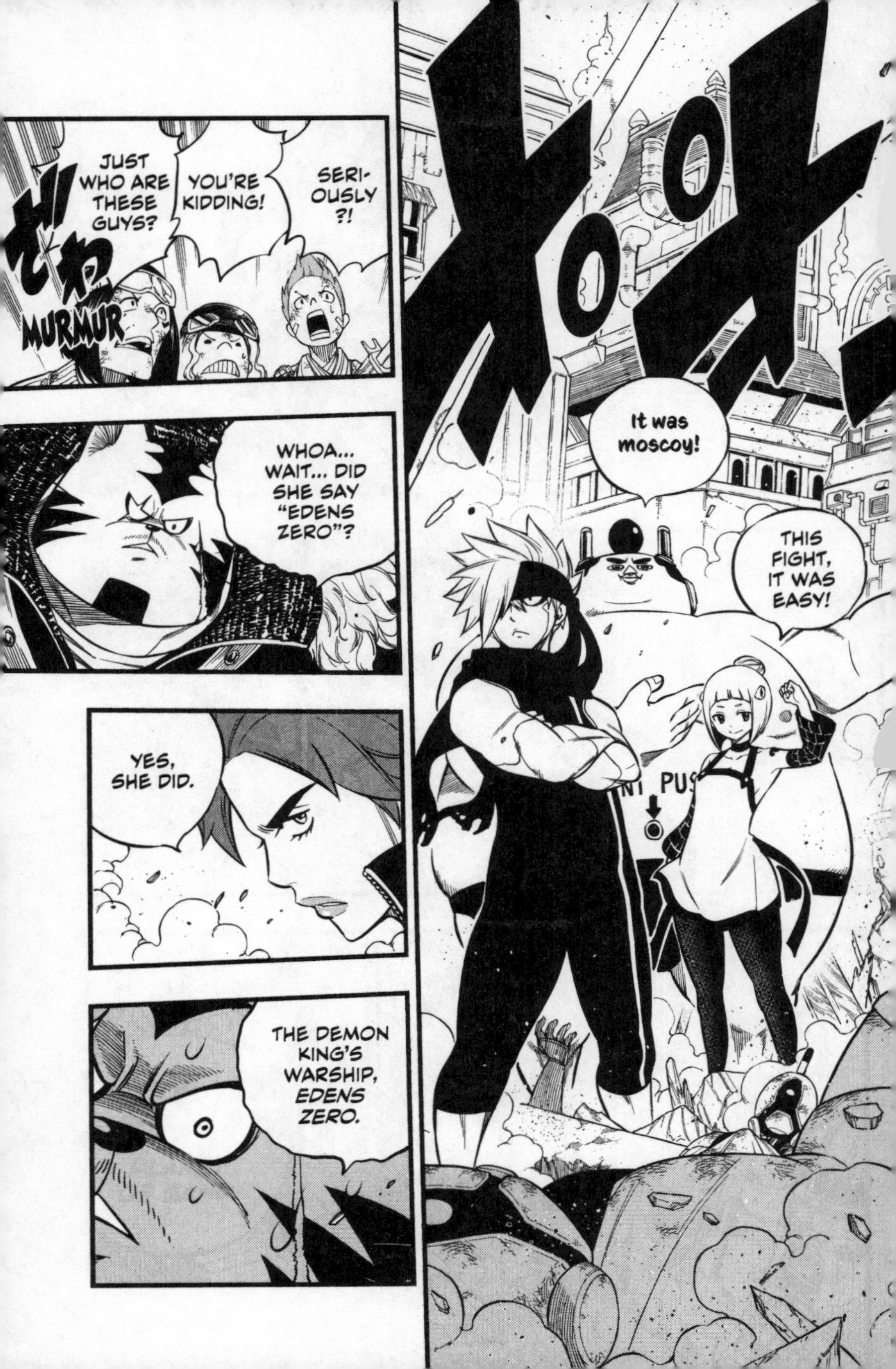
It was moscoy!
THIS FIGHT, IT WAS EASY!
PUS
SERI-OUSLY?!
YOU'RE KIDDING!
JUST WHO ARE THESE GUYS?
MURMUR
WHOA... WAIT... DID SHE SAY "EDENS ZERO"?
YES, SHE DID.
THE DEMON KING'S WARSHIP, EDENS ZERO.

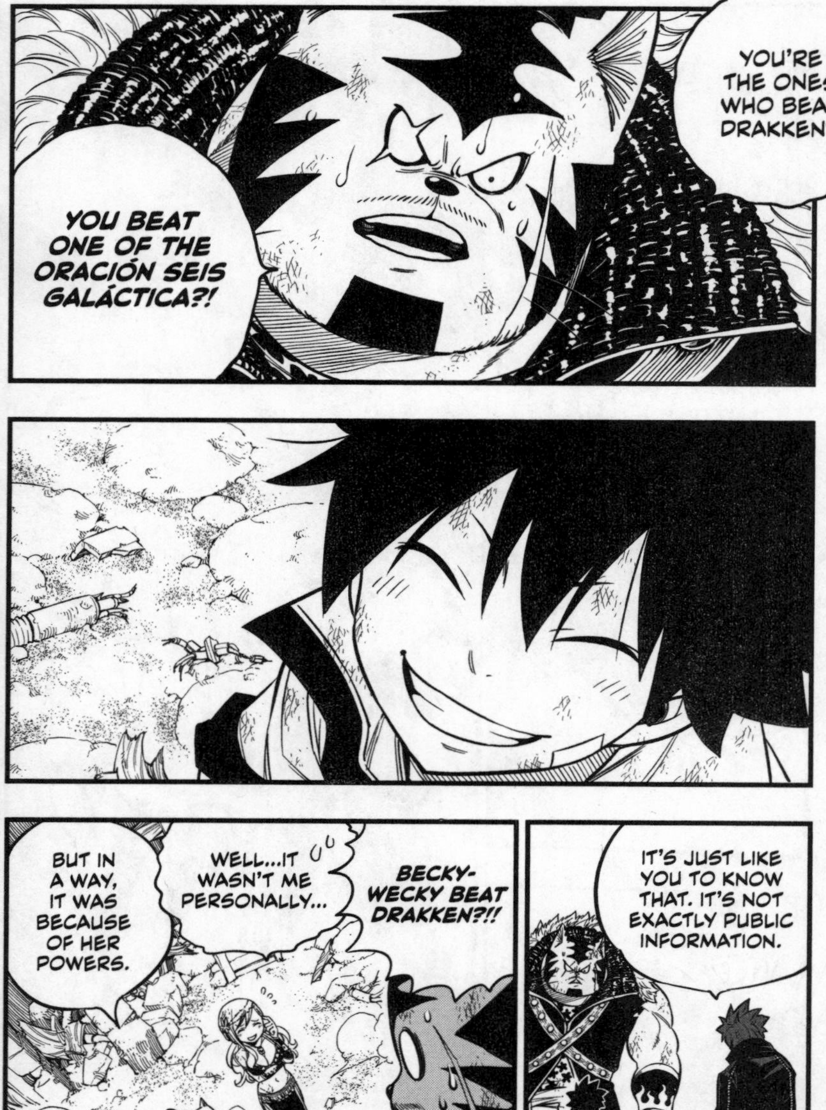
YOU'RE THE ONES WHO BEAT DRAKKEN?
YOU BEAT ONE OF THE ORACIÓN SEIS GALÁCTICA?!
IT'S JUST LIKE YOU TO KNOW THAT. IT'S NOT EXACTLY PUBLIC INFORMATION.
BECKY-WECKY BEAT DRAKKEN?!!
WELL...IT WASN'T ME PERSONALLY...
BUT IN A WAY, IT WAS BECAUSE OF HER POWERS.

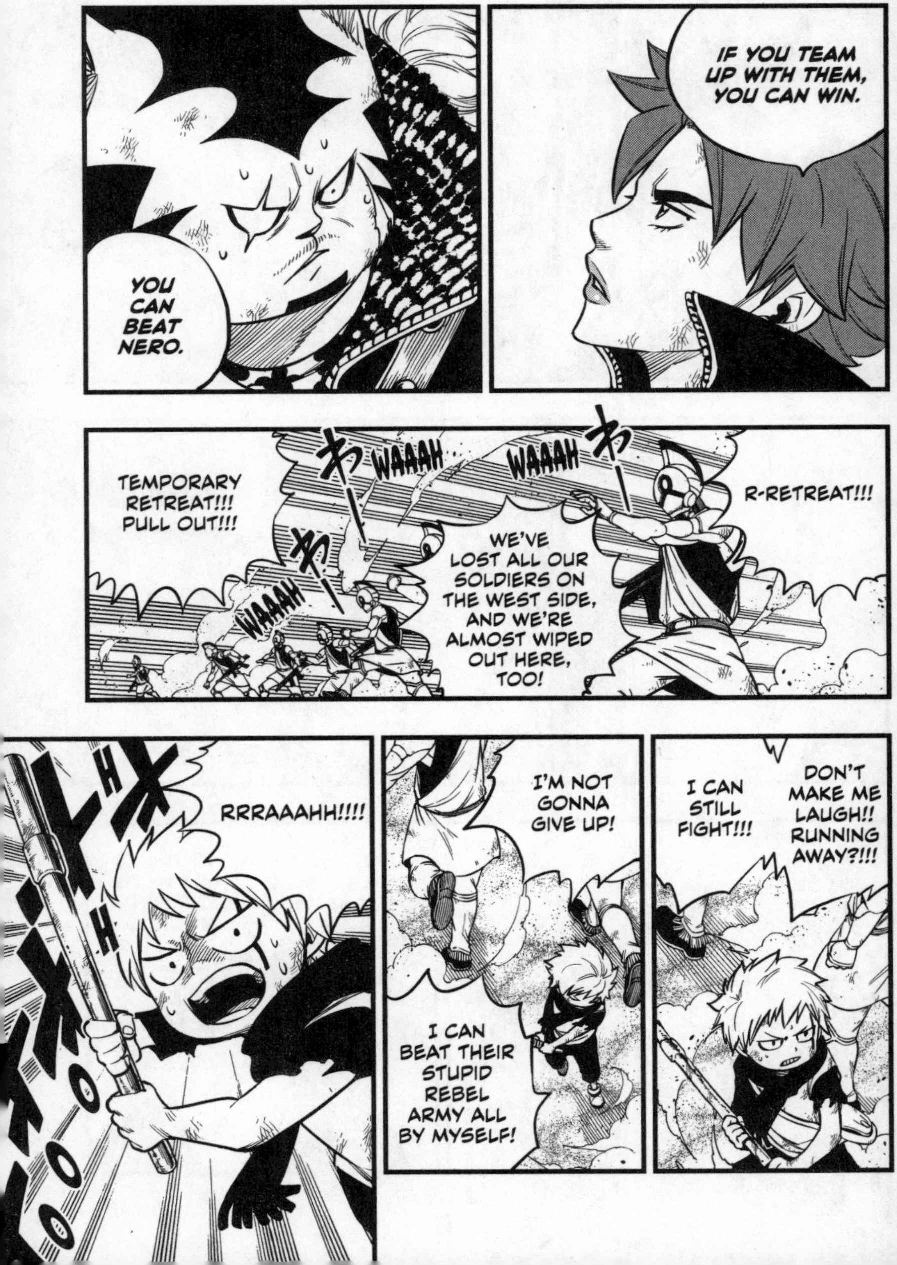

IF YOU TEAM UP WITH THEM, YOU CAN WIN.
YOU CAN BEAT NERO.
R-RETREAT!!!
WAAAH
WAAAH
WE'VE LOST ALL OUR SOLDIERS ON THE WEST SIDE, AND WE'RE ALMOST WIPED OUT HERE, TOO!
TEMPORARY RETREAT!!! PULL OUT!!!
WAAAH
DON'T MAKE ME LAUGH!! RUNNING AWAY?!!!
I CAN STILL FIGHT!!!
I'M NOT GONNA GIVE UP!
I CAN BEAT THEIR STUPID REBEL ARMY ALL BY MYSELF!
RRRAAAHH!!!!

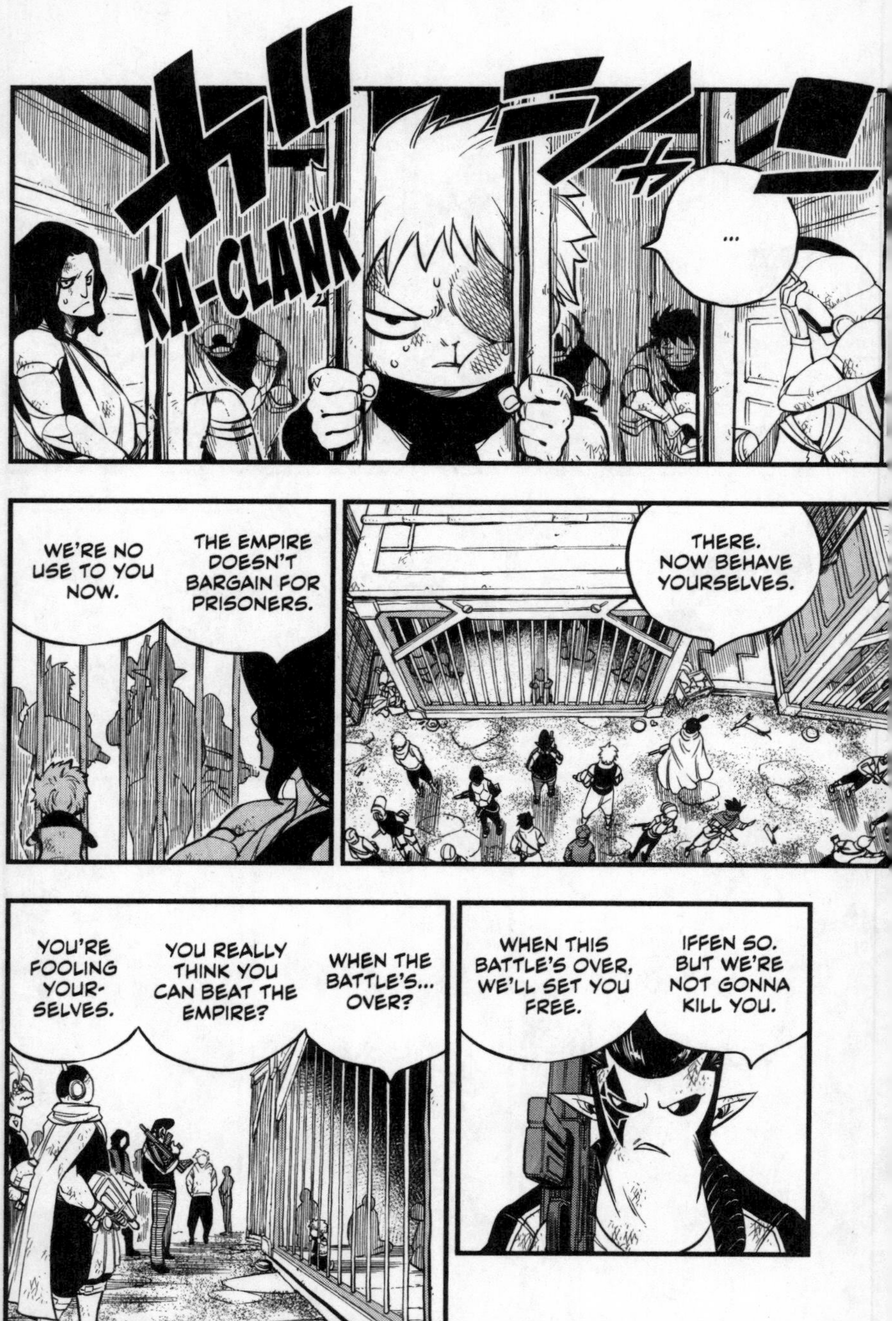
...
KA-CLANK
THERE. NOW BEHAVE YOURSELVES.
THE EMPIRE DOESN'T BARGAIN FOR PRISONERS.
WE'RE NO USE TO YOU NOW.
IFFEN SO. BUT WE'RE NOT GONNA KILL YOU.
WHEN THIS BATTLE'S OVER, WE'LL SET YOU FREE.
WHEN THE BATTLE'S... OVER?
YOU REALLY THINK YOU CAN BEAT THE EMPIRE?
YOU'RE FOOLING YOUR-SELVES.

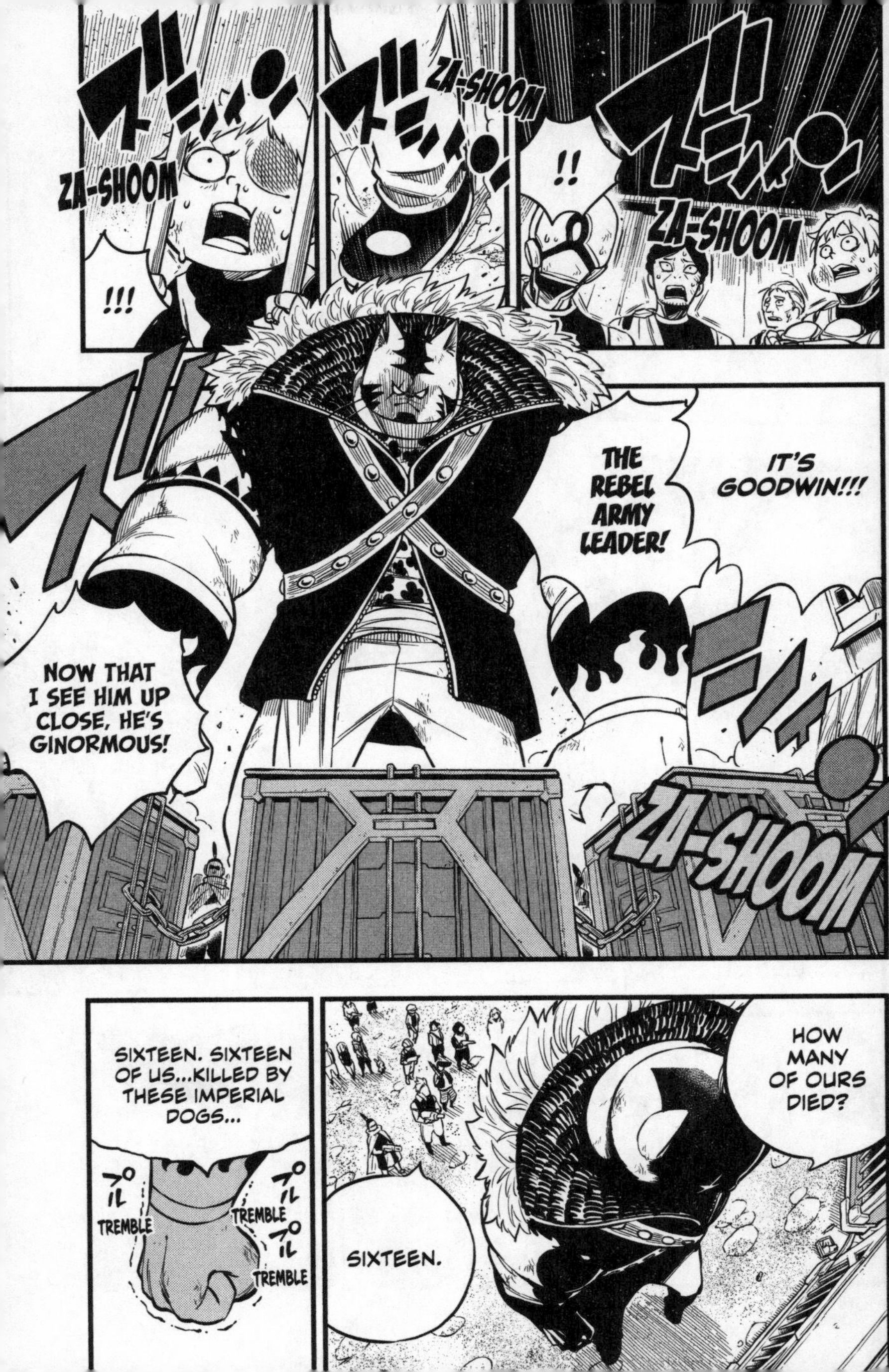

ZA-SHOOM
!!
ZA-SHOOM
ZA-SHOOM
!!!
IT'S GOODWIN!!!
THE REBEL ARMY LEADER!
NOW THAT I SEE HIM UP CLOSE, HE'S GINORMOUS!
ZA-SHOOM
HOW MANY OF OURS DIED?
SIXTEEN.
SIXTEEN. SIXTEEN OF US...KILLED BY THESE IMPERIAL DOGS...
TREMBLE
TREMBLE
TREMBLE

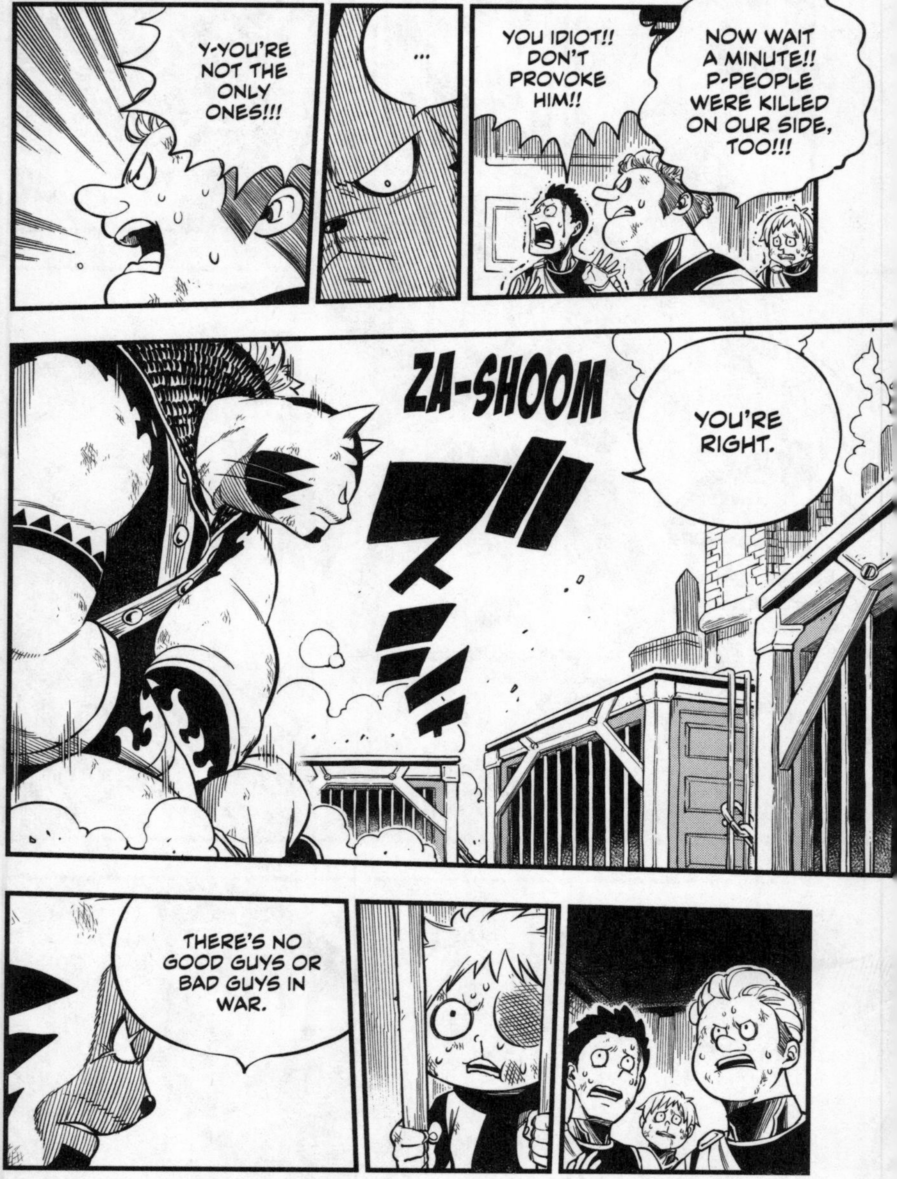
NOW WAIT A MINUTE!! P-PEOPLE WERE KILLED ON OUR SIDE, TOO!!!
YOU IDIOT!! DON'T PROVOKE HIM!!
...
Y-YOU'RE NOT THE ONLY ONES!!!
YOU'RE RIGHT.
ZA-SHOOM
THERE'S NO GOOD GUYS OR BAD GUYS IN WAR.

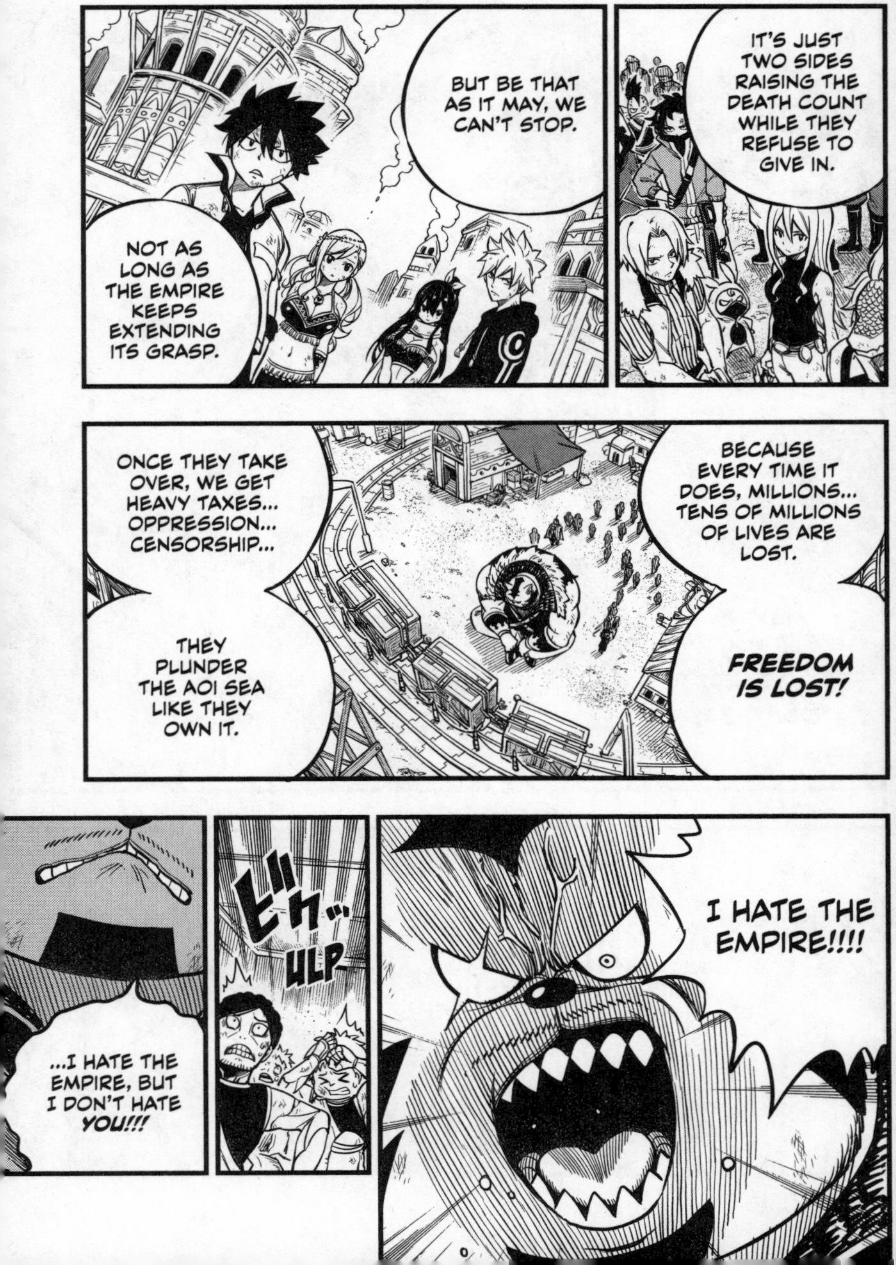
IT'S JUST TWO SIDES RAISING THE DEATH COUNT WHILE THEY REFUSE TO GIVE IN.
BUT BE THAT AS IT MAY, WE CAN'T STOP.
NOT AS LONG AS THE EMPIRE KEEPS EXTENDING ITS GRASP.
BECAUSE EVERY TIME IT DOES, MILLIONS... TENS OF MILLIONS OF LIVES ARE LOST.
FREEDOM IS LOST!
ONCE THEY TAKE OVER, WE GET HEAVY TAXES... OPPRESSION... CENSORSHIP...
THEY PLUNDER THE AOI SEA LIKE THEY OWN IT.
I HATE THE EMPIRE!!!!
ULP
...I HATE THE EMPIRE, BUT I DON'T HATE YOU!!!

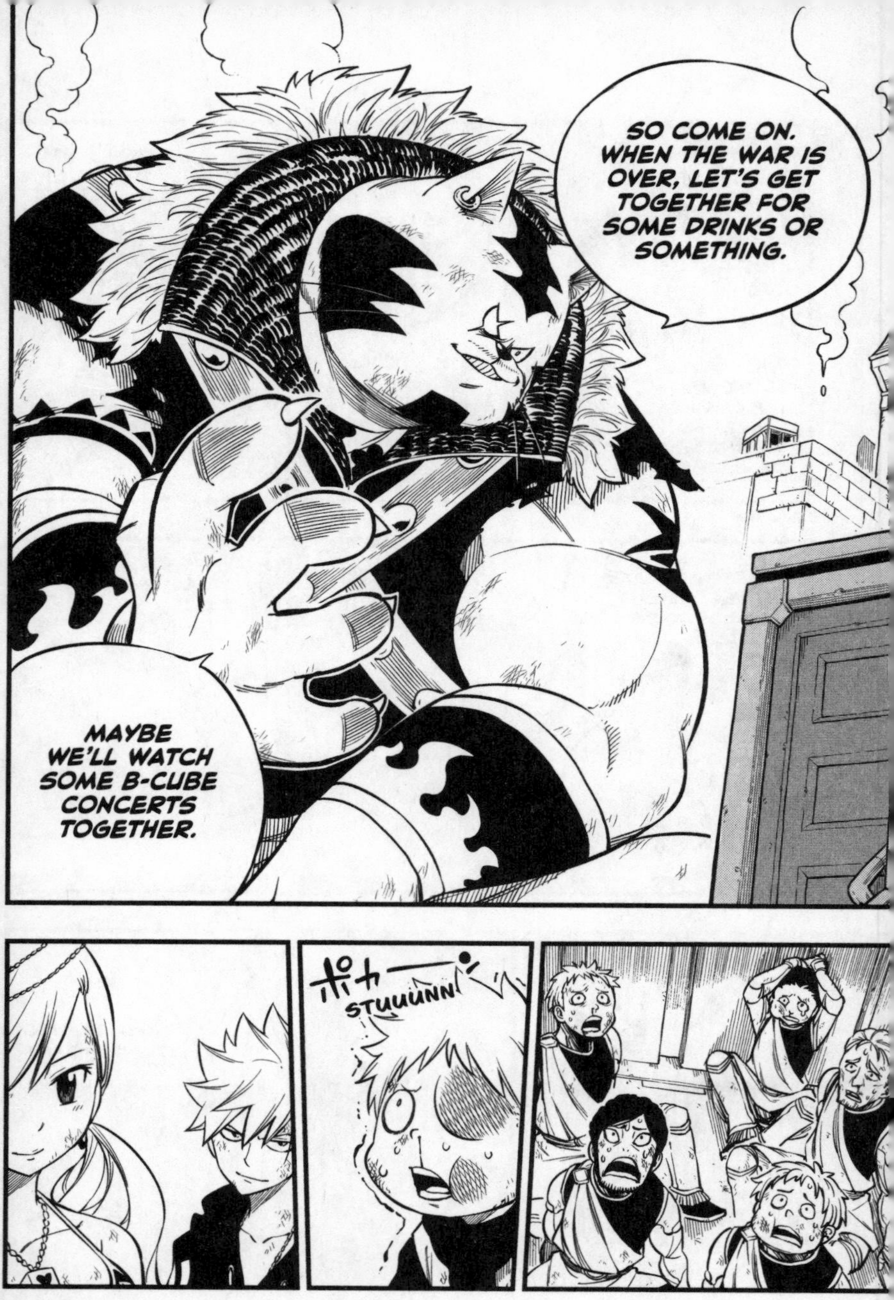
SO COME ON. WHEN THE WAR IS OVER, LET'S GET TOGETHER FOR SOME DRINKS OR SOMETHING.
MAYBE WE'LL WATCH SOME B-CUBE CONCERTS TOGETHER.
ポカーン
STUUUNN

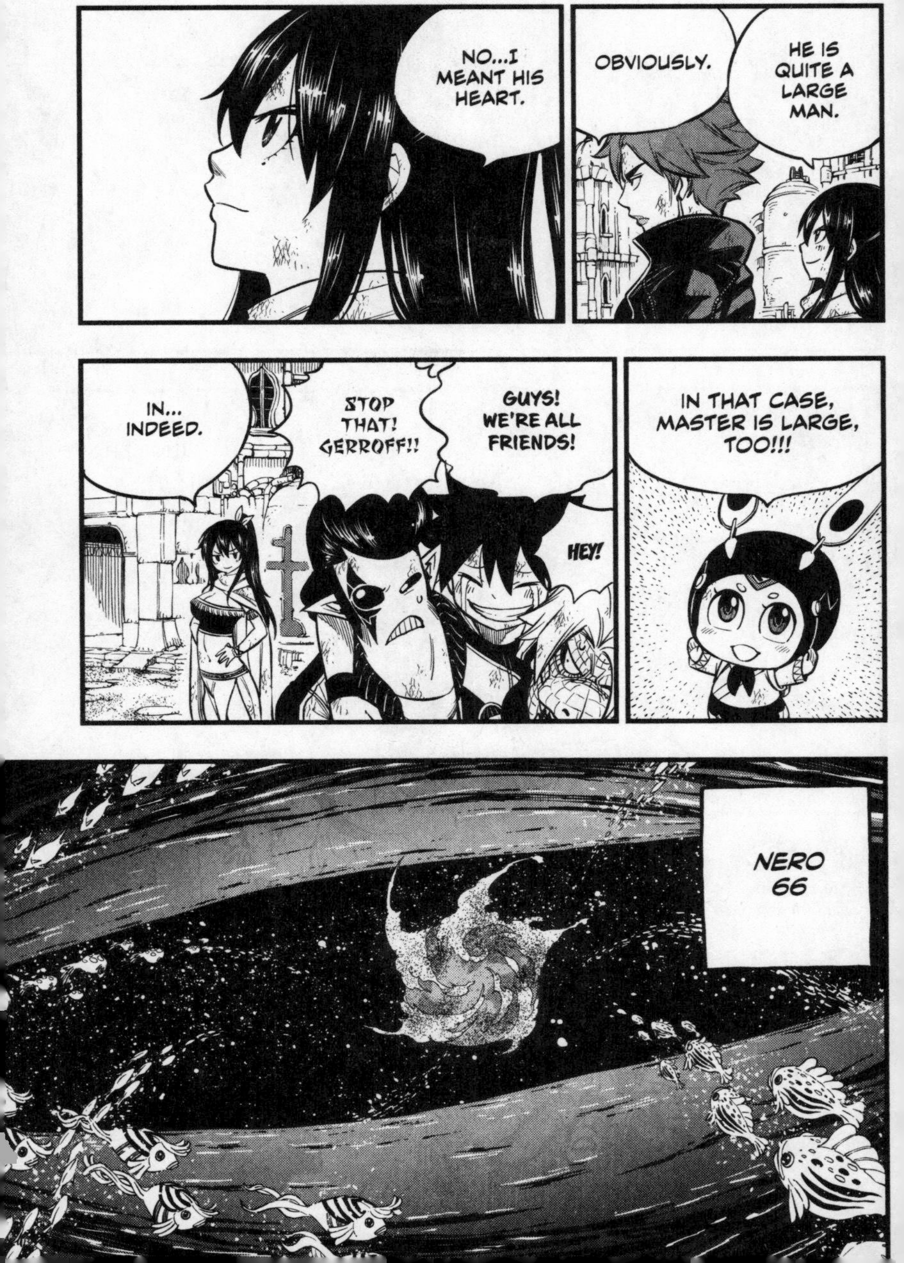
HE IS QUITE A LARGE MAN.
OBVIOUSLY.
NO...I MEANT HIS HEART.
IN THAT CASE, MASTER IS LARGE, TOO!!!
GUYS! WE'RE ALL FRIENDS!
HEY!
STOP THAT! GERROFF!!
IN... INDEED.
NERO 66

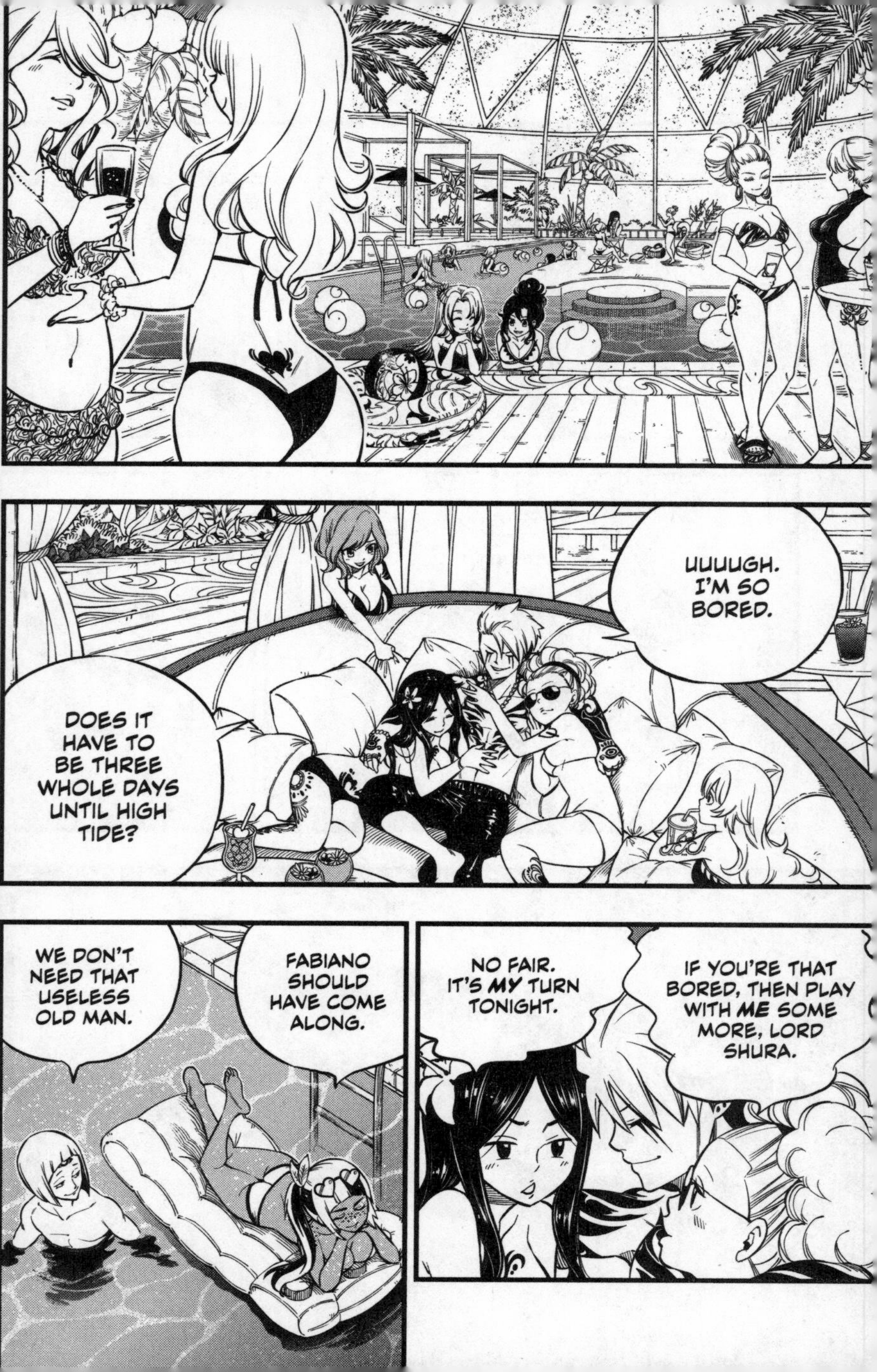
UUUUGH. I'M SO BORED.
DOES IT HAVE TO BE THREE WHOLE DAYS UNTIL HIGH TIDE?
IF YOU'RE THAT BORED, THEN PLAY WITH **ME** SOME MORE, LORD SHURA.
NO FAIR. IT'S **MY** TURN TONIGHT.
FABIANO SHOULD HAVE COME ALONG.
WE DON'T NEED THAT USELESS OLD MAN.

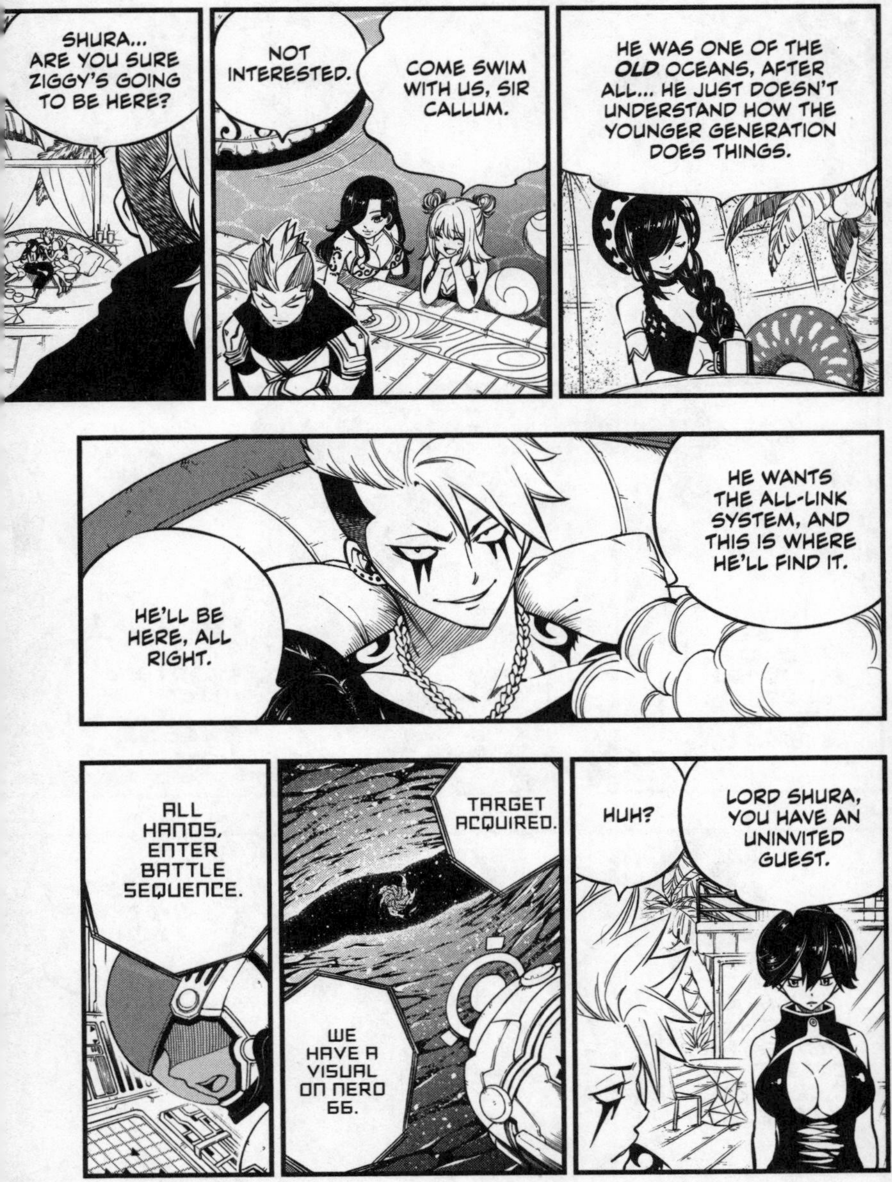
HE WAS ONE OF THE *OLD* OCEANS, AFTER ALL... HE JUST DOESN'T UNDERSTAND HOW THE YOUNGER GENERATION DOES THINGS.
COME SWIM WITH US, SIR CALLUM.
NOT INTERESTED.
SHURA... ARE YOU SURE ZIGGY'S GOING TO BE HERE?
HE WANTS THE ALL-LINK SYSTEM, AND THIS IS WHERE HE'LL FIND IT.
HE'LL BE HERE, ALL RIGHT.
LORD SHURA, YOU HAVE AN UNINVITED GUEST.
HUH?
TARGET ACQUIRED.
WE HAVE A VISUAL ON NERO 66.
ALL HANDS, ENTER BATTLE SEQUENCE.

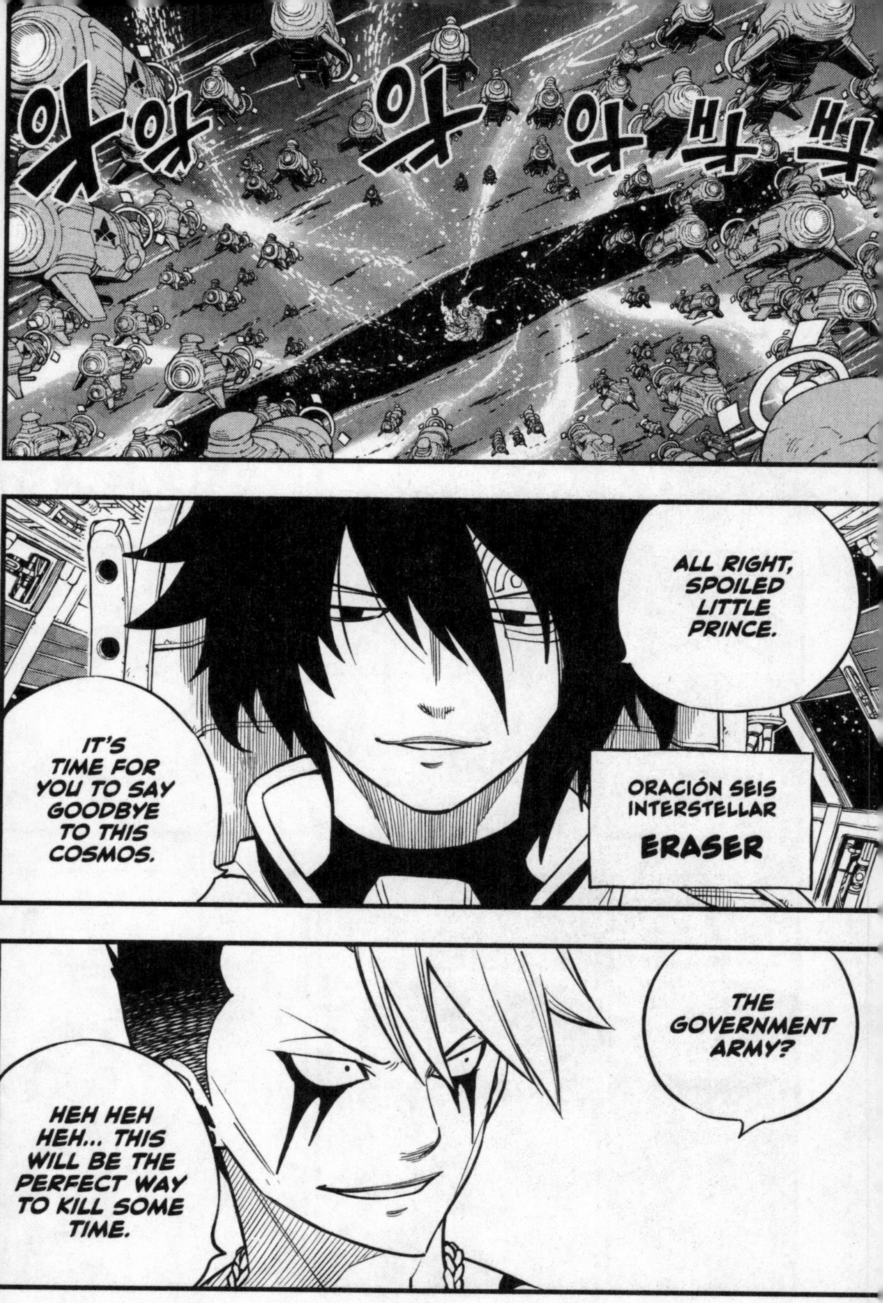
ALL RIGHT, SPOILED LITTLE PRINCE.
ORACIÓN SEIS INTERSTELLAR
ERASER
IT'S TIME FOR YOU TO SAY GOODBYE TO THIS COSMOS.
THE GOVERNMENT ARMY?
HEH HEH HEH... THIS WILL BE THE PERFECT WAY TO KILL SOME TIME.

EDENS ZERO

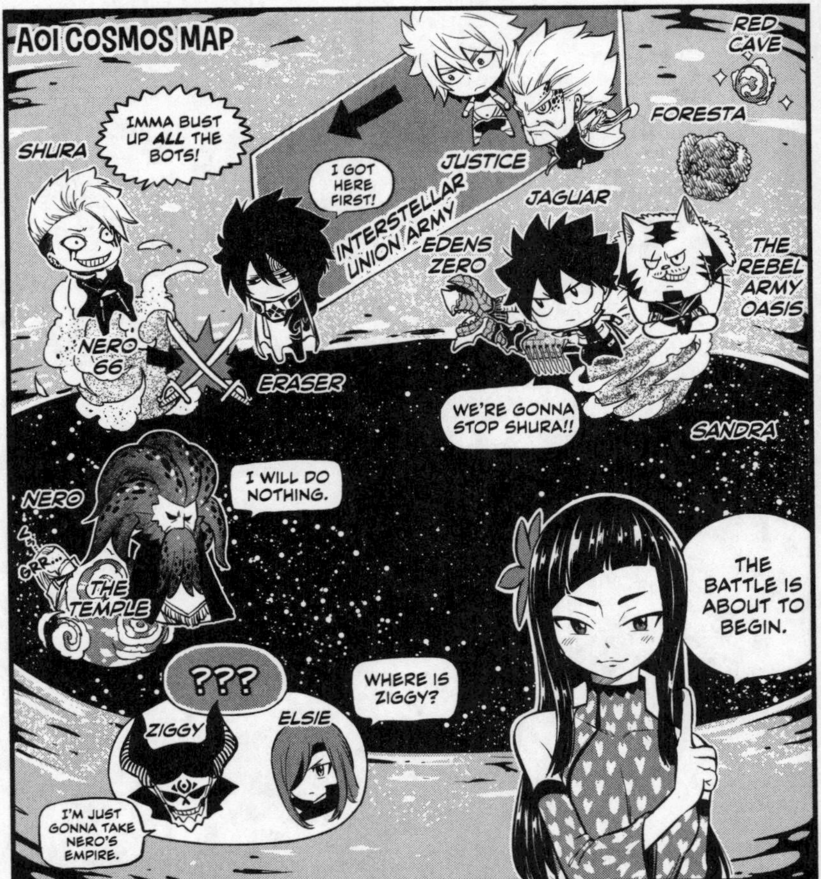
AOI COSMOS MAP
RED CAVE
FORESTA
JUSTICE
INTERSTELLAR UNION ARMY
I GOT HERE FIRST!
IMMA BUST UP ALL THE BOTS!
SHURA
THE REBEL ARMY OASIS
JAGUAR
EDENS ZERO
NERO 66
ERASER
WE'RE GONNA STOP SHURA!!
SANDRA
THE BATTLE IS ABOUT TO BEGIN.
I WILL DO NOTHING.
NERO
GRR...
THE TEMPLE
WHERE IS ZIGGY?
ELSIE
???
ZIGGY
I'M JUST GONNA TAKE NERO'S EMPIRE.

CHAPTER 139: WHITE FLASH

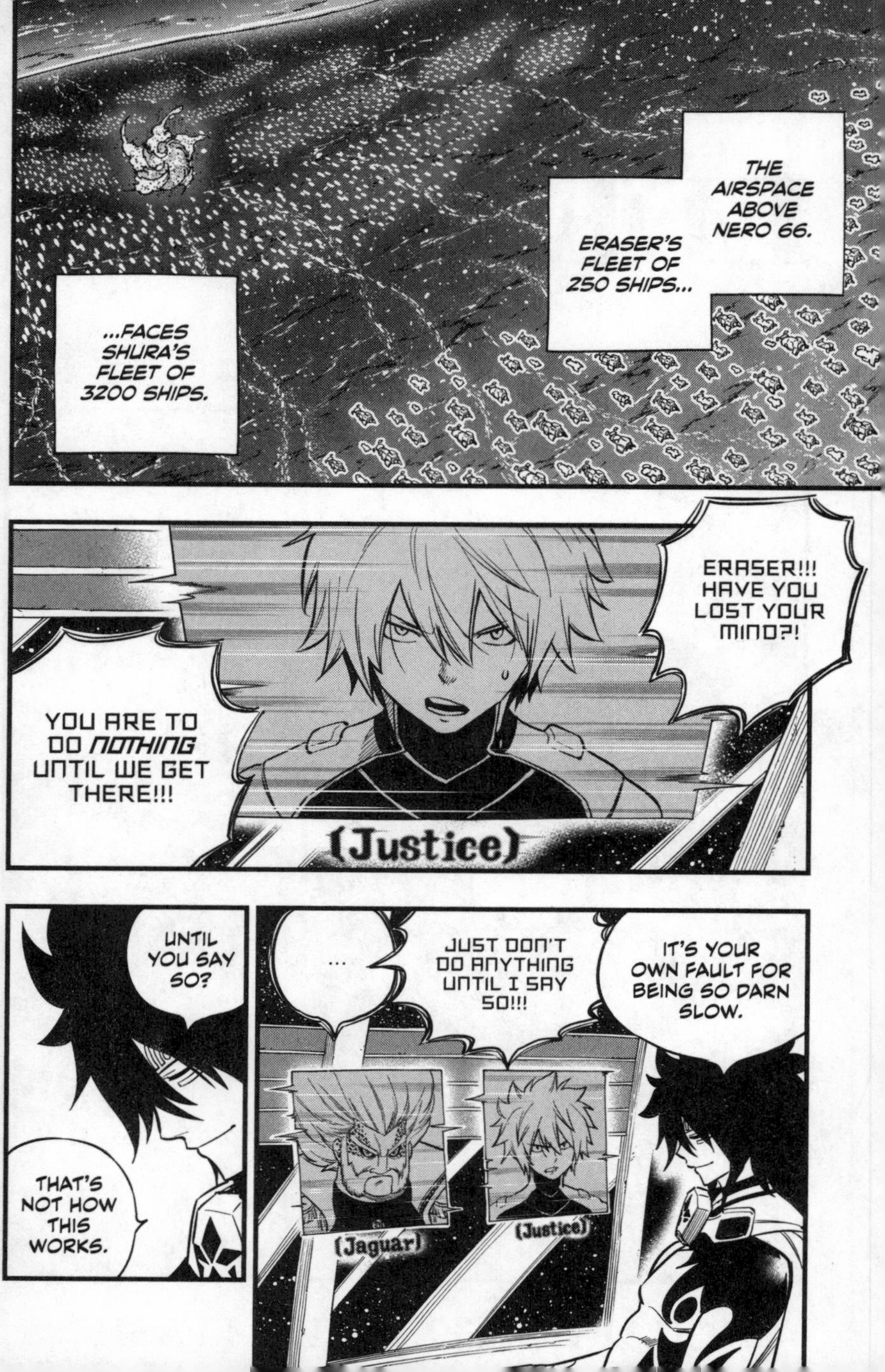
THE AIRSPACE ABOVE NERO 66.
ERASER'S FLEET OF 250 SHIPS...
...FACES SHURA'S FLEET OF 3200 SHIPS.
ERASER!!! HAVE YOU LOST YOUR MIND?!
YOU ARE TO DO *NOTHING* UNTIL WE GET THERE!!!
(Justice)
IT'S YOUR OWN FAULT FOR BEING SO DARN SLOW.
JUST DON'T DO ANYTHING UNTIL I SAY SO!!!
...
(Justice)
(Jaguar)
UNTIL YOU SAY SO?
THAT'S NOT HOW THIS WORKS.

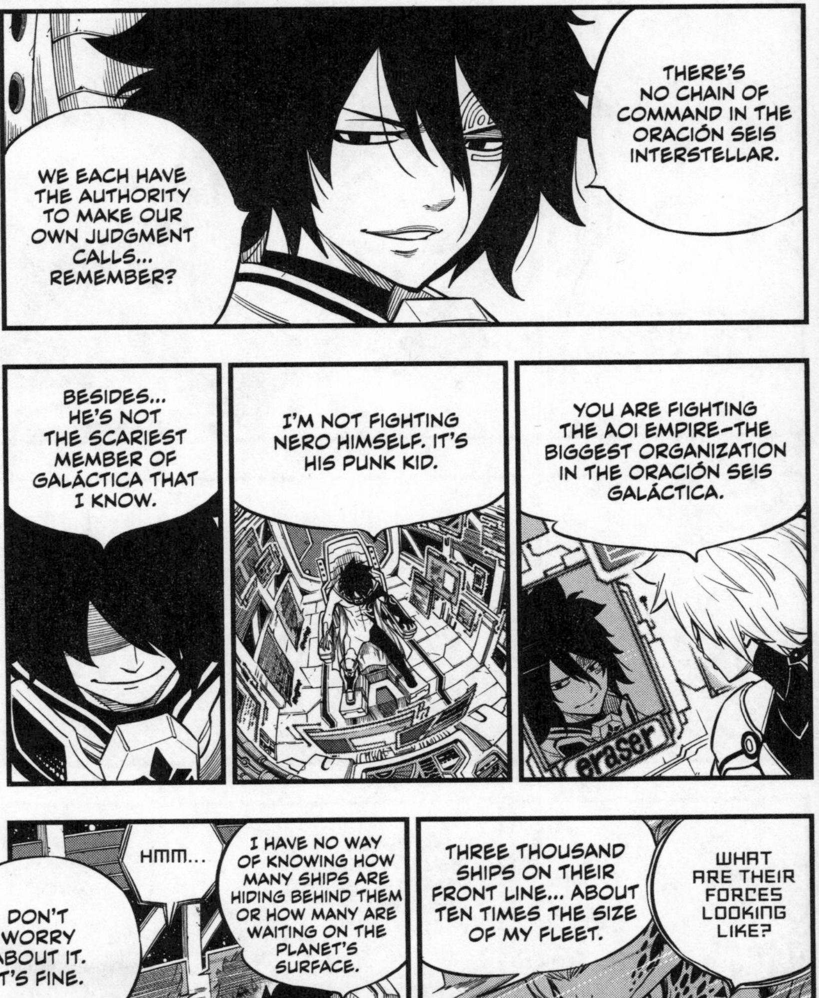
THERE'S NO CHAIN OF COMMAND IN THE ORACIÓN SEIS INTERSTELLAR.
WE EACH HAVE THE AUTHORITY TO MAKE OUR OWN JUDGMENT CALLS... REMEMBER?
YOU ARE FIGHTING THE AOI EMPIRE—THE BIGGEST ORGANIZATION IN THE ORACIÓN SEIS GALÁCTICA.
eraser
I'M NOT FIGHTING NERO HIMSELF. IT'S HIS PUNK KID.
BESIDES... HE'S NOT THE SCARIEST MEMBER OF GALÁCTICA THAT I KNOW.
WHAT ARE THEIR FORCES LOOKING LIKE?
THREE THOUSAND SHIPS ON THEIR FRONT LINE... ABOUT TEN TIMES THE SIZE OF MY FLEET.
I HAVE NO WAY OF KNOWING HOW MANY SHIPS ARE HIDING BEHIND THEM OR HOW MANY ARE WAITING ON THE PLANET'S SURFACE.
HMM...
DON'T WORRY ABOUT IT. IT'S FINE.

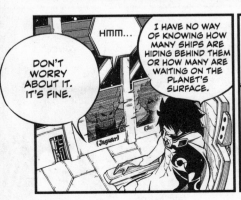

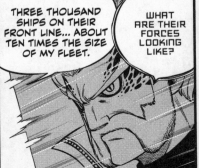

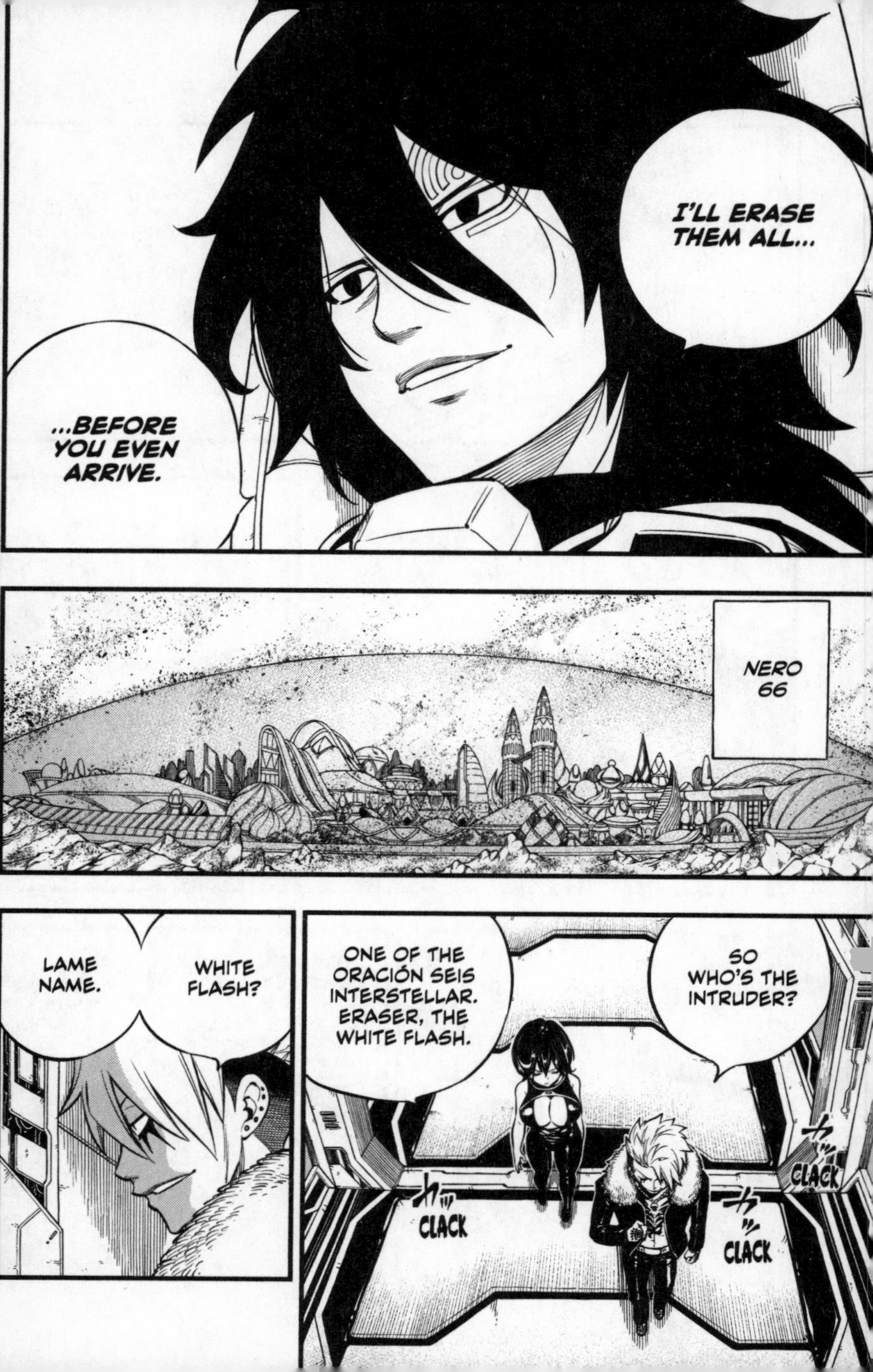
I'LL ERASE THEM ALL...
...BEFORE YOU EVEN ARRIVE.
NERO 66
SO WHO'S THE INTRUDER?
ONE OF THE ORACIÓN SEIS INTERSTELLAR. ERASER, THE WHITE FLASH.
CLACK
CLACK
CLACK
WHITE FLASH?
LAME NAME.

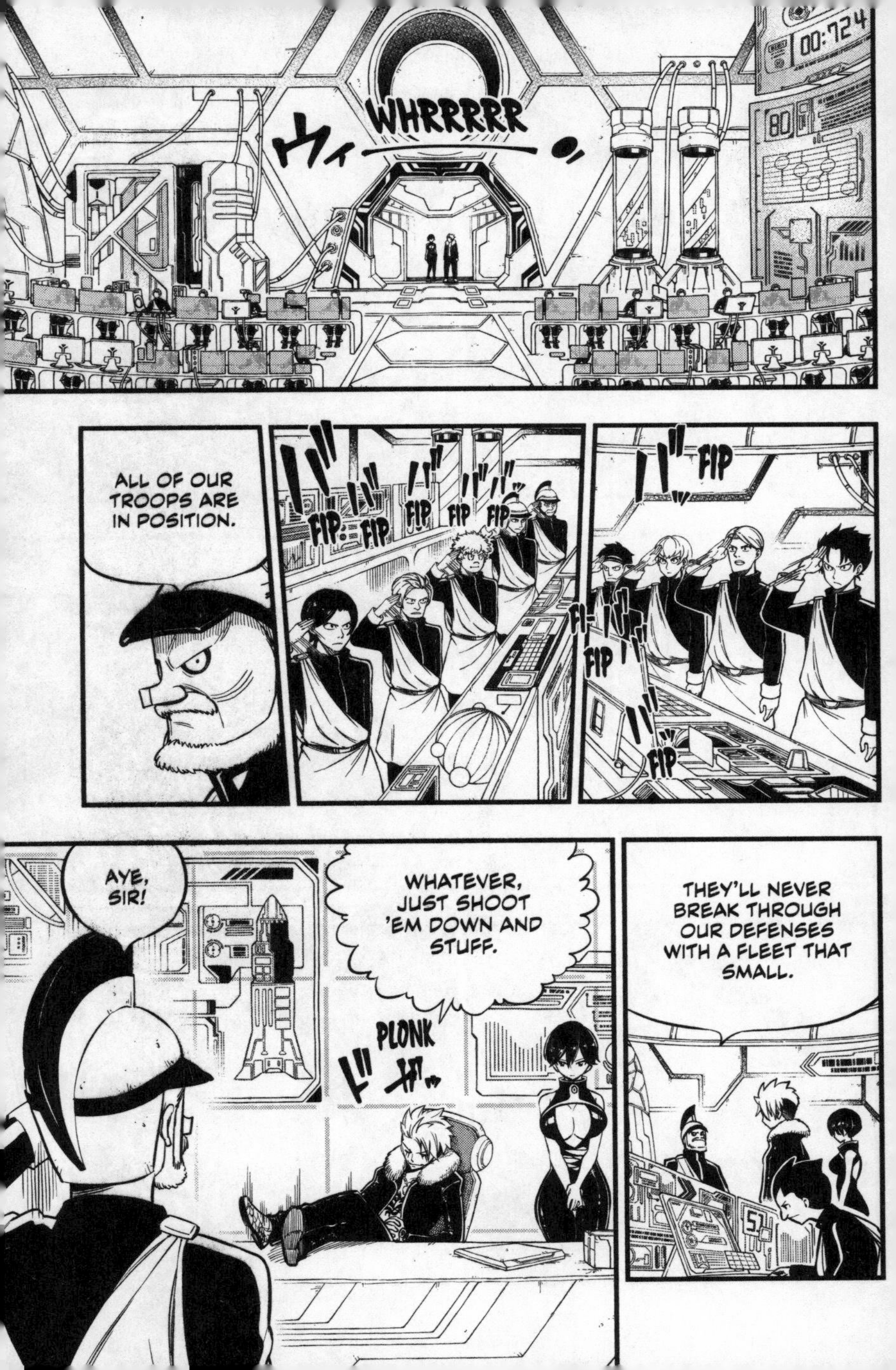

00:724
WHRRRRR
FIP
FI-
FIP
FIP
FIP
FIP
FIP
FIP
FIP
ALL OF OUR TROOPS ARE IN POSITION.
THEY'LL NEVER BREAK THROUGH OUR DEFENSES WITH A FLEET THAT SMALL.
WHATEVER, JUST SHOOT 'EM DOWN AND STUFF.
PLONK
AYE, SIR!

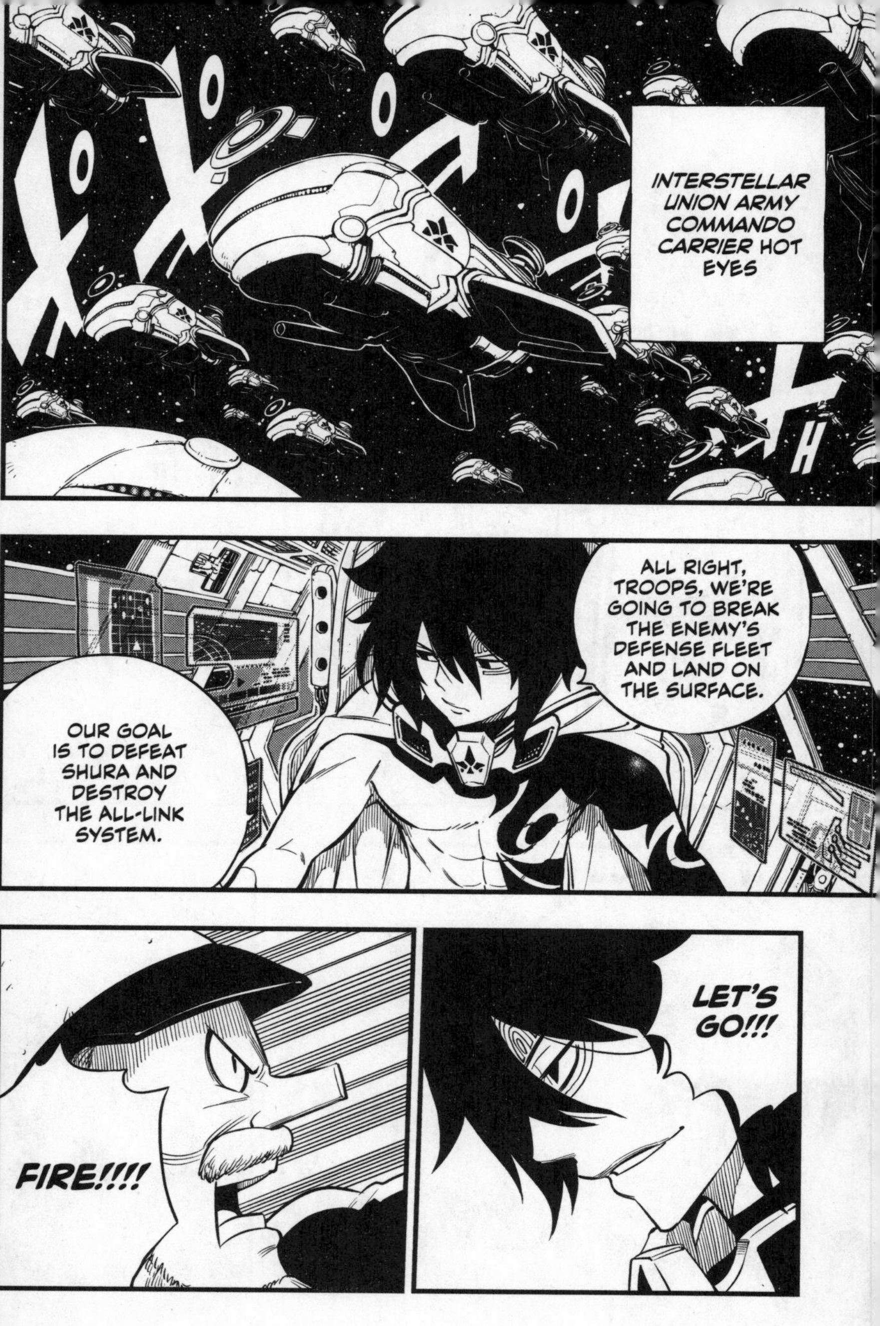
INTERSTELLAR UNION ARMY COMMANDO CARRIER HOT EYES
ALL RIGHT, TROOPS, WE'RE GOING TO BREAK THE ENEMY'S DEFENSE FLEET AND LAND ON THE SURFACE.
OUR GOAL IS TO DEFEAT SHURA AND DESTROY THE ALL-LINK SYSTEM.
LET'S GO!!!
FIRE!!!!

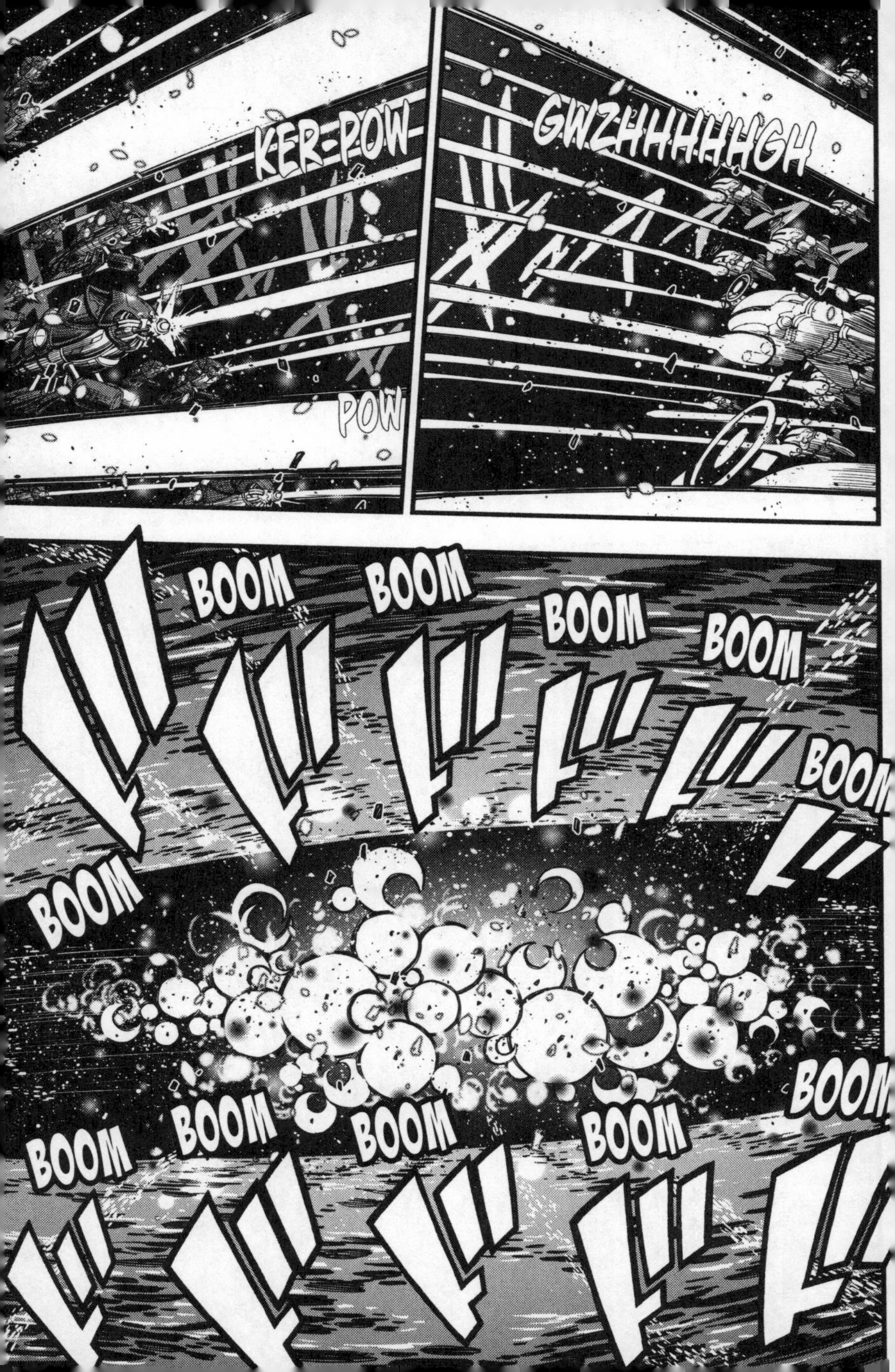
GWZHHHHHGH
KER-POW
POW
BOOM
BOOM
BOOM
BOOM
BOOM
BOOM
BOOM
BOOM
BOOM
BOOM
BOOM

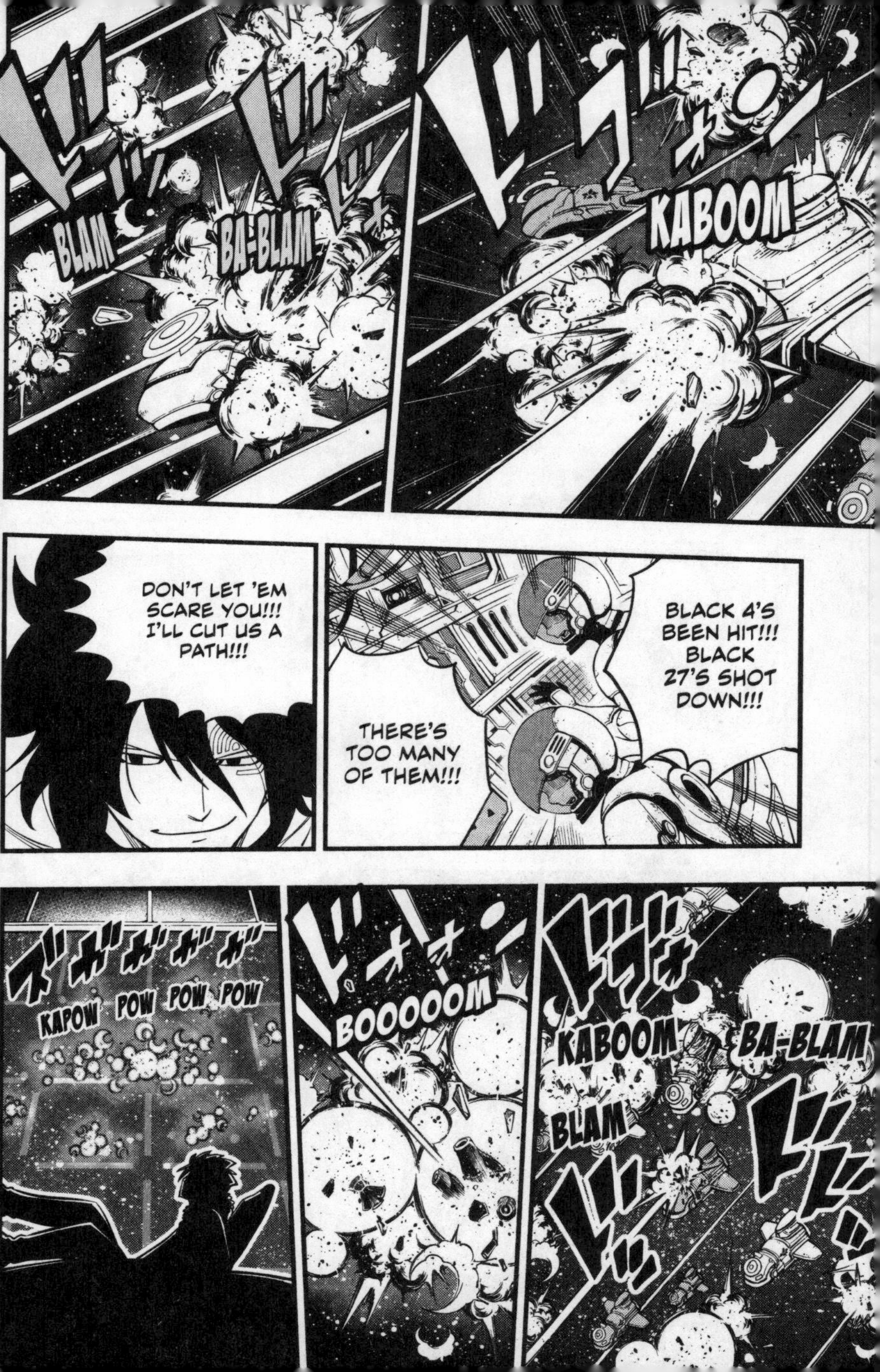
KABOOM
BA-BLAM
BLAM
BLACK 4'S BEEN HIT!!! BLACK 27'S SHOT DOWN!!!
THERE'S TOO MANY OF THEM!!!
DON'T LET 'EM SCARE YOU!!! I'LL CUT US A PATH!!!
BA-BLAM
KABOOM
BLAM
BOOOOOM
KAPOW POW POW POW

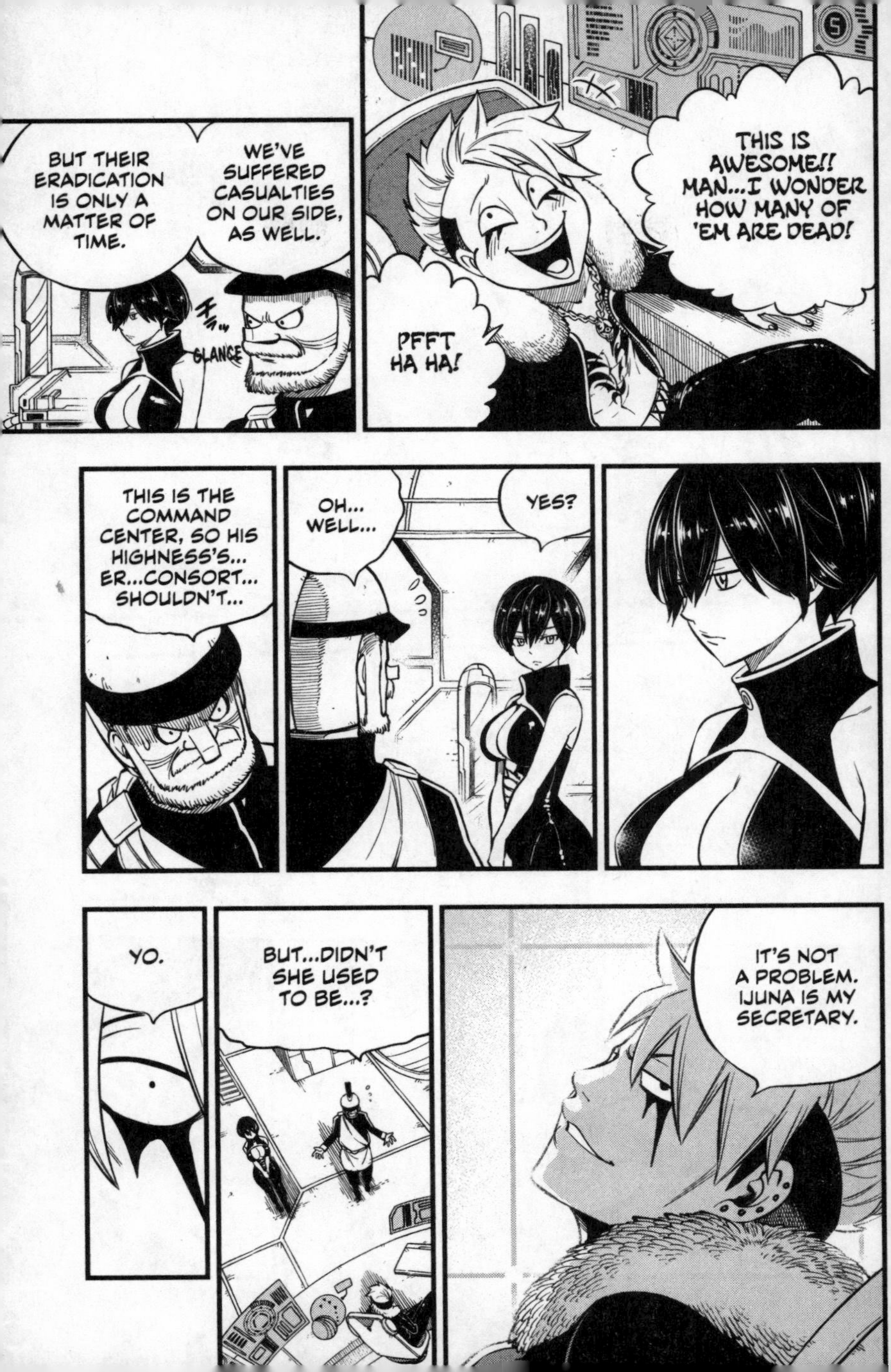
THIS IS AWESOME!! MAN...I WONDER HOW MANY OF 'EM ARE DEAD!
PFFT HA HA!
WE'VE SUFFERED CASUALTIES ON OUR SIDE, AS WELL.
BUT THEIR ERADICATION IS ONLY A MATTER OF TIME.
GLANCE
YES?
OH... WELL...
THIS IS THE COMMAND CENTER, SO HIS HIGHNESS'S... ER...CONSORT... SHOULDN'T...
IT'S NOT A PROBLEM. IJUNA IS MY SECRETARY.
BUT...DIDN'T SHE USED TO BE...?
YO.

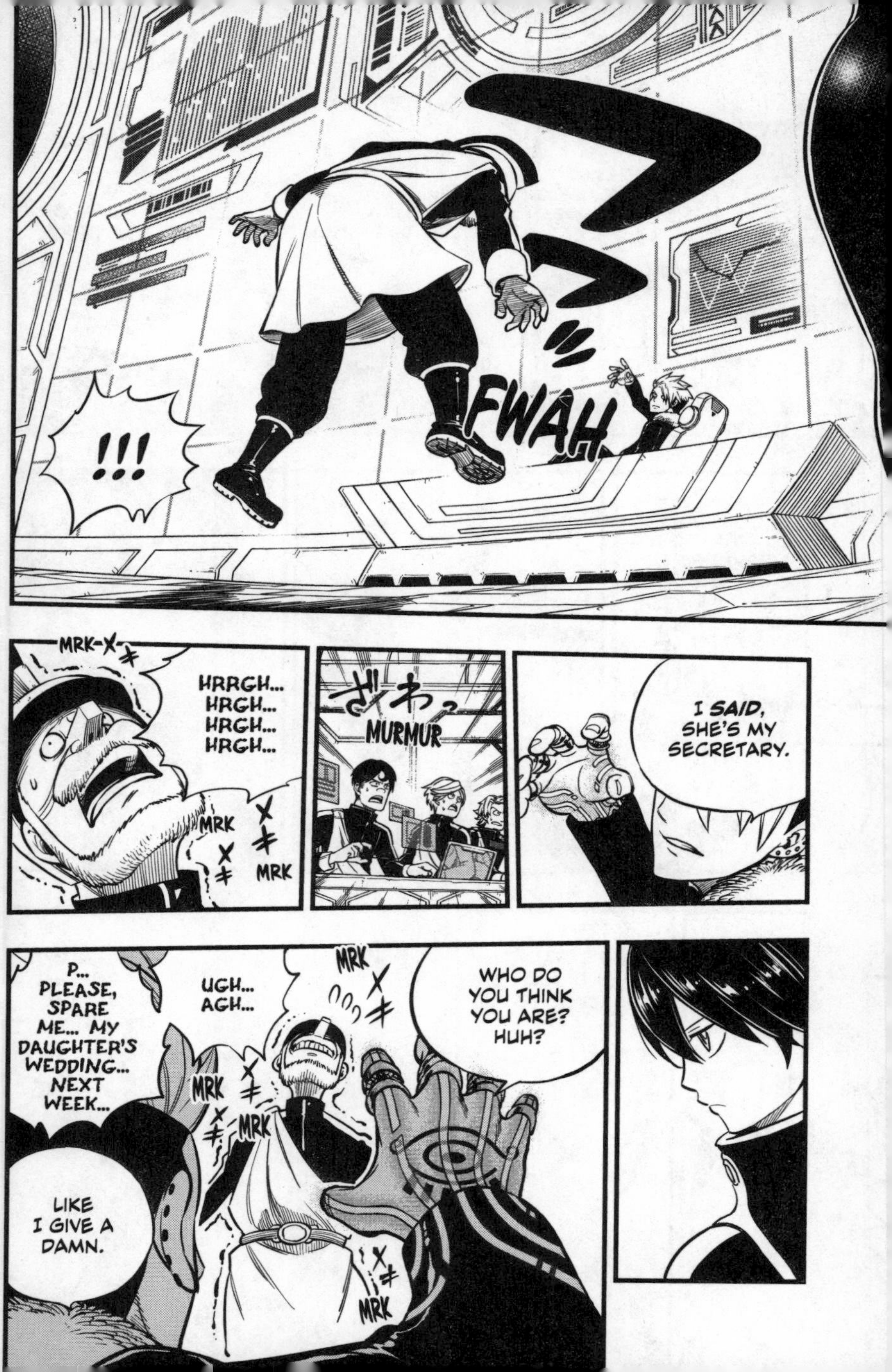
FWAH
!!!
I SAID, SHE'S MY SECRETARY.
ざわっ
MURMUR
MRK-
HRRGH... HRGH... HRGH... HRGH...
MRK
MRK
MRK
WHO DO YOU THINK YOU ARE? HUH?
UGH... AGH...
P... PLEASE, SPARE ME... MY DAUGHTER'S WEDDING... NEXT WEEK...
MRK
MRK
LIKE I GIVE A DAMN.
MRK

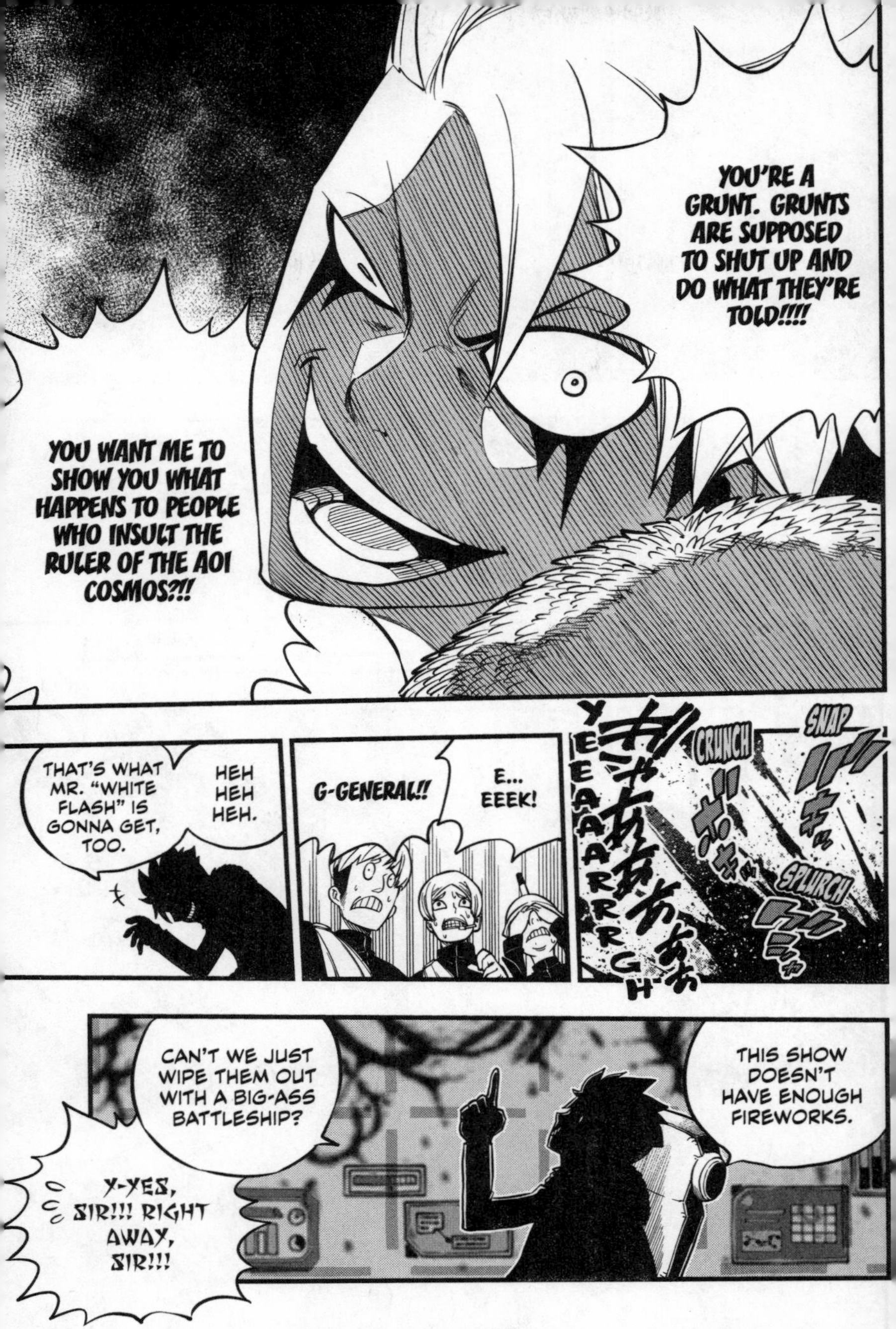

YOU'RE A GRUNT. GRUNTS ARE SUPPOSED TO SHUT UP AND DO WHAT THEY'RE TOLD!!!!
YOU WANT ME TO SHOW YOU WHAT HAPPENS TO PEOPLE WHO INSULT THE RULER OF THE AOI COSMOS?!!
SNAP
CRUNCH
SPLURCH
YEEAAAARRRRGH
E... EEEK!
G-GENERAL!!
HEH HEH HEH.
THAT'S WHAT MR. "WHITE FLASH" IS GONNA GET, TOO.
THIS SHOW DOESN'T HAVE ENOUGH FIREWORKS.
CAN'T WE JUST WIPE THEM OUT WITH A BIG-ASS BATTLESHIP?
Y-YES, SIR!!! RIGHT AWAY, SIR!!!

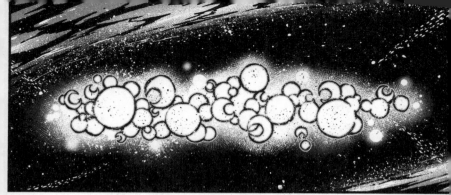

LARGE BATTLESHIP APPROACHING, STRAIGHT AHEAD!!!

THAT'S...!!!

RUMBLE

IT'S A KRAKEN-CLASS CRUISER!

RUMBLE

RUMBLE

ONE OF THE EMPIRE'S CAPITAL SHIPS!!!!

RUMBLE

RUMBLE

RUMBLE

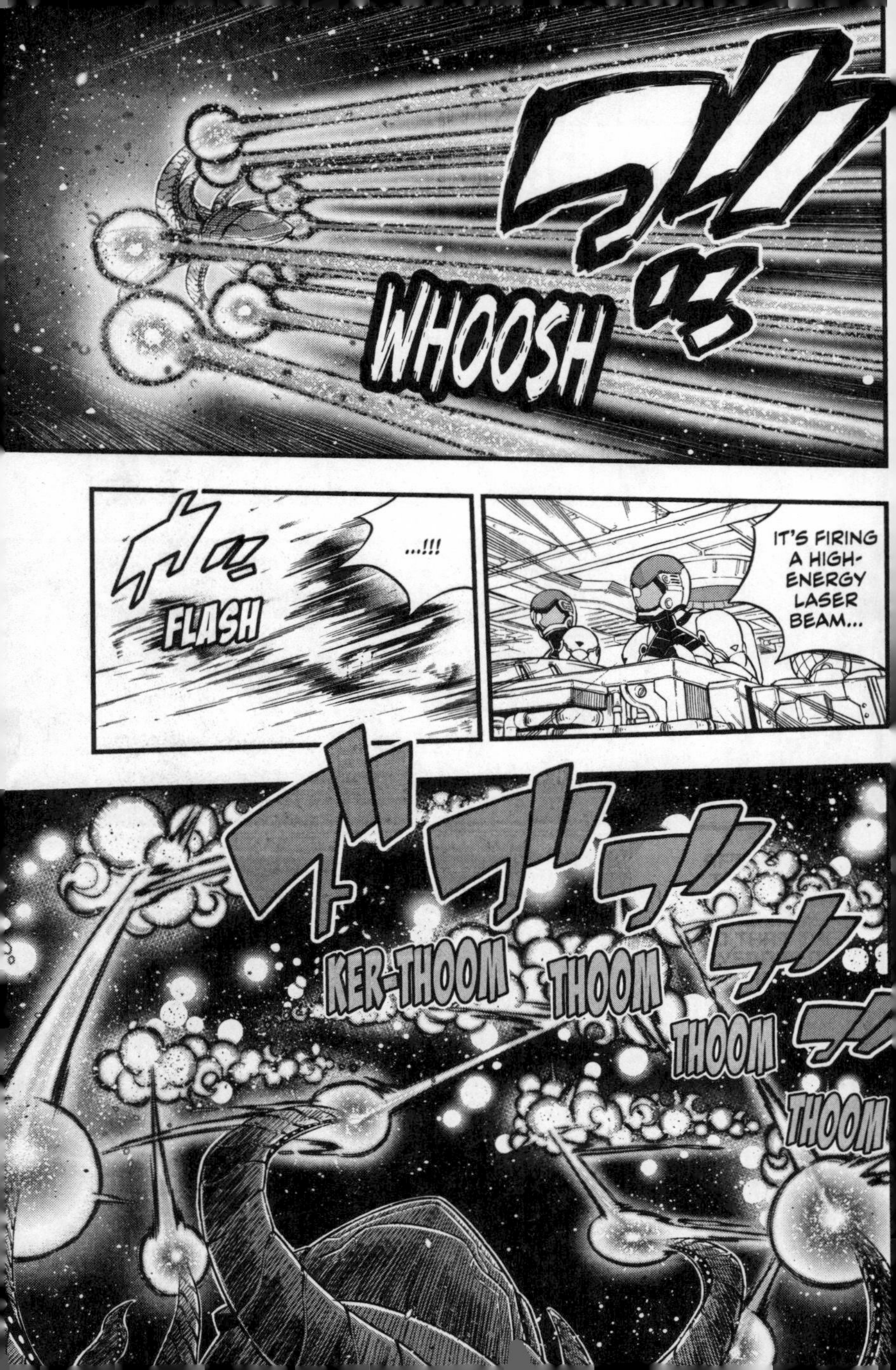
WHOOSH
IT'S FIRING A HIGH-ENERGY LASER BEAM...
...!!!
FLASH
KER-THOOM
THOOM
THOOM
THOOM

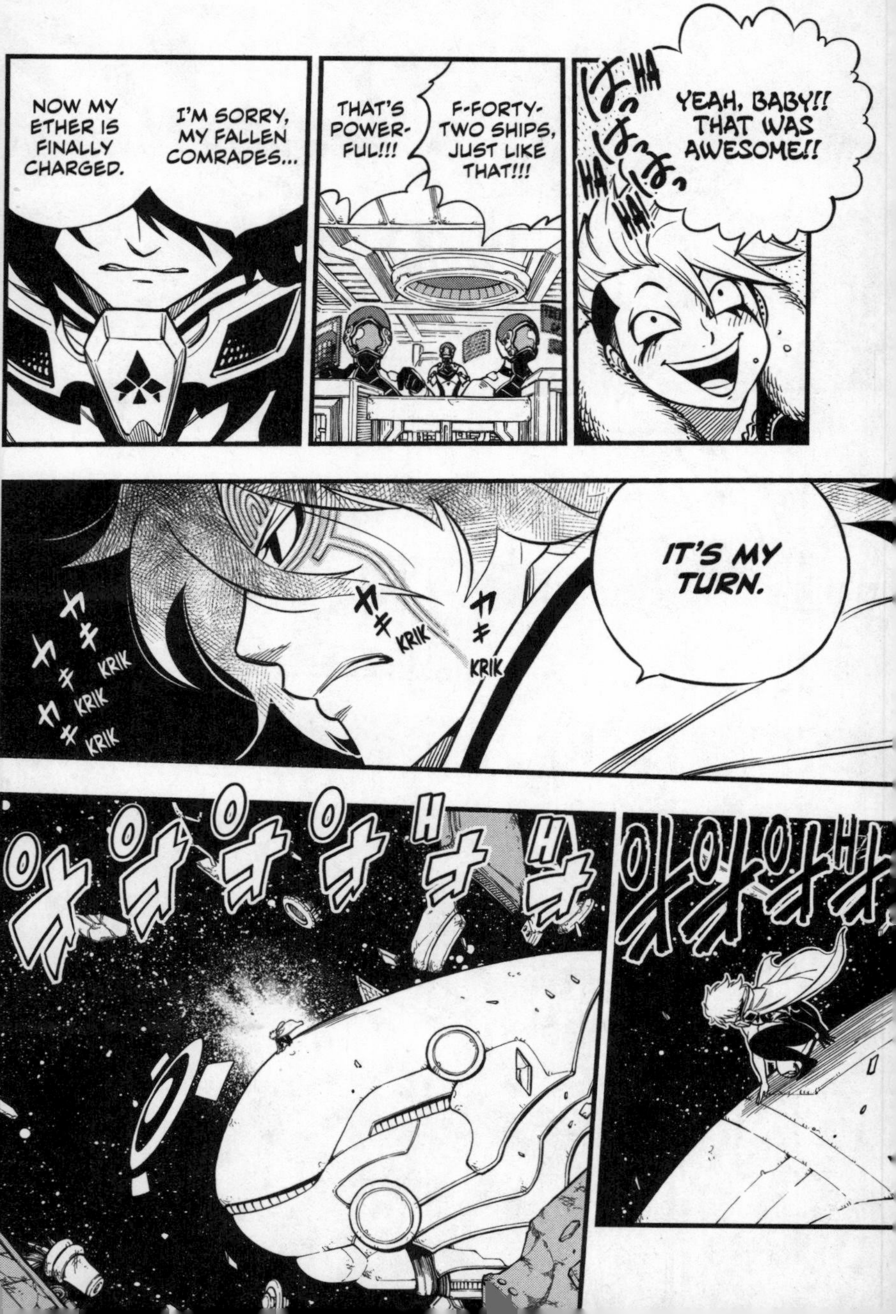

HA HA HA HA!
YEAH, BABY!! THAT WAS AWESOME!!
F-FORTY-TWO SHIPS, JUST LIKE THAT!!!
THAT'S POWERFUL!!!
I'M SORRY, MY FALLEN COMRADES...
NOW MY ETHER IS FINALLY CHARGED.
IT'S MY TURN.
KRIK KRIK
KRIK KRIK KRIK
OOOOHH
OOOOHH

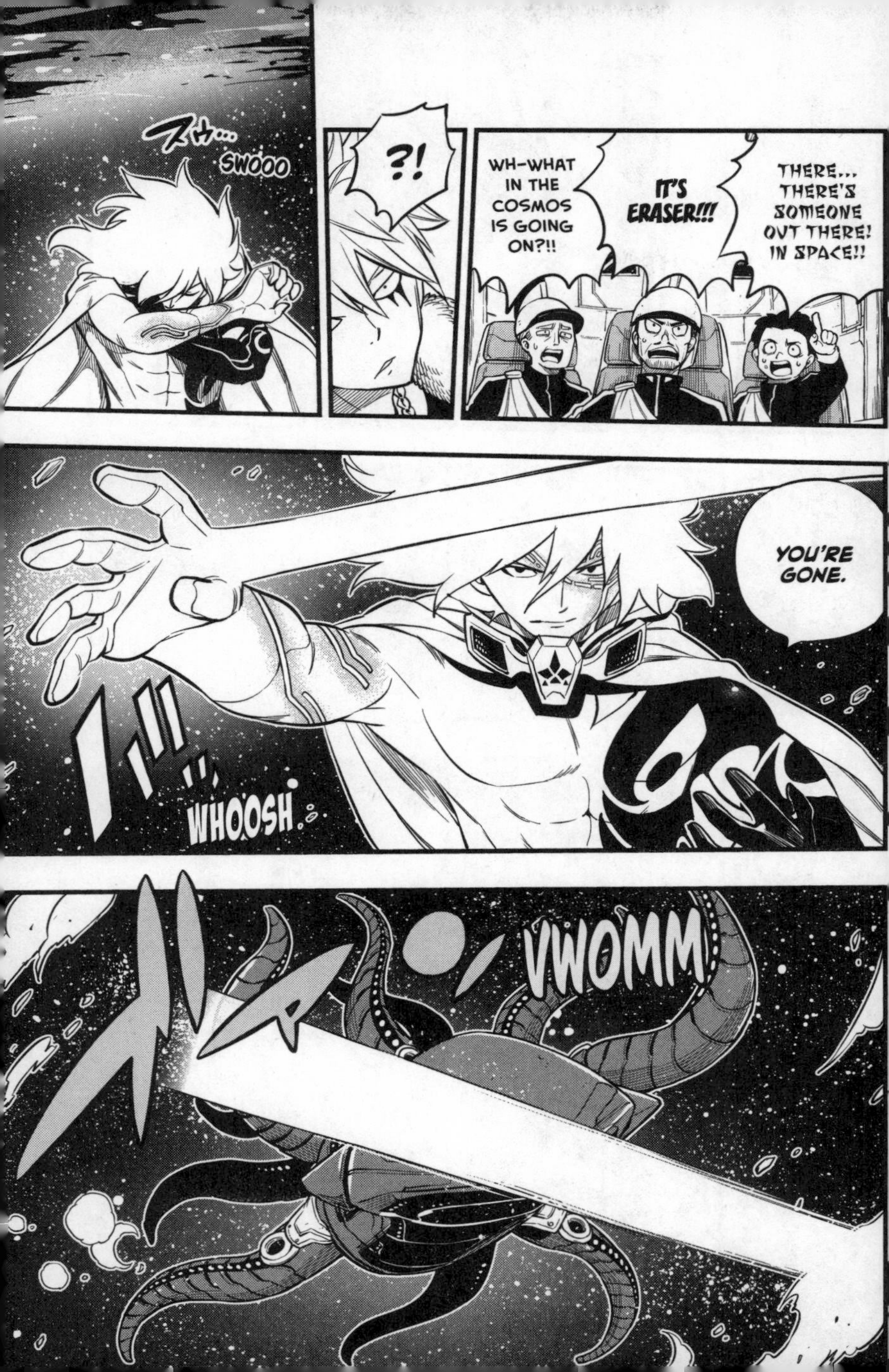
THERE... THERE'S SOMEONE OUT THERE! IN SPACE!!
IT'S ERASER!!!
WH-WHAT IN THE COSMOS IS GOING ON?!!
?!
スゥ...
SWOOO
YOU'RE GONE.
WHOOSH
VWOMM

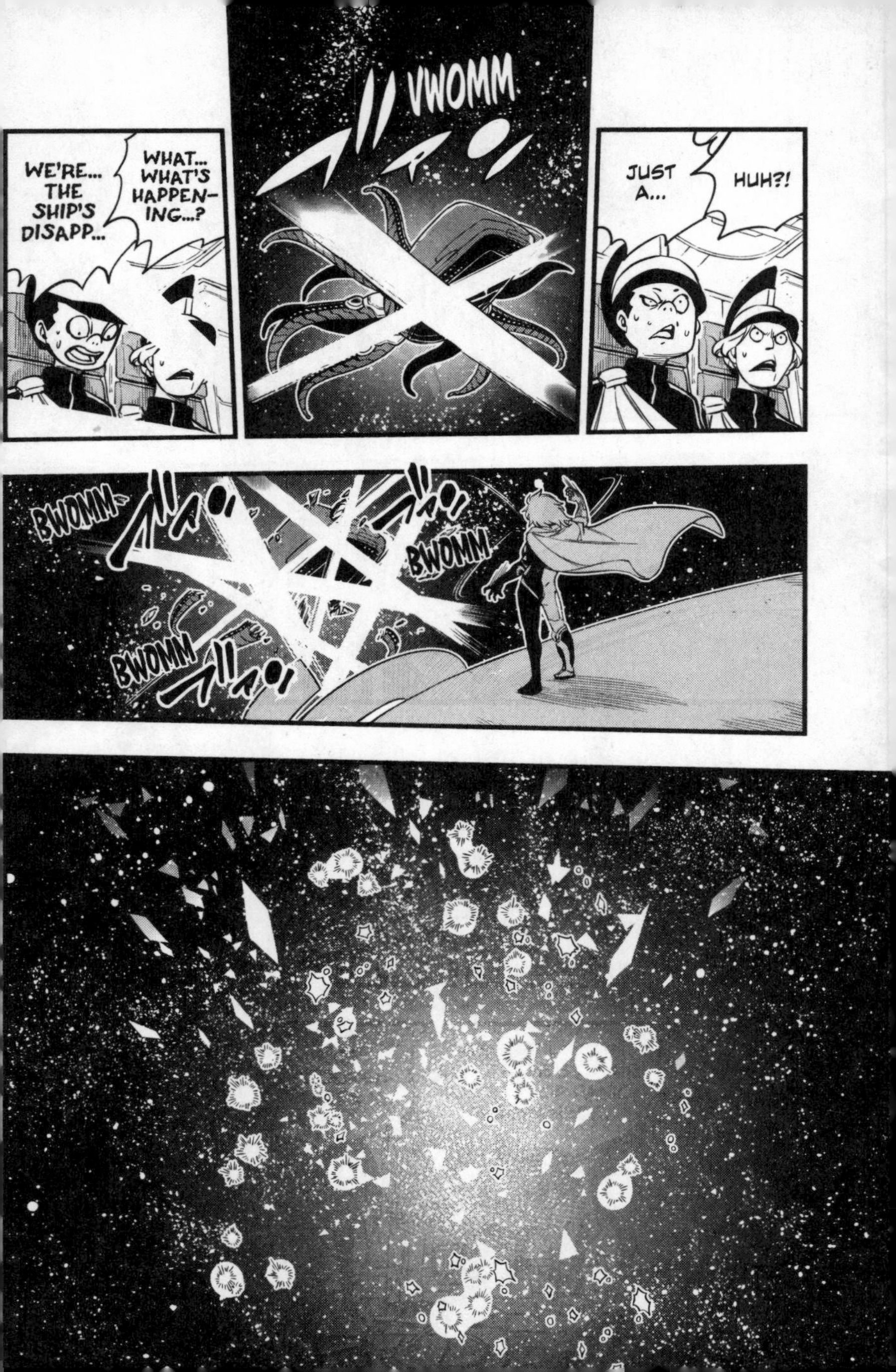
HUH?!
JUST A...
VWOMM
WHAT... WHAT'S HAPPENING...?
WE'RE... THE SHIP'S DISAPP...
BWOMM
BWOMM
BWOMM

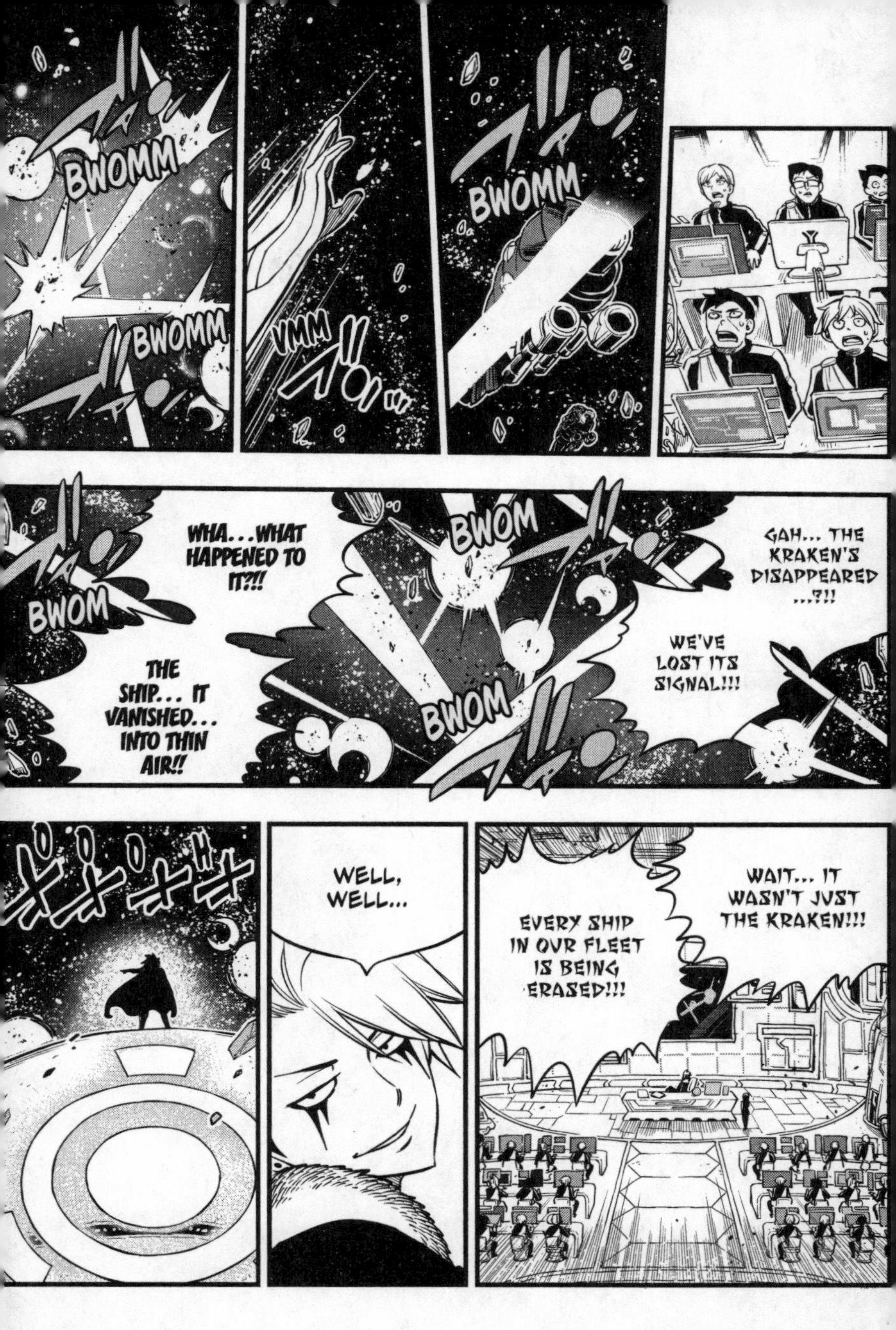
BWOMM
VMM
BWOMM
BWOMM
GAH... THE KRAKEN'S DISAPPEARED ...?!!
BWOM
WHA...WHAT HAPPENED TO IT?!!
WE'VE LOST ITS SIGNAL!!!
BWOM
BWOM
THE SHIP... IT VANISHED... INTO THIN AIR!!
WAIT... IT WASN'T JUST THE KRAKEN!!!
EVERY SHIP IN OUR FLEET IS BEING ERASED!!!
WELL, WELL...

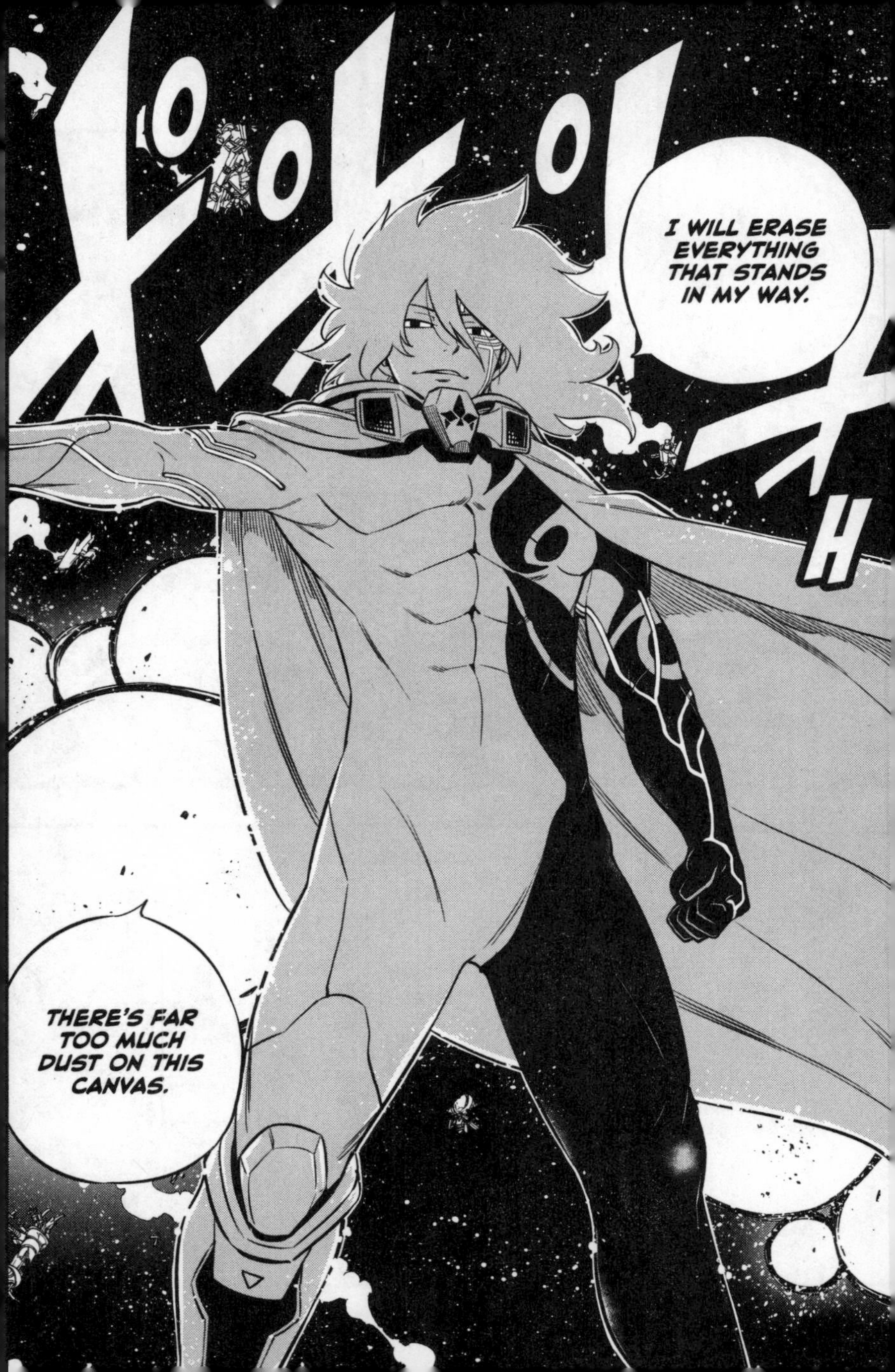
I WILL ERASE EVERYTHING THAT STANDS IN MY WAY.
THERE'S FAR TOO MUCH DUST ON THIS CANVAS.

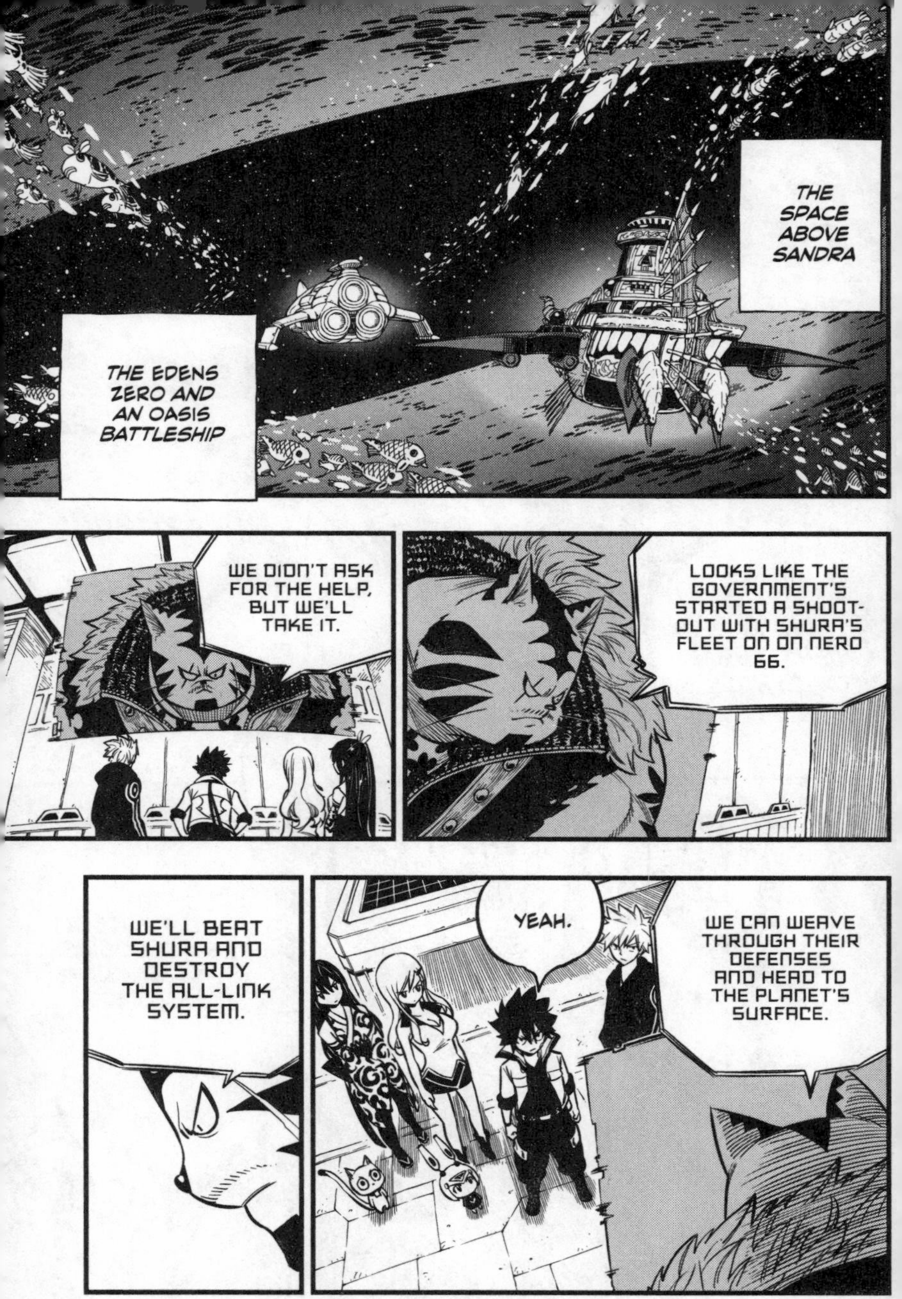
THE SPACE ABOVE SANDRA
THE EDENS ZERO AND AN OASIS BATTLESHIP
LOOKS LIKE THE GOVERNMENT'S STARTED A SHOOT-OUT WITH SHURA'S FLEET ON ON NERO 66.
WE DIDN'T ASK FOR THE HELP, BUT WE'LL TAKE IT.
WE CAN WEAVE THROUGH THEIR DEFENSES AND HEAD TO THE PLANET'S SURFACE.
YEAH.
WE'LL BEAT SHURA AND DESTROY THE ALL-LINK SYSTEM.

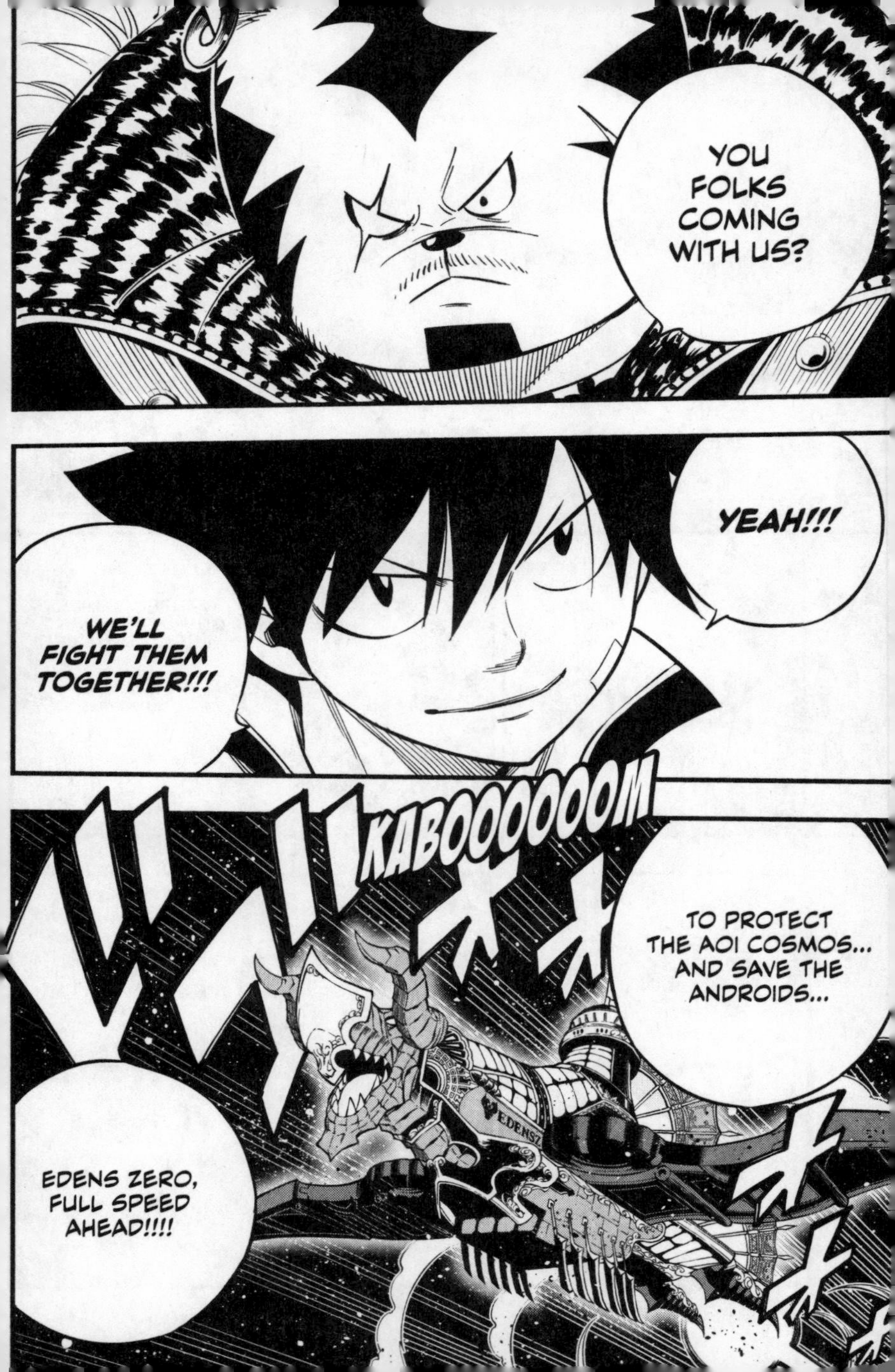
YOU FOLKS COMING WITH US?
YEAH!!!
WE'LL FIGHT THEM TOGETHER!!!
KABOOOOOOM
TO PROTECT THE AOI COSMOS... AND SAVE THE ANDROIDS...
EDENS ZERO, FULL SPEED AHEAD!!!!

EDENS ZERO

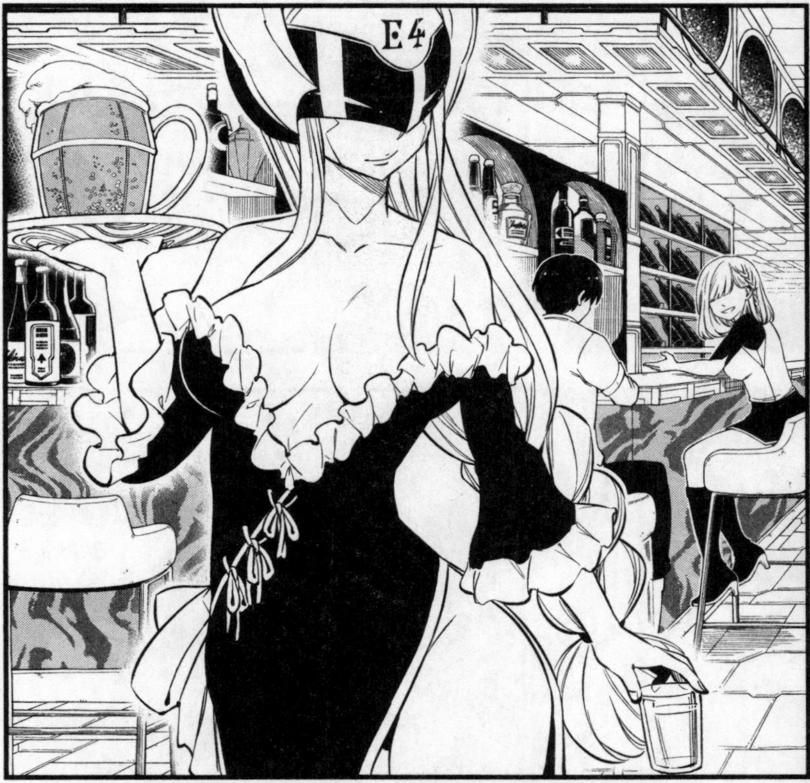
E4

CHAPTER 140: CHARGE!! TO PLANET NERO 66

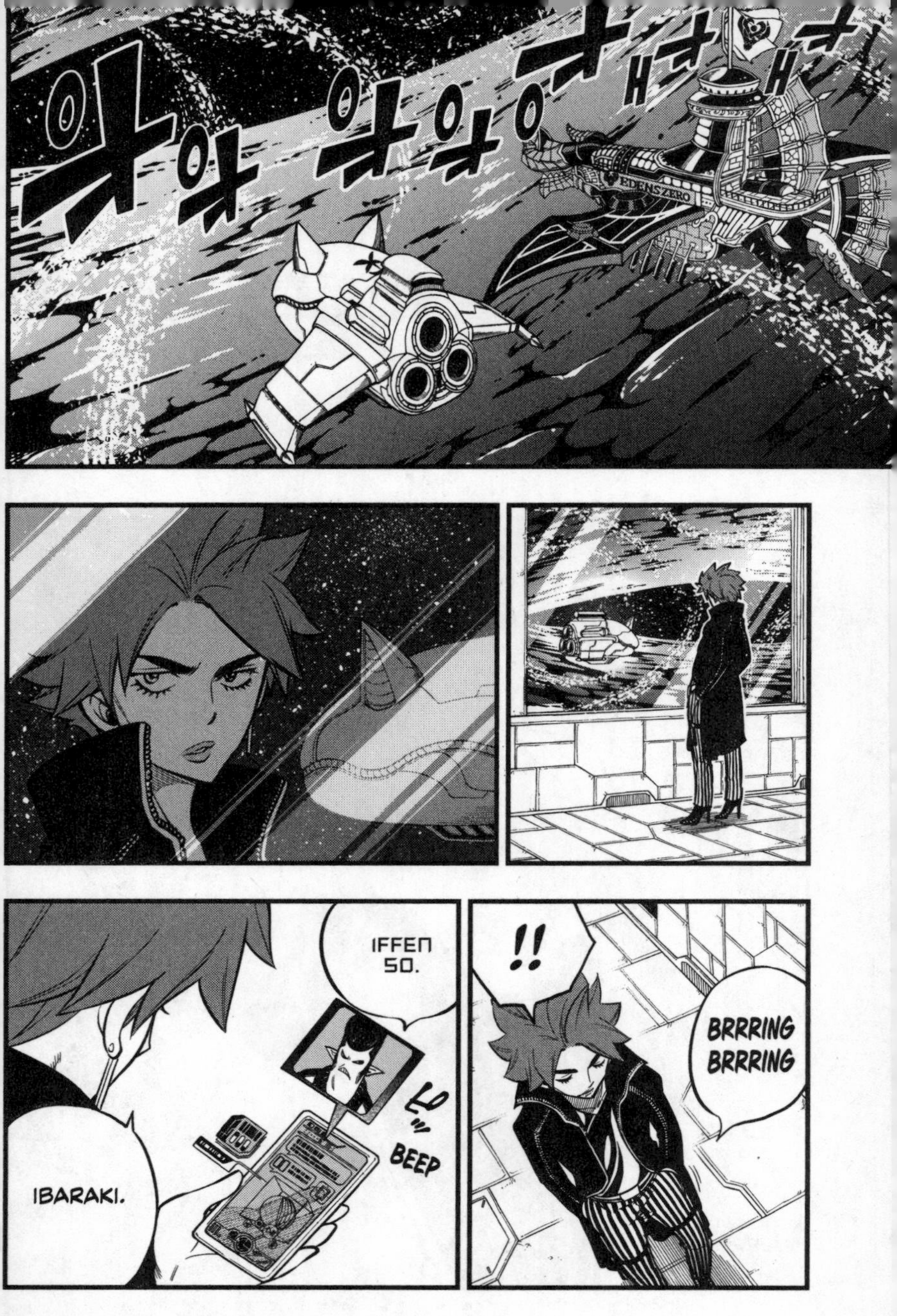
!!
BRRRING BRRRING
IFFEN SO.
BEEP
IBARAKI.

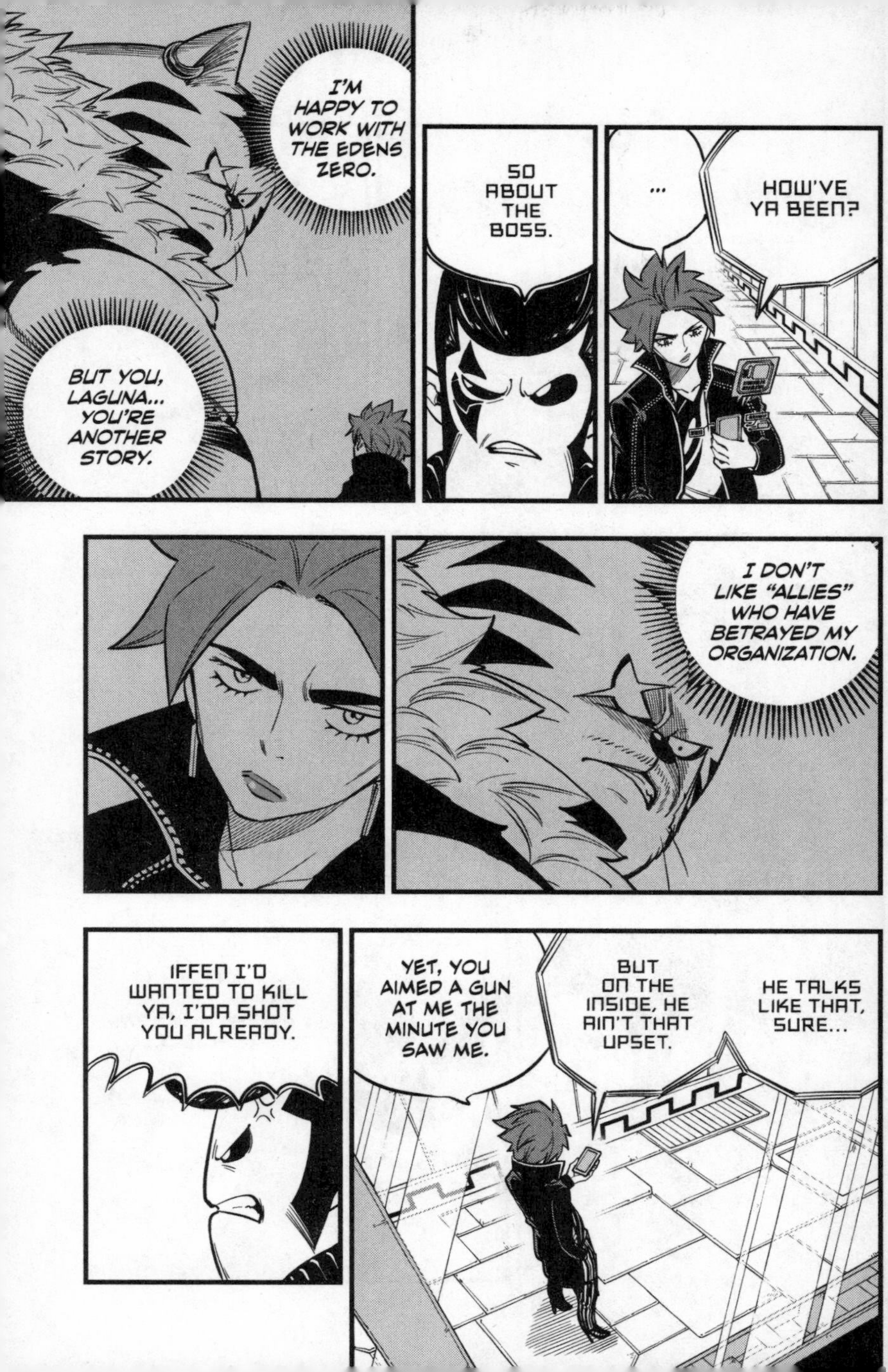
HOW'VE YA BEEN?
...
SO ABOUT THE BOSS.
I'M HAPPY TO WORK WITH THE EDENS ZERO.
BUT YOU, LAGUNA... YOU'RE ANOTHER STORY.
I DON'T LIKE "ALLIES" WHO HAVE BETRAYED MY ORGANIZATION.
HE TALKS LIKE THAT, SURE...
BUT ON THE INSIDE, HE AIN'T THAT UPSET.
YET, YOU AIMED A GUN AT ME THE MINUTE YOU SAW ME.
IFFEN I'D WANTED TO KILL YA, I'DA SHOT YOU ALREADY.

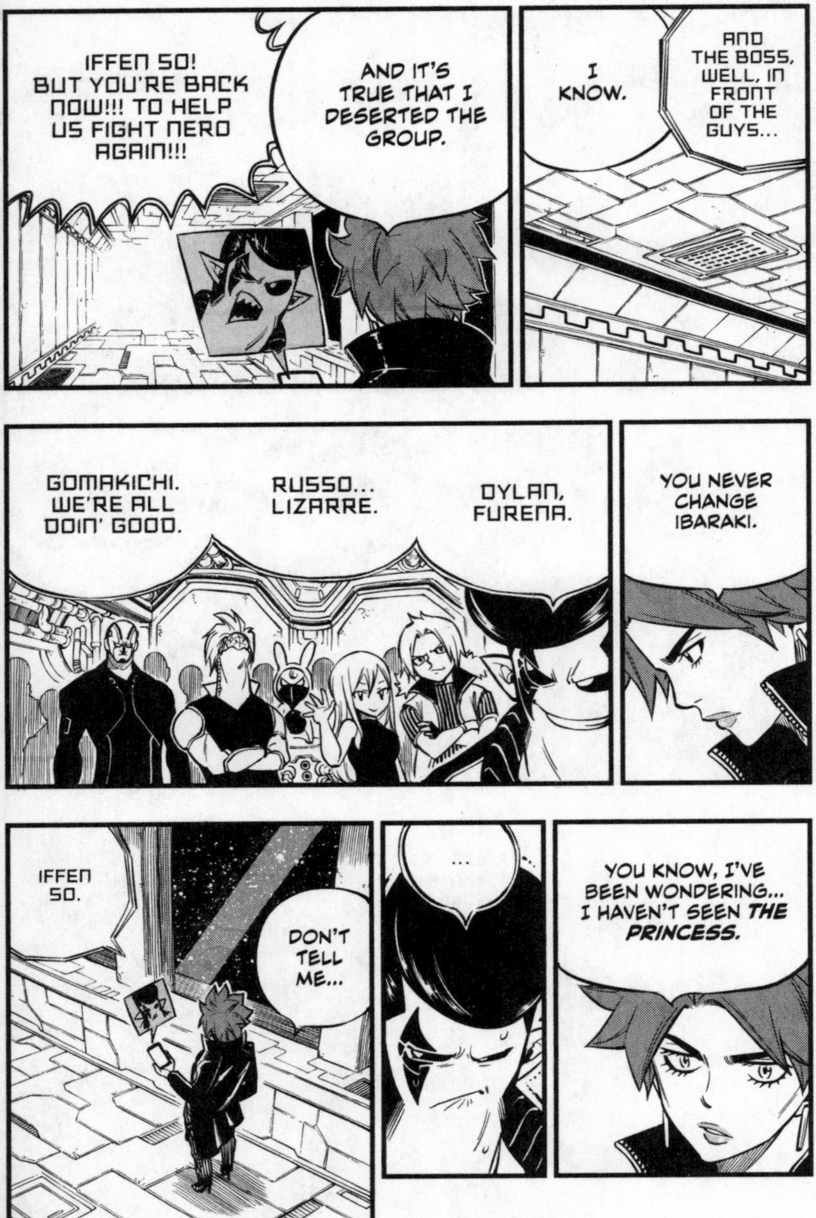
AND THE BOSS, WELL, IN FRONT OF THE GUYS...
I KNOW.
AND IT'S TRUE THAT I DESERTED THE GROUP.
IFFEN SO! BUT YOU'RE BACK NOW!!! TO HELP US FIGHT NERO AGAIN!!!
YOU NEVER CHANGE IBARAKI.
DYLAN, FURENA.
RUSSO... LIZARRE.
GOMAKICHI. WE'RE ALL DOIN' GOOD.
YOU KNOW, I'VE BEEN WONDERING... I HAVEN'T SEEN *THE PRINCESS.*
...
DON'T TELL ME...
IFFEN SO.

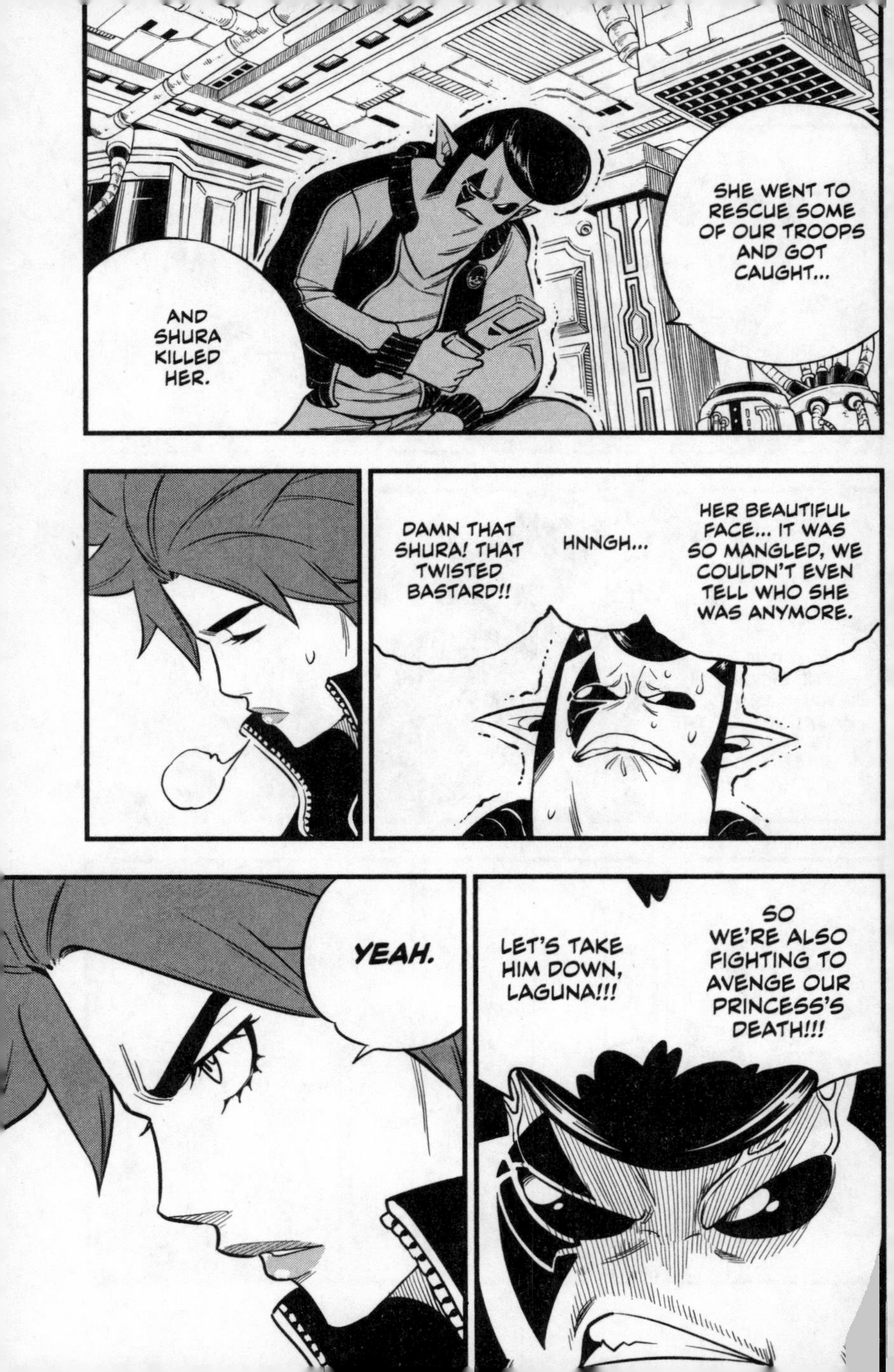
SHE WENT TO RESCUE SOME OF OUR TROOPS AND GOT CAUGHT...
AND SHURA KILLED HER.
HER BEAUTIFUL FACE... IT WAS SO MANGLED, WE COULDN'T EVEN TELL WHO SHE WAS ANYMORE.
HNNGH...
DAMN THAT SHURA! THAT TWISTED BASTARD!!
SO WE'RE ALSO FIGHTING TO AVENGE OUR PRINCESS'S DEATH!!!
LET'S TAKE HIM DOWN, LAGUNA!!!
YEAH.

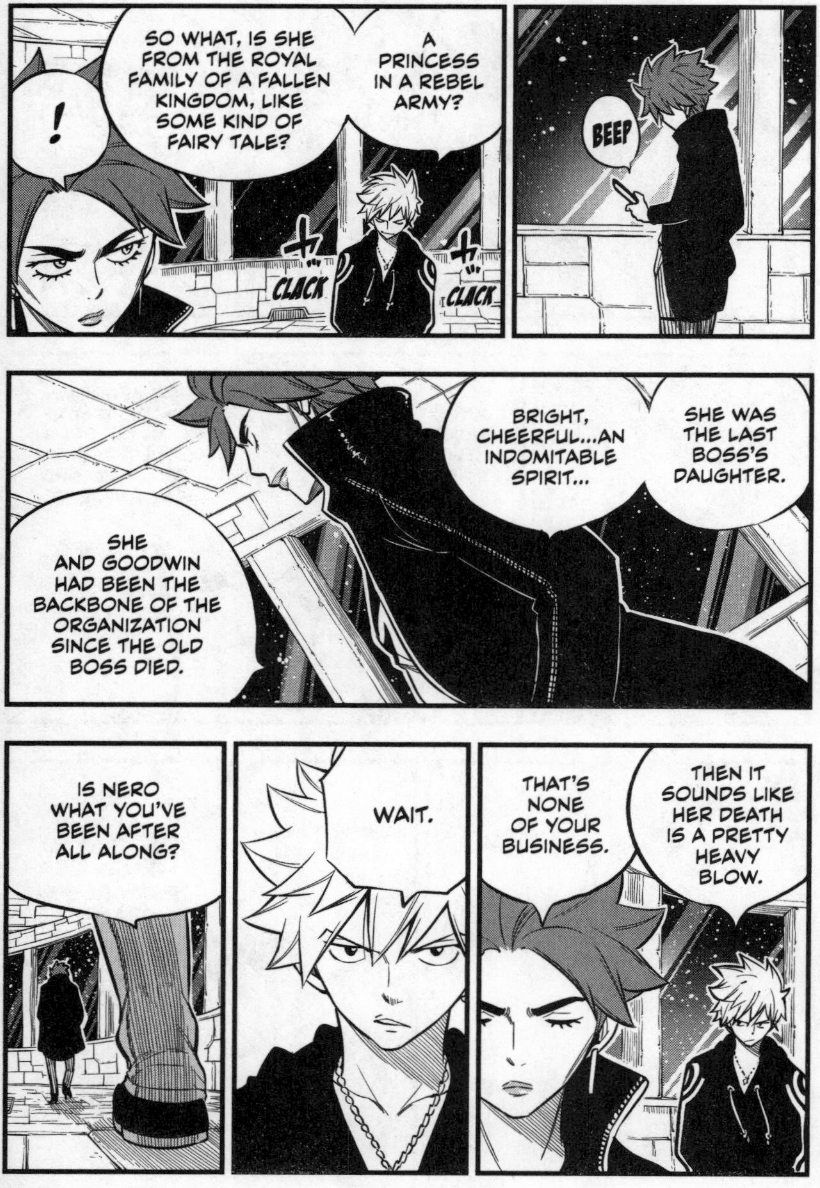
BEEP
A PRINCESS IN A REBEL ARMY?
SO WHAT, IS SHE FROM THE ROYAL FAMILY OF A FALLEN KINGDOM, LIKE SOME KIND OF FAIRY TALE?
!
CLACK
CLACK
SHE WAS THE LAST BOSS'S DAUGHTER.
BRIGHT, CHEERFUL...AN INDOMITABLE SPIRIT...
SHE AND GOODWIN HAD BEEN THE BACKBONE OF THE ORGANIZATION SINCE THE OLD BOSS DIED.
THEN IT SOUNDS LIKE HER DEATH IS A PRETTY HEAVY BLOW.
THAT'S NONE OF YOUR BUSINESS.
WAIT.
IS NERO WHAT YOU'VE BEEN AFTER ALL ALONG?

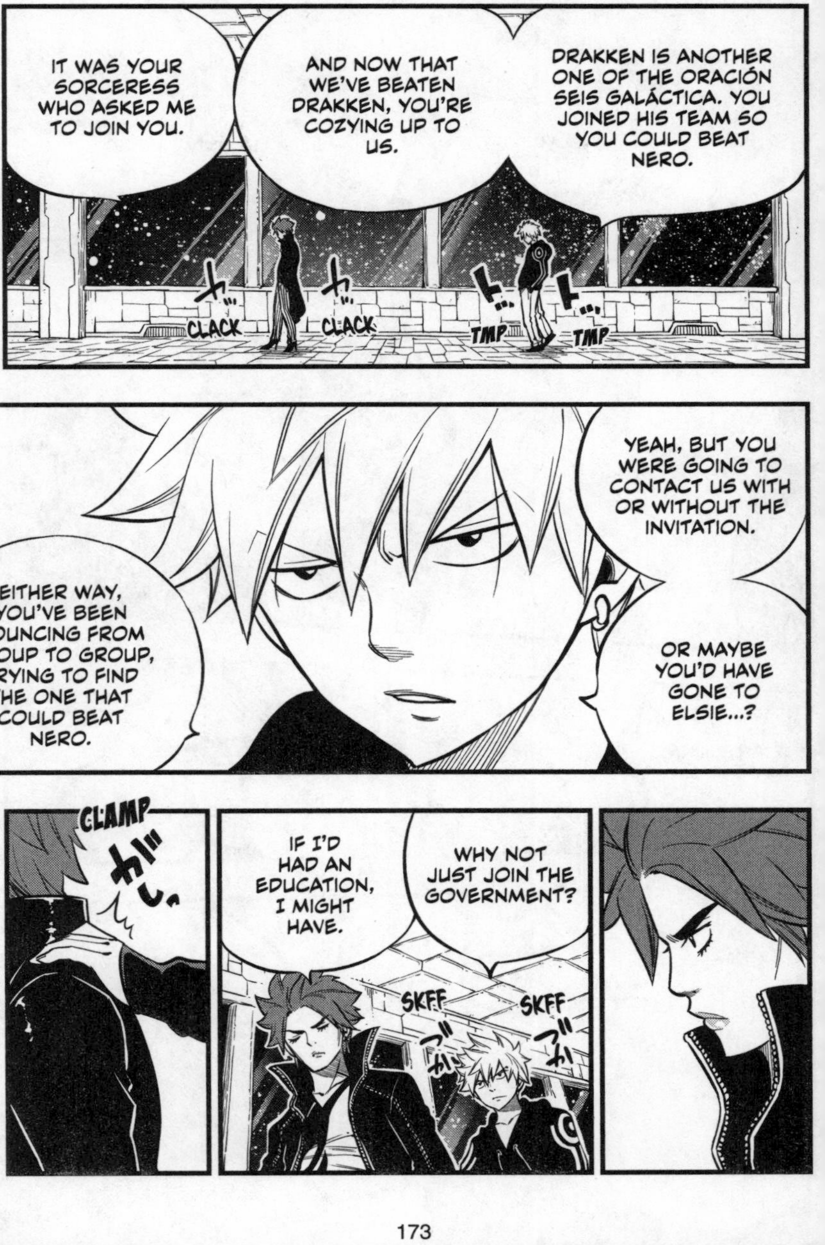
DRAKKEN IS ANOTHER ONE OF THE ORACIÓN SEIS GALÁCTICA. YOU JOINED HIS TEAM SO YOU COULD BEAT NERO.
AND NOW THAT WE'VE BEATEN DRAKKEN, YOU'RE COZYING UP TO US.
IT WAS YOUR SORCERESS WHO ASKED ME TO JOIN YOU.
TMP
TMP
CLACK
CLACK
YEAH, BUT YOU WERE GOING TO CONTACT US WITH OR WITHOUT THE INVITATION.
OR MAYBE YOU'D HAVE GONE TO ELSIE...?
EITHER WAY, YOU'VE BEEN BOUNCING FROM GROUP TO GROUP, TRYING TO FIND THE ONE THAT COULD BEAT NERO.
WHY NOT JUST JOIN THE GOVERNMENT?
IF I'D HAD AN EDUCATION, I MIGHT HAVE.
SKFF
SKFF
CLAMP

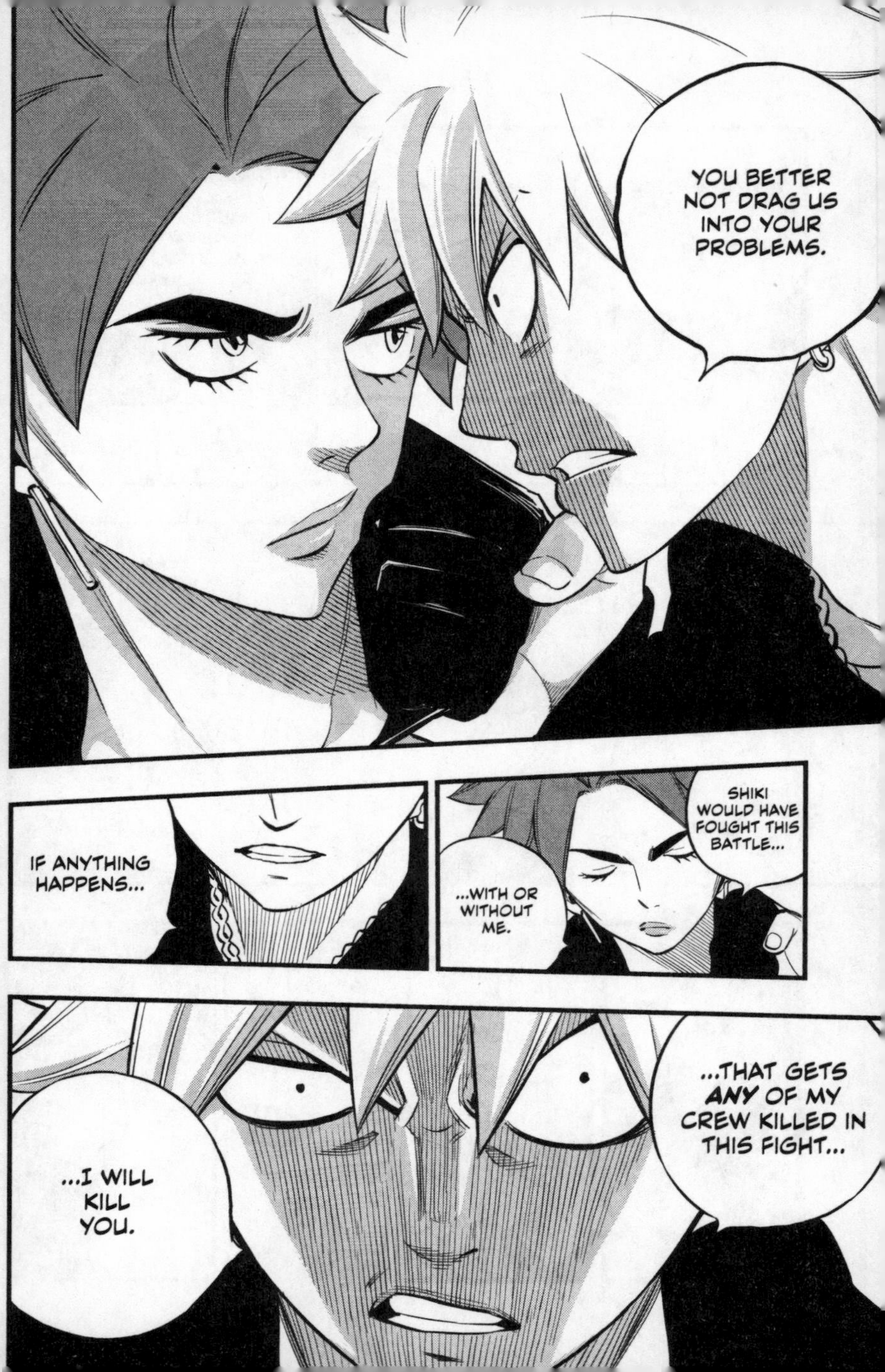
YOU BETTER NOT DRAG US INTO YOUR PROBLEMS.
SHIKI WOULD HAVE FOUGHT THIS BATTLE...
...WITH OR WITHOUT ME.
IF ANYTHING HAPPENS...
...THAT GETS ANY OF MY CREW KILLED IN THIS FIGHT...
...I WILL KILL YOU.

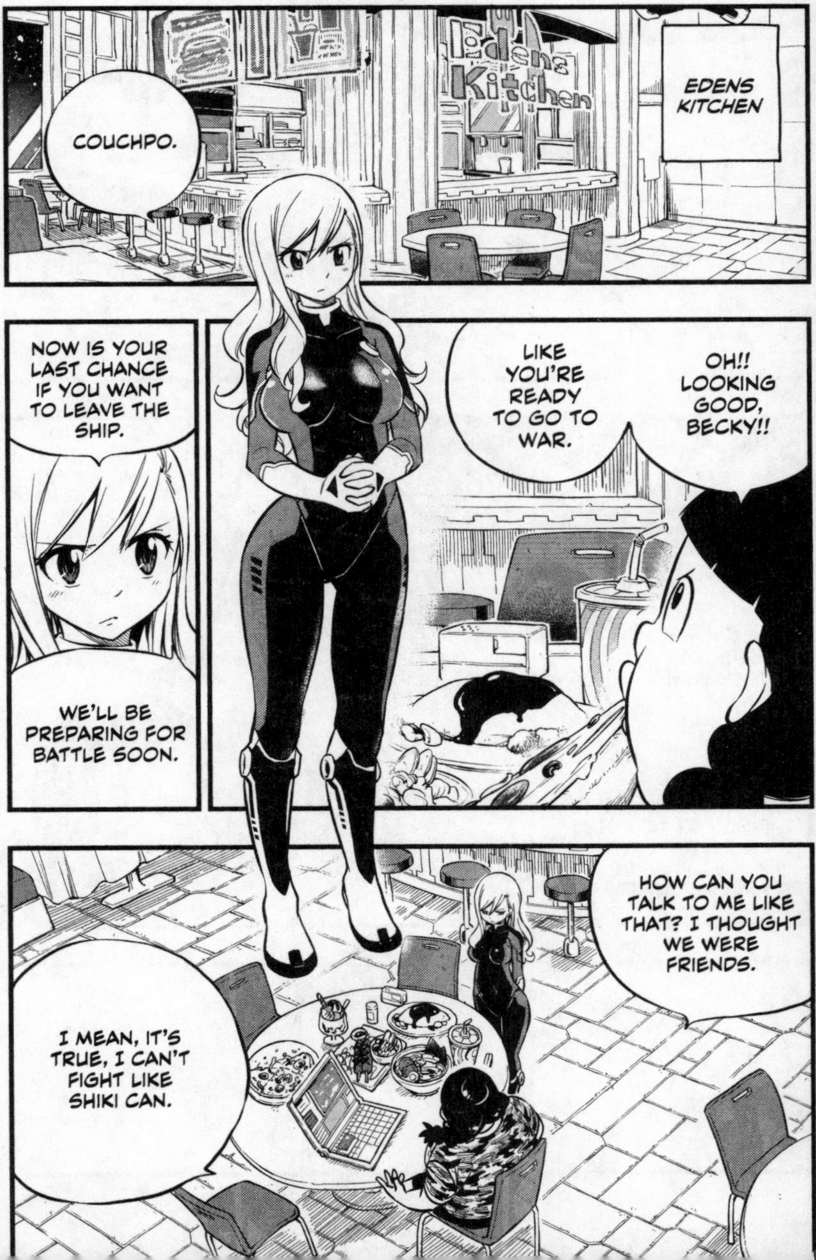
EDENS KITCHEN
Edens Kitchen
COUCHPO.
OH!! LOOKING GOOD, BECKY!!
LIKE YOU'RE READY TO GO TO WAR.
NOW IS YOUR LAST CHANCE IF YOU WANT TO LEAVE THE SHIP.
WE'LL BE PREPARING FOR BATTLE SOON.
HOW CAN YOU TALK TO ME LIKE THAT? I THOUGHT WE WERE FRIENDS.
I MEAN, IT'S TRUE, I CAN'T FIGHT LIKE SHIKI CAN.

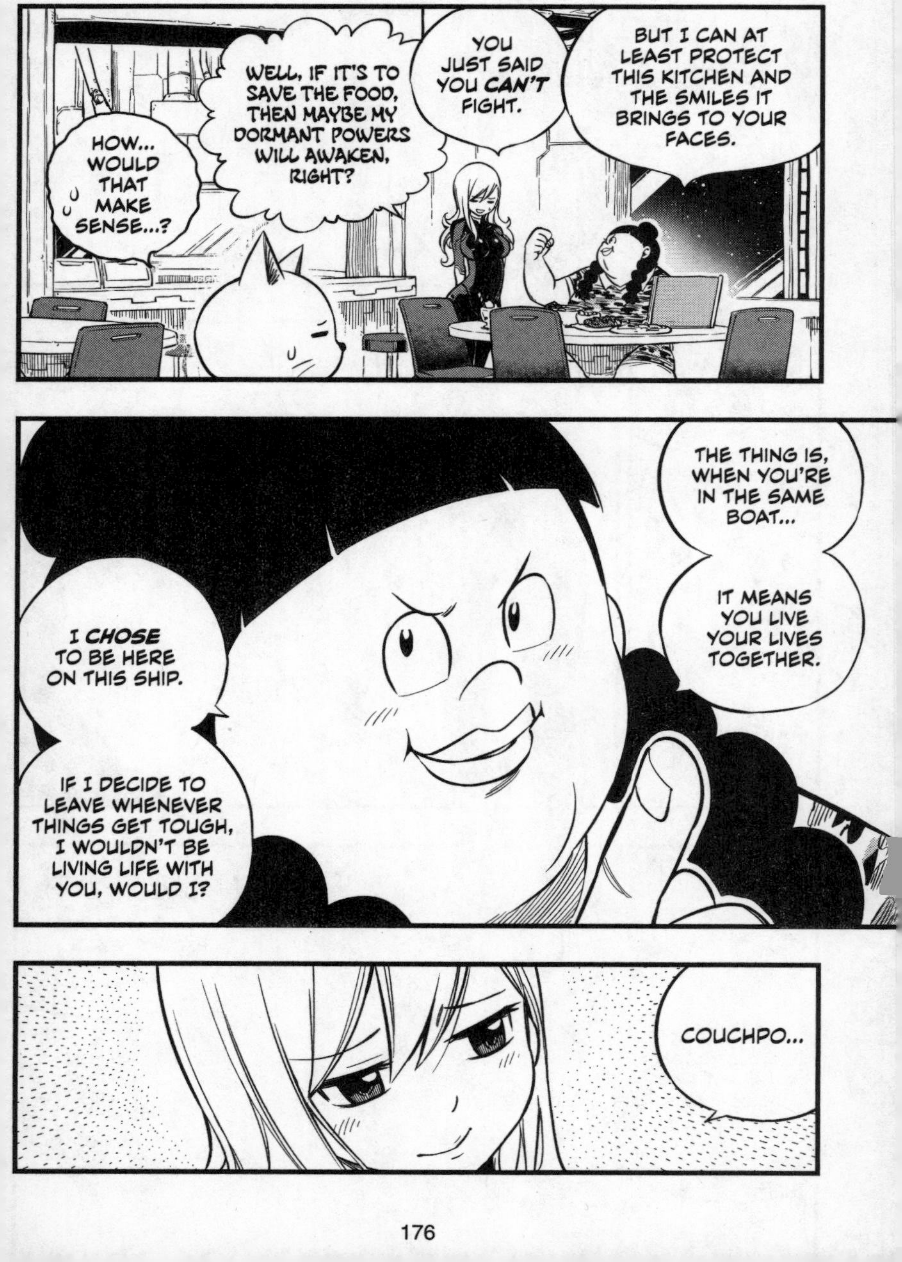
BUT I CAN AT LEAST PROTECT THIS KITCHEN AND THE SMILES IT BRINGS TO YOUR FACES.
YOU JUST SAID YOU CAN'T FIGHT.
WELL, IF IT'S TO SAVE THE FOOD, THEN MAYBE MY DORMANT POWERS WILL AWAKEN, RIGHT?
HOW... WOULD THAT MAKE SENSE...?
THE THING IS, WHEN YOU'RE IN THE SAME BOAT...
IT MEANS YOU LIVE YOUR LIVES TOGETHER.
I CHOSE TO BE HERE ON THIS SHIP.
IF I DECIDE TO LEAVE WHENEVER THINGS GET TOUGH, I WOULDN'T BE LIVING LIFE WITH YOU, WOULD I?
COUCHPO...

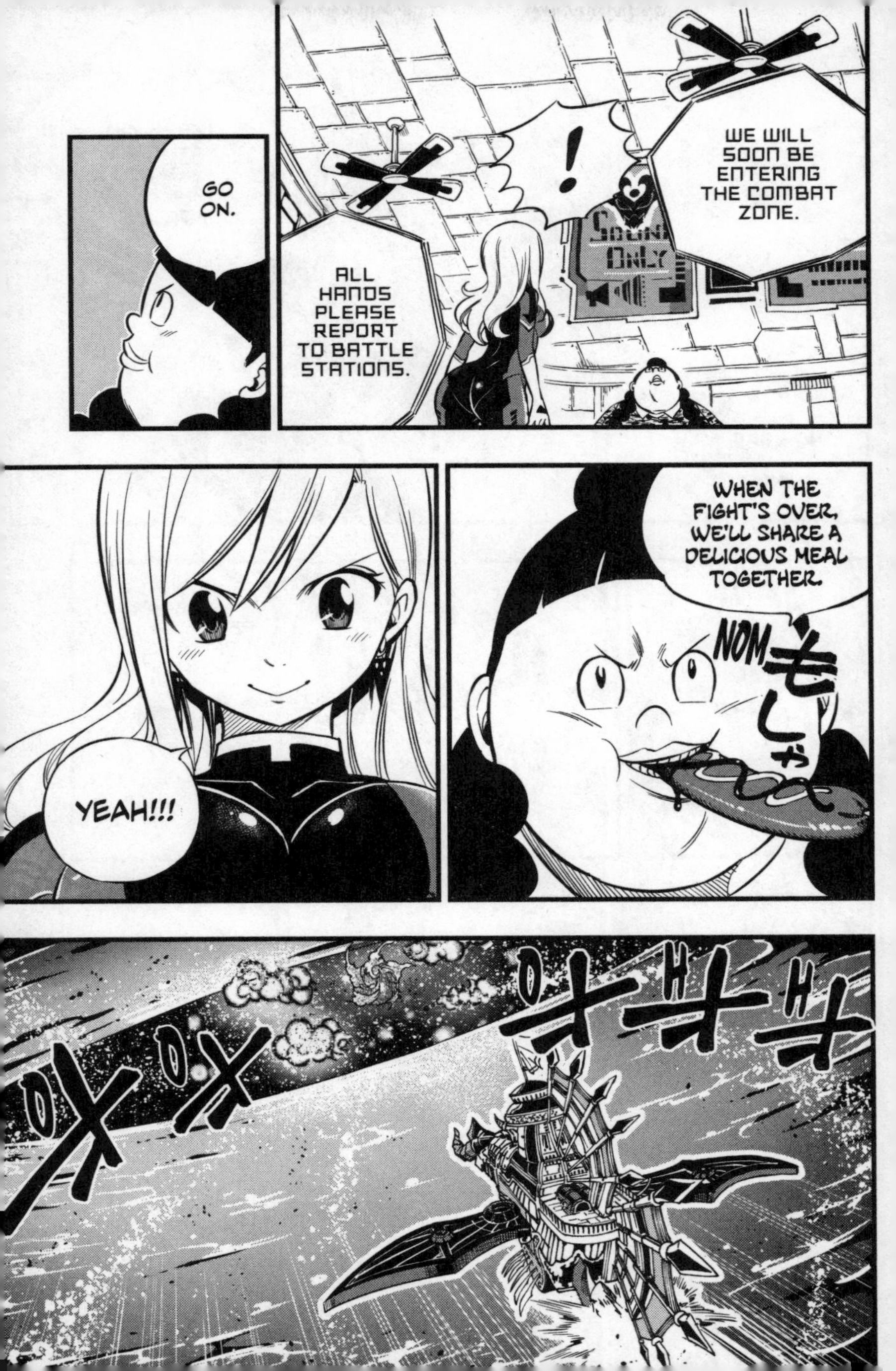
!
WE WILL SOON BE ENTERING THE COMBAT ZONE.
ALL HANDS PLEASE REPORT TO BATTLE STATIONS.
GO ON.
WHEN THE FIGHT'S OVER, WE'LL SHARE A DELICIOUS MEAL TOGETHER.
NOM もしゃ
YEAH!!!

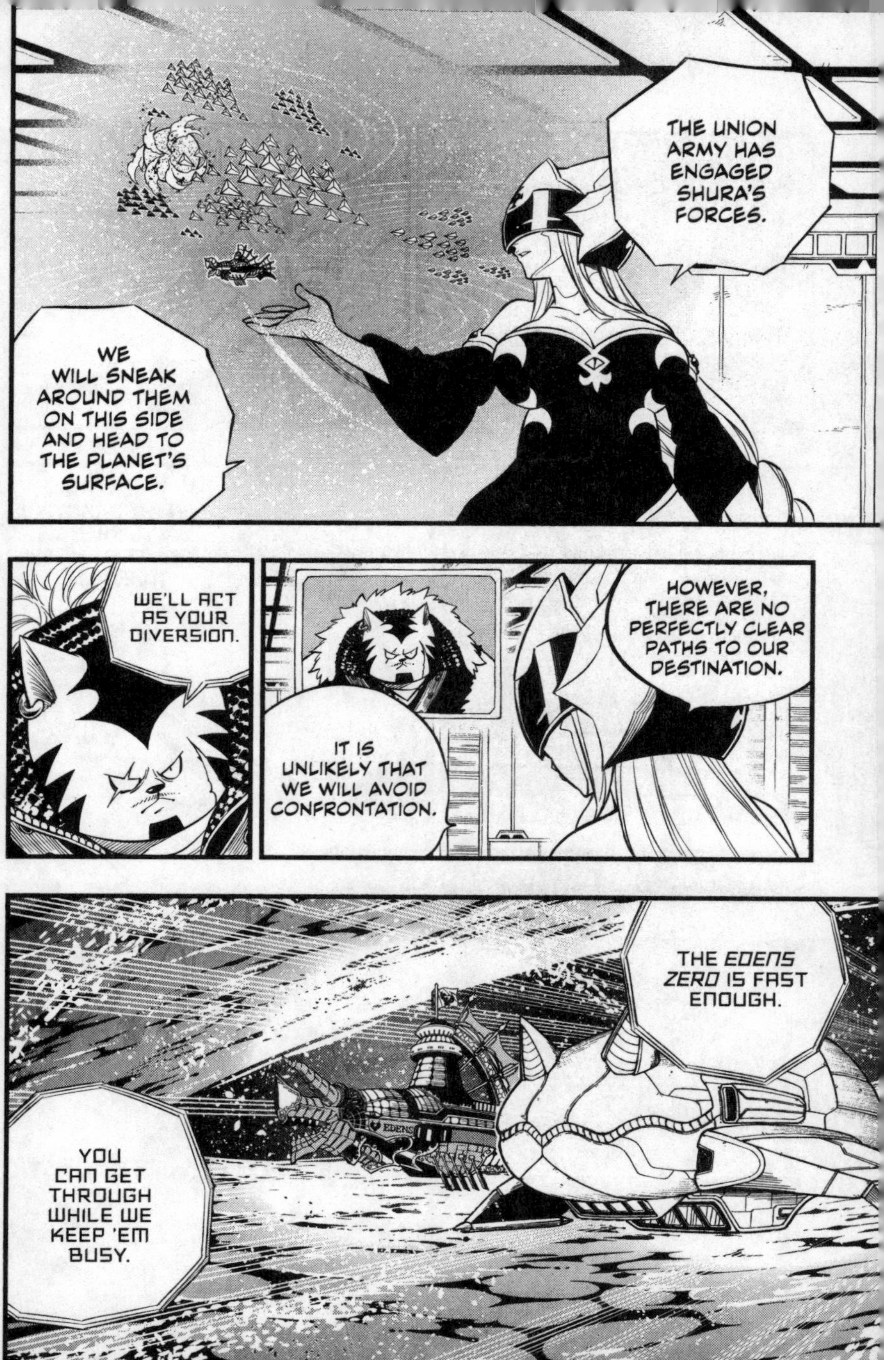
THE UNION ARMY HAS ENGAGED SHURA'S FORCES.
WE WILL SNEAK AROUND THEM ON THIS SIDE AND HEAD TO THE PLANET'S SURFACE.
HOWEVER, THERE ARE NO PERFECTLY CLEAR PATHS TO OUR DESTINATION.
IT IS UNLIKELY THAT WE WILL AVOID CONFRONTATION.
WE'LL ACT AS YOUR DIVERSION.
THE *EDENS ZERO* IS FAST ENOUGH.
YOU CAN GET THROUGH WHILE WE KEEP 'EM BUSY.

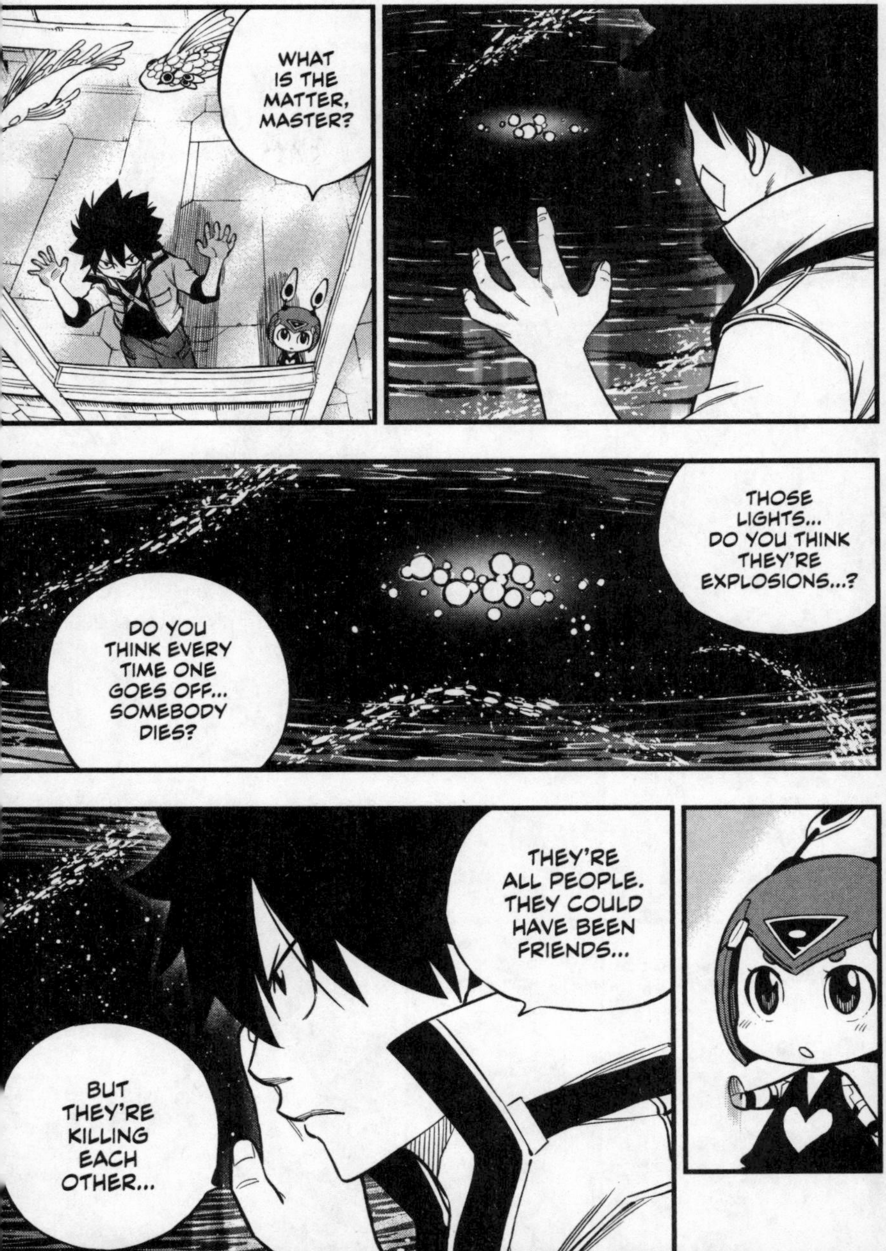
WHAT IS THE MATTER, MASTER?
THOSE LIGHTS... DO YOU THINK THEY'RE EXPLOSIONS...?
DO YOU THINK EVERY TIME ONE GOES OFF... SOMEBODY DIES?
THEY'RE ALL PEOPLE. THEY COULD HAVE BEEN FRIENDS...
BUT THEY'RE KILLING EACH OTHER...

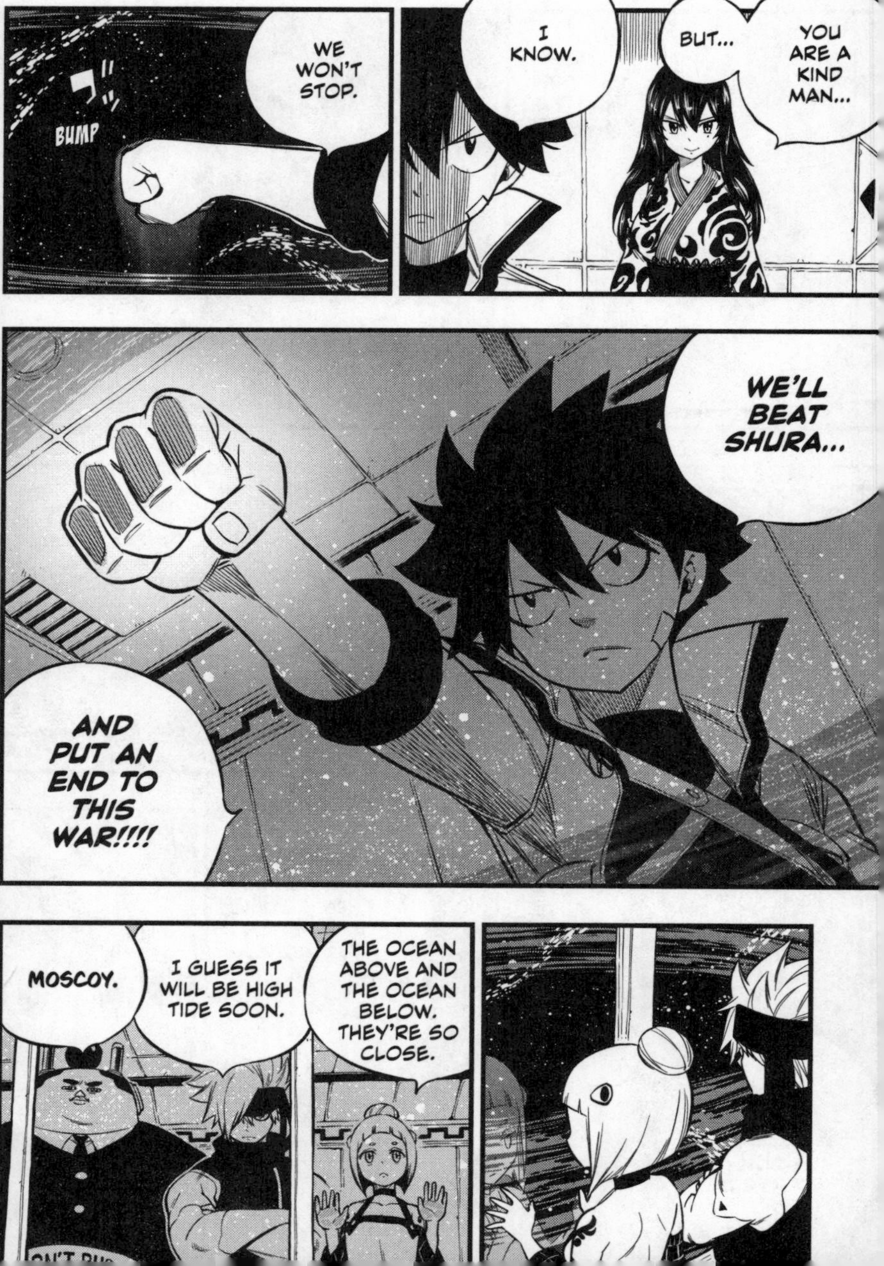
YOU ARE A KIND MAN...
BUT...
I KNOW.
WE WON'T STOP.
BUMP
WE'LL BEAT SHURA...
AND PUT AN END TO THIS WAR!!!!
THE OCEAN ABOVE AND THE OCEAN BELOW. THEY'RE SO CLOSE.
I GUESS IT WILL BE HIGH TIDE SOON.
MOSCOY.

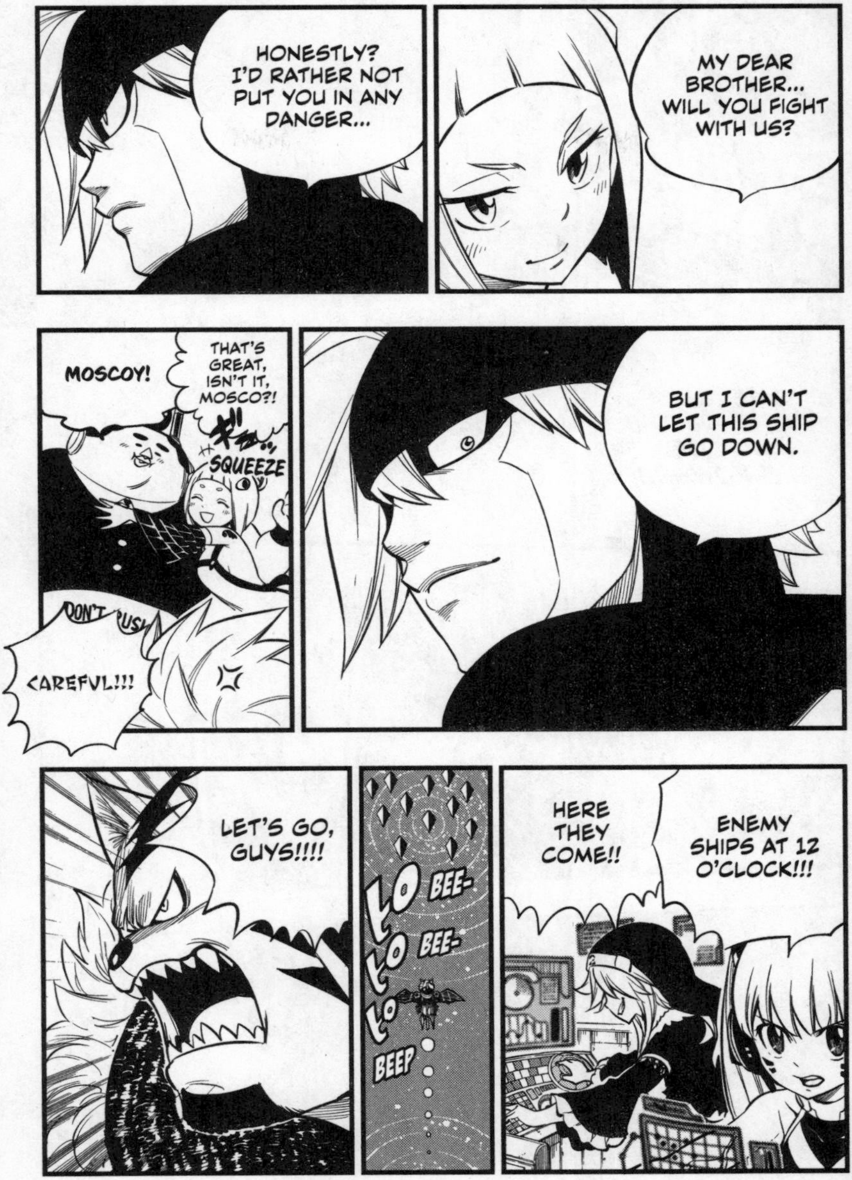
MY DEAR BROTHER... WILL YOU FIGHT WITH US?
HONESTLY? I'D RATHER NOT PUT YOU IN ANY DANGER...
BUT I CAN'T LET THIS SHIP GO DOWN.
THAT'S GREAT, ISN'T IT, MOSCO?!
MOSCOY!
SQUEEZE
DON'T RUSH
CAREFUL!!!
ENEMY SHIPS AT 12 O'CLOCK!!!
HERE THEY COME!!
BEE-
BEE-
BEEP
LET'S GO, GUYS!!!!

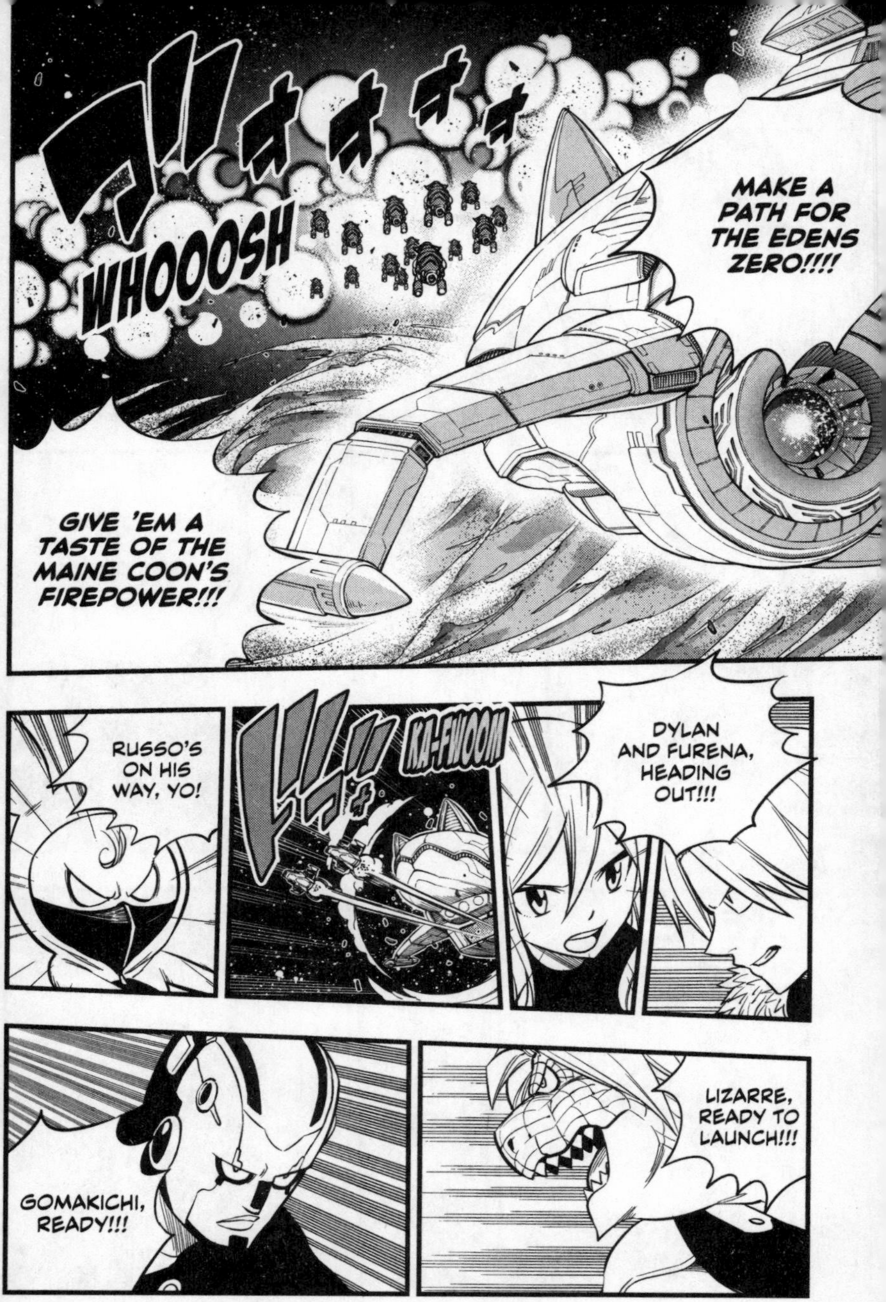
MAKE A PATH FOR THE EDENS ZERO!!!!
WHOOOSH
GIVE 'EM A TASTE OF THE MAINE COON'S FIREPOWER!!!
DYLAN AND FURENA, HEADING OUT!!!
KA-FWOOM
RUSSO'S ON HIS WAY, YO!
LIZARRE, READY TO LAUNCH!!!
GOMAKICHI, READY!!!

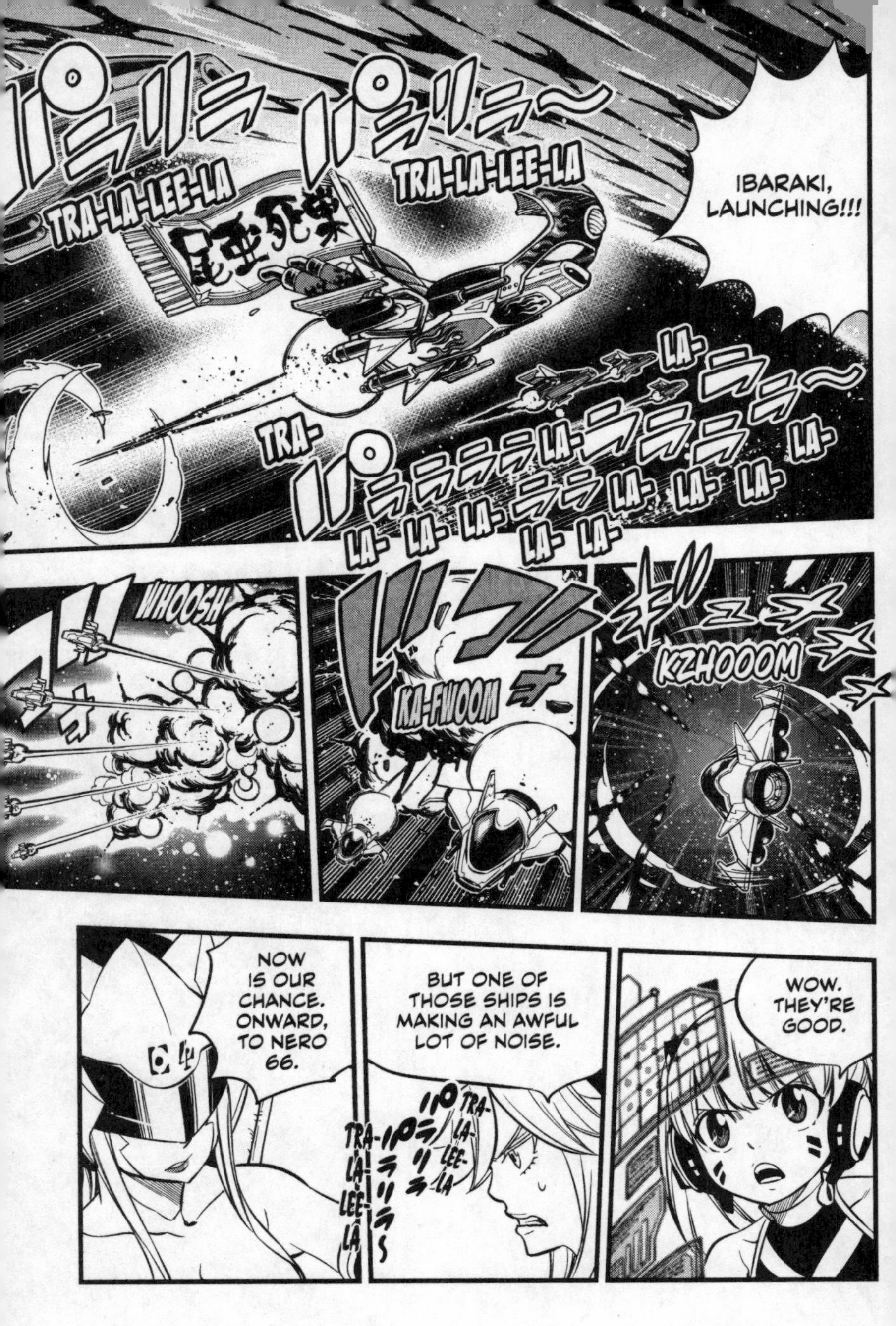
IBARAKI, LAUNCHING!!!
TRA-LA-LEE-LA
TRA-LA-LEE-LA
TRA- LA- LA- LA- LA- LA- LA- LA- LA- LA- LA- LA- LA-
KZHOOOM
KA-FWOOM
WHOOSH
WOW. THEY'RE GOOD.
BUT ONE OF THOSE SHIPS IS MAKING AN AWFUL LOT OF NOISE.
TRA-LA-LEE-LA
TRA-LA-LEE-LA
NOW IS OUR CHANCE. ONWARD, TO NERO 66.

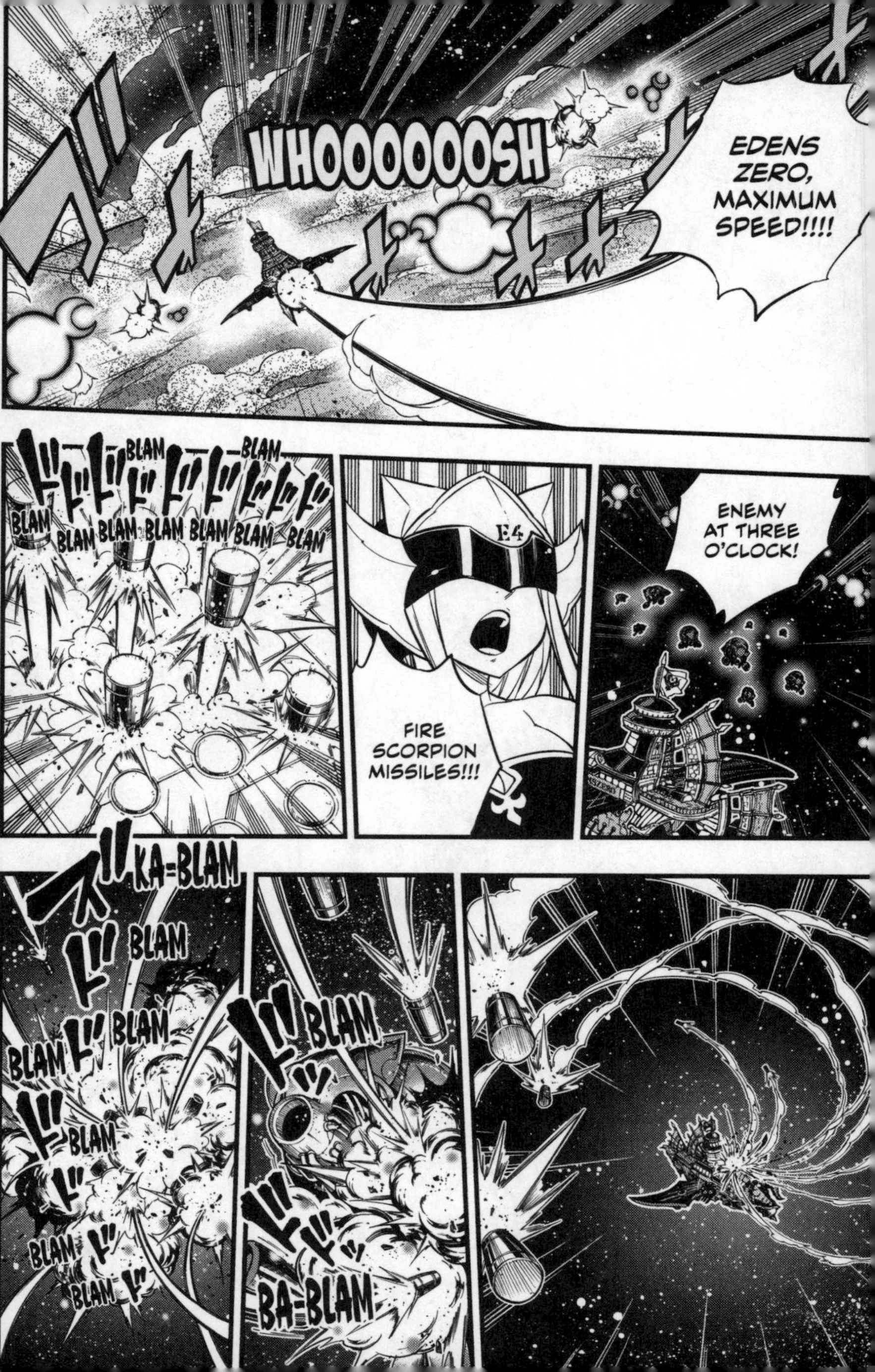
EDENS ZERO, MAXIMUM SPEED!!!!
WHOOOOOOSH
ENEMY AT THREE O'CLOCK!
E4
FIRE SCORPION MISSILES!!!
BLAM BLAM
BLAM BLAM BLAM BLAM BLAM BLAM BLAM
BLAM
BA-BLAM
KA-BLAM
BLAM
BLAM BLAM
BLAM
BLAM
BLAM

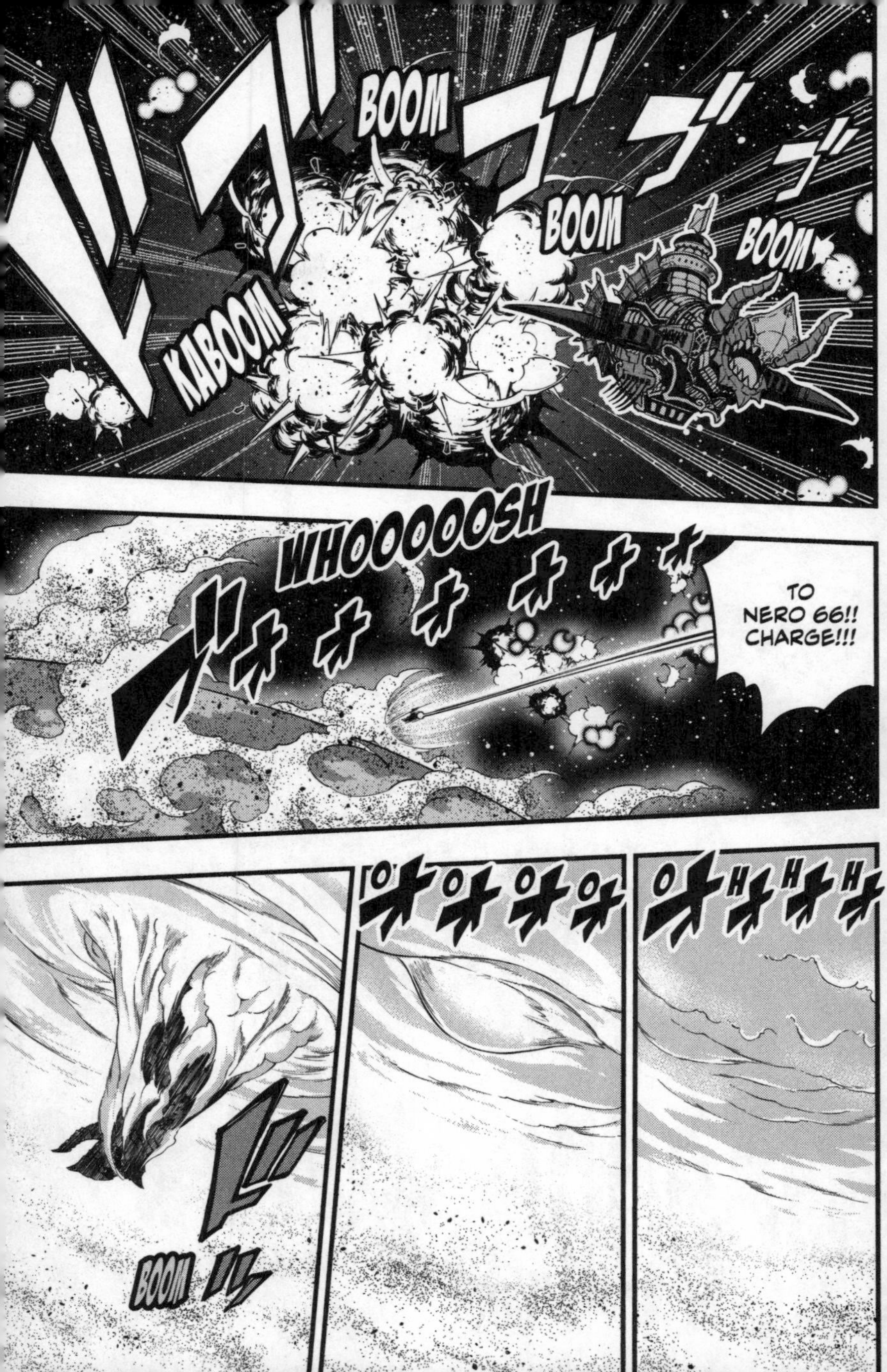
BOOM
BOOM
BOOM
KABOOM
TO NERO 66!! CHARGE!!!
WHOOOOOSH
BOOM

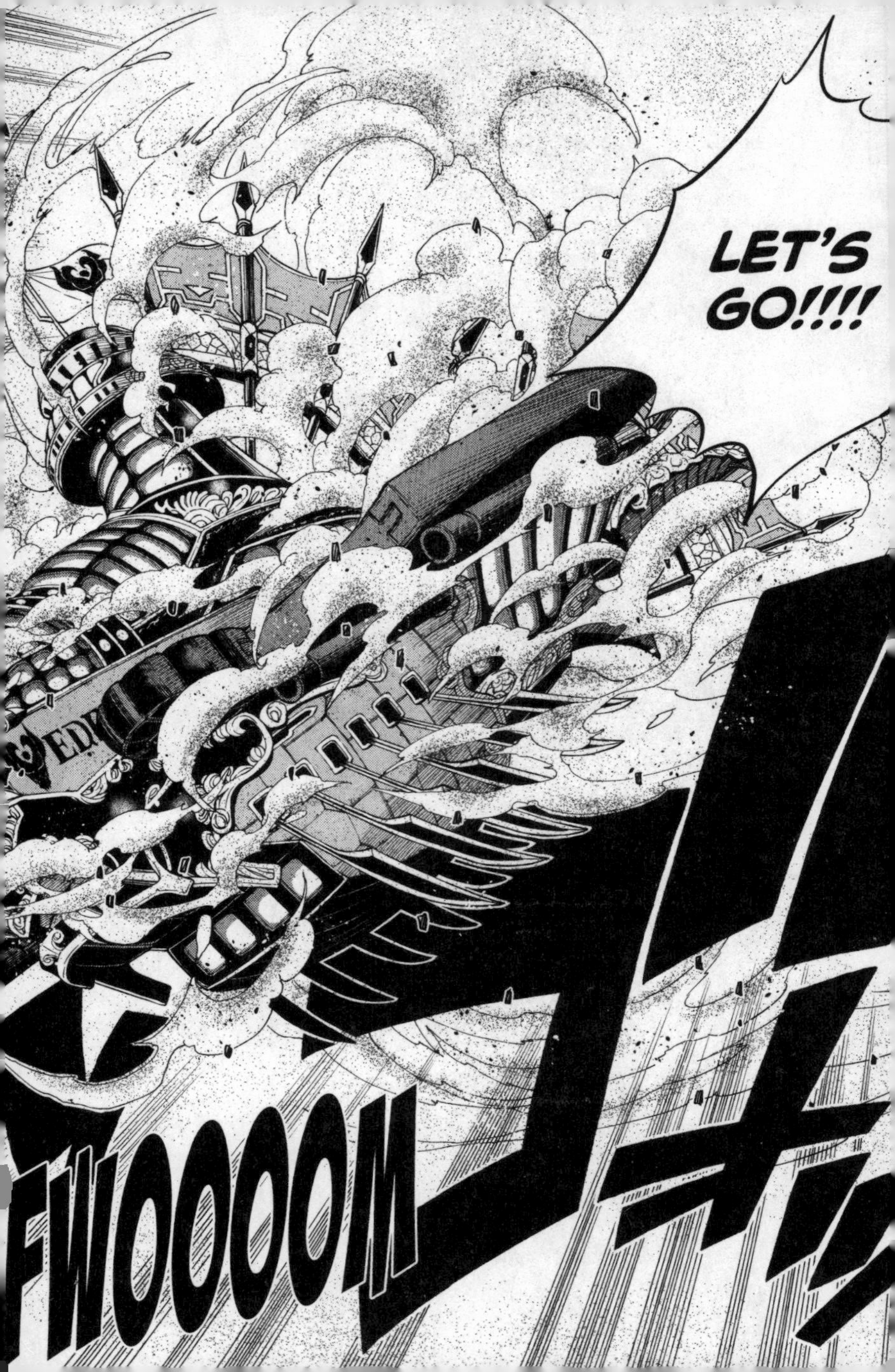
LET'S GO!!!!
FWOOOOM

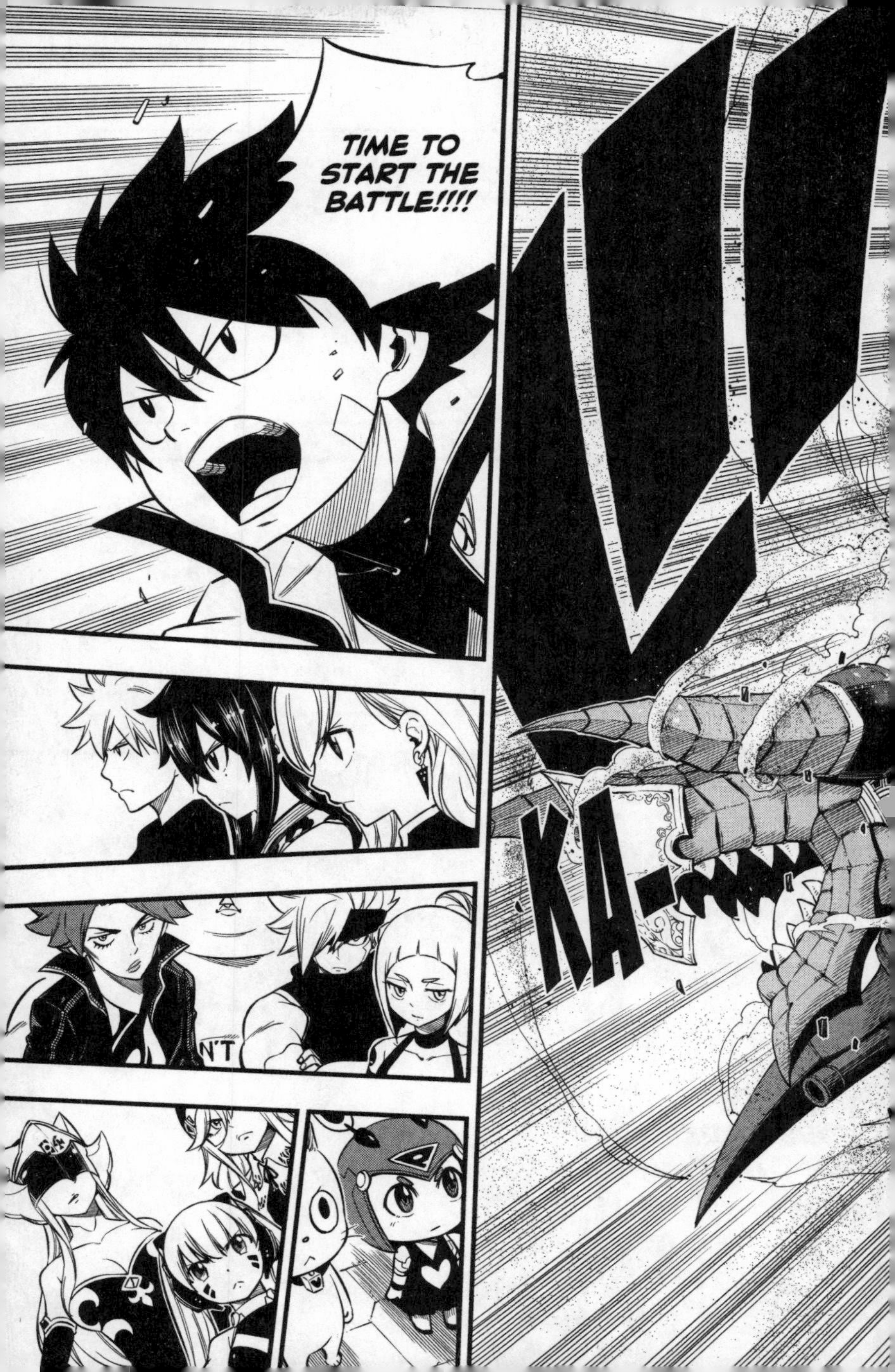
KA-
TIME TO START THE BATTLE!!!!

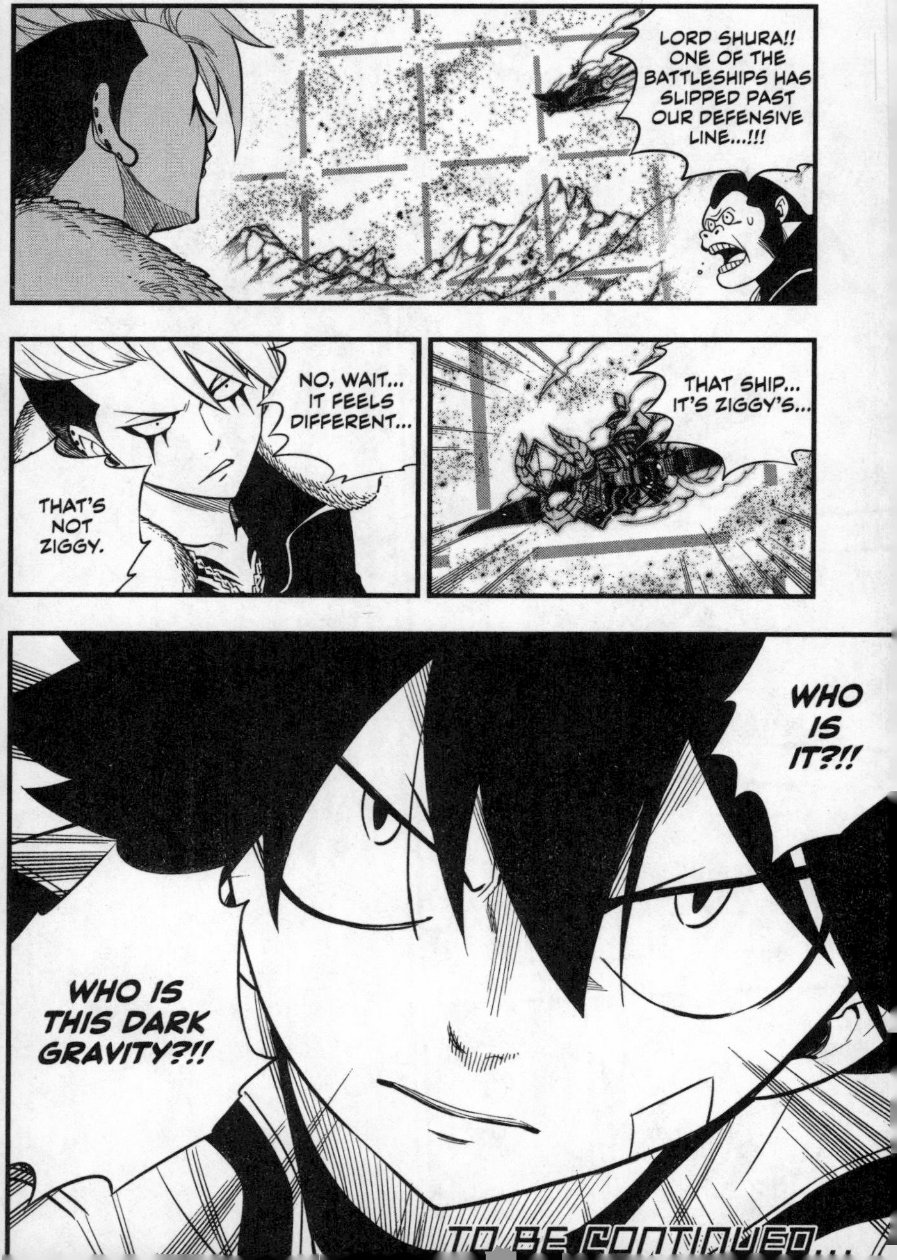
LORD SHURA!! ONE OF THE BATTLESHIPS HAS SLIPPED PAST OUR DEFENSIVE LINE...!!!
THAT SHIP... IT'S ZIGGY'S...
NO, WAIT... IT FEELS DIFFERENT...
THAT'S NOT ZIGGY.
WHO IS IT?!!
WHO IS THIS DARK GRAVITY?!!
TO BE CONTINUED...

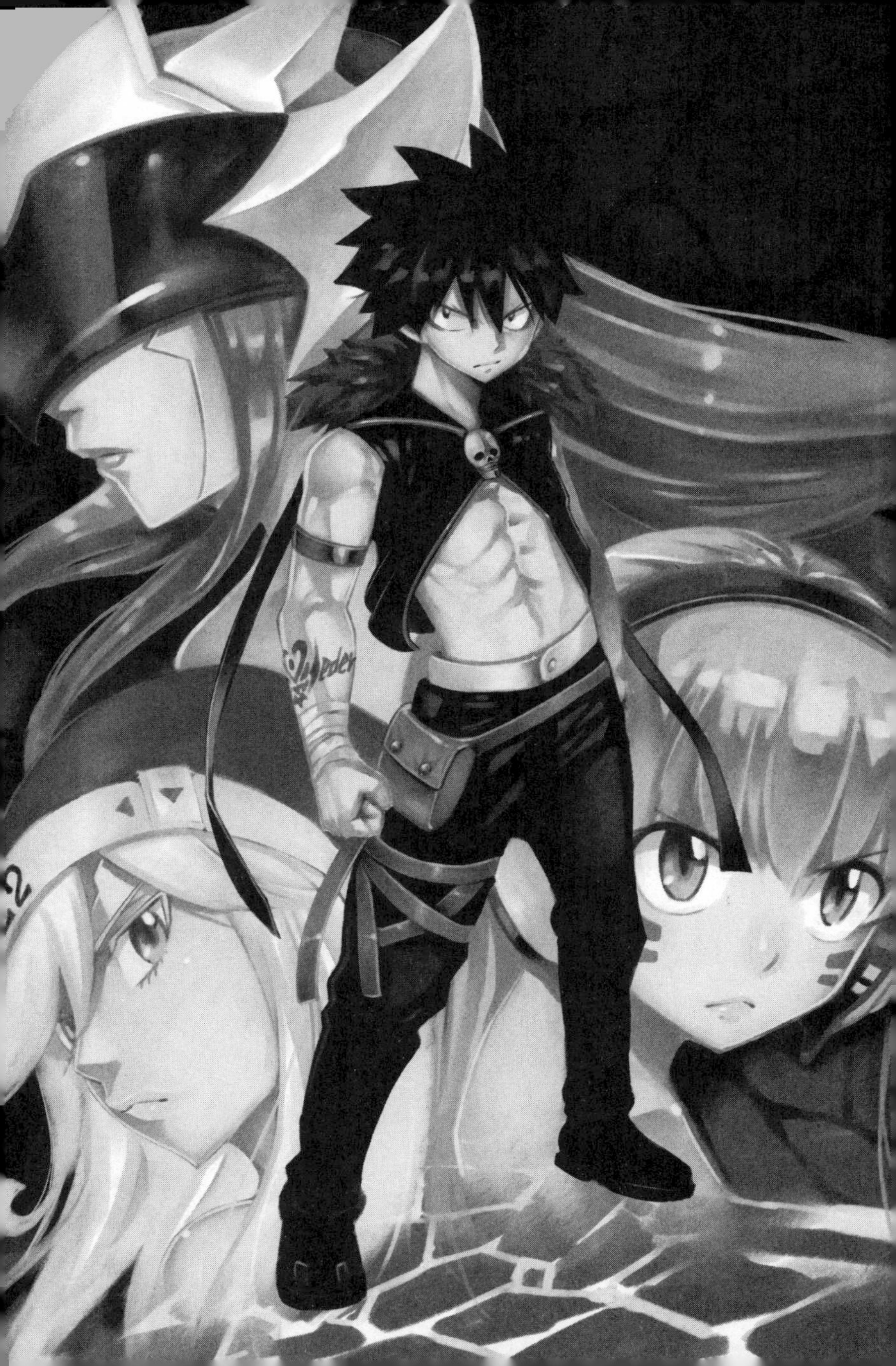

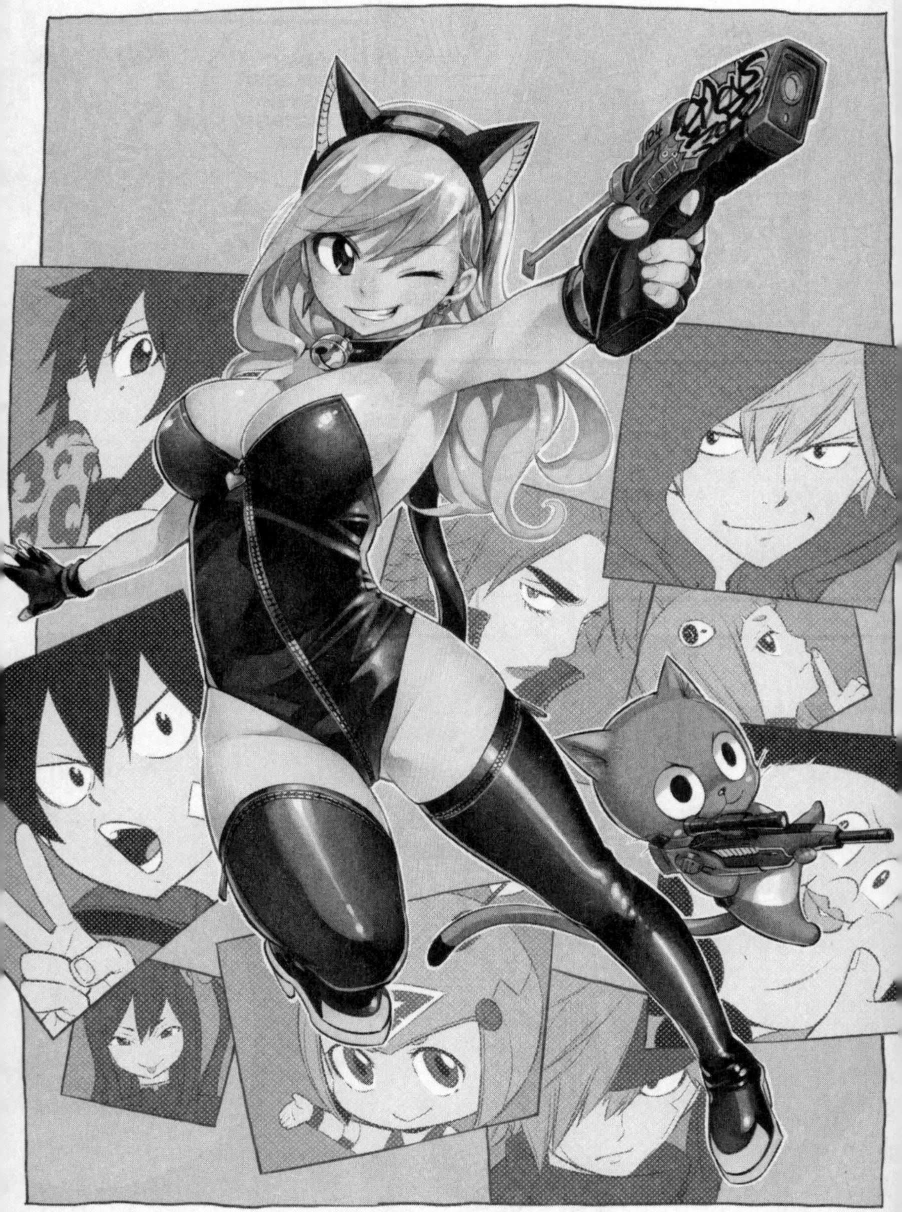

AFTERWORD

Since I'm doing a space story, I was like, "I'm gonna draw starfighter and destroyer battles in space!", but when I actually started drawing one, I understood very deeply why that never happens in any weekly shonen manga magazine.

To put it simply, the art cost is high, you use up a lot of panels, and you have fewer panels with characters' faces in them.

No wonder nobody does 'em (ha ha). You can use some tricks to make it work, but it requires a different kind of drawing than the human vs. human battles that I've been so used to doing for so long. Gotta make it easy to look at, easy to follow, and awesome-looking. I kept that in mind, so it was like I was a beginner all over again, and it was even kind of fun.

I hired a few more staff members a little while ago in anticipation of the space battles, but when I'm doing a chapter that doesn't have space battles, I kind of have more staff than I know what to do with.

Still, there are several jobs in addition to manga at my studio, so it's just as hectic as ever. I am very grateful to my staff.

As for what we do other than manga, there are video recordings and events to attend. Illustrations for companies. Video game character designs. Supervising games that I'm involved with. Approving merchandise. Writing for a different manga *(100 Years Quest)*. I have several character designs for other projects I can't disclose yet, so I'm pretty busy if I do say so myself. With this much work to do, of course it's terrible for my editors, and the other day they finally upped the number to four (at Shonen Magazine it's usually one or two). To be honest, I thought, "That's too many!", but we'd never get all the work done without all four of them, so I'll be working with four editors for a while now. I'm always grateful to my editors, too.

Now, changing the subject, the Aoi Cosmos arc is reaching its climax, and I'm planning some scenes and plot points that aren't really typical of my manga, so I'm really nervous to see if the fans will accept it. But I decided that it's necessary to make it even better later on, so I think things are going to get pretty dark soon. When I talked to my editors about what's going to happen, then, as expected, they were divided on whether or not I should do it. It's some pretty serious stuff, so it's not surprising. And of course, I'm a professional, so I'm not going to insist on doing things my way; I want to create my manga while thinking about what I want to do, but putting more emphasis on how I can make my readers happy. So the upcoming story my get pretty grim, but depending on how we work it out, there's still a fairly decent chance it could turn out pretty mild. Now, what is going to happen next? I hope you're all looking forward to it!

A Kodansha Comics Trade Paperback Original
EDENS ZERO 16 copyright © 2021 Hiro Mashima
English translation copyright © 2022 Hiro Mashima

All rights reserved.

Published in the United States by Kodansha Comics, an imprint of Kodansha USA Publishing, LLC, New York.

Publication rights for this English edition arranged through Kodansha Ltd., Tokyo.

First published in Japan in 2021 by Kodansha Ltd., Tokyo.

ISBN 978-1-64651-445-8

Printed in the United States of America.

www.kodansha.us

1st Printing
Translation: Alethea Nibley & Athena Nibley
Lettering: AndWorld Design
Editing: David Yoo
Kodansha Comics edition cover design by Phil Balsman

Publisher: Kiichiro Sugawara

Director of publishing services: Ben Applegate
Director of publishing operations: Dave Barrett
Associate director, publishing operations: Stephen Pakula
Publishing services managing ditors: Madison Salters, Alanna Ruse
Production managers: Emi Lotto, Angela Zurlo